W9-ATR-374

STORM
CENTER

STORM CENTER

The Supreme Court in American Politics

DAVID M. O'BRIEN

UNIVERSITY OF VIRGINIA

W · W · *Norton & Company*

New York · London

*The text of this book is composed in Caledonia, with display type set in Centaur.
Composition and manufacturing by the Maple-Vail Book Manufacturing Group. Book
design by Marjorie J. Flock.*

FIRST EDITION

Library of Congress Cataloging-in-Publication Data
O'Brien, David M.
  Storm center.

  Bibliography: p.
  Includes indexes.
  1. United States. Supreme Court. 2. Political
questions and judicial power—United States. 3. Judicial
process—United States. I. Title.
KF8742.027 1986   347.73'26   85–19869
                    347.30735

ISBN 0-393-02330-3

W. W. Norton & Company, Inc., 500 Fifth Avenue, New York, N.Y. 10110
W. W. Norton & Company Ltd., 37 Great Russell Street, London WC1B 3NU

2 3 4 5 6 7 8 9 0

For Benjamin

Contents

Illustrations

Tables and Charts

Preface

THE Supreme Court, Justice Oliver Wendell Holmes observed, is a "storm centre" of political controversy. The Court stands as a temple of law—an arbitrator of political disputes, an authoritative organ of law, and an expression of the American ideal of "a government of laws, not of men." But it remains a fundamentally political institution. Behind the marble facade, the justices compete for influence; the Court itself is locked in a larger struggle for power in society. This book is about the political struggles among the justices and between the Court and rival political forces in the country.

As a political institution, the Court wields an antidemocratic and countermajoritarian power. Those who sit on the high bench are not elected and are rarely held directly accountable for their decisions. Their power and prestige stem from the authority to interpret the Constitution but rest with public expectations of expertise, independence, impartiality, and reasoned judgment. The justices constitute a kind of secular priesthood, yet the Court is not a meritocracy. Presidents invariably try to pack the Court and, as Chapter 2 shows, thereby influence public policy beyond their limited time in the Oval Office. On the bench, however, justices are sovereign. They frequently disappoint their presidential benefactors and find it difficult to refrain from off-the-bench activities. Rather than leave the world of politics behind, justices form a small political elite with enormous power, a unique history, and the awesome responsibility of maintaining the constitutional principles of free government and human dignity.

Life in the marble temple constrains judicial behavior and the politics of making law. In historical perspective, Chapter 3 examines the institutional dynamics of the Court, the changing working relations among the justices, and the way the Burger Court has become increasingly bureaucratic in response to growing caseloads. Unlike any other federal court, the Supreme Court now has virtually complete discretion over its selection of cases and sets its own agenda for policy-making. The justices' control over deciding what to decide and the processes by which they select cases are examined in Chapter 4. In explaining how justices decide cases and the process of opinion writing, Chapter 5 shows why there is now less collective deliberation than there used to be and how the Court has come to function more like a legislative body. Critics of unpopular rulings have often castigated the Court for being a "super legislature." I aim to show that the Court has instead come to *function* more like a legislative body. As one justice puts it, "decisions have become more of an event, rather than a process." The justices now place less of a premium on collegial deliberations leading to institutional decisions and delegate more responsibilities to larger staffs within the Court. These and other institutional trends in turn lead to less certainty, stability, and predictability in the law.

Although the Court has come to function like a roving commission monitoring the governmental process, it rulings are not self-executing. The Court depends on other political institutions and on public opinion to carry out its decisions. But those forces may also curb the Court. The limitations of

Supreme Court policy-making are considered in the final chapter, but the basic conclusion may be stated at the outset: the Court is a guardian of the substantive value choices in the Constitution, but by itself holds less power to change the country than either liberals or conservatives often claim. Major confrontations in constitutional politics, like those over school desegregation, school prayer, and abortion, are determined as much by what is possible in a system of free government and in pluralistic society as by what the Court says. The Court's influence on American life rests on a paradox. Its political power is at once anti-democratic and countermajoritarian. Yet that power, which flows from giving meaning to the Constitution, truly rests, in Chief Justice Edward White's words, "solely upon the approval of a free people."

Acknowledgments

I N RESEARCHING and writing this book, I incurred a large number of debts. It is fair to say that I might never have embarked on the project had it not been for Chief Justice Warren Burger and his assistant, Mark Cannon. The opportunities they afforded me as a judicial fellow, and then as a research associate, in the Office of the Administrative Assistant to the Chief Justice were invaluable. Both later took an interest in the book and generously spent time talking with me and clarifying various matters. Although they may not agree with all my views, I remain grateful for the insights and kindness they gave me.

The experience at the Court provided a perspective, but only began my inquiry. The inquiry led to an examination of the private papers of fifty-five justices (over half of all the justices who ever sat on the high bench), as well as the papers of six Presidents. While most of the collections are open to the public, access to some requires special permission. For their permission to use certain collections, I am grateful to Justice William J. Brennan, Jr., Paul Freund, Eugene Gressman, William E. Jackson, Mrs. Carolyn Agger Fortas, Mrs. Hugo Black, and Hugo Black, Jr.

Assistance at various libraries was crucial to the study. David Wigdor and his splendid staff in the Manuscripts Division of the Library of Congress were always helpful. Paul Freund, Erika Chadbourn, and Judith Mellins made my stays at the Harvard Law School Library fruitful. Others who deserve mention for their attention and assistance are Bill Cooper of the University of Kentucky Library; Nancy Bressler and Jean Holiday of the Seeley G. Mudd Manuscripts Library at Princeton University; Patricia Bodak Stark of the Yale University Library; Dale Mayer of the Herbert Hoover Presidential Library; Carole Knobil of Special Collections at the Universtiy of Texas School of Law Library; Cynthia Fox of the National Archives and Records Service; Marjorie Barritt of the Bentley Historical Library at the University of Michigan; Michael Kohl of Special Collections at Clemson University; Karen Rohrer at the Dwight D. Eisenhower Library; Nancy Smith of the Lyndon Baines Johnson Library; Charles Warren Ohrvall of the Harry S. Truman Library; Dallas R. Lindgren of the Minnesota Historical Society; Gail Galloway and Diane Williams of the Curator's Office of the Supreme Court of the United States; and David Pride of the Supreme Court Historical Society. No less helpful were the staffs of the Manuscripts Division of Alderman Library at the University of Virginia; the John Marshall Papers Project at the College of William and Mary; the John Fitzgerald Kennedy Library; the Gerald R. Ford Library; the Hoover Institution on War, Revolution, and Peace; the Franklin D. Roosevelt Library; the Columbia Oral History Project and the Rare Books and Manuscripts Division in Butler Library at Columbia University; and the library of the Cardozo School of Law at Yeshiva University.

The justices' papers did not end my inquiry, but instead raised further questions. Interviews and discussions of my tentative conclusions saved me from some (though possibly not all) errors of judgment. For their time and insights, I am indebted to Chief Justice Warren Burger and Justices William J. Brennan, Jr., Sandra Day O'Connor, Lewis F. Powell, Jr., William H. Rehnquist, Potter Stewart, and John Paul Stevens. I am also grateful to Mark Cannon, William T. Gossett, Jr., Fred Graham, Sidney Fine, Paul Freund, Alpheus T. Mason, Walter Murphy, and Benno Schmidt. Justices Harry Blackmun, Thurgood Marshall, and Byron White graciously corresponded with me about the book.

Without the support of a number of individuals and organizations, the research could not have been undertaken. Two grants from the American Philosophical Society got the project under way. The Gerald R. Ford Foundation, the Hoover Presidential Library Association, the Lyndon Baines Johnson Foundation, and the Harry S. Truman Institute made possible the examination of presidential papers. The National Endowment for the Humanities provided a small travel grant. Marshall Robinson and Peter de Janosi of the Russell Sage Foundation, patient supporters of my projects, provided opportunities that contributed to this work. At the University of Virginia, Kenneth Thompson and the Committee on Summer Research Grants, and Dean Merrill Peterson and the Virginia Research Policy Council, provided additional support at crucial times. Henry J. Abraham, Gordon E. Baker, Alpheus T. Mason, Jack Peltason, Philip Phibbs, and C. Herman Pritchett wrote the necessary letters of recommendation. Bunny Stinnett and Kathy Fast faithfully typed the manuscript, and William Mandel and William J. O'Brien did their share of photocopying materials.

The book benefited from the comments of John Schmidhauser and Martin Shapiro. There are not words to repay my teacher, C. Herman Pritchett, for reading two drafts and (as always) offering encouragement. I am no less indebted to my colleague Henry J. Abraham for reading drafts of chapters and supporting me in ways that only he knows. At Norton, Donald

Fusting, Hilary Hinzmann, and Amanda Adams were tough and immensely helpful, for which I am especially grateful.

And last I thank my wife, Claudine, editor-in-residence and, for so many reasons, editor-in-chief.

                                                    D.M.O.

Charlottesville, Virginia
December 5, 1985

STORM
CENTER

ONE

A Struggle for Power

O N A HOT NIGHT in August 1969, Norma McCorvey, a twenty-one-year-old carnival worker nicknamed Pixie, was returning to her motel on a side road outside Augusta, Georgia. On her way back to her room, she was gang-raped by three men and a woman. The carnival and Pixie moved on to Texas. There, several weeks later, Pixie found herself pregnant. A high school dropout, who was divorced and had a five-year-old daughter and little money, Norma McCorvey unsuccessfully sought an abortion. Texas, like most other states at the time, prohibited abortions unless necessary to save a woman's life. "No legitimate doctor in Texas would touch me," she has remembered. "I found one doctor who offered to abort me for $500. Only he didn't have a license, and I was scared to turn my body over to him. So there I was—pregnant, unmarried, unemployed, alone and stuck."[1] A lawyer friend, Henry McCloskey, Jr., agreed to find someone to adopt the baby. He also introduced her to two recent graduates of the University of Texas Law School, Sarah Weddington and Linda Coffee. The three women decided to challenge the constitutionality of the Texas law forbidding all abortions not necessary "for the purpose of saving the life of

the mother." McCorvey never saw the child she bore and
gave up for adoption. And "Pixie" became "Jane Roe" in a test
case against Henry Wade, the criminal district attorney for
Dallas County, Texas. Her case eventually led to the Supreme
Court's landmark ruling in *Roe v. Wade* (1973). In the controversy aroused by the decision, and in the tortuous way the
decision was reached, *Roe v. Wade* exemplifies the Supreme
Court's central place in American politics.

Abortion, the Court, and American Politics

Little public attention was paid on May 4, 1971, when *Roe
v. Wade* appeared on the Court's order list. It was one of only
163 from more than 4,500 cases on the docket granted oral
argument and to be decided the next term. The *New York
Times* simply reported that the Court "agreed to consider if
state anti-abortion laws violate the constitutional rights of
pregnant women by denying their right to decide whether or
not to have children." In the end, the Court's decision would
affect the laws in virtually every state. At the time, though,
there was no way of predicting whether or how the Court
would decide the issue.

Just one month earlier, in *United States v. Vuitch* (1971),
a bare majority had upheld the District of Columbia's statute
prohibiting abortions unless "necessary for the preservation
of the mother's life or health." By upholding the statute, the
Court increased the availability of abortions in Washington,
but it did not address the question of whether women have a
constitutional right to obtain abortions. Chief Justice Burger
and Justices John Harlan, Byron White, and Harry Blackmun
joined Hugo Black's opinion for the Court. Black ruled that
the law was not unconstitutionally vague in allowing abortions
for "health" reasons. The most liberal member of the Court,
William Douglas, dissented. He thought the law was "void

for vagueness" since it was uncertain whether psychological considerations—such as anxiety and the stigma of having an unwanted or illegitimate child—counted as health factors entitling women to have abortions. The District of Columbia statute, however, unlike the Texas law adopted in 1854, was one of the most liberal in the country at the time, since it allowed abortions not only to save the woman's life but also to maintain her physical and psychological well-being.

The movement to liberalize abortion laws had grown throughout the turbulent 1960s with the "sexual revolution" and demands for women's rights. Yet, the legal reforms pushed by women's pro-choice advocates were in some respects little more than a return to the legal status of abortions a century earlier. Until the mid-nineteenth century, most states permitted abortions, except after quickening—the first movement of the fetus—and then an abortion was usually considered only a minor offense. After the Civil War, anti-abortionists persuaded states to toughen their laws. Every state, except Kentucky, had made abortion a felony by 1910. The overwhelming majority of the states permitted abortions only to save a woman's life. But by the late 1960s, fourteen states had liberalized laws to permit abortions when the woman's health was in danger, when there was a likelihood of fetal abnormality, and when the woman had been a victim of rape or incest. Four states—Alaska, Hawaii, New York and Washington—had gone so far as to repeal all criminal penalties for abortions performed in early pregnancy.

By the time oral arguments were heard in 1971, Black and Harlan had retired. Black had been a leading liberal and Harlan one of the most conservative members within the Court. But neither looked kindly on claims to a constitutional right to an abortion. At the conference discussion of *Vuitch*, Black would not go along "with a woman's claim of [a] constitutional right to use her body as she pleases." Burger shared that view. He rejected any "argument that [a] woman has [an] absolute right to decide what happens to her own body."[2] Without Black and Harlan, the Court was diminished. President Richard Nixon's last two nominations, Powell, and Rehnquist, had not yet been confirmed by the Senate.

On December 13, 1971, Chief Justice Burger opened the Court's oral argument session with the simple announcement "We will hear arguments in No. 18, *Roe* against *Wade.*" Sarah Weddington was remarkably calm in her first appearance before the high bench. She began by reviewing the lower court's holding that the Texas abortion law violated a woman's right to continue or terminate a pregnancy. But Burger interrupted to ask whether the issues had already been decided by the ruling in *Vuitch v. United States.* Weddington explained that *Vuitch* upheld a law that permitted abortions when necessary to the health or the life of a woman. The Texas law was more restrictive; it allowed abortions only when necessary to save the life of the woman. Doctors were not free to consider the effects of pregnancy on the woman's mental or physical health. *Vuitch* was not considered binding in Texas, and doctors were being prosecuted for performing abortions other than those necessary to save the woman's life. Women who sought to terminate unwanted pregnancies had to go to New York, the District of Columbia, or some other state with liberal abortion laws. Women like Jane Roe, who were poor and for whom abortions were not necessary to saving their lives, had no real choice. They faced either unwanted childbirth or medically unsafe self-abortions that could result in their death. The cruel irony of the law, moreover, was that women who performed self-abortions were guilty of no crime. The Texas law authorized the prosecution only of doctors who perform abortions, not of the women who seek or perform their own abortions. The victims of the law were women and, Weddington pointed out, "[i]t's so often the poor and disadvantaged in Texas who are not able to escape the effect of the law."

Weddington's argument was diverted when Justice White

observed, "[S]o far on the merits, you've told us about the important impact of the law, and you made a very eloquent policy argument against it." But he added, "[W]e cannot here be involved simply with matters of policy, as you know." White wanted to know what the constitutional basis was for a woman's right to have an abortion and for the Court's overturning the Texas law. Appropriate arguments could be drawn from the Ninth Amendment's guarantee of "rights retained by the people," Weddington responded, or the "protection for rights of persons to life, liberty, and the pursuit of happiness" [*sic*] under the Fourteenth Amendment. If "liberty" is meaningful, she concluded, "that liberty to these women would mean liberty from being forced to continue the unwanted pregnancy."

"It's an old joke, but when a man argues against two beautiful ladies like this, they are going to have the last word." There was no laughter in the courtroom, however, at that opening remark by Jay Floyd, the assistant attorney general of Texas, who was before the Court to defend the abortion law. His southern accent and manner embellished the values and position he was trying to defend. This controversy is not one for the courts, he argued, and arguments about freedom of choice are misleading. Floyd pressed the point:

There are situations in which, of course as the Court knows, no remedy is provided. Now I think she makes her choice prior to the time she becomes pregnant. That is the time of the choice. It's like, more or less, the first three or four years of our life we don't remember anything. But, once a child is born, a woman no longer has a choice, and I think pregnancy then terminates that choice. That's when.

After Weddington's presentation of the realities of abortion in Texas, the argument sounded surreal, strangely out of date and out of place, especially since Norma McCorvey had been raped. One of the justices impatiently shot back, "Maybe she makes her choice when she decides to live in Texas." Laughter almost drowned out Floyd's feeble reply, "There is no restriction on moving."

"What is Texas' interest? What is Texas' interest in the statute?" demanded Justice Marshall. The state has "recognized the humanness of the embryo, or the fetus," Floyd explained, and has "a compelling interest because of the protection of fetal life." Yet, interjected Justice Stewart, "Texas does not attempt to punish a woman who herself performs an abortion on herself." "That is correct," Floyd continued,

And the matter has been brought to my attention: Why not punish for murder, since you are destroying what you—or what has been said to be a human being? I don't know, except that I will say this. As medical science progresses, maybe the law will progress along with it. Maybe at one time it could be possible, I suppose, statutes could be passed. Whether or not that would be constitutional or not, I don't know.

But, Stewart countered, "we're dealing with the statute as it is. There's no state, is there, that equates abortion with murder? Or is there?" There was none, Floyd admitted and then hastened to emphasize that, though courts had not recognized the unborn as having legal rights, states have a legitimate interest in protecting the unborn. As to a woman's choice on abortion, Floyd reiterated, "[W]e feel that this choice is left up to the woman prior to the time she becomes pregnant. This is the time of choice."[3]

When *Roe* was discussed in the justices' private conference, Burger noted that the case had not been very well argued. He also thought because the case presented such a "sensitive issue," it should be set for reargument so that Powell and Rehnquist could participate and a full Court reach a decision. As chief justice, he led the discussion, observing that the Texas law was "certainly arcane," though not unconstitutional. He was inclined to the view that the law should fall for vagueness. Senior Associate Justice Douglas spoke next. He disagreed and had no doubt that the statute was unconstitutional. For Douglas, the Texas law not only was vague but also impinged on a woman's right of privacy. Brennan and Stewart agreed, as later did Marshall. White came out on the other side. He could not go along with the argument that women have a constitutional right of privacy, giving them a choice on abortion. A right of privacy is not specifically mentioned in the Constitution. And White did not find persuasive arguments that a right of privacy is one of the unenumerated rights retained by the people under the Ninth Amendment, and protected by the Fourteenth Amendment's provision that no state may deprive any person of life, liberty, or property without due process of law. Blackmun, then the newest member of the Court, spoke last: "Don't think there's an absolute right to do what you will with [your] body." But this statute was poorly drawn, Blackmun observed. It's too restrictive—it "doesn't go as far as it should and impinges too far on [Roe's] Ninth Amendment rights."[4] Blackmun appeared in the middle, but inclined toward the position of Douglas, Brennan, Stewart, and Marshall.

After conference the chief justice, if he is in the majority, by tradition assigns a justice to write the opinion justifying the Court's decision. On the abortion cases, Burger appeared to be in the minority, but he nonetheless gave the assignment to Blackmun. When Douglas complained, Burger responded that the issues were so complex and the conference discussion so diverse "that there were, literally, not enough columns to mark up an accurate reflection of the voting" in his docket book. He "therefore marked down no vote and said this was a case that would have to stand or fall on the writing, when it was done."[5]

Assigned to write the Court's opinion in late December 1971, Blackmun did not circulate a first draft until May 18, 1972. The draft immediately troubled Douglas and Brennan. Though striking down the abortion law, Blackmun's opinion did so on Burger's view that the law was vague rather than on the majority's view that it violated a woman's constitutional right of privacy. Douglas and Brennan wanted to know why the opinion failed to address the core issue, "which would make reaching the vagueness issue unnecessary." Blackmun claimed that he was "flexible as to results." He was simply trying his "best to arrive at something which would command a court." With "hope, perhaps forlorn, that we might have a unanimous Court," he explained, "I took the vagueness route."[6]

A "freshman" in his second year on the Court and assigned to write a very difficult opinion, Blackmun found himself in the middle of the cross-pressures of a growing dispute. Blackmun was psychologically and intellectually torn. On the one hand, Burger had been his longtime friend and had recommended his appointment to the Court; on the other, Blackmun was attracted to Douglas's position on the issue of abortion. He began thinking that it might be better to have the case reargued the next term, as Burger and White had suggested. "Although it would prove costly to [him] personally, in the light of energy and hours expended," Blackmun concluded, he would move for reargument. He explained that "on an issue so sensitive and so emotional as this one, the country deserves the conclusion of a nine-man, not a seven-man court, whatever the ultimate decision may be."[7]

Douglas was taken aback by the prospect of Nixon's last two appointees participating: the final decision might go the other way. If Blackmun withdrew his motion for reargument, it would fail. But if he didn't, there would be trouble. The vote would be four to three against reargument, and that could lead to a heated confrontation. Douglas appealed to Blackmun not to vote for reargument. Instead of complaining about the initial draft opinion, Douglas commended Blackmun by letter for his "yeoman service" in a difficult area and emphasized that he had "a firm 5 and the firm 5 will be behind you" on the opinion. Brennan followed with a similar note.[8]

By tradition, only those justices participating in a case may vote on its reargument, but then came a memorandum from Powell. He noted that during his first months when decisions were made on rearguments he had taken "the position then, as did Bill Rehnquist, that the other seven Justices were better qualified to make those decisions." However, Powell further explained, "The present question arises in a different context. I have been on the Court for more than half a term. It may be that I now have a duty to participate in this decision." He and Rehnquist would vote for a rehearing.[9] That made a majority of five for carrying *Roe* over to the next term.

Douglas was shocked and threatened: "If the vote of the Conference is to reargue, then I will file a statement telling what is happening to us and the tragedy it entails."[10] That would only have intensified tensions. Douglas was finally persuaded not to publicize his outrage and instead simply to note that he dissented from the Court's order for reargument. Blackmun also decided to spend the summer further researching the complex issues in this increasingly vexing case.

On October 11, 1972, the Court heard rearguments. For a second time, Weddington stood before the high bench to ask that it rule that women have a right to choose to continue or terminate a pregnancy. Since *Vuitch,* she pointed out, more than 1,600 Texas women had gone to New York City for abortions, and there were "many other women going to other parts of the country." But Weddington's arguments were repeatedly interrupted by questions from the bench about the rights of the unborn. Justice White put it bluntly, "[W]ould you lose your case if the fetus was a person?" That would require a balancing of interests, Weddington replied, but that was not at issue here, since it had not been asserted that a fetus has any constitutional rights. The issue was simply a conflict between the constitutional rights of women and the statutory interests of the state. The state would have to establish that the fetus is a "person" under the Fourteenth Amendment or some other part of the Constitution, before it would have a compelling interest in prohibiting abortions and require the Court to strike a balance with women's constitutional rights.

"That's what's involved in this case? Weighing one life against another?" White again asked toward the end of Weddington's oral argument time. No, she insisted in her concluding exchange with the justices:

STEWART: Well, if—if it were established that an unborn fetus is a person, with the protection of the Fourteenth Amendment, you would have almost an impossible case here, would you not?

WEDDINGTON: I would have a very difficult case.

STEWART: I'm sure you would. So, if you had the same kind of thing, you'd have to say that this would be the equivalent—after the child was born, if the mother thought it bothered her health any having the child around, she could have it killed. Isn't that correct.

WEDDINGTON: That's correct. That—

BURGER: Could Texas constitutionally, in your view, declare that— by statute, that the fetus is a person, for all constitutional purposes, after the third month of gestation?

WEDDINGTON: I do not believe that the State legislature can determine the meaning of the Federal Constitution. It is up to this Court to make that determination.

Chief Justice Burger then called Robert C. Flowers, who had replaced Floyd and as assistant attorney general represented Texas before the Court. From the outset, Flowers faced a steady barrage of questions about whether a fetus is a "person" under the Constitution. He was driven to concede that no case had recognized the fetus as a "person" and that the Fourteenth Amendment extends protection only to those born or naturalized in the United States. At the prodding of White, he was forced to agree that the case would be lost if the fetus is not recognized as a "person." Yet, Flowers continued to insist that the unborn are entitled to constitutional protection. In response to questions from Justices Marshall and Rehnquist, however, he could not supply any medical evidence that a fetus is a "person" at the time of conception. Finally, Flowers confessed that he knew of no way "that any court or any legislature or any doctor anywhere can say that here is the dividing line. Here is not a life; and here is a life, after conception."

Whether a fetus is a "person," Flowers argued, is an issue that should be left to the state legislatures. But that argument underscored the Court's dilemma and aroused Stewart:

Well, if you're right that an unborn fetus is a person, then you can't leave it to the legislature to play fast and loose dealing with that person. In other words, if you're correct, in your basic submission that an unborn fetus is a person, then abortion laws such as that which New York has are grossly unconstitutional, isn't it?

Liberal abortion laws, Flowers urged, allow "the killing of people." But, put this way, the matter could not be left to the states, for it ran against the logic of constitutional law to say that a fetus is a "person" in one state but not in another. It is the Court's responsibility to interpret the Constitution. If the Court struck down the Texas law, it would invite attacks by those who believe that the fetus is a "person" entitled to constitutional protection. But, even though there may be good, moral arguments for recognizing the personhood of an unborn, there was no constitutional basis for ruling that way. Neither the text nor the history of the drafting of the Constitution and the Fourteenth Amendment revealed that the unborn are "persons" with constitutionally protected rights. Scientific evidence was not helpful, and the reform of abortion laws in almost half of the states supported the conclusion that the unborn were not generally considered legal persons. If Texas's century-old law were upheld on the ground that the unborn are "persons" under the Constitution, then the Court would be making law that ran counter to the text and history of the Constitution as well as legal and social trends, and would thus force it to strike down all of the recently enacted state laws permitting abortions.

Weddington had a few minutes to give a final rebuttal, but most of her time was consumed by questions from Burger, who returned to whether *Vuitch* had not already settled the issues here. Again, she reiterated, the issue of a woman's right to decide whether to terminate an unwanted pregnancy had not been decided in *Vuitch*, and that issue had divided the lower federal courts; nine decisions had favored women in upholding the constitutionality of liberal abortion laws, and five had not. The issue was one that the Court could not avoid or leave to the lower courts or state legislatures. The issue was basically one of human dignity, that of a woman's struggle for power and for the right to have some control over her own life. Norma McCorvey had been raped and then forced to bear an unwanted child because of the Texas law and because she was too poor to go elsewhere for an abortion. "We are not here to advocate abortion," Weddington concluded.

We do not ask this Court to rule that abortion is good, or desirable in any particular situation. We are here to advocate that the decision as to whether or not a particular woman will continue to carry or will terminate a pregnancy is a decision that should be made by that individual; that, in fact, she has a constitutional right to make that decision for herself; and that the State has shown no interest in interfering with that decision.

About a month after the Court heard rearguments, Blackmun had finished a new draft of his opinion for *Roe*. "It has been an interesting assignment," he observed when circulating the draft that eventually became the Court's final opinion. The opinion struck down the abortion law, but now along the lines originally advanced by Douglas and Brennan at conference. The opinion announced that the constitutional right of privacy is "broad enough to encompass a woman's decision whether or not to terminate her pregnancy." During the rest of November and most of December, Blackmun continued to rework portions of the opinion in light of other justices' comments. On December 21, he sent around his final draft. Douglas, Brennan, Marshall, and Stewart immediately agreed to join. Soon after the Christmas holidays, Powell also signed on, commending Blackmun for his "exceptional scholarship."[11] By mid-January, Burger had also agreed, though he would add a short concurring opinion, saying that he did not support "abortion on demand." Rehnquist and White were the only dissenters.

States could no longer categorically proscribe abortions or make them unnecessarily difficult to obtain. The promotion of maternal care and the preservation of the life of a fetus were not sufficiently "compelling state interests" to justify restrictive abortion laws. During roughly the first trimester (three months) of a pregnancy, the decision on abortion is that of a woman and her doctor. During the second, the Court ruled, states may regulate abortions, but only in ways reasonably related to its interest in safeguarding the health of women. In the third trimester, states' interests in preserving the life of the unborn become compelling, and they may limit, even ban, abortions, except when necessary to save a woman's life.

At conference, Blackmun had warned that the opinion "will probably result in the Court's being severely criticized." He therefore took special care in preparing the statement announcing the decision that he would read from the bench on January 23, 1973, and even had copies made available for reporters in the hope that they would not go "all the way off the deep end."[12]

But immediate press coverage was muted. President Lyndon Johnson died the day the ruling came down, and so the announcement of the landmark decision shared the headlines in the *New York Times, Los Angeles Times, Chicago Tribune,* and other major newspapers.

Reactions outside the media, however, were intense and mixed. The president of the Planned Parenthood Federation of America, Dr. Alan Guttmacher, hailed the ruling as "a wise

and courageous stroke for the right of privacy, and for the
protection of a woman's physical and emotional health." Others, especially Catholics, took quite a different view. The justices "have made themselves a 'super legislature,' " New York's
Cardinal Cooke charged. "Whatever their legal rationale, seven
men have made a tragic utilitarian judgment regarding who
shall live and who shall die."[13] "Apparently the Court was
trying to straddle the fence and give something to everybody," concluded Philadelphia's Cardinal John Krol after
reading the opinion: "abortion on demand before three months
for those who want that, somewhat more restrictive abortion
regulations after three months for those who want that."[14]

Underlying these reactions was the irony of the Court ruling liberally even though it was packed with "strict construc-
tionists." The final ruling was handed down by a Court that
President Nixon had tried to remold in his own image. As a
presidential candidate in 1968 Nixon had attacked the "liberal
jurisprudence" of the Warren Court (1953–1969) for being
unfaithful to the text of the Constitution. Nixon's four
appointees—Warren Burger, Harry Blackmun, Lewis Powell
and William Rehnquist—were all selected for their conservative "strict constructionist" judicial philosophy. Strict con-
structionists hold that constitutional interpretation should be
confined to a literal reading of the Constitution informed by
an understanding of its historical context. Yet only Rehnquist
and Kennedy appointee White dissented from the Court's
ruling that women have a constitutional right to have abortions.

Even those who favored the ruling sharply criticized *Roe*
for resting on a constitutional right of privacy. Scholars attacked
the legal analysis and reliance on scientific and medical evidence in the opinion.[15] The Court had created the right of
privacy out of whole constitutional cloth, when striking down
laws limiting the availability of contraceptives in *Griswold v.
Connecticut* (1965). In *Griswold,* Douglas held that a consti-

tutional right of privacy may be found in the "penumbras," "emanations," or "shadows" of various guarantees of the Bill of Rights. A right of associational privacy may be found in the penumbra of the First Amendment. The Third Amendment's prohibition against the quartering of soldiers "in any house" without the consent of the owner, Douglas claimed, is another facet of constitutionally protected privacy. The Fourth Amendment explicitly guarantees the right "of the people to be secure in their persons, houses, papers, and effects, against unreasonable searches and seizures." The Fifth Amendment's safeguard against self-incrimination also "enables the citizen to create a zone of privacy." Finally, Douglas noted, the Ninth Amendment provides that "[t]he enumeration in the Constitution, of certain rights, shall not be construed to deny or disparage others retained by the people." Douglas's penumbra theory of a right of privacy was, perhaps, too imaginative to persuade many court watchers. And *Roe* went even further. A woman's interests in abortion appeared to have little to do with those privacy interests identified in *Griswold* with various guarantees of the Bill of Rights. Rather than privacy per se, abortion basically involves a woman's liberty under the Constitution.[16]

Other court watchers critical of *Roe* took their cue from Rehnquist's dissenting opinion. They attacked the Court for becoming a "super legislature" in determining when a state's interests are compelling enough to override a woman's interests in obtaining an abortion. In overturning most abortion laws, the Court held that states' interests become compelling only at the point of "viability"—the point at which the fetus is "potentially able to live outside the mother's womb, albeit with artificial aid." For states' rights advocates like Rehnquist, the Court impermissibly imposed its own view on state legislatures.

For still others, the Court committed a more fundamental sin: it had written the rights of the unborn out of the Constitution. "In my opinion," Utah's Republican Senator Orrin Hatch proclaimed, "this is clearly the *Dred Scott* issue of this century."[17] In *Dred Scott v. Sandford* (1857) the Court held that under the Constitution blacks were not "persons" entitled to its protection. Chief Justice Roger Taney also held that Congress had unconstitutionally enacted the Missouri Compromise, prohibiting slavery in the Louisiana Territory, except in Missouri. The Court thereby exacerbated tensions between the North and the South and hastened the movement toward the Civil War. In *Roe*, the Court did not resolve the question of when life begins, but held that the unborn do not enjoy protection under the Fourteenth Amendment's guarantee that no state may "deprive any person of life, liberty, or property, without due process of law." The Constitution does not define "person," and, the Court reasoned, the use of the word in the text of the Constitution, as well as the rather permissive abortion practices in the early nineteenth century, indicates that "the word 'person,' as used in the Fourteenth Amendment, does not include the unborn."

Advocates of planned parenthood and pro-choice views celebrated the ruling, while groups like the National Right to Life Committee denounced the Court for sanctioning an increase in the number of abortions. The number of illegal abortions declined from nearly 750,000 before *Roe* to an estimated 10,000 in 1980. Yet, the number of legal abortions grew from 744,610 in the year following the decision to over 1.5 million in 1981. In 1982–1983 there were an average of 426 abortions per 1,000 births in the United States. The District of Columbia had the highest ratio of abortions to births, with 1,517 for every 1,000 live births. New York led the states with a ratio of 731 abortions to every 1,000 births, while in Utah there were only 100 abortions for every 1,000 births.[18]

Hundreds of thousands of letters arrived at the Court, some congratulating but most condemning the justices. Blackmun received more than 45,000 letters, and he was seriously trou-

Demonstration on the steps of the Supreme Court Building protesting rulings on abortion. *(Washington Post)*

bled by attacks on him as the "Butcher of Dachau, murderer, Pontius Pilate, Adolph Hitler." Threats were made on his life. A decade later, a group called the Army of God bombed offices of Planned Parenthood around the country. Security at the Court was increased and more protection given to the justices when they traveled to and from the Court.

Opponents of *Roe* organized to elect representatives to enact new laws and constitutional amendments to overturn the decision. In the three years after *Roe,* thirty-four states passed new abortion laws. Some were in conformity with the Court's ruling—requiring, for example, that abortions be performed by licensed physicians—but many others sought to limit the impact of *Roe.* States tried to restrict the availability of abortions in several ways: by requiring the informed consent of a husband or that of parents for a minor's abortion, by forbidding the advertising of abortion services, and by withholding state funds for abortions not medically necessary.[19]

Like most Supreme Court policy-making, *Roe* left numerous questions unanswered and afforded ample opportunities for thwarting the implementation of its mandate. But the Court for the most part struck down state and local attempts to limit the impact of *Roe.*[20] Even after the retirements of Douglas and Stewart—and the appointments of John Paul Stevens in 1975 and Sandra Day O'Connor in 1981—the Court continued to affirm its ruling in *Roe.* In *City of Akron v. Akron Center for Reproductive Health* (1983), the Court struck down an informed-consent requirement for abortions. O'Connor, joined only by Rehnquist and White, dissented and suggested a willingness to reverse *Roe.* But Powell countered that the majority would not yield to pressure from within or from outside the Court. *Roe* "was considered with special care" and "joined by the Chief Justice and six other Justices," Powell emphasized. "Since *Roe* was decided," he asserted, "the Court repeatedly and consistently has accepted and applied the basic principle that a woman has a fundamental right to make the highly personal choice whether or not to terminate her pregnancy." Unless the Court's composition changed further, it would not overturn *Roe*.

An annual "March for Life," attracting greater followings each year in picketing the Court on the anniversary of *Roe*, came to symbolize that abortion had risen to the national political agenda of the 1980s. After 1973, constitutional amendments were introduced in every Congress to limit or overturn the ruling. Some proposed "right-to-life" amendments would simply return to the pre-*Roe* practice of allowing the states to freely regulate abortions. Others, introduced by Senators Hatch and Jesse Helms, would amend the Constitution to recognize the unborn as "persons" with protected rights. Still other bills aimed to limit the federal courts' jurisdiction over abortion and, more successfully, to withdraw funding from welfare programs for nontherapeutic abortions.[21] By 1980, abortion was an issue in presidential politics as well. The Republican platform and President Ronald Reagan supported a constitutional amendment "to restore protection of the right to life for unborn children." Reagan promised to appoint to the federal bench only individuals opposed to abortion.

Roe invited a heated political controversy among special-interest groups over abortion policy. But the general public remained ambivalent. Approximately 46 percent of the public favored the decision; 45 percent opposed it. A decade later, 41 percent agreed that it should be possible for a married woman who did not want to have any more children to obtain an abortion; 49 percent disagreed. Rather consistently since 1973, public opinion polls show that over 80 percent approve of abortions if the woman's health is endangered, if the pregnancy was due to rape or incest, and if there is a likelihood of fetal abnormality. Over 60 percent oppose a constitutional amendment to make abortions illegal.[22]

No Longer the Least Dangerous Branch

Like other rulings on major issues of policy, *Roe* invited criticism that the Court is no longer, in Alexander Hamilton's words, "the least dangerous" branch. Rather, critics charge, the Court has become a "super legislature." But the Court's responsibility has always been to interpret the Constitution.

The role and power of the Court have changed with American politics. The Court first struck down an act of Congress in *Marbury v. Madison* (1803), when Chief Justice John Marshall interpreted the Judiciary Act of 1789 to have impermissibly expanded the Court's original jurisdiction under Article III of the Constitution. The Marshall Court also overturned a number of state laws and thereby legitimated the power of the national government and its own power of judicial review. But the Court did not challenge Congress again until the Taney Court's decision in *Dred Scott v. Sandford* in 1857.

Since the late nineteenth century, the Court has assumed a major role in monitoring the governmental process. The Court regularly overturns acts of Congress, of the states, and even of local and municipal governments. The table on page 43 illustrates the trend toward more judicial activism, or willingness to overturn decisions of other political institutions.[23] *Roe v. Wade* dramatically exemplifies this trend, because it placed the Court at the center of a great national controversy. But it is by no means an isolated case.

Over the last thirty years the Court, regardless of its composition, has increasingly asserted its power. The ideologically conservative Burger Court, for example, has been more activist than the liberal Warren Court. The trend is likely to continue regardless of future appointments and attempts to curb the Court. The reasons why this is so are the subject of this book. The controversial appointment of justices and their struggles for influence, the ever more bureaucratic structure of the Court, and the pressure of important cases like *Roe v. Wade* have given the Supreme Court a new, more difficult role to play in American political life.

DECISIONS OF THE SUPREME COURT OVERRULED AND
ACTS OF CONGRESS HELD UNCONSTITUTIONAL, 1789–1984;
AND STATE LAWS AND MUNICIPAL ORDINANCES
OVERTURNED, 1789–1980

Year	Supreme Court Decision Overruled	Acts of Congress Overturned	State Laws Overturned	Ordinances Overturned
1789–1800, Pre-Marshall				
1801–1835, Marshall Court	3	1	18	
1836–1864, Taney Court	6	1	21	
1865–1873, Chase Court	3	10	33	
1874–1888, Waite Court	11	9	7	
1889–1910, Fuller Court	4	14	73	15
1910–1921, White Court	6	12	107	18
1921–1930, Taft Court	5	12	131	12
1930–1940, Hughes Court	14	14	78	5
1941–1946, Stone Court	24	2	25	7
1947–1952, Vinson Court	11	1	38	7
1953–1969, Warren Court	46	25	150	16
1969–1986, Burger Court	50	34	192	15

TWO

The Cult of the Robe

THERE is no reason in the world why a President should not 'pack' the Court"—"appoint people to the Court who are sympathetic to his political and philosophical principles."[1] So Justice William Rehnquist answered Democratic charges that the 1984 reelection of President Ronald Reagan could change the direction of Supreme Court policymaking. Because justices serve for life, they furnish Presidents with historic opportunities to influence the direction of national policy well beyond his own term.

The myth occasionally circulates that appointments should be made strictly on merit. Attorney General Ramsey Clark, for instance, confided to President Lyndon Johnson, "I think a most significant contribution to American government would be the non-political appointment of judges."[2] Yet, Johnson's appointments of Abe Fortas and Thurgood Marshall were political, as those of all other Presidents have been.

Once on the bench, justices often forget their political history and complain that Presidents don't know enough about the Court to make intelligent appointments, Justice Felix Frankfurter, for one, felt that President John Kennedy and his attorney general, Robert Kennedy, chose inferior judges.

"What does Bobby understand about the Supreme Court? He understands about as much about it as you understand about the undiscovered 76th star in the galaxy. . . . He said Arthur Goldberg was a scholarly lawyer. I wonder where he got that notion from."[3] What perturbed Frankfurter was that the Kennedy administration did "not adequately appreciate the Supreme Court's role in the country's life and the functions that are entrusted to the Supreme Court and the qualities both intellectual and moral that are necessary to the discharge of its functions." Distinguished individuals were accordingly passed over, in Frankfurter's opinion, in favor of such "wholly inexperienced men as Goldberg and White, without familiarity with the jurisdiction or the jurisprudence of the Court either as practitioners or scholars or judges."[4]

Judges and scholars perpetuate the myth of merit. The dean of Stanford Law School and former clerk to Chief Justice Earl Warren, John Hart Ely, when Justice Douglas's seat became open in 1975, wrote to President Gerald Ford, "Should the Court over time come to be viewed as just another political branch, America will have lost, irretrievably lost, something that is entirely unique and extremely valuable." It is crucial, he insisted, "that the process of selection be one that is structured—and, at least as important, that it be perceived by the public—as not primarily political."[5]

The reality is that every appointment is political. Merit competes with other political considerations like personal and ideological compatibility, with the forces of support or opposition in Congress and the White House, and with demands for representative appointments on the basis of geography, religion, race, gender, and ethnicity.

The Myth of Merit

The Supreme Court is not a meritocracy. This is so for essentially two reasons: the difficulties of defining merit and the politics of judicial selection.

Any definition of "judicial merit" is artificial. Henry Abraham, a leading scholar on the appointment of justices, proposes following six criteria of judicial merit: demonstrated judicial temperament; professional expertise and competence; absolute personal and professional integrity; an able, agile, lucid mind; appropriate professional educational background or training; and the ability to communicate clearly, both orally and in writing.[6] Yet, justices themselves have difficulty defining such qualities as "judicial temperament." Judicial merit is perhaps reducible only to the standard of "obscenity" offered by Justice Potter Stewart: "I know it when I see it."[7]

A disproportionate number of justices are appointed from prominent positions in the legal profession, the executive branch, and lower federal and state courts. The prior positions of the 102 justices who have served on the Court are as follows:[8]

Private legal practice	25
Federal bench	21
Executive branch	21
State bench	21
U.S. Senate	6
State governorship	3
House of Representatives	2
Law school professorship	2
Miscellaneous	1

But legal education and previous judicial experience have not been necessary for appointment to or achievement on the bench. In the first seventy-five years of the nineteenth century, law schools as we know them did not exist, and up until World War I the majority of the legal profession learned law through apprenticeship. Not until 1957, when Justice Charles Whittaker replaced Justice Stanley Reed, did all sitting members of the Court hold law degrees. Lack of prior judicial experience has not been a barrier either. No fewer than 80 of the 102 justices who sat in the Court had less than ten years of previous federal or state court experience. In the last century, 36 percent of the justices had no prior judicial experience, and even more (44 percent) have had none this century. Judicial inexperience does not result in failure on the bench. Six chief justices had no prior experience—Marshall, Taney, Chase, Waite, Fuller, and Warren—as well as some outstanding associate justices, including Joseph Story, Louis Brandeis, Harlan Stone, Charles Evans Hughes, Felix Frankfurter, Robert Jackson, and William Rehnquist.

Judicial selection, as Justice Stone put it, is like a "lottery" from a pool of more or less qualified individuals. One of Stone's close friends, the Harvard law professor and political scientist Thomas Reed Powell, was even more blunt: "[T]he selection of Supreme Court Justices is pretty much a matter of chance."[9] Political associations and personal friendships often determine the fate of candidates for the Court. Powell saw this illustrated in the fact that

[President] Taft met [his appointee Mahlon] Pitney at a dinner given to advance Swazye's prospects and preferred him to Swayze; . . . that [Justice Joseph] McKenna was a personal associate of [President William] McKinley; that [Justice William] Day also was and that his appointment by [President Theodore] Roosevelt was a legacy from McKinley; that [Justice Pierce] Butler was known to Taft in the Canadian Railways Valuation work and was a Catholic who could be substituted for Manton without having to turn down a Catholic . . . that [Justice Stone] had been in college with [President Calvin] Coolidge; that [Justice] Brandeis had a closer relation with [President Woodrow] Wilson than with members of the Boston Bar, etc.[10]

Meritorious individuals are thus passed over. Paul Freund, a respected Harvard law professor and clerk for Justice Brandeis in 1932, is one who was denied a deserved seat on the high bench. During the Kennedy administration, Freund was offered the solicitor generalship, but he declined it. The Kennedys were accordingly unwilling to give him a lifetime appointment to the Court. As Attorney General Robert Kennedy explained, when discussing why Freund and others had not been nominated, "Some of these other people we didn't know, and we did know that Byron White had ability and that Arthur Goldberg had ability. We'd worked with them, they'd worked with us, so why not appoint them rather than somebody that someone else said was good but that neither my brother nor I knew? That was the basis of it."[11]

Later, insiders in the Johnson White House and others continued to push for Freund's appointment. Even though he was then in his sixties, Freund, insisted the presidential adviser James Rowe, "is, without question, easily the most qualified man in the United States to sit on the Supreme Court."[12] When he was seventy (well beyond the usual age of mid-fifties for most appointees), his nomination for Justice Douglas's seat was again urged on the ground that any appointment by the unelected "accidental President" Ford would be controversial. Freund's "nomination would be perceived as apolitical," and he would serve, if even for a short time, with distinction.[13] He was nonetheless passed over again.

No appointment has been more widely acclaimed as meritorious than that of Benjamin Cardozo, yet it was primarily due to political expediency. Frankfurter, for one, proclaimed, "The appointment of Cardozo is the noble fruit of a large-minded statesmanship on the President's part."[14] When telling President Hoover of the large number of letters he received hailing the appointment, Stone noted, "The interesting thing about Judge Cardozo's appointment is that, although there is nothing political in it, it will prove, I believe, to be of immense political advantage to the President. No appointment he has made has been better received."[15]

A leading liberal and chief judge on the New York Court of Appeals, Cardozo was indubitably distinguished. But he had been passed over several times before the Republican President Hoover nominated him in 1932. He had been mentioned for the seat vacated by William Day in 1922. Leaders of the New York Bar continued to push him for positions filled by Presidents Warren Harding and Calvin Coolidge.[16] Cardozo was first considered by Hoover when Edward Sanford died in 1930. The President wanted to appoint someone from the West, since there was no representation of that region on the Court at the time. However, Hoover's adviser George Wickersham failed to find anyone from that region who merited serious consideration. Wickersham proposed naming Attorney General William Mitchell, the Pennsylvania attorney Owen Roberts, or the prominent attorney and unsuccessful 1924 presidential candidate John W. Davis. Hoover's close friend Justice Stone sent his list of candidates. At the top was Cardozo; at the bottom was the conservative North Carolina circuit court of appeals judge John J. Parker.[17] The President went down the list, eliminating potential nominees on the basis of their geographical location and political leanings, and finally settled on Judge Parker.[18]

Hoover's nomination was immediately attacked by the American Federation of Labor and other labor organizations, because one of Parker's decisions was interpreted as anti-union. The National Association for the Advancement of Colored People also lobbied against his confirmation, because they thought he was an enemy of black voting rights. After a six-week battle, the Senate for the first time in the twentieth century rejected a nomination to the Court, by the narrow margin of forty-one to thirty-nine. The respected Republican attorney Owen Roberts was subsequently nominated and confirmed. Hoover was badly embarrassed by the defeat of Parker. When the opportunity arose to make his next and last appointment, in 1932, he nominated Cardozo, for his reputation was unimpeachable, his nomination politically opportune, and his confirmation certain.

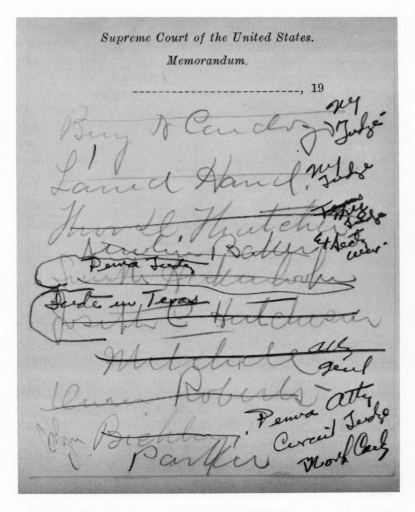

**Note from Justice Harlan Stone, recommending individuals for appointment to the
Supreme Court in 1930, with President Herbert Hoover's notes.** *(Herbert Hoover
Presidential Library)*

Politics conspired to assure Cardozo's appointment, just as it may defeat meritorious candidates. White House politics defeated the selection of Freund, though he unquestionably deserved a seat on the bench. Politics in the Senate defeated Parker, yet he served with distinction for another twenty-eight years on the court of appeals and was again considered for an appointment during the Roosevelt and Truman administrations.[19] The verdict on candidates for the Court turns less on merit than on political visibility, support, and circumstance.

Process of Appointment

The appointment of justices is guided by the Constitution and the competitive politics of the nomination and confirmation process. Article II, Section 2, of the Constitution stipulates that the President "shall nominate, and by and with the Advice and Consent of the Senate, shall appoint" members of the federal judiciary.* The Senate's power to reject nominees is the crucial obstacle that a President must overcome. Twenty-four nominees to the Court have fallen prey to partisan politics, either because of the nominee's political views or because the Senate wanted to deny "lame duck" Presidents appointments to the high court. Thanks to the tradition of "senatorial courtesy," which began in the 1840s, the Senate may also refuse to confirm an individual opposed by the senators of the President's party and the nominee's home state. Only two nomi-

---

*In contrast with the system of appointing federal judges, the methods of selecting state court judges are rather complex. They vary from state to state, and among different courts within particular states. The methods of selection include popular—partisan and nonpartisan—election; appointment by governors or legislatures; and some combination of both methods, or so-called merit systems. In the merit system, a nonpartisan commission provides lists of nominee from which the governor or legislature makes appointments; then, after one year of service, the judges have names placed on a ballot and voters decide whether they should be retained.[20]

nees—George Williams in 1873 and G. Harrold Carswell in
1970—suffered defeat because of mediocre judicial records and
lack of professional qualifications.

The influence of the Senate has declined in the selection
of Supreme Court justices but not in that of lower federal
court judges. Presidents in fact trade lower-court judgeships
for legislation and good relations.[21] Federal judgeships are
opportunities for the Senate, no less than for the President,
to influence national policy and confer political patronage. The
tradition of senatorial courtesy guarantees patronage. During
President Jimmy Carter's administration, "merit" commissions were created in an effort to minimize the influence of
the Senate over lower-court judgeships. But the commissions
did not work well and were abandoned when Reagan took
office. Some senators simply refused to give up control over
their patronage appointments. As Mississippi's Senator James
Eastland told Carter's attorney general Griffin Bell, "I'll hand
you a slip of paper with one name on it, and that'll be the
judge." Bell, a former court of appeals judge, knew from first-
hand experience the vested interests in "senatorial courtesy."
"Becoming a federal judge wasn't very difficult," he recalled
of his own appointment to the federal bench. "I managed John
F. Kennedy's presidential campaign in Georgia. Two of my
oldest friends were the senators from Georgia. And I was
campaign manager and special unpaid counsel for the governor."[22]

The appointment process has become essentially a bargaining process in which the influence of the Senate is greater
in regard to lower-court judgeships and that of the President
is greater in regard to the Supreme Court. At the level of
federal district courts, in Attorney General Kennedy's words,
"Basically, it's senatorial appointment with the advice and
consent of the President."[23] Presidents have greater discretion at the level of circuit courts of appeals, whose jurisdiction
spans several states. They may play senators off against each

other by claiming the need for representation of different political parties, geographical regions, religions, races, and the like within a circuit. "In the case of the Supreme Court Justices," Hoover's attorney general, William Mitchell, observed, "with the whole country to choose from, the Senators from one state or another are in no position even if they were so inclined, to attempt a controlling influence. Such an appointment is not a local matter, and the entire nation has an equal interest and responsibility."[24] But the Senate as a whole still has the power to influence the selection of, and even to defeat, a President's nominee.

Most Presidents delegate responsibility to their attorney general and close advisers for selecting candidates and getting them through the Senate. The assistant attorney general in charge of the Office of Legal Policy usually begins by compiling a list of candidates from recommendations by White House staff, congressmen, governors, state and local bar associations, and individuals wanting to be considered or suggesting others. A committee of the president's top advisers narrows the number per position down to two or three, on the basis of a political evaluation and (until the Reagan administration) informal approval by the American Bar Association (ABA). An exhaustive FBI investigation is then initiated and a formal evaluation by the ABA requested. Once these reports are reviewed, a recommendation is sent to the President. If he approves, it is formally submitted to the Senate. The Senate Judiciary Committees sends a "blue slip" to the senators of the same state as the nominee for their approval. If there is no objection, a confirmation hearing—typically lasting only a few minutes—is held before a subcommittee of the Judiciary Committee, which finally moves confirmation by the full Senate.

Presidents are now less involved in the process of appointing justices. Their greater reliance on staff has brought the possibility of more infighting at the White House. Appoint-

ments have become less a personal presidential decision than
a hard choice from among candidates promoted by various
vested-interests groups. The appointment of John Paul Stevens in 1975 illustrates the diverse pressures within the contemporary presidency.

In an irony of history, the opportunity to fill the seat of
the outspoken liberal Justice Douglas fell to the Republican
President Ford. As a congressman, Ford had sought to impeach
Douglas in 1970. Yet, Ford had no electoral mandate. He had
been appointed Vice-president by President Nixon and had
moved into the Oval Office when Nixon resigned rather than
face impeachment in 1974. With his own possible election
and place in history in mind, Ford faced the forces of competing interests within the White House and the watchful eye of
liberal senators. There was considerable pressure on him to
appoint the first woman to the Court. Conservatives in the
administration, like Ford's presidential adviser and head of
the American Enterprise Institute, William Baroody, however, urged the nomination of the Yale law professor and AEI
associate Robert Bork. Bork, later appointed by Reagan to the
Court of Appeals for the District of Columbia Circuit, served
as Nixon's solicitor general and acting attorney general during
the Watergate episode. "He is young and is a strict Constructionist and," wrote Arizona's Senator Barry Goldwater, "would
give continuity to the kind of Court that you want for at least
twenty-five years." But, for precisely those reasons, the nomination of such a conservative associated with the disgraced
Nixon administration would have been extremely controversial. It might have been defeated by Democrats in the Senate
and hurt Ford's bid for the 1976 election. As a moderate
Republican, Ford leaned toward the advice of Attorney General Edward Levi, who was on leave from the University of
Chicago School of Law and who promoted the elevation of
Stevens, a Nixon appointee to the federal court of appeals in
Chicago. After conferring with Senator Charles Percy of Illi-

nois, Senate Judiciary Committee Chairman Eastland, and others, Ford made a pragmatic, rather than ideologically controversial, nomination.[25]

The nomination and confirmation process thus involves numerous political compromises and much "horse-trading." The role of the ABA in that process deserves special attention. Its evaluations certify the legal qualification of nominees and thus become political bargaining chips. The ABA's Standing Committee on Federal Judiciary began screening prospective candidates for the Court with the nomination of William Brennan in 1956, rating them as "qualified'" or "unqualified." This system continued until the appointment of Harry Blackmun in 1970. Criticism of the Senate's rejection of Nixon's nomination of Clement Haynsworth and G. Harrold Carswell—whom the committee had ranked as "highly qualified" and "qualified," respectively—led to a change in the ABA system of rating. Nominees for the Court are now rated "highly qualified," "not opposed," or "not qualified." (Nominees for lower courts are rated "exceptionally well qualified," "well qualified," "qualified," or "not qualified").[26] After Blackmun's appointment, Nixon's attorney general John Mitchell refused to submit any further candidates to the ABA committee, because of an unfavorable news story about possible nominees for the seats of retiring Justices John Harlan and Hugo Black. The ABA committee nonetheless conducted its own investigation of Nixon's last two appointments to the Court: it unanimously endorsed Lewis F. Powell, a former ABA president, as "one of the country's best lawyers available," and it gave William Rehnquist, a Nixon administration assistant attorney general, nine votes for a "highly qualified" ranking and three "not opposed" votes for his appointment. With Ford's nomination of Stevens in 1975, the ABA reestablished its formal role in the confirmation process.

The prestige of the ABA serves to legitimize the qualifications of nominees, but does not alter the basic politics of appointments. A former member of the ABA committee, Leon Jaworski, points out that the ABA typically functions as a "buffer" between the White House and the Senate. Senators may be told, "Well, the American Bar Association has turned [your candidate] down, who can we agree on now?"[27] The ABA rule that a nominee not be over the age of sixty, for instance, was frequently invoked by the Kennedys to avoid having to appoint senators' nominees of whom they disapproved. Yet, the rule proved no obstacle to the appointment of the highly qualified but sixty-four-year-old Sarah Hughes as circuit court judge. As Johnson's attorney general put it, "A gentlemen never asks a lady her age."[28]

The ABA committee is not above politics, either in rating nominees or in being lobbied by senators, White House officials, and justices. When his former law clerk was nominated for a court of appeals judgeship, Powell did not hesitate to lobby for J. Harvie Wilkinson. The committee eventually rated Wilkinson "qualified," even though he did not meet the ABA's standard of twelve years of legal practice and trial experience.[29]

Political Trade-offs

Packing the Court has come to mean not merely filling the bench with political associates and ideological kin but accommodating the demands for other kinds of symbolic political representation. Some people maintain that merit rather than political favoritism should govern appointments, and others, like Justice Stone, lament that "the view has come to prevail that in addition to political considerations, considerations of race, religion and sectional interests should influence the appointment."[30] In fact, it is neither merit nor representative factors like geography, religion, race, and gender that proves controlling; instead, it is the competing political considerations in presidential attempts to pack the Court.

IDEOLOGICAL COMPATIBILITY AND GEOGRAPHY

President George Washington initiated the practice of appointing only ideological kin to the Court. When Thomas Jefferson won the election in 1800, President John Adams wanted to ensure the preservation of Federalist philosophy in the national government and appointed his secretary of state, John Marshall, as chief justice. It fell to Andrew Jackson in 1835 to appoint Marshall's successor, and he immediately turned to his longtime supporter and secretary of the treasury, Roger B. Taney. President Lincoln, in turn, appointed his secretary of the treasury, Salmon Chase, to fill Taney's seat in 1864.

Presidents invariably let the swing of elections control appointments and make little effort to balance the Court by crossing party lines. The party affiliations of those who have served on the Court largely reflect those of their presidential benefactors: thirteen Federalists, one Whig, eight Democratic-Republicans, thirty-eight Republicans, and forty-two Democrats.

Only one Democratic President crossed party lines to fill a vacancy on the Court. Stone, a Republican, had been elevated to the post of chief justice by FDR. But after FDR filled eight seats with Democrats and died in the spring of 1945, Truman faced considerable pressure to name a Republican to the seat of retiring Justice Roberts. Although the selection of Harold Burton, a Republican senator, was inspired by political pressure, Truman was perfectly comfortable with his appointment, because they had been close friends for over a decade.[31]

Republican presidents have more frequently named Democrats, but only when it was politically expedient or as a reward for personal and ideological compatibility. The first crossover appointment was made by President John Tyler, a nominal Whig. After several rejections of earlier nominees, he named the Democrat Samuel Nelson in 1845, just before the Democratic President James Polk took office. Elected by a minority of the popular vote, President Lincoln appointed California's Stephen Field as a gesture to northern and western Democrats in an effort to broaden political support. Benjamin Harrison was defeated for reelection in 1892, and he named Howell Jackson within days of the inauguration of the Democratic President Grover Cleveland. President William Taft elevated Justice White to the post of chief justice and appointed his friend and ideological kin Horace Lurton. His other Democratic appointee, Joseph Lamar, was the only pure crossover to achieve political balance within the Court. Presidents Harding and Eisenhower appointed Butler and Brennan because of their Catholic affiliation and reportedly conservative views. Nixon named Powell, a Democratic-Republican from Virginia, for his conservative and "strict constructionist" views.

Geography used to figure prominently in appointments. During the founding period, geographical representation was considered crucial to establishing the legitimacy of the Court and the national government. Congress encouraged geographical diversity by requiring the justices to ride circuit. From the appointment of John Rutledge from South Carolina in 1789 until the retirement of Hugo Black in 1971, with the exception of the Reconstruction decade of 1866–1876, there was always a southerner on the bench. Until 1867, the sixth seat was reserved as the "southern seat." Until Cardozo's appointment in 1932, the third seat was reserved for New Englanders.

As the country expanded westward, Presidents were inclined to give representation to new states and regions. After the Civil War, the influx of immigrants and the gradual nationalization of the country diminished the importance of geographical regions. Congress's elimination of circuit riding in 1891 reinforced the declining influence of geography. A few appointments in this century turned on geography, but they were exceptional. President Taft selected Willis Van Devanter from Wyoming in 1910, because he was determined to have a westerner on the court. After he became chief justice, Taft continued to lobby Presidents Harding and Coolidge on the need for geographical balance on the Court.[32]

The appointment of Wiley Rutledge in 1943 illustrates how little geography influences appointments to the modern Court. From FDR's first appointment in 1937, Rutledge, dean of Iowa's law school, was mentioned as a possible nominee because he was a westerner. In 1936, before his own appointment to the high bench, Senator Hugo Black recommended him "as possible material for the Supreme Court." But in 1939 even Black supported the President's decision to pass over Rutledge: "[M]any circumstances," he wrote, "combine to make Felix Frankfurter the only possible nominee at this time, and the balancing of the Court geographically ought to be held back till the next vacancy occurs."[33] Rutledge and geography were repeatedly pushed aside until FDR's last appointment to the Court.[34] Even then, FDR had other reasons for the appointment. Frankfurter made a pest of himself by lobbying for the appointment of Judge Learned Hand, and Roosevelt set his mind against him. During a dinner conversation, Douglas has recalled, FDR said, "Well, this time your Brother Frankfurter has overplayed his hand." He then asked, "Well, in what respect?" The President responded, "Nineteen people have seen me or called me saying that I must appoint Learned Hand. By God, I am not going to do it." Later that evening, Irving Brant, a St. Louis newspaper editor and friend of the President, came by to urge Rutledge's nomination, as he had done many times before. This time, FDR agreed: "That's my man."[35]

Rutledge's appointment shows that geography is not insurmountable. When the justice from the Deep South, Hugo Black, was still on the bench, Haynsworth of South Carolina

and Carswell of Florida were nominated. Nixon claimed that
southerners "deserve representation on the Court."[36] But, after
the Senate refused to confirm both, Nixon named Harry
Blackmun from Minnesota even though his earlier appointee,
Burger, was from that same state. Blackmun was a conservative Republican and "best man" at Burger's wedding. Burger
had recommended his appointment, and in their first years
on the Court together the two were known as "the Minnesota
Twins." Geography also did not dissuade Reagan from
appointing Rehnquist's former Stanford law school classmate
Sandra Day O'Connor, though both were from Arizona. Geographical diversity remains important in the selection of lower
federal appellate court judges; balance is sought on the basis
of population, caseload, and the number of judges from different states in a circuit.[37] But geographical representation on
the Court is less compelling: only thirty-one states have been
represented by the 102 members of the Court. Over half came
from seven states—thirteen from New York; ten from Ohio;
eight from Massachusetts; six each from Pennsylvania, Tennessee, and Virginia; and five from Kentucky.

RELIGION, RACE, GENDER, AND BEYOND

Religion, race, and gender have historically been barriers
to rather than bases for appointments to the Court. The overwhelming majority (91) of the 102 justices have come from
established Protestant religions: 54 from old-line faiths—
Episcopalian, Unitarian, Congregationalist, and Quaker—and
37 from others, such as Baptists, Methodists, Lutheran, and
Disciples of Christ. Of the remaining 11, 6 were Catholics and
5 Jews.

Religion has political symbolism, but it played little role
in judicial selection until the twentieth century. The "Catholic seat" and the "Jewish seat" were created accidentally, rather
than by presidential efforts to give the Court religious balance. Representation, of course, is purely symbolic. Catholics

and Jews do not have well-defined positions, for example, on statutory interpretation. Nor does the appointment of a Catholic or a Jew guarantee that the views of each faith will be reflected in the voting of representative justices. Brennan, a Catholic, did not heed Church teachings when voting in *Roe v. Wade* to uphold a woman's right to obtain an abortion. Religious and racial considerations, moreover, appear "highly indefensible and dangerous" to the extent that more-qualified individuals are passed over. Frankfurter contended that such considerations are "not only irrelevant for appointments to the bench, but mischievously irrelevant—that to appoint men on the score of race and religion [is] playing with fire."[38]

The first Catholic, Chief Justice Taney, was appointed in 1835, but religion had little to do with Jackson's selection of his friend and adviser. Thirty years after Taney's death, the next Catholic was named. Edward White was appointed in 1894, but again religion played a minor role; though in 1910 President Taft was urged to promote him to the post of chief justice because he was "a democrat, a Catholic, and [was] from the South."[39] From White's appointment until 1949, the Court always included one, and usually two, Catholics: Joseph McKenna served from 1898 to 1925; Pierce Butler from 1922 to 1939; and Frank Murphy from 1940 to 1949. For over thirty years (from 1894 to 1925), there were two Catholics on the Court, even though Catholics lacked the political influence they later acquired in the New Deal coalition. Roosevelt rewarded Catholic supporters with an unprecedented number of lower federal court judgeships, but he did not do the same with his appointments to the Court.[40] When Murphy died in 1949, Truman did not feel compelled to appoint another Catholic. None sat on the high bench until Eisenhower's appointment of Brennan in 1956. Devoted to bipartisanship, Eisenhower wanted "a very good Catholic, even a conservative Democrat," in order to "show that we mean our declaration that the Court should be nonpartisan."[41]

In 1853, President Millard Filmore offered a position to Judah Benjamin, but Benjamin wanted to stay in the Senate. Not until President Wilson's appointment of Brandeis in 1916 did the Court acquire its first Jewish justice. Opposition was not necessarily anti-Semitic, but based largely on antagonism toward Brandeis's progressive legal views and reform politics. Seven prior ABA presidents, including William Howard Taft, proclaimed that Brandeis was "not a fit person to be a member of the Supreme Court of the United States."[42] After Brandeis's appointment, there developed an expectation of a "Jewish seat." With the confirmation of Cardozo in 1932 and his subsequent replacement by Frankfurter, two Jewish justices sat on the Court until Brandeis retired in 1939. When Frankfurter stepped down in 1962, the Jewish factor mattered, and Kennedy named Arthur Goldberg, his secretary of labor.[43] Three years later, Johnson persuaded Goldberg to become ambassador to the United Nations, and his vacancy was filled by the President's friend Abe Fortas. Since Fortas's resignation in 1969, no other Jew has sat on the Court.

Although politically symbolic, religious representation on the Court never amounted to a quota system. Catholics and Jews were more often selected because of personal and ideological compatibility with the President. "There is no such thing as a Jewish seat," Goldberg observed, though his religion was a factor that Johnson considered when coaxing him to leave the Court. "The question of whether or not this appointee should be Jewish concerns me," Attorney General Nicholas Katzenbach told the President:

I think most Jews share with me the feeling that you should not seek a Jewish appointment for the "Jewish seat" on the court. It is somewhat offensive to think of religion as a qualification, and you will recall that after Mr. Justice Murphy's death there was no Catholic on the Court for a period of eight years. At the same time, I think it undesirable for there to be no Jew on the Court for too long a period and I think it would be desirable if a Jew were appointed to the Court before 1968. . . . On balance, I think, if you appoint a Jew he should be so outstanding as to be selected clearly on his own merits as an individual. [44]

Johnson was intent on appointing Fortas, regardless of his religion. The two had known each other since the New Deal, and in 1964 LBJ had unsuccessfully urged Fortas to become attorney general. Fortas also initially declined appointment to the Court because he wanted "a few more years of activity."[45] Johnson persisted, and in the end Fortas reluctantly agreed to enter the marble temple.

In 1967, Johnson's advisers told him the time had come for the appointment of a black to the Court.[46] The symbolism of appointing a black was never lost on the President, nor had LBJ's commitment to naming Thurgood Marshall ever waned. As director of the NAACP Counsel of Legal Defense and Education Fund, Marshall gained national recognition while arguing the landmark school desegregation case, *Brown v. Board of Education* (1954). In 1961, Kennedy named him to the U.S. Court of Appeals for the Second Circuit. Subsequently, Johnson persuaded him to give up the judgeship and become his solicitor general. LBJ wanted "that image, number one," of having a black solicitor general, Marshall has recalled. The President told him at the time, "You know this has nothing to do with any Supreme Court appointment. I want that distinctly understood. There's no quid pro here at all. You do your job. If you don't do it, you go out. If you do it, you stay here. And that's all there is to it."[47] That, of course, was not all there was to it. The solicitor generalship offers experience in representing the government before the Court and a strategic basis for elevation to the high bench. As Cornelius Vanderbilt, Jr., remarked, when congratulating the President on the appointment, "This is *great* news! Also it is *very* clever politics."[48]

Marshall was not the first black to be seriously considered

for the Court. Twenty years earlier, rumors had circulated that William Hastie might be named. Dean of Howard University Law School and later a court of appeals judge, Hastie was given more serious consideration during the Kennedy administration. Attorney General Kennedy recalled that Hastie had been his first choice for the vacancy eventually filled by Byron White. Kennedy talked with both Earl Warren and Douglas about the nomination. Warren "was violently opposed to having Hastie on the Court," according to Kennedy. Warren added, "He's not a liberal, and he'll be opposed to all the measures that we are interested in, and he would just be completely unsatisfactory."[49] "Hastie is a very fine person," Douglas observed, but "he is sort of a pedestrian type of person, very conservative."[50] On the basis of merit, the presidential adviser Jim Rowe and others argued, Hastie deserved the appointment, since he was "much more of a legal scholar than Marshall."[51] The Kennedys decided against the nomination. They had just suffered the defeat of their proposed Department of Housing and Urban Development as a result of "political error" of announcing that, if the department were established, Robert Weaver would be named its secretary and become the first black cabinet member.[52] Such opposition to the naming of blacks to prominent government posts reinforced Johnson's commitment to appoint Marshall. There were other leading blacks, but Johnson felt that Marshall had paid his political dues.

Political pressure for the appointment of a woman had been building for decades and intensified in the 1970s with the battle over the adoption of the Equal Rights Amendment to the Constitution. During the Truman administration, the respected federal court of appeals judge Florence Allen was mentioned for an appointment.[53] Later, Johnson was urged to consider Barbara Jordan or Sarah Hughes, among other women.[54] Nixon also considered nominating a woman. But he claimed "that in general the women judges and lawyers qualified to be nomi-

Justice Sandra Day O'Connor, the first woman appointed to the Supreme Court, and Chief Justice Warren Burger. *(Timothy Murphy of U.S. News / World Report)*

nated for the Supreme Court were too liberal to meet the strict contructionist criterion" he had set for his appointees.[55] In fact, Nixon submitted the name of Judge Mildred Lillie to the ABA judiciary committee in 1971, but she was unanimously ranked "not qualified." Ford's advisers compiled a list of over twenty women attorneys and judges, including Sandra Day O'Connor, for possible nomination to the vacancy created by the retirement of Douglas.[56]

In 1980, Reagan made a campaign promise to appoint a woman. Less than a year later, he fulfilled that pledge by naming Sandra Day O'Connor. In May 1981, Justice Stewart privately told the President that he would retire at the end of the term. A two-month search concluded with a woman who shared Reagan's view that "the role of the courts is to interpret the law, not to enact new law by judicial fiat." O'Connor had risen through the ranks of Republican politics, from assistant state attorney general to a seat in the Arizona state senate, where she was majority leader, and to a state appellate court judgeship. Her nomination was supported by both senators from Arizona and Chief Justice Burger and Justice Rehnquist. The Democratic representative Morris Udall endorsed her nomination with the comment that she was "about as moderate a Republican as you'll ever find being appointed by Reagan." And the president of the National Organization of Women, Eleanor Smeal, claimed "a major victory for women's rights."

Religion, race, and gender are politically symbolic and largely reflect changes in the electorate. In the future, such considerations are likely to compete with expectations for more ethnic representation on the Court—for the appointment of an Italian, Hispanic, or Asian. Still, they will remain less important than personal and ideological compatibility in presidential attempts to pack the Court.

Packing the Court

The presidential impulse to pack the Court with politically compatible justices is irresistible. The "tendency to choose a known, rather than an unknown evil," as Stone put it, "can never be eliminated from the practical administration of government."[57] Yet, Court packing depends on the politics of the possible—on presidential prestige and political expediency. The politics of packing the Court is well illustrated by the appointments of Roosevelt, Truman, Eisenhower, and Nixon.

With the exception of George Washington, no President has had more opportunities to pack the Court than Franklin Roosevelt. He made eight appointments and elevated Justice Stone to the chief justiceship. Although Nixon later achieved remarkable success in remolding the Court in his own image with his four appointments, Roosevelt succeeded more than any other President in packing the Court. Moreover, perhaps no other President before Nixon had as great a contempt for the Court. Nixon vehemently opposed the "liberal jurisprudence" of the Warren Court and named only those who he believed shared his "strict constructionist" philosophy. Roosevelt attacked the conservative economic politics of the Court in the 1930s for thwarting the country's recovery from the Great Depression.

During FDR's first term, the Court invalidated most of the early New Deal program. Yet, the President had no opportunity to fill a seat on the bench. After his landslide reelection in 1936, Roosevelt proposed judicial reforms allowing him to expand the size of the Court to fifteen by appointing a new member for every justice over seventy years of age. In the spring of 1937 when the Senate Judiciary Committee was debating his "Court-packing plan," the Court abruptly upheld major pieces of New Deal legislation. The Court had been badly divided five to four in striking down progressive New Deal legislation. Sutherland, McReynolds, Butler, and Van Devanter—the "Four Horseman"—voted together against economic legislation, while Stone and Cardozo followed Brandeis in supporting progressive economic legislation. Hughes and Roberts were the "swing votes," the latter, more conservative justice casting the crucial fifth vote to strike down FDR's programs. Roberts then changed his mind. In March he abandoned the Four Horsemen in *West Coast Hotel Co. v. Parrish* (1937) to uphold Washington state's minimum-wage law. Two weeks later, in *National Labor Relations Board v. Jones & Laughlin Steel Corporation* (1937), he again switched sides to affirm a major piece of New Deal legislation, the National Labor Relations Act. The Court's "switch in time that saved nine" was widely speculated to have been due to FDR's Court-packing plan. But, even though the rulings did not come down until the spring, Roberts had switched his vote at conference in December 1936, two months before FDR announced his plan. The reversal of the Court's position nonetheless contributed to the Senate Judiciary Committee's rejection of FDR's proposal in May. Then Willis Van Devanter—one of the President's staunchest opponents—told the President that he would resign at the end of the term. FDR had the first of eight appointments in the next six years to infuse his own political philosophy into the Court. Although his plan to enlarge the size of the Court failed, FDR eventually succeeded in packing the Court.

When FDR made his first appointment, he was angry at the Senate for defeating his plan to enlarge the Court and angry at the Court for destroying his program for recovery. For the appointment, FDR chose Senator Hugo Black, who had led the unsuccessful fight for the Court-packing plan. Roosevelt, recalled Robert Jackson, wanted to "humiliate [the Senate and the Court] at a single stroke by naming Black." Only in extraordinary circumstances would the Senate refuse to confirm one of its own. "The Senate would have to swallow

Sunday
February 14, 1937

The New York Times

Retrogravure
Picture Section **9**

Nine or Fifteen? The Nation's Eyes Turn to the Supreme Court

The Hughes Court, Supreme Court Building, and Court Room. Clockwise from upper left (*photos credit the* New York Times *except as noted*): **Harlan Fiske Stone, James C. McReynolds, Charles Evans Hughes** (*Harris & Ewing*); **Owen Roberts** (*F. Bachrach*); **Louis Brandeis** (*Harris & Ewing*); **Willis Van Devanter** (*Underwood & Underwood*); **Benjamin Cardozo; George Sutherland and Pierce Butler** (*Harris & Ewing*).

hard and approve," Jackson observed. "The Court would be humiliated by having to accept one of its most bitter and unfair critics and one completely alien to the judicial tradition."[58]

At Black's confirmation hearings, rumors began to circulate that he had been a member of the Ku Klux Klan in the mid-1920s, when the Klan membership reached its peak of over four million and virtually assured the election of Democrats in the Deep South. When evidence of Black's prior Klan membership materialized after his confirmation, the revelation confirmed for many that the appointment had been an act of revenge. Roosevelt claimed "that he had not know of any Klan link when he appointed Black to the Court." Black went on national radio to explain briefly, though not to apologize for, his membership in the Klan from 1922 to 1925. Although he denied having any knowledge of the KKK association, Roosevelt must have known. Black, moreover, left a note in his private papers to "correct for posterity any idea about Pres. Roosevelt's having been fooled about my membership in the Klan." He recollected,

President Roosevelt, when I went up to lunch with him, told me that there was no reason for my worrying about having been a member of the Ku Klux Klan. He said that some of the best friends and supporters he had in the State of Georgia were strong members of the organization. He never in any way, by word or attitude, indicated any doubt about my having been in the Klan nor did he indicate any criticism of me for having been a member of that organization. The rumors and statements to the contrary are wrong.[59]

Roosevelt's subsequent appointments all turned on the ideological litmus test of support for the New Deal. When the conservative westerner George Sutherland retired in 1938, the President momentarily considered nominating another senator—either South Carolina's James Byrnes, later appointed in 1941, or Indiana's Sherman Minton, who was forced to await Truman's selection in 1949. But he worried about taking too

Justice Hugo Black in his chambers. Black was President Roosevelt's first appointee to the Court and a leader of liberals on the Court. *(Supreme Court Historical Society, National Geographical Society)*

many supporters from the Senate. Attorney General Hommer
Cummings urged the elevation of Solicitor General Stanley
Reed. Reed was from Kentucky, and the President initially
remarked, "Well, McReynolds is from Kentucky, and Stanley
will have to wait until McReynolds is no longer with us."
Cummings countered that McReynolds was "closely identified with New York City" because of his earlier law practice
and that Reed's record justified his nomination. Roosevelt
agreed: "Tell Stanley to make himself so disagreeable to
McReynolds that the latter will retire right away."[60]

Reed joined the Court in 1938, but McReynolds did not
retire until 1941, and the pressure for an appointee from the
West steadily grew. In 1938 Cardozo died. The vacancy would
be hard to fill, for "Cardozo was not only a great Justice, but
a great character, a great person and a great soul . . . held in
reverence by multitudes of people and," Cummings observed,
"whoever followed him, no matter how good a man he might
be would suffer by comparison."[61] Roosevelt long contem-
plated appointing Frankfurter to Brandeis's seat. Anticipating
"a terrible time getting Frankfurter confirmed," he had earlier unsuccessfully urged Frankfurter to become solicitor general. "I want you on the Supreme Court, Felix," Roosevelt
told him, "but I can't appoint you out of the Harvard Law
School. What will people say? 'He's a Red. He's a professor.
He's had no judicial experience.' But I could appoint you to
the Court from the Solicitor General's office."[62] When Cardozo died, he at first told Frankfurter, "I've got to appoint a
fellow west of the Mississippi—I promised the party leaders
he'd be a Westerner the next time."[63] A number of western-
ers were considered, but FDR found lesser-known candidates
unacceptable. Frankfurter was appointed, despite criticism that
it would put two Jews and an excessive number of justices
from the Atlantic seaboard on the Court.

Geography did not dissuade Roosevelt from then filling
Brandeis's seat in 1939 with his Securities and Exchange

Commission chairman, William O. Douglas. At first, Senator Lewis Schwellenbach was considered, but opposition emerged from the other senator from the state of Washington. Frank Murphy had replaced Cummings as attorney general and urged the President to disregard pressure for the selection of a westerner. "Members of the Supreme Court are not called upon nor expected to represent any single interest or group, area or class of persons," Murphy insisted. "They speak for the country as a whole. Considerations of residential area or class, interest, creed or racial extraction, ought therefore be subordinate if not entirely disregarded."[64] Brandeis had recommended Douglas. Born in Minnesota and raised in Yakima, Washington, Douglas claimed Connecticut as his legal residence because he had taught at Yale Law School before joining the SEC. There was accordingly opposition to naming another nonwesterner, but powerful Senate leaders like Idaho's William Borah endorsed the nomination. Douglas later recalled, "When Roosevelt named me he didn't name me from the State of Washington, but he stuck to the record, and named me from Connecticut."[65]

When the midwesterner Pierce Butler died in 1939, there was even greater pressure on Roosevelt to appoint a westerner and a Catholic. Butler was a Catholic, and Catholics were a crucial part of the New Deal coalition. Roosevelt settled on Attorney General Murphy—a Catholic, an affable "Irish mystic," and a former governor of Michigan. Murphy's midwestern Catholic background, however, was only a politically useful rationalization. No less important, morale within the Department of Justice was abysmally low. Murphy was not intellectually equipped to handle the position of attorney general. White House Press Secretary Stephen Early, among others, viewed him "as a complete washout." His appointment was another example of the President's lack of concern for the Court.[66] Roosevelt was not unaware of Murphy's faults. Assistant Attorney General Robert Jackson told him, "Mr.

President, I don't think that Mr. Murphy's temperament is
that of a judge." His elevation to the Court was nevertheless
politically opportune. The President explained to Jackson, "It's
the only way I can appoint you Attorney General."[67]

Roosevelt promised later to make Jackson chief justice, if
he accepted the attorney generalship. Jackson reluctantly
agreed. In 1941, McReynolds retired and Chief Justice Hughes
informed the President that he would step down at the end of
the term. FDR had the opportunity to fill two more seats and
to appoint Jackson. Hughes suggested that the chief justiceship go to Stone. He had long aspired to the position and been
disappointed because his friend President Hoover passed him
over when appointing Hughes.[68] Frankfurter preferred Jackson but agreed that Stone was "senior and qualified profes-
sionally to be C.J." He also told FDR that the elevation of
Stone, a Republican, would inspire confidence in him "as a
national and not a partisan President."[69] In July, Senator Byrnes
was named to McReynolds's seat, Stone elevated to the post
of chief justice, and Jackson nominated associate justice. When
trying to mollify Jackson, the President noted that Stone was
within a couple of years of retirement and explained, "I will
have another chance at appointment of a Chief Justice, at which
time you'd already be over there [in the court] and would be
familiar with the job." At the moment, the arrangement
appeared politically advantageous: "one Republican for Chief
Justice and two Democrats will not be too partisan."[70] Roosevelt, however, made his last appointment little over a year
later. Byrnes was persuaded to leave the Court to become
director of the Office of Economic Stabilization, and Rutledge
got his seat on the Court.

Roosevelt's appointments illustrate the importance of
presidential prestige. FDR was able to overcome pressures
imposed on Presidents for political, geographic, and religious
representation on the Court. He turned a conservative Court
into a liberal one and changed the direction of the Court's

policy-making. As a legacy of FDR's liberalism, Black and Douglas remained on the Court until the 1970s and helped forge the Warren Court's decisions on school desegregation, reapportionment, and criminal procedure.

Chief Justice Stone's death in 1946 presented a ready-made controversy over a successor, but President Truman found a politically expedient solution. The Roosevelt Court had become badly divided. Black led the liberals—Reed, Douglas, Murphy, Rutledge, and Burton—against Jackson and Frankfurter, who tended to advance the basic conservatism of Roberts and Stone. The Black-Jackson disputes were deep-seated, ideological, and personal. When Stone died, senior Associate Justice Black temporarily assumed the responsibilities of chief justice. Having long labored under Roosevelt's promise to make him chief justice, Jackson immediately became vindictive, convincing himself that his rival would be named chief justice. Unpersuaded by the President's assurances that he had not talked with Black about the position, Jackson made public a telegram sent to the chairman of the House and Senate Judiciary Committees attacking Black and airing the animosities within the Court.[71]

Outraged by the Black-Jackson controversy, Truman lamented, "The Supreme Court has really made a mess of itself."[72] He decided to appoint his friend Fred Vinson. Roosevelt had appointed Vinson to the Court of Appeals for the District of Columbia Circuit in 1938 and director of the Office of Economic Stabilization during World War II. In 1945, Truman successively made him federal loan administrator, director of the Office of War Mobilization and Reconversion, and, finally, secretary of the treasury. Vinson was a loyal friend and an experienced politician with "an uncanny knack of placating opposing minds."[73] That was precisely what Truman thought the Court needed: an outsider and proven negotiator, rather than an insider and legal scholar. What the Court required was someone to keep the justices in line. As William Rogers,

Eisenhower's deputy attorney general, later observed, "Fred Vinson would not have been on the Court but for the fact that he was a successful politician."[74]

The appointments of Chief Justices Earl Warren and Warren Burger both sprang from the 1952 Republican Convention. Why did Eisenhower appoint Warren? Douglas, among

Chief Justice Fred Vinson and his close friend President Harry S. Truman on the way to an Army-Navy game. *(University of Kentucky, Special Collections)*

others, insisted that Vice-President Nixon and Senator William Knowland of California viewed Warren—an extremely popular governor with bipartisan support in California—as "an unorthodox, off-beat kind of Republican." They "went to Eisenhower when Vinson died, and urged that Eisenhower name Warren as Chief Justice because Nixon and Knowland wanted to get Warren out of the State of California so that they could take over the Republican machine."[75] But the story is too simple to be true.[76] Shortly after the election in November 1952, Eisenhower indicated to Warren that he could have the "first vacancy" on the Court. Later, in the summer of 1953, he persuaded Warren to leave the governorship and become solicitor general so as to gain experience arguing cases before the Court. When Vinson died that summer, his job was immediately offered to Warren.[77]

Eisenhower was committed to appointing Warren because he "was firmly convinced the prestige of the Supreme Court had suffered severely in prior years, and that the only way it could be restored was by the appointment to it of men of nationwide reputation, of integrity, competence in the law, and in statesmanship." He also refused to appoint anyone over sixty-four years of age, and that barred several prominent jurists. As California's favorite-son candidate for the presidency in 1952, Warren had "national stature" and, in Eisenhower's opinion, "unimpeachable integrity," "middle-of-the-road views," and "a splendid record during his years of active law work" as state attorney general. "If the Republicans as a body should try to repudiate" his appointment, the President vowed, "I shall leave the Republican Party and try to organize an intelligent group of independents, no matter how small."[78]

Warren's popularity and role in the 1952 Republican Convention impressed Eisenhower. But what happened at that convention also set the political stage for the eventual appointment of Warren Burger as chief justice. General Eisenhower and Senator Robert Taft (the son of Chief Justice William Taft) were leading contenders, though it remained uncertain right up to the convention who would win the nomination. Herbert Brownell, Eisenhower's campaign manager, was convinced that his candidate could not win without the support of the favorite-son candidates Warren of California and Harold Stassen of Minnesota. Just before the convention opened, a dispute arose over whether contested delegates could vote on their seating at the convention. If they were allowed to vote, Brownell believed, Taft would have the nomination. If they were not, no candidate could expect a majority on the first ballot, but Eisenhower's chances of getting the nomination would be better. Brownell proposed and secured a "fair play" amendment to the rules of the convention; it forbade any contested delegate from voting, with the result that the Taft candidacy began to disintegrate before the convention opened. During negotiations over the "fair play" amendment, Brownell and Stassen's campaign manager, Warren Burger, came to know and admire each other. Burger worked to get the Minnesota delegation to agree on the amendment. No less helpful was the freshman senator Richard Nixon, who made a moral appeal to the California delegation to vote for the "fair play" amendment. Although pledged as a delegate to support Warren, Nixon was committed to seeing that Eisenhower got the nomination. Warren reluctantly agreed to the amendment, even though it hurt his chances of winning the nomination if there were a deadlock at the convention. When it then looked as though Eisenhower could win the nomination on the first ballot if either the California or Minnesota delegations swung over to him, Burger and others pressed Stassen to turn his delegates over to Eisenhower. Stassen "objected strenuously to it," and his adviser Bernard Shanley later recalled telling "him it was going to happen whether he liked it or not."[79] Toward the end of the first roll-call vote, Stassen released the Minnesota delegation to Eisenhower, giving him a first-ballot nomination, while members of the California delegation continued to support Warren.

Warren's "statesmanship" at the convention impressed Eisenhower. Warren had not opposed the "fair play" amendment, as he might have done. Since he had not turned over any of his delegates on the floor of the convention, Eisenhower felt "there was no possibility of charging that his appointment was made as payment for a political debt."[80] Stassen and his advisers went into the Eisenhower-Nixon administration: Stassen as head of foreign aid, Shanley as special counsel to the President, and Burger as assistant attorney general under Attorney General Brownell. Burger further developed his friendship with Brownell and in 1956 was appointed to the prestigious Court of Appeals for the District of Columbia Circuit.

In 1969, President Nixon's first choice to fill the seat of retiring Chief Justice Warren was Brownell. However, since Brownell "had been Eisenhower's Attorney General in 1957 at the time of the Little Rock school crisis," he concluded that confirmation would be difficult, for "many Southerners were still deeply embittered by his role in the use of federal troops to enforce integration." Nixon's attorney general Mitchell told Brownell that "confirmation would be messy," and the latter withdrew from consideration.[81] Nixon could not nominate Mitchell, since that would open him to the charge of "cronyism"—a charge that Republicans had just used to defeat Johnson's effort to promote Fortas to the chief justiceship. The battle over Fortas hurt the morale of the Court. Justice Potter Stewart, another Eisenhower appointee, told the President that under the circumstances it would be unwise for him to be elevated to the position. Nixon also thought about appointing the former New York governor Thomas E. Dewey, but he was too old. The President wanted someone who had judicial experience but was young enough to serve at least ten years. Most important, he wanted someone who shared his own "strict constructionist" philosophy of constitutional interpretation. The President knew Burger from the days of the Eisenhower administration and had read his speeches on law and order. But Nixon was not close to Burger, and so his nomination would not raise charges of cronyism. After conferring with Mitchell, Brownell, and others, he named Burger to be Warren's successor.

Events set in motion by the 1952 Republican Convention,

President Dwight D. Eisenhower and Chief Justice Earl Warren with Vice-President Richard Nixon, who later appointed Warren Burger chief justice. *(Dwight D. Eisenhower Presidential Library)*

combined with perceived presidential compatibility and political expediency, made Warren and then Burger chief justice. Warren's Court revolutionized constitutional law and American society: with the unanimous 1954 school desegregation ruling, *Brown v. Board of Education;* with the 1962 ruling in *Baker v. Carr* that announced the "reapportionment revolution" guaranteeing equal voting rights; and with a series of rulings on criminal procedure that extended the rights of the accused. Eisenhower later called his appointment of Warren "the biggest damn-fooled mistake" he had ever made. Nixon sought to rectify the mistake. Burger came to the Court with the agenda of reversing the "liberal jurisprudence" of the Warren Court and restoring "law and order."

Betrayed by Justice

"Whenever you put a man on the Supreme Court he ceases to be your friend. I'm sure of that." Lamenting that "packing the Supreme Court simply can't be done," Truman confessed, "I've tried and it won't work."[82] Like other disappointed Presidents, Truman felt he misjudged his appointee. "Tom Clark was my biggest mistake. No question about it." With characteristic bluntness, he expressed his disillusionment:

That damn fool from Texas that I first made Attorney General and then put on the Supreme Court. I don't know what got into me. He was no damn good as Attorney General, and on the Supreme Court . . . it doesn't seem possible, but he's been even worse. He hasn't made one right decision that I can think of. . . . It's just that he's such a dumb son of a bitch.[83]

In a letter to Douglas, Truman further explained that he could not "see how a Court made up of so-called 'Liberals' could do what that Court did to" him in *Youngstown Sheet & Tube Co. v. Sawyer* (1952).[84] Six members—including two of his appointees, Clark and Burton—held that he had exceeded his power by seizing steel mills in order to avert a nationwide strike that, he claimed, threatened the country's war effort in Korea. Vinson and Minton, his other two appointees, dissented along with Reed. The ruling was Truman's "*Dred Scott* decision." He felt that it "seriously hamstrung" the modern presidency.[85]

Clark's desertion was especially troubling since, earlier as attorney general, Clark had advised Truman that he had the power to deal with such emergencies. That was not the first time, however, that an appointee changed his mind on an important constitutional question after coming to the Court. Lincoln's secretary of the treasury, Salmon Chase, wrote the Legal Tender Acts, allowing the use of paper money to repay the Union's debts incurred in the Civil War. But, after his confirmation as chief justice, he struck them down in *Hepburn v. Griswold* (1870) and then dissented when a new majority overturned that decision a year later in the *Legal Tender* cases (1871). Justice Jackson likewise reversed himself on a position he had taken as attorney general, explaining simply, "The matter does not appear to me now as it appears to have appeared to me then."[86]

Like most Presidents, Truman expected loyalty. Clark was considered part of Truman's "official family," and his sense of having been personally betrayed ran deeper than his disagreement with *Youngstown*. In the fall of 1953, after Truman left office, Attorney General Brownell continued the 1952 Republican campaign attack against the Roosevelt and Truman administrations for being soft on communism. Brownell charged that Harry Dexter White, a former assistant under Secretary of the Treasury Vinson, was a Soviet spy. Brownell, countered Truman, "lied" and "fully embraced, for political advantage, McCarthyism."[87] The House Un-American Activities Committee subsequently subpoenaed Truman, and he refused to testify. Clark, who as attorney general had approved all White House appointments, refused not only to testify but even to defend the President publicly. In 1949, Justices Reed and Frankfurter testified as character witnesses in Alger Hiss's trial for perjury and espionage. Frankfurter claimed it was his "duty" to testify in behalf of his former student and clerk to Justice Holmes. Other justices strongly objected to members of the Court appearing at trials or before congressional investigating committees.[88] But Truman could not accept Clark's refusal to stand up for him when Brownell issued his attack.[89]

Justices frequently disappoint their presidential benefactors. Two years after joining the Court, Holmes disappointed President Theodore Roosevelt by voting against his administration's antitrust policies. The President was prompted to observe that he "could carve out of a banana a Judge with more backbone than that!"[90] Franklin Roosevelt "thought that Judge Frankfurter was going to be flaming liberal, but he turned out in many areas to be a rank conservative." Clark also recalled how Eisenhower was "very much disturbed over Chief Justice Warren and Justice Brennan."[91] Byron White disappointed the Kennedys.[92] Nixon was surprised when Burger voted in *United States v. Nixon* (1974) to deny his claim of executive privilege as a shield against having to turn over the "Watergate tapes." And Blackmun undoubtedly also proved a disappointment because of his authorship of the ruling on abortion in *Roe v. Wade*.

Presidential efforts to pack the Court are only partially successful, for a number of reasons. "Neither the President nor his appointee can foresee what issues will come before the Court during the tenure of the appointees," Justice Rehnquist has pointed out. "Even though they agree as to the proper resolution of [past or] current cases, they may well disagree as to future cases involving other questions when, as judges, they study briefs and hear arguments. Longevity of the appointees, or untimely deaths such as those of Justice Murphy and Justice Rutledge, may also frustrate a President's expectations; so also may the personal antagonism developed between strong-willed appointees of the same President." Fundamentally, Presidents are disappointed because they fail to understand "that the Supreme Court is an institution far more dominated by centrifugal forces, pushing towards individuality and independence, than it is by centripetal forces pulling for hierarchical ordering and institutional unity."[93]

There is no denying that Presidents influence Supreme Court decision making through their appointments. One or two appointments can make a crucial difference in the direction of Supreme Court policy-making.[94] But life in the marble temple also frustrates presidential attempts to influence the direction of Supreme Court policy-making. "The Court functions in a way," Jackson concluded, "that is pleasing to an individualist." Each justice gets to the Court "under his own steam" and, Douglas observed, becomes "a sovereign in his own right."[95] Unlike the presidency, the Court does not have a "mission." Phrases like "the Court as an institution" and "the Court as a team," Frankfurter concluded, amount to question-begging clichés.[96] Each member serves justice in his or her own way. When Blackmun first arrived at the Court, for example, he voted almost 90 percent of the time with Burger, his old friend and fellow Nixon appointee. But Blackmun now votes over 70 percent of the time with Brennan, the Court's most liberal member. Justices change and react differently to life in the marble temple.

Off-the-Bench Activities

The myth of the cult of the robe—that justices are "legal monks" removed from political life—has been perpetuated by justices like Frankfurter who hypocritically proclaim, "When a priest enters a monastery, he must leave—or ought to leave—all sorts of worldly desires behind him. And this Court has no excuse for being unless it's a monastery."[97]

The reality is that justices are political actors and find it more or less hard to refrain from outside political activities. Off-the-bench activities are the norm. More than seventy of those who have sat on the Court advised Presidents and congressmen about matters of domestic and foreign policy, patronage appointments, judgeships, and legislation affecting the judiciary.[98] Even more justices have made their views on public policy known through speeches and publications.[99]

POLITICAL CAMPAIGNING AND CONSULTING

Justice O'Connor turned down an invitation to appear as guest of honor of the National Federation of Republican Women at the 1984 Republican Convention. Her decision was consistent with the low visibility of contemporary justices. For much of the Court's early history, though, justices used their positions for political advantage. Chief Justices Jay and Marshall served for brief periods as secretary of state, and Oliver Ellsworth accepted the post of minister to France. Several other justices campaigned for friends seeking governorships and the presidency. Chief Justice Chase sought the presidency in 1868, and throughout the rest of the century numerous justices worked actively for presidential candidates. With the growing institutional prestige and responsibilities of the Court in this century, fewer justices sought greener political pastures. Hughes resigned as associate justice after he was nominated Republican presidential candidate in 1916, whereas Douglas, Vinson, and Warren declined opportunities to run as national political candidates.

A far more prevalent activity has been consulting on public policy. Justices on the pre-Marshall Court frequently offered advice. Yet, when President Washington formally requested the Court's views on a treaty in 1793, they responded that there were "considerations which afford strong arguments against the propriety of our extra-judicially deciding such questions."[100] The letter of 1793 remains a precedent for the Court's not rendering advisory opinions. But justices have not

felt precluded from giving their individual views on issues of
public policy.

In this century, all chief justices served as presidential
consultants. Taft pursued the broadest range of activities. He
helped shape the 1924 Republican Party platform and regularly advised Presidents Harding and Coolidge on everything
from patronage appointments and judicial reform to military
expenditures and legislation.[101] Stone was an intimate adviser
of Hoover, joining his "Medicine Ball Cabinet," at which policy questions as well as an exercise ball were thrown around.
When Roosevelt came into office, Stone thought that his
advisory role would end, but he cultivated a relationship with
FDR and continued to offer advice on problems with the Court
and even on the Department of Justice's strategies and conduct of criminal prosecutions.[102]

Vinson was an intimate adviser of Truman, frequently conferring with him by telephone in the evenings or on fishing
trips to Key West.[103] Eisenhower met with Warren and asked
his attorney general to seek his advice on pending cases before
the Court.[104] Both the Kennedy and the Johnson administrations came to Warren for advice on judicial appointments and
other matters. According to Nixon's White House aide John
Ehrlichman, Burger "sent a steady stream of notes and letters
to Nixon" in his campaign to reform judicial administration.
Ehrlichman also claimed, though both Nixon and Burger deny,
that the President and Attorney General Mitchell also sought
to keep "in touch with Burger" and "openly discussed with
the Chief Justice the pros and cons of issues before the
Court."[105]

Just as justices seek to influence Presidents, the latter may
try to influence them. Warren recalled two such instances.
The first occurred at the White House when *Brown v. Board
of Education* was being considered. At a dinner, the newly
appointed chief justice sat next to the President and within
speaking range of John W. Davis, who was representing the

segregation states before the Court in *Brown*. During dinner conversation, the President stressed "what a great man Mr. Davis was." Afterward, he took Warren by the arm, and as they walked to another room, and spoke of the southern states in the segregation cases, he observed, "These are not bad people. All they are concerned about is that their sweet little girls are not required to sit in school along side some big over-grown Negroes." The second incident occurred in the first months of the Nixon administration, shortly after the Court ruled against the government in some wiretapping cases. Attorney General Mitchell worried that other pending cases might be overturned. He sent the Department of Justice's public information officer, Jack C. Landau, to talk with Brennan and Warren. If the Court disapproved of the government's wiretapping practices, Landau told them, the electronic surveillance of over forty-eight foreign embassies might be jeopardized. Warren was appalled at "this surreptitious attempt to influence the Court."[106]

Isn't it wrong for justices and Presidents to consult with each other? The traditional view was well expressed by Senator Sam Ervin, during the confirmation hearing on the nomination of Fortas as chief justice in 1968:

I just think it is the height of impropriety for a Supreme Court justice, no matter how close he may have been to the President, to advise him or consult with him on matters, public matters, that properly belong within the realm of the executive branch of Government, and which may wind up in the form of litigation before the Court.[107]

History, however, is replete with justices advising Presidents, and standards of judicial propriety evolve. Ultimately, the crucial point is whether off-the-bench activities bring the Court into a political controversy. Fortas's relationship with LBJ and the battle over his confirmation as chief justice illustrate the politics of off-the-bench activities.

Fortas's relationship with LBJ was by no means unprecedented. It stemmed from the days of the New Deal and was
shaped by the experience of those associated with the inner
circle of Democratic politics dating back to the Roosevelt
administration. After graduating from and teaching for a year
at Yale Law School, Fortas went to Washington in 1934 as an
assistant in the Securities and Exchange Commission. The
commitment and interaction among New Deal lawyers left an
indelible imprint on Fortas, no less than on Johnson, who saw
himself as FDR's protégé.

FDR's consultation with members of the Court established a model for the Fortas-Johnson relationship. In his first
term, FDR relied on advice from Brandeis, who had been an
adviser to President Wilson. "I need Brandeis everywhere,"
Wilson observed, "but I must leave him somewhere."[108] A
respected "prophet of reform," Brandeis stood as a "judicial
idol" for New Deal lawyers. During the early years of the
New Deal, as the political scientist Bruce Murphy has shown,
Brandeis used Frankfurter as his "scribe," his intermediary
for promoting his ideas in the Roosevelt administration.[109] But
the "Brandeis / Frankfurter connection" was neither secret nor
deemed newsworthy or improper in Washington political cir-
cles.[110]

When Roosevelt filled vacancies on the Court, he continued to feel free to turn to his appointees for advice. Shortly
after leaving the post of solicitor general, Reed sent a note
requesting a meeting with the President and revealed the
attitude of the Roosevelt Court toward their President. "If it
is not too much of an intrusion," he wrote, "[our meeting] will
help me to maintain, in some degree, my understanding of
your objectives."[111] After Frankfurter joined the Court, he
continued his advisory relationship, though his constant med-
dling sometimes backfired. Frankfurter also competed for
influence with others on the Court. Stone, Black, and Douglas advised the President on judicial appointments and other

matters of public policy. Murphy frequently met with FDR to discuss the war in the Pacific; and Byrnes, during his brief stay on the bench, continued to offer advice on the constitutionality of legislation.[112] Unlike Frankfurter, Douglas continued, after FDR's death, to offer advice to Truman, Kennedy, and Johnson on concerns ranging from saving the redwoods in the West and protecting the environment to increased Soviet influence in the Middle East and the wisdom of a diplomatic recognition of China.[113] When a President like FDR and justices find commonality of purpose and personal and ideological compatibility, consultations are inevitable and questions of propriety overlooked.

Johnson's relationship with Fortas was more intimate and extensive than that of FDR and his Court. The President considered Fortas to be in his elite group of foreign policy advisers. Regularly joining White House meetings on the Vietnam War, Fortas attended more cabinet meetings than the man he replaced on the bench, UN Ambassador Arthur Goldberg, who was one of the few "doves" in the administration.[114] "Should we get out of Vietnam?" was the central question at the November 2, 1967, meeting of the foreign policy advisers (and a question continually debated throughout LBJ's term). "The public would be outraged if we got out," Fortas observed. "What about our course in North Vietnam?" The President asked, "Should we continue as is; go further, moderate it; eliminate the bombing?" Both "hawks" on the war, "Fortas and Clark Clifford recommended continued bombing as we are doing." Less than a year later, in the spring of 1968, the North Vietnamese successfully penetrated South Vietnam in the so-called Tet offensive. General William Westmoreland demanded more troops. Goldberg pressed for a bombing halt and a more vigorous initiative to bring about peace negotiations. Protest against the Vietnam War was steadily mounting. LBJ was at the crossroads of a major decision affecting the war and his presidency. At a March meeting, Goldberg pushed for direct talks with Hanoi and for a "cessation of the bombing" of North Vietnam. Fortas opposed a pause in the bombing. He urged the President to explain in a speech to the American people in need for troop reinforcement and for American "strength and resoluteness" in the war. Less than

Justice Abe Fortas, with National Security Adviser Clark Clifford, advising President Lyndon Johnson in the Oval Office of the White House. (*Lyndon B. Johnson Presidential Library*)

ten days later, Johnson announced the most critical decision of his presidency. Bombing would continue, but only in the area south of Hanoi, where the North Vietnamese had a large military force and from where they launched invasions of South Vietnam. He thus opened the possibility for negotiations with the Hanoi government. But he also announced his decision not to seek reelection.[115]

Fortas was no less active in the formulation of domestic

policy. He attended meetings on fiscal policy, labor legislation, election reform, and campaign financing, often offering his views on matters that would eventually come before the courts.[116] Senator Thurston Morton remembered making a telephone call to learn LBJ's position on pending legislation and being told, "Well, the President is away, but Mr. Justice Fortas is here and he's managing the bill for the White House."[117] Fortas also helped write LBJ's speeches and messages to Congress on civil rights and criminal justice reform, and he recommended individuals for appointments as attorney general and to federal judgeships.[118]

Fortas's nomination for the post of chief justice was defeated, but not primarily because of his advising LBJ. Even after it was revealed that he accepted $15,000 for teaching a seminar entitled "Law and the Social Environment" at American University, the public supported confirmation by a two-to-one margin.[119] Several factors contributed to his defeat. Johnson overestimated his influence after announcing that he would not seek reelection. Anticipating Nixon's victory in the 1968 election, Republican senators wanted to deny LBJ any appointments to the Court. White House advisers also told LBJ that it was a mistake to name another close personal friend, Homer Thornberry, to fill the vacancy created by Fortas's promotion.[120]

Senate opposition focused on Fortas's judicial record and his support of the Warren Court's "liberal jurisprudence." Virginia's Senator Harry F. Byrd contended, "[T]he Warren Court has usurped authority to which it is not entitled and is not serving the best interests of our nation. Mr. Fortas appears to have embraced the Warren philosophy, which philosophy I strongly oppose."[121] Senator Eastland asserted, "[T]he main thrust of Justice Fortas' philosophy as expressed in his opinions is to tear down those ideas, ideals, and institutions that have made this country great. . . ."[122]

Defeat, Fortas told Warren, ultimately came from the

"bitter, corrosive opposition to all that has been happening in
the Court and the country: the racial progress, and the insistence upon increased regard for human rights and dignity in
the field of criminal law." "Other elements," he added, "contribute to the mix, but it's my guess that they are minor."[123]
Shortly before he asked LBJ to withdraw his nomination, Fortas explained to Harlan that he had "not been a governmental
'busybody' " and that he "never 'volunteered' suggestions or
participation in the affairs of State." "On the other hand," he
went on, "I felt that I had no alternative to complying with
the President's request for participation in the matters where
he sought my help—or more precisely, sought the comfort of
hearing my summation before his decision—That's about what
it amounted to in the case of President Johnson–Justice Fortas." He had no regrets about his off-the-bench activities and
could not believe that he "injured the Court as an institution."[124]

Less than a year later, Fortas resigned from the Court. He
did so because of further publicity that he had accepted $20,000
in 1965 as an adviser to the Wolfson Family Foundation, which
was devoted to community relations and racial and religious
cooperation. Fortas had terminated his relationship with the
foundation during his first year on the Court and had returned
the $20,000. He conceded "no wrong doing." But, Fortas told
Warren, "the public controversy relating to my association
with the Foundation is likely to continue and adversely affect
the work and position of the Court." The Court's prestige, he
concluded, "prompts my resignation which, I hope, by ter-
minating the public controversy, will permit the Court to proceed with its work without harassment of debate concerning
one of its members."[125]

SPECIAL ASSIGNMENTS

Justices have either volunteered or given in to presidential pressure to assume the duties of quasi-diplomats, arbitra-

tors of foreign and domestic controversies, and heads of commissions. The practice began when Jay and Ellsworth served as special envoys to Great Britain and France. During the Civil War era, Samuel Nelson was an intermediary for peace proposals to southern states. In 1876, however, a controversy over off-the-bench public service seriously threatened the Court's prestige. Congress established a commission to resolve the disputed presidential election of 1876 between the Republican Rutherford Hayes and the Democrat Samuel Tilden. The commission included three Republican and two Democratic senators, two Republican and three Democratic representatives, and five justices—two from each party and the fifth, the Republican Joseph Bradley, designated by the Court. When Bradley cast the deciding vote giving the election to Hayes, attacks on the partisanship of the Court were inexorrable.

Justices were more reluctant to assume special assignments after the controversy over the Hayes-Tilden commission. A number still served on nonpartisan commissions and investigatory bodies. But the potential for controversy and the burden of work at the Court in this century persuaded many to resist pressures for taking on additional duties. Stone was prevailed on by his brethren not to accept Hoover's offer of chairmanship of the Law Enforcement Commission. He declined FDR's plan to make him "rubber czar" during World War II, when rubber products were in short supply and needed for the military; and he turned down Truman's proposal that he head the National Traffic Safety Commission.[126] The patriotic spirit sparked by World War II nonetheless led several justices to accept off-the-bench assignments. Roberts chaired the Commission to Investigate the Pearl Harbor Disaster. Murphy was especially persistent in his endeavor to be helpful. When he was denied a military commission because of his age, he joined the army reserves. He went to boot camp during summer recess, begged FDR for special military assign-

ments, and, much to the ire of Chief Justice Stone, drew a
salary both as a justice and as a commissioned army officer.[127]

Jackson's absence from the bench while serving as chief
prosecutor at the Nuremberg trials of Nazi war crimes created
serious problems and taught a lesson about the dangers of off-
the-bench activities. Within the Court, his acceptance of the
post was opposed, his absence was resented, and his vote on
cases where the others divided four to four was extremely
aggravating. Antagonism toward Jackson ran deep and made
it manifest to the brethren that, in Burton's words, "the failure of any member to bear his full share of the work immediately results in increasing the burdens of the other members
of the Court."[128]

Justices have since been exceedingly reluctant to assume
additional time-consuming duties. Warren was hard-pressed
and finally gave in to LBJ's request that he head the commission to investigate the assassination of President Kennedy.
Burger, however, takes great pleasure in his responsibilities
as chancellor of the Smithsonian Institution, for instance, and
has traveled to China and the Soviet Union on cultural
exchanges as titular head of the federal judiciary.

CONGRESSIONAL LOBBYING

Judicial lobbying for legislation has a long history. On legislation affecting the administration of justice in particular, Chief
Justice Burger has insisted, "the separation of powers concept
was never remotely intended to preclude cooperation, coordination, communication and joint efforts."[129]

Virtually all major legislation affecting the Court's jurisdiction was drafted by justices and was the result of their lobbying. Jay, Iredell, and Johnson lobbied for modifications in the
Judiciary Act of 1789 and for the elimination of circuit riding.
Story advised his friend in the House of Representatives, Daniel
Webster, on judicial reform and drafted legislation on criminal punishment, bankruptcy, and the jurisdiction of federal
courts. In the 1840s, John Catron actively lobbied for judicial

improvements.[130] Chief Justices Chase and Samuel Miller later pushed bills that would give the Court relief from its growing caseload. The latter wrote in 1872, "I have prepared and carried through the House a bill curtailing our jurisdiction and facilitating its exercise. I can do no more, and shall leave the responsibility where it belongs."[131] Miller's proposals achieved some success in 1875 and 1879, but Chief Justice Waite and Fuller and others continued to press for the elimination of circuit-riding duties and for the expansion of the Court's discretionary power to decide which cases should be granted review. Their lobbying finally succeeded when Congress passed the Circuit Court of Appeals Act in 1891, which eliminated circuit riding and created courts of appeals.

Chief Justice Taft championed major reforms in judicial administration. "If you go pussyfooting," the former President and unblushing judicial lobbyist observed, "my experience convinces me that you will fail."[132] Relying on Van Devanter, Day, and McReynolds to draft proposed legislation, Taft successfully lobbied Congress to enact the Judges' Bill, or Judiciary Act of 1925, which established the basic jurisdiction of the modern Supreme Court.[133] Hughes was more reserved but no less shrewd. When Roosevelt sent his Court-packing plan to Congress, Hughes responded with a letter to the Senate Judiciary Committee implying that all the justices opposed the plan. As he hoped, Senator Burton Wheeler proclaimed that the justices were "unanimous with reference to the letter of the Chief Justice." The letter was skillfully written to give that impression, but Hughes had in fact talked only with Van Devanter and Brandeis. Cardozo and Stone strongly disapproved of Hughes's action and would have refused to sign the letter.[134]

Since Taft, chief justices have used a number of organizations in lobbying Congress. The Judicial Conference, established in 1922 and chaired by the chief justice, is the principal policy-making body of the federal judiciary. The conference meets twice a year and brings together senior chief judges from each appellate court and (since 1957) one district court judge from each circuit. It develops rules of procedure for federal courts and recommends or responds to proposed legislation affecting the courts. [135] The Administrative Office of the United States Courts, created in 1939, studies federal caseloads and helps implement recommendations of the chief justice and the Judicial Conference. Within the Administrative Office, Burger created an office of legislative affairs to assist in drafting legislation and lobbying the House and Senate Judiciary Committees. The Federal Judicial Center, established in 1969, undertakes research projects aimed at improving the administration of justice and also assists the chief justice and the Judicial Conference.

Chief justices have a number of other ways of co-opting congressmen and mobilizing support. After Taft, Burger has been the most active in lobbying Congress and getting the assistance of the ABA in promoting his proposals. Beginning in 1978, Burger, his administrative assistant, and the directors of the Administrative Office and the Federal Judicial Center have met with the attorney general and representatives of the Department of Justice, as well as with members of the House and Senate Judiciary Committees, in colonial Williamsburg, Virginia, at a "Seminar on Judicial Administration" sponsored by the Brookings Institution. The occasion allows Burger and his staff to press for legislative changes. [136] By delegating more of the congressional liaison work to his administrative assistant and the legislative affairs office, Burger has been able to pursue a broad range of projects and devote his own time to "hard-sell" luncheons and to more-personal appeals to pivotal congressmen and presidential advisers.

Independence and Accountability

Justices enjoy a remarkable degree of independence. Article III of the Constitution prohibits Congress from diminishing their salary and provides for lifetime tenure, subject to "good behavior." Article II contains the threat of removal by impeachment in the House of Representatives and a trial and conviction by the Senate for "high crimes and misdemeanors."

Salaries have historically ranged somewhat below that of leading members of the legal profession, and so service may involve some financial sacrifice. A pay raise in 1985 brought the salary of associate justices to $104,100 and that of the chief justice to $108,400, as compensation for his additional administrative responsibilities. Three members of the Burger Court (the chief justice, Powell, and O'Connor) are millionaires as a result of their prior legal practices and investments; Marshall is the poorest because of his limited income as an NAACP public interest lawyer.

Removal from office has never been a serious threat. Impeachment is a "mere scarecrow," concluded Thomas Jefferson, after the unsuccessful 1805 effort to convict Samuel Chase for expounding Federalist philosophy while riding circuit. Forty-five federal judges have been subject to impeachment proceedings, but only nine faced trials and only four were convicted. Chase and Douglas were the only two Supreme Court justices to confront the possibility of impeachment. Chase was acquitted. Two impeachment resolutions against Douglas failed to pass the House. Douglas was attacked in 1953 for his temporary stay of the executions of the convicted spies Julius and Ethel Rosenberg, and then again in 1970.

The drive to remove Douglas in 1970 illustrates the political difficulties of impeachment. After Fortas resigned in 1969 and Nixon's first two nominees to fill his seat were defeated, House Republicans sought to impeach Douglas in retaliation. A 1966 *Los Angeles Times* story had disclosed that Douglas was receiving $12,000 a year as a consultant to the Parvin Foundation, which funded seminars on Latin America and on combating the forces of international communism. In light of Fortas's resignation and his association with the Wolfson

Foundation, Douglas's activity became newsworthy again. A week after Fortas resigned from the Court, Douglas resigned from the Parvin Foundation.

To the House Republican leader, Gerald Ford, the activities of Fortas and Douglas stretched the ABA's canon of judicial ethics that a "judge's official conduct should be free from impropriety and *the appearance of impropriety.*" Although Douglas's relationship with the Parvin Foundation has been known, the allegation of impropriety was politically opportune for Republicans.

What really disturbed Ford and others was Douglas's lifestyle and judicial philosophy. Ford, as his legislative assistant Robert Hartmann has recalled, "disapproved of Douglas the way a Grand Rapids housewife would deplore the behavior of certain movie stars. The old man [Douglas] took too many wives and he seemed to encourage any new fad in youthful rebellion."[137] He joined the Court's rulings extending First Amendment protection to ostensibly obscene materials. And his publishing agent permitted Ralph Ginsberg, convicted for publishing obscene and libelous magazines, to print an excerpt from one of Douglas's books in *Avant Garde.* Ford alleged a conflict of interest when Douglas participated in the Court's decision (denying) review of Ginsberg's conviction. Antagonism grew, and House Republicans pressed Ford to do something when an excerpt of Douglas's book *Points of Rebellion* appeared in *Evergreen,* a magazine identified with left-wing radicals.

When Ford finally went to the floor of the House to call for a special committee to investigate Douglas, Representative Andrew Jacobs, a Democrat, beat him to the punch by introducing a resolution for impeachment. Under the rules of the House, the matter immediately went to the Judiciary Committee, which at the time was controlled by Democrats. After the committee found no grounds for impeachment, Ford called it a "travesty." He continued to maintain that "over the past decade Justice Douglas' extensive extra-judicial earnings and activities have impaired his usefulness and clouded his contribution to the United States Supreme Court."[138] Yet, the momentum for impeachment had declined by the time of the committee's report. The Senate had confirmed Blackmun, Nixon's third nominee for Fortas's seat. Douglas's association with the Parvin Foundation no longer appeared extraordinary in view of the revelation during Blackmun's confirmation hearing that, as a federal appellate court judge, he was associated with the Mayo Clinic and the Kahler Corporation Foundation, among others, and was a trustee of (Chief Justice Burger's alma mater) the William Mitchell College of Law.

The drive to remove Douglas was also made difficult by disagreement on the standard for removing justices. A number of congressmen contend that judges may be removed for failure to maintain "good behavior" or for "willfull misconduct in office, willful and persistent failure to perform duties in the office, habitual intemperance, or other conduct prejudicial to the administration of justice that brings the judicial office into disrepute." By contrast, impeachment requires conviction for an indictable criminal offense. During his attempt to remove Douglas, Ford claimed that the two standards are essentially the same and depend on "historical context and political climate." A justice may be removed, Ford contended, for "whatever a majority of the House of Representatives [decides] at a given moment in history."[139] That position would severely limit judicial independence and make members of the Court sensitive to political opposition in Congress. But the Founding Fathers sought to ensure judicial independence by making removal possible only by impeachment, and no federal judge has ever been impeached except for a criminal offense.

Although impeachment is rare, neither the Court nor the justices are totally unaccountable. The Court is institutionally accountable for its policy-making (as will be discussed further in Chapter 6). Other political institutions and public opinion may thwart and openly defy particular rulings. Justices are subject to the norms of life in the marble temple. A kind of internal institutional accountability is imposed by the processes of decision making and by the competition for influence among the justices. Lower-court judges and leading members of the legal profession impose an additional measure of professional accountability through personal communications and legal publications. Justices also look to their place in history: how their judicial record compares with that of others who sat and will sit on the high bench. Like all political actors, they desire, in the words of Adam Smith, "not only to be loved, but to be lovely."

THREE

Life in the Marble Temple

T HE 'VILLANEOUS' sea-sickness which generally afflicts me in a Stage [coach] has yielded, in some degree, to my suffering from the extreme cold," Justice Levi Woodbury wrote his wife in the 1840s. "I think I never again, at this season of the year, will attempt this mode of journeying. Beside the evils before mentioned I have been elbowed by old women—jammed by young ones—suffocated by cigar smoke—sickened by the vapours of bitters and w[h]iskey—my head knocked through the carriage top by careless drivers and my toes trodden to a jelly by unheeding passengers." In the early nineteenth century, a Supreme Court justice earned much of his pay on rough roads. Justices had to ride circuit and twice a year travel to Washington for the Court's sessions. Travel on horseback or by carriage was a hardship, "amid clouds of dust and torrents of rain," and involved long stays in taverns away from family and friends. Justice Woodbury's wife constantly complained about his long absences, and once on his return he found that his wife had gone on vacation without him. "Why do you talk of regret at my necessary absence on the Circuit to support my family and object to my going to Washington," the devoted justice pleaded, "and are still so unwilling to stay with me when at home?"[1]

The Supreme Court is a human institution that has adapted to changing conditions. "The great tides and currents which engulf the rest of men," Justice Benjamin Cardozo noted, "do not turn aside in their course, and pass judges by."[2] Justices no longer ride circuit, and the caseload now keeps them in Washington for much of the year. These changes have been shaped by American society and politics. But they have also been shaped, in very basic ways, by the institutionalization of the Supreme Court.

Institutionalization is a process by which the Court establishes and maintains its internal procedures and norms and defines and differentiates its role from that of other political branches. Institutionalization reflects justices' interactions, vested interests, and responses to the Court's distinctive history and changing political environment. It remains a central force conditioning judicial behavior. Whereas the early Court struggled to create procedural norms and an institutional identity, the structure and processes of the contemporary Court have become increasingly bureaucratic. Since the appointment of Chief Justice Burger, the number of support and professional staff has grown, and the division of labor and responsibility within the Court has increased.

Before the Marble Temple

In its first decade (1790–1800), the Court had little business, frequent turnovers in personnel, no chambers or staff of its own, no fixed customs, and no clear institutional identity. It indeed appeared, in Alexander Hamilton's words, to be "the least dangerous" branch. When the Court initially convened, on February 1, 1790, only Chief Justice John Jay and two other justices arrived at the Exchange Building in New York City, where they were to meet. It adjourned until the following day, when Justice John Blair and Attorney General Edmund Randolph arrived from Virginia. The other two appointed justices of the first Court never arrived: Robert Harrison resigned before the next session, and John Rutledge, though he sat on the circuit court for one year, resigned when appointed chief justice of his state, South Carolina. Its business largely limited to the admission of attorneys who would practice before its bar, the Court concluded its first session in ten days and its second, held in August, in two. Later that year, the capital of the United States moved from New York City to Philadelphia. Thereafter, the Court met in Independence Hall, known as The State House, and in Old City Hall, where it shared the courtroom of the Mayor's Court until the capital again moved, to Washington, D.C., in 1800.

In these first years, the justices wore English wigs and colored robes. The wigs soon became controversial and were abandoned; Thomas Jefferson pleaded, "For Heaven's sake, discard the monstrous wig which makes the English Judges look like rats peeping through bunches of oakum!"[3] Colored robes lasted until the chief justiceship of John Marshall, whose Court, like all subsequent Courts, dressed in black. The justices also adopted, but gradually abandoned, the English practice of rendering seriatim opinions, whereby every justice would give his own opinion on each case.

With few cases, the Court held two sessions a year, one in February and one in August, neither lasting more than two or three weeks. As the workload increased, sessions became somewhat longer, and an annual session, or term, as it is called, was established. By 1840, the Court was convening in January and sitting until March. Yet sessions remained rather short and by the end of the 1860s lasted only about seventeen weeks a year.[4] Because of an increasing workload throughout the later nineteenth century, Congress moved the beginning of each term back in stages to its present opening day on the first Monday in October. The term now runs through to the fol-

lowing June or July, depending on when the Court concludes
its business.

The problems presented by frequent changes in personnel, few customs, and short sessions were exacerbated by the
requirement, under the Judiciary Act of 1789, that the justices ride circuit. Twice a year each justice would hold court,
in the company of district judges, in his circuit of the country
in order to hear appeals from the trial courts. Circuit riding
was the principal means by which the people of the new country became acquainted with the Court, but the justices had to
travel long distances on horseback. Justice James Iredell's
southern circuit not only carried him through North and South
Carolina and Georgia but twice a year also took him back north
to attend the Court's sessions. He likened himself to a "trav-
elling postboy." In 1792, the justices urgently requested the
President and Congress to find an alternative to circuit riding,
insisting that it was "too burdensome" and unfair for them "to
pass the greater part of their days on the road, and at inns,
and at a distance from their families."[5] Chief Justice Jay complained that serving on the Court "was in a degree intolerable
and therefore almost any other office of a suitable rank and
emolument was preferable." Rather than ride circuit, Justice
Thomas Johnson resigned.

Circuit riding was not merely burdensome; it also diminished the Court's prestige, for a decision by a justice on circuit
could afterward be reversed by the whole Court. As Jay
observed, "The natural tendency of such fluctuations is obvious;
nor can they otherwise be avoided than by confining the Judges
to their proper place, *viz.* the Supreme Court."[6] Jay subsequently resigned to become envoy to England and later
declined reappointment as chief justice, because he "was not
perfectly convinced that under a system so defective [the Court]
would obtain the energy, weight and dignity which were
essential to its affording due support for the National Government, nor acquire the public confidence and respect which,

as the last resort of justice of the nation, it should possess."[7]

The development of institutional identity and esprit de corps within the Court was necessarily difficult because the justices resided primarily in their circuits rather than in Washington, and often felt a greater allegiance to their circuits than to the Court.[8] Justices not only faced the problem of divided loyalties but also had opportunities for teaching, practicing law, and consulting in their circuits, thereby supplementing (if not surpassing) their judicial salaries.[9] Accordingly, the important distinction between official status and personal interests was far from clearly drawn, and, perhaps inevitably, some justices felt little or no institutional allegiance. Though Congress periodically altered circuit-riding duties, the responsibilities and burdens continued to plague the justices throughout the nineteenth century; they even grew for those who had to travel west of the Mississippi.[10]

When the capital moved to Washington, D.C., in 1800, no building or courtroom was specifically provided for the Court. Between 1801 and 1809, the justices convened in various rooms in the basement of the Capitol until remodeling took place, and the Court met for a year in Long's Tavern. In 1810, the justices returned to the Capitol but now met in a room designed for their use. At the time, the room was also shared by the circuit court and the Orphan's Court of the District of Columbia. The courtroom, however, was rendered unusable in the War of 1812 when the British burned the Capitol on August 24, 1814. For two years, the Court met in a rented house, the Bell Tavern. In 1817, the Court moved back into the Capitol, where it held its sessions in a small room, "little better than a dunjeon," until its courtroom was restored in 1819. A newspaper reporter in 1824 described the courtroom as being

not in a style which comports with the dignity of [the Court], or which bears a comparison with the other Halls of the Capitol. In the first place, it is like going down a cellar to reach it. The room is on the basement story in an obscure part of the north wing. In arriving at it, you pass a labyrinth, and almost need the clue of Ariadne to guide you to the sanctuary of the blind goddess. A stranger might traverse the dark avenues of the Capitol for a week, without finding the remote corner in which Justice is administered to the American Republic. [11]

In this room the Court nevertheless met until 1860, when it moved upstairs to the room previously occupied by the Senate. In the old Senate Chamber, preserved on the ground floor of the Capitol today, the Court met for three-quarters of a century, until the completion of its own building in 1935.

Coincident with the move into the Capitol, John Marshall assumed the position of chief justice, presiding over the Court for the next thirty-four years, until 1835. The Court's internal norms were as uncertain as its institutional identity, but Marshall managed to establish regularized procedures and enhance the Court's prestige. In contrast to the first decade, the entire first half of the nineteenth century saw a remarkable degree of continuity in the Court: seventeen of the twenty-two justices who served were on the bench for fifteen years or more. During this period, with decisions like *Marbury v. Madison,* the Court established, more or less delineated, and maintained its own institutional boundaries, thereby differentiating its role from that of other political institutions. To be sure, the public had little interest in the judicial process, other than attending an occasional session of the Court. Still, after 1811 *Niles' Register* and a few other Washington, New York, and Philadelphia newspapers began covering the Court's decisions. No less important, after 1821 the Court for the first time provided for the filing of written briefs by attorneys, though until 1833 it did not require the printing of records. Briefs and records were rarely preserved until after 1854. Only after 1870 do the yearly sets in the Supreme Court Library become complete. [12]

For most of the nineteenth century, life remained transitory in the Court, as in the Washington community—in the early part of the century, Washington was the capital of the country in search of a city. The justices continued to reside in their districts and to stay in boardinghouses while attending sessions of the Court. Chief Justice Taney (1836–1864) was the first to reside permanently in the city, and as late as the 1880s most justices did not bring their families or maintain homes there. The justices had no offices and shared the law library of Congress in the Capitol. They relied on a single Clerk of the Court to answer correspondence, manage the docket, collect fees, and locate boarding rooms for them on their annual visits. The Marshal of the Court also worked for other courts in the District of Columbia. On days when the Court heard oral arguments, which ran from eleven in the morning to three or four in the afternoon and often carried over for several days, the Marshal would announce the sitting of the justices with the now traditional introduction:

Oyez! Oyez! Oyez! All persons having business before the Honorable, the Supreme Court of the United States, are admonished to draw near and give their attention, for the Court is now sitting. God save the United States, and this Honorable Court.

From across the hall, where they had put on their robes in the presence of spectators, the justices would proceed into the courtroom following the chief justice in order of their seniority. There they would sit at a long straight bench, the chief justice in the center and the others on both sides in alternating order of their seniority. The Reporter recorded arguments and compiled and published the final decisions at his own expense and for his own profit. The Court had no other employees or assistants until the 1860s, when each justice acquired a messenger or servant. Not before the 1880s did the justices gain a secretary or law clerk.[13]

The development of the Court's institutional identity, regularized procedures, and norms of decision making flowed largely from the creative skills of "the Great Chief Justice," John Marshall. Few fixed customs bound Marshall, and his

associates shared his federalist philosophy. Being chief justice
gave him special prerogatives: presiding at public sessions,
leading discussion and directing the order of business in private conferences, either writing or assigning to another the
Court's opinion, and serving as the executive officer of the
Court and the titular head of the federal judiciary. But although
the office of chief justice entitled Marshall to lead, his person-
ality—inventive, shrewd, exacting yet amiable and unassum-
ing—enabled him to mass the Court. For other justices, it
was "both easy and agreeable to follow his lead" as well as
"both hard and unpleasant to differ with him."[14]

John Marshall's great legacy has been the Court's ongoing
collegiality. Although he once thought that the Court had
"external & political enemies enough to preserve internal
peace," Marshall sought to maintain "harmony of the bench"
by ensuring that all justices roomed in the same boarding-
house.[15] He thus turned the disadvantage of transiency into
strategic opportunity. After a day of hearing oral arguments,
the justices would dine together and around seven o'clock begin
discussing cases. Marshall used the talks to achieve his over-
riding institutional goal—unanimity. He perceived that unanimous decisions would build the Court's prestige. He
discouraged dissenting opinions, sought to accommodate
opposing views, and wrote the overwhelming number of the
Court's opinions, even when he disagreed with a ruling.[16]
Defending his practice, Marshall observed,

> The course of every tribunal must necessarily be, that the opin-
> ion which is to be delivered as the opinion of the court, is previously
> submitted to the consideration of all the judges; and, if any part of
> the reasoning be disapproved, it must be so modified as to receive
> the approbation of all, before it can be delivered as the opinion of
> all.[17]

Justice William Johnson of South Carolina, one of President Jefferson's appointees, took a different view. When Jefferson urged him to press for a return to the practice of

individual opinions, Johnson's lengthy reply explained how difficult Marshall made it to disagree:

> While I was on our State-bench I was accustomed to delivering seriatim Opinions in our Appellate Court, and was not a little surprised to find our Chief Justice in the Supreme Court delivering all the opinions in Cases in which he sat, even in some Instances when contrary to his own Judgement and Vote. But I remonstrated in vain; the Answer was he is willing to take the trouble and it is a Mark of Respect to him. I soon however found out the real Cause. Cushing was incompetent. Chase could not be got to think or write— Paterson was a slow man and willingly declined the Trouble, and the other two [Chief Justice Marshall and Justice Bushrod Washington] are commonly estimated as one Judge. Some Case soon occurred in which I differed from my Brethren, and I felt it a thing of Course to deliver my Opinion. But, during the rest of the Session I heard nothing but Lectures on the Indecency of Judges cutting at each other, and the Loss of Reputation which the Virginia Appellate Court has sustained by pursuing such a Course. At length I found that I must either submit to Circumstances or become such a Cypher in our Consultations as to effect no good at all. I therefore bent to the Current, and persevered until I got them to adopt the Course they now pursue, which is to appoint someone to deliver the Opinion of the Majority, but to leave it to the rest of the Judges to record their Opinions or not ad Libitum.[18]

The Taney Court emulated the Marshall Court's collegial decision-making practices. Justice John McLean provides the following view of the Court's conferences in that period:

> Before any opinion is formed by the Court, the case after being argued at the Bar is thoroughly discussed in consultation. Night after night, this is done, in a case of difficulty, until the mind of every judge is satisfied, and then each judge gives his views of the whole case, embracing every point of it. In this way the opinion of the judges is expressed, and then the Chief Justice requests a particular judge to write, not his opinion, but the opinion of the Court. And after the opinion is read, it is read to all of the judges, and if it does not embrace the views of the judges, it is modified and corrected.[19]

The justice assigned to write the Court's opinion would read his draft at conference but not circulate a printed version. Thus, the justices would typically agree only on the main points of the decision and not on the precise wording of the Court's opinion. The decision would be announced and the opinion read the next day. This practice discouraged dissenting and concurring opinions alike. Occasionally, other justices complained, most notoriously about Taney's opinion in *Dred Scott*, that the opinion read from the bench and the final printed version differed from that agreed to in conference.[20] In the latter part of the nineteenth century, this complaint helped lead to the practice of circulating draft opinions for comments and changes before a final vote and announcement.

Chief Justice Charles Evans Hughes once characterized *Dred Scott* as one of the Court's "self-inflicted wounds." That decision and the Civil War changed the Court as well as the country. During Reconstruction, the capital became a city, the Court's workload steadily increased, and terms lengthened. The justices deserted boardinghouses for fashionable hotels along Pennsylvania Avenue. Instead of dining together and discussing cases after dinner, they held conferences on Saturdays and announced decisions on Mondays. (The Warren Court started delivering opinions on any day of open session, and the Burger Court moved conferences back to Fridays.) Justices still dined in company, but more frequently they were joined by members of the Court's bar, with whom they frequently discussed pending cases.[21]

After 1860, the Court met upstairs in the old Senate Chamber in the Capitol between the new chambers of the Senate and those of the House of Representatives. The justices still had no offices of their own. In the 1920s, Justices George Sutherland and Edward Sanford and a few others managed to secure small rooms on the gallery floor of the Capitol. During the chief justiceships of Salmon Chase (1864–1873) and Morrison Waite (1874–1888), conferences were held downstairs in a "consultation" room which also served as a library. Chief Justice Melville Fuller (1888–1910) proudly held conferences at his home. The red-brick house had boarded the Marshall Court in 1831 and 1833.[22] Fuller also inaugurated the customary handshake among the justices before they ascend the bench or begin conference deliberations. These

The Supreme Court in session in the old Senate Chamber of the United States Capitol, where the Court held its sessions from 1860 until 1935, when it moved into the building that now houses the Court. *(Office of Curator, Supreme Court of the United States)*

marks of conviviality aside, however, Fuller was unlike his predecessor Waite in spurning Washington social life. His successor, Chief Justice Edward White (1910–1921), was similarly austere.

By the turn of the century, the justices resided in the capital and for the most part worked at home. Congress provided funds for each justice to maintain a working library and employ a messenger and a secretary or law clerk. At a big desk in his library, for instance, Holmes read and slowly, illegibly wrote his opinions with a sputtering ink pen. He had no typewriter. "How I loathe conveniences," Holmes cherished saying.[23] Former Secretary of State Dean Acheson, who clerked for Justice Louis Brandeis, recalled, "Poindexter, the messenger, and I constituted the whole office staff; and Poindexter, half the household staff as well."[24] Law clerks worked in a variety of capacities, from assisting in legal work to serving cocktails at weekly social gatherings. Relations among the justices varied widely, for each worked principally alone at home. Brandeis and Holmes were neighbors and had a warm, lifelong friendship. James McReynolds, a bachelor, was abrasive and worked poorly with others; he even had trouble keeping law clerks.[25]

Since the early part of this century, the Court's collegial procedures have depended less on sociability than on institutional norms and majority rule. The court now functions on the basis of a shared or pooled interdependence. The chief justice has a special role in maintaining certain rules and routines, in scheduling and coordinating conferences, and in assigning and announcing opinions. But the deliberative process—the conference discussions, the voting, and the circulation of draft opinions—entails a mutual adjustment among equals. The Court, Frankfurter once noted, "is an institution in which every man is his own sovereign."[26] The justices' independence, as well as the need for mutual adjustment, was reinforced by the fact that each justice now resided in Washington and worked primarily and independently at home, with little or no assistance. The justices had come to function like "nine little law firms," as Justice Robert Jackson later observed. This was a matter of great pride for justices like Brandeis, who said, "The reason the public thinks so much of the Justices of

Justice Oliver Wendell Holmes in his library at home where he worked.
(Harvard Law School)

the Supreme Court is that they are almost the only people in Washington who do their own work."[27]

When William Howard Taft became chief justice in 1921, he set out to construct the Court's own building. His associates balked.[28] In 1896, the justices had unanimously rejected a congressional proposal to move them from the Capitol to the more spacious Congressional Library Building across the street.[29] On Taft's Court, Brandeis thought that there was a more than symbolic importance to the Court's sitting at the center of the Capitol, midway between House and Senate. And he abhorred the opulence of Taft's design. By contrast, Taft envisioned a building that would symbolize the Court's prestige and independence.

Taft tirelessly lobbied Congress and in 1925 persuaded the Senate to fund his marble temple. He died before the completion of the building in 1935, to a cost of slightly less than ten million dollars. Built in the Greek Corinthian style, the four stories above the ground featured Vermont marble outside and Alabama marble in the interior corridors and in the Great Hall at the entrance; Georgian marble was used for four inner courtyards surrounding the main-floor courtroom, constructed of marble from Italy, Spain, and Africa. Handcrafted American white oak was used throughout the building, with particularly impressive carvings on the arches and ceiling of the library.

The main floor holds two large conference rooms, offices for the Marshal and the solicitor general of the United States, and a lawyers' lounge. Circling the four courtyards and the courtroom at the center are the justices' chambers—each a suite of three to four rooms—with the chambers of the chief justice, the justices' robing room, and a private conference room directly behind the courtroom. One floor up are the Office of the Reporter of Decisions, the Legal Office, and the justices' dining room, with smaller private dining rooms on each side. The remaining rooms on the floor house law clerks and records. On the third floor is the library. Half a floor above the library, there is now a basketball court, commonly referred to as the "highest court in the land," where law clerks and occasionally Justice Byron White play basketball and where Justice Sandra O'Connor and some twenty female employees hold an exercise class each morning. On the ground floor, opened to the public by Chief Justice Burger, the curator displays historical exhibits, and the Supreme Court Historical Society has a kiosk. The offices of the Clerk, the Public Information Officer, the Director of Personnel and Organizational Development, the Administrative Assistant to the Chief Justice, and the Curator; the police; and a barbershop, seamstress, nurse, and public cafeteria are also on the ground floor. Below, there are a parking garage for the justices and the Court's printing shop, carpentry shop, and laundry.

Though Chief Justice Taft managed to persuade four other justices—a bare majority—to support his lobbying for the building,[30] he would have found it difficult to get them to move into the marble temple. Chief Justice Hughes himself later referred to the building as simply "a place to hang my hat," and Stone reportedly commented snidely that the justices would look like nine black beetles in the temple of Karnak. When a guest at one of the Brandeis Sunday teas remarked that Stone was complaining about the building and about the acoustics and lighting in the courtroom, Brandeis, recalled his law clerk Paul Freund, replied hotly, "Well, he voted for it!" Although the Hughes Court (1930–1941) held its sessions and conferences there, Brandeis and the others stayed in their home offices. Hugo Black became, in 1937, the first to move in, leading the way for President Roosevelt's seven other appointees. Still, even when Harlan Fiske Stone was elevated from associate to chief justice, he continued to work primarily at home (1941–1946).[31] The Vinson Court (1946–1953) first saw all nine justices regularly working in the building.

In the Marble Temple

Completion of the marble temple preceded by two years FDR's attack on the Court as a "super-legislature" for its invalidation of early New Deal legislation. The building, as Taft envisioned, indeed symbolized the Court's changed role in American politics—its move from being "the least dangerous" to being a coequal branch of government. "The function of the Supreme Court," Taft and later chief justices affirmed, had become "not the remedy of a particular litigant's wrong, but the consideration of cases whose decision involves principles, the application of which are of wide public or governmental interest, and which should be authoritatively declared by the final court."[32] The modern Supreme Court is not, as it once was, a tribunal for the resolution of private disputes; instead, it is an institution devoted to public policy-making through constitutional and statutory interpretation.

The marble temple, however, is more than a symbol of the modern Court. Once again the institutional life of the Court changed. The building further removed and insulated the justices from the political life in the Capitol. The building nonetheless reinforces basic institutional norms—in particular, along with the justices' psychological interdependence and independence from outside political accountability, the norms of secrecy, tradition, and collegiality.

Isolation from the Capitol and the close proximity of the justices' chambers within the Court promotes secrecy, to a degree that is remarkable, given the rather frequent disclosures in the nineteenth century by justices to Presidents, congressmen, and attorneys. The decision in *Dred Scott*, for instance, was leaked well before its announcement from the bench; and Chief Justice Chase later informed the secretary of the treasury "about two weeks in advance of the delivery of the opinions" in the *Legal Tender* cases.[33] Once justices spent most of their time in the same building, they became more careful about their revelations and certainly more conscious of the consequences of rumors that they had revealed votes or the outcome of cases.[34] The norm of secrecy conditions the employment of the justices' staff and has become more important as the number of employees increases. Messengers were excluded from the justices' conferences because of a leak about the *Carbonic Gas* case, and in 1919 Justice Joseph McKenna's clerk was indicted for disclosing the vote in a pending case to speculators on the New York Stock Exchange.[35] In 1979, Burger had an employee in the Court's printing office transferred for

Members of the Taft Court in 1929 examining a model of the building that now houses the Supreme Court. From left to right, Justices Brandeis and Van Devanter, Chief Justice Taft, and Justices Holmes, Butler, Sanford, and Stone. *(The Bettmann Archive)*

alleged leaks to an ABC news reporter, and several times in recent years sexually explicit material in obscenity cases has disappeared from the building.[36]

The Court has a profound sense of history and tradition. Brass spitoons still flank chairs on the bench, and goose-quill pens and pewter inkwells grace the tables for participating counsel. There have, of course, been changes in the justices' chambers and in other aspects and practices of the Court. From 1790 to 1972, the justices sat in a straight line. Burger modified the straight bench to a half-hexagonal shape, so that the justices seated on the two wings could better hear and see both attorneys and one another. Previously, the Warren Court had amplifying equipment installed because of poor acoustics in the courtroom. Pages abandoned knickers for gray trousers and dark blue blazers in 1963. The tail coat required of attorneys was also abandoned, as was, in 1981, the practice of addressing a member of the Court as "Mr. Justice." In 1982, after a complaint, the Court started using the term "Esquire" when addressing female and male attorneys. Down through Chief Justice Warren's time, almost all of the justices' messengers were black—virtually the only black employees in the Court until the first black page was appointed in 1954.[37] The first black law clerk, William Coleman, was chosen by Frankfurter in 1948. The first woman was picked by Douglas in 1944, but no others were until Black selected the daughter of his New Deal friend and Washington lawyer-lobbyist Thomas ("Tommy the Cork") Corcoran in 1966. Under Chief Justice Burger, the racial, ethnic, and religious character of Court employees became more diverse, and employment became more professional with the posting of job openings, the establishment of pay scales and time sheets for Court personnel, and the creation of an officer of personnel and organizational development.[38]

While altering working relations among the justices, the building to some extent also reinforces collegiality. Justices collectively decide (usually by majority vote) not only cases but also changes in procedures and other organizational matters. In Chief Justice Waite's time, for instance, the justices agreed (over two dissents) that the Reporter should live in Washington during the term and not participate in pending cases while the Court is in session. [39]

Most matters come to a vote: the printing of Court opinions within the building, the transcribing of oral arguments, the posting in the robing room of opinions to be announced, and the setting of salaries for the Court's officers. [40] Burger, however, has not always brought important matters before the conference. For instance, the Court began having oral arguments recorded in 1955. Recordings were made available from the National Archives three years after the date of oral argument and solely for educational purposes. In 1977, a CBS news story aired on television portions of the oral arguments in *New York Times Co. v. United States* (1971)—in which a bitterly divided Court ruled that the government's injunction against the publication of the "Pentagon Papers" (a top-secret history of America's involvement in the Vietnam War) was a prior restraint on freedom of speech in violation of the First Amendment. Subsequently, without a conference vote, Burger no longer permitted the recordings to be transferred to the National Archives. (Transcripts of oral arguments are still made available, but they do not indicate which justices are asking what questions.) Although Burger in 1983 and 1985 urged Congress to create an intercircuit tribunal, to which the Court might refer cases and thereby relieve its workload, no conference was held, though some justices wanted to discuss the proposal and the Court's workload problem. Some members of the Burger Court also favor having video-tape recordings of oral arguments, which after five or ten years would be made available to scholars and the public, but Burger has been opposed to having a conference discussion of the matter and opposes having cameras in the courtroom.

Justice Stanley Reed, President Franklin Roosevelt's second appointee to the Court, in his chambers, overlooking the United States Capitol. *(University of Kentucky, Special Collections)*

Majority rule on organization matters occasionally proves unsatisfactory, for as Frankfurter observed,

> Of course votes—a majority vote—must decide judicial business, and such votes must be acted upon. But very different considerations apply to the family life of the Court—the way it should carry on in its corporate life, its relations to the other branches of Government, to the Bar, and the public. In such matters, the controlling considerations are those that relate to the best way of assuring inner harmony, whatever intellectual differences there may be. And that means not votes but accommodation—the give-and-take of comradeship, accommodation to the purpose and not mere counting of heads. [41]

After his retirement, Chief Justice Warren recollected, "When you are going to serve on a court of that kind for the rest of your productive days, you accustom yourself to the institution like you do to the institution of marriage, and you realize that you can't be in a brawl every day and still get any satisfaction out of life."[42] But the Court is much less collegial now, and the justices socialize less with each other. There was a time when, on the days that oral arguments were heard, the justices would have lunch together. Burger, O'Connor, and Stevens are the only ones who now regularly meet for lunch.

Even though the Court depends on accommodation and compromise, it is also, in Justice Powell's words, "one of the last citadels of jealously preserved individualism."[43] Some justices have no friends on the bench. McReynolds refused to sign letters of tribute from the Court to Justices Brandeis, Cardozo, and John Clarke on their retirement. Black refused to sign any joint letter from the justices of tribute to Owen Roberts that expressed regret "that our association within the daily work of the Court must come to an end."[44]

The internal dynamics and institutional life of the Court reflect the norms, vested interests and interplay of personalities among the justices and their staffs. The modern Court functions more or less like nine little law firms, but life in the

marble temple has also become more bureaucratic. As caseloads have increased dramatically over the last twenty-five
years, the number of law clerks has more than tripled and the
number of other employees has increased by 65 percent.[45]
Most of the justices' chambers have grown in proportion.

Justice and Company—Nine Little Law Firms

When Potter Stewart joined the Court, he expected to
find "one law firm with nine partners, if you will, the law
clerks being the associates." But Justice Harlan told him, "No,
you will find here it is like nine firms, sometimes practicing
law against one another."[46] Each justice and his staff works in
rather secluded chambers with virtually none of the direct
daily interaction that occurs in lower federal appellate courts.
No one today follows Frankfurter's practice of sending clerks—
"Felix's happy hotdogs"—scurrying around the building. "As
much as 90 percent of our total time," Powell has underscored, "we function as nine small, independent law firms":

I emphasize the words *small* and *independent*. There is the equivalent of one partner in each chamber, three or four law clerks [seven
of the justices each use four clerks, the Chief Justice employs an
additional special assistant or senior clerk, while Justices William
Rehnquist and John Paul Stevens rely on three and two, respec-
tively], two secretaries, and a messenger. The informal interchange
between chambers is minimal, with most exchanges of views being
by correspondence or memoranda. Indeed, a justice may go through
an entire term without being once in the chambers of all of the other
eight members of the Court.[47]

A number of factors isolate the justices. The Court's members decide together, but the justices deliberate alone. Their
interaction and decision making depend on how each and all
of the nine justices view their roles and common institutional
goals. According to Harlan, "decisions of the Court are not

the product of an institutional approach, as with a professional decision of a law firm or policy determination of a business enterprise. They are the result merely of a tally of individual votes cast after the illuminating influences of collective debate."[48] By contrast, Burger has emphasized, "In this Court we only act together, even when we do not agree. To do our task, we must consult on each step and stage, and almost daily, as the decisions evolve."[49] Intellectual and personal compatibility and leadership may determine whether justices embrace Burger's institutional, consensual approach to their work, or follow Harlan and stress their own policy objectives. At worst, as Harry Blackmun has observed, the justices are "all primadonnas."[50]

Justices "stay at arm's length," in Byron White's view, and rely on formal printed communications partly because the workload discourages justices "from going from chamber to chamber to work things out." Powell has also remarked that "collegiality diminishes as the caseload increases."[51] This is particularly troubling for new members of the Court.

The growing caseload has affected the contemporary Court in several ways. By Chief Justice Stone's time, it was well established for each justice to have one law clerk and for the chief justice, to have one additional clerk. During Vinson's chief justiceship, the number increased to two and more or less remained the same through the years of the Warren Court. Beginning in 1970, the number gradually grew to three and to four, with Burger having a fifth senior clerk. The number of secretaries likewise increased, at first in place of additional clerks and later to help the growing number of clerks.[52] The Legal Office was created in 1975 to assist the justices; subsequently, the staff of research librarians was increased and the secretarial pool was enlarged.

Computer technology also affects the operation of the chambers. In the late 1970s, each chamber acquired a photocopying machine and five or more terminals for word processing and computerized legal research in the library. Justices once circulated eight carbon copies—called flimsies—of their draft opinions for comments and return by other justices. But they now send and receive, in duplicate, drafts and other justices' comments; typically, justices respond with a one-page, one-line reply such as "Please join me" or "I am still with you."[53]

The justices' chambers tend to resemble, in Justice Rehnquist's words, "opinion writing bureaus."[54] Each chamber now averages about seven people: the justice, three to four law clerks, two secretaries, and a messenger. Burger's chambers are larger: four law clerks, a senior clerk or special assistant, four secretaries, a messenger-clerk, and a chauffeur; in addition to six others in the Office of the Administrative Assistant to the Chief Justice. The managing of chambers and supervising of paperwork consumes more time than in the past and keeps the justices apart. They talk less to each other and read and write more memoranda and opinions.

Law Clerks in the Chambers

Law clerks have been in the Court just over a century. As the Court's caseload increased, the justices acquired more clerks and delegated more of their work. But in addition to relieving some of the justices' workload pressures, clerks bring fresh perspectives to the Court. For young lawyers one or two years out of law school, the opportunity of clerking is invaluable for their later careers. After their year at the Court, clerks go on to teach at leading law schools or to work for prestigious law firms.

On his appointment in 1882, Horace Gray initiated (at first at his own expense) the practice of hiring each year a graduate of Harvard Law School as "secretary" or law clerk. When Oliver Wendell Holmes succeeded Gray, he continued the practice, and other justices gradually followed him. Most justices have had clerks serve for only one year. There are some notable exceptions: one clerk for Pierce Butler served sixteen years; McKenna's first clerk worked for twelve; Frank Murphy kept Eugene Gressman for six; and Owen Roberts had a husband-and-wife team as his permanent clerk and secretary. Chief Justices Stone and Vinson had overlapping terms for one of their two clerks each year; and Burger has had his special assistant sign on for three to four years.

The selection of clerks is entirely a personal matter and may be one of the most important decisions that a justice makes in any given year.[55] The selection process varies with each justice. Burger alone lets his special assistant and several of his former law clerks interview and select his clerks. Four considerations appear to enter into everyone's selection process: The justice's preference for (1) certain law schools, (2) special geographic regions, (3) prior clerking experience on certain courts or with particular judges, and (4) personal compatibility.

Following Gray and Holmes, Brandeis, Frankfurter, and Brennan, in his early years on the bench, chose graduates of Harvard Law School. Taft and Vinson selected graduates from Yale and Northwestern, respectively. Other justices likewise tend to draw on their alma maters. Though graduates from Ivy League schools still continue to be selected in disproportionately large numbers, there is now a greater diversity. Of the thirty-four clerks in the 1983 term (including one for retired Justice Stewart), for example, eleven graduated from Harvard; four each from Yale and the University of Virginia; two each from Stanford and Michigan; and one each from Chicago, Pennsylvania, Columbia, Indiana, Minnesota, New York University, Southern Methodist University, Washington and Lee, Brigham Young University, the University of Denver, and the University of Puget Sound.

Several justices have favored particular geographic regions when selecting clerks. Douglas and Warren tended to select individuals from the West, Charles Whittaker those from the

Midwest, and Black those from the South and, in particular, from Alabama. As one former clerk remarked, "The perfect clerk for Justice Black was an Alabama boy who went to Alabama Law School. If that wasn't possible, then someone from the South who went to a leading law school."[56]

As the Court's caseload and involvement with constitutional and statutory interpretation grew, the justices started drawing clerks from lower federal or state courts. Consequently, formal legal education may carry no more weight than clerking for a respected judge or on a leading court in the country. Of sixty-eight clerks during 1982–1984, twenty-six came from the Court of Appeals for the District of Columbia Circuit, twelve from the second circuit, eight from the fifth, and six from federal district courts; the remainder were from other federal appellate courts and one state supreme court. Some leading federal judges frequently send clerks on to the Court. During any two years, six clerks work for each federal appellate judge. In 1982–1984, six who clerked with J. Skelly Wright, five with Malcolm Wilkey, and three each with David Bazelon and Amalya Kearse were chosen to serve on the Court. Apparently, the justices choose clerks for their legal training and experience and not because of ideological affinity with particular federal judges.[57]

The position and duties of clerks naturally vary with the justice. Oliver Wendell Holmes initially had little casual contact with his clerks, but when his eyesight began to fade in his later years they served as companions and often read aloud to him. According to Walter Gellhorn, Stone "made one feel a co-worker—a very junior and subordinate co-worker, to be sure, but nevertheless one whose opinions counted and whose assistance was valued."[58] Likewise, Harold Burton told his law clerks that he wanted each "to feel a keen personal interest in our joint product," and he encouraged "the most complete possible exchange of views and the utmost freedom of expression of opinion on all matters to the end that the best possible product may result."[59] Earl Warren's law clerks communicated with him almost always by memorandum.[60] Some justices prefer to work more or less alone, and some like Douglas and Burger simply do not establish relationships easily. By contrast, Brennan, Blackmun, Powell, Rehnquist, and Stevens set up rather warm working relationships with their clerks. The level of work and responsibility depends on the capabilities and the number of the clerks and varies from justice to justice and over the course of the clerkship year.

At one extreme, perhaps, is Dean Acheson, who said of his working with Brandeis, "He wrote the opinion; I wrote the footnotes."[61] At the other are clerks like Butler's, Byrnes's, and Murphy's who draft almost all of a justice's written work. Indeed, within the Court, Murphy's law clerks were snidely referred to as "Mr. Justice Huddleson" and "Mr. Justice Gressman."[62] In one instance, Rutledge wrote to the chief justice, "After discussion with Justices Black and Douglas and Justice Murphy's clerk, Mr. Gressman, it has been agreed that I should inform you that the four of us" agree that the petition should be granted review and that "the case should be set for argument forthwith." On another occasion, Gressman wrote Rutledge, "I have tried in vain to reach Justice Murphy. But I know that he would want to join Black's statement if he files it. It certainly expresses his sentiments. I feel it perfectly O.K. to put his name on it—he would want it that way, especially since you are putting your name on it."[63]

Most clerks' role falls somewhere between these two extremes. Stone let his clerks craft footnotes that often announced novel principles of law.[64] Stone's technique, in the view of his clerk Herbert Wechsler, was like that of "a squirrel storing nuts to be pulled out at some later time."[65] Frankfurter had his clerks prepare lengthy memoranda, such as the ninety-one-page examination of segregation prepared by Alexander Bickel in 1954, as well as some of his better-known opinions, such as his dissent in the landmark reapportionment case, *Baker v. Carr* (1962).[66] From the perspective of other justices, Frankfurter also "used his law clerks as flying squadrons against the law clerks of other Justices and even against the Justices themselves. Frankfurter, a proselytizer, never missed a chance to line up a vote."[67]

A justice's background, facility in writing, dedication, and age affect his style of work and his reliance on law clerks. Few are academic lawyers like Stone, "a New England wood carver" devoted to craftsmanship. Most come from an administrative-political background, where they learned law in government law offices and were accustomed to the assistance of large staffs. As two of his former clerks observed, "The fact that [Chief Justice Vinson] wasn't going to sit down with a blank yellow pad and start from scratch was characteristic of an administrator." Moreover, unlike someone like Frankfurter, he "was not a legal scholar who took great delight in the intellectual approach to the law for its own sake."[68] Exceptional are justices who have the ability of a Douglas or a Jackson to write quickly and with flair. Reed, for one, struggled to write what he wanted to say. "Wouldn't it be nice if we could write the way we think," he once lamented.[69] Like many of his successors, Reed for the most part relied on his clerks for first drafts— "the clerk had the first word and he had the last word."[70]

Most justices now delegate the preliminary writing of opinions to their clerks. Earl Warren's practice, for instance, was to have one of his clerks do a first draft of an opinion. Warren would meet with the clerk and sketch an outline of the main points to be included in the opinion. Later, he would give the clerk's draft a "word for word edit" in order to get his own style down. Justice Rehnquist follows a similar pattern. He usually has one of his clerks do a first draft as quickly as possible and without bothering about style. Rehnquist reworks the opinion—using some, none, or all of the draft—to get his own thoughts and style down. The draft opinion then typically circulates three or four times among the clerks in his chambers, before Rehnquist sends it to the other justices for their comments.[71]

Even though they delegate the preliminary opinion writing, justices differ in their approach when revising first drafts. If a clerk's draft is "in the ball park," they often edit rather than rewrite. But some, like Burton, virtually rewrite their clerks' drafts, while others, like Reed, tend to insert paragraphs in the draft opinions prepared by their clerks. As one former clerk recalled, Reed simply "didn't like to start from the beginning and go to the ending." Consequently, his opinions tend to read like a dialogue with "a change of voice from paragraph to paragraph."[72] Reed's patchwork opinions did not stem from excessive delegation of responsibility or lack of dedication. At least in his early years on the Court, he took opinion writing seriously but found that words did not flow easily for him. "The problem with Stanley," Frankfurter once said, "is that he doesn't let his law clerks do enough of the work. The trouble with Murphy is that he lets them do too much of the work."[73] In time, as Reed grew older and the pressures of the caseload increased, he, like others on the Court, found it necessary to delegate more and more opinion writing to law clerks.

Though there are differences in the duties and manner in which clerks function, certain responsibilities are now commonly assigned in all chambers. Clerks play an indispensable role in the justices' deciding what to decide. As the number of filings each year rose, justices delegated the responsibility of initially reading all filings: appeals, which require mandatory review, and petitions for certiorari—"pets for cert.," as Justice Holmes referred to them—which seek review but may be denied or granted at the Court's own discretion. Clerks then write a one- to two-page summary of the facts, the questions presented, and the recommended course of action—that is, whether the case should be denied, dismissed, or granted full briefing and plenary consideration.

This practice originated with the handling of indigents'
petitions—in forma pauperis petitions, or "Ifp's"—by Chief
Justice Hughes and his clerks. Unlike paid petitions and
appeals, which are filed in multiple copies, petitions of indigents are typically filed without the assistance of an attorney
in a single, handwritten copy. From the time of Hughes through
that of Warren, these petitions were solely the responsibility
of the chief justice and his law clerks (and this also explains
why the chief justice had one more law clerk than the other
justices). Except when an Ifp raised important legal issues or
involved a capital case, Chief Justice Hughes as a matter of
course neither circulated the petition to the other justices nor
placed it on the conference list for discussion. Stone, Vinson,
and Warren had their law clerks' certiorari memos routinely
circulated to the other chambers. Chief justices, of course,
differ in how carefully they study Ifp's. Hughes and Warren
were especially conscientious and scrupulous about Ifp's; the
latter told his clerks, "[I]t is necessary for you to be their
counsel, in a sense."[74] As the number of Ifp's and other filings
grew, they became too much for the chief's chambers to handle alone. They were thus distributed along with other paid
petitions and jurisdictional statements to all chambers for each
justice's consideration. Accordingly, almost all filings, with the
exception of those handled by the Legal Office, are now circulated to the chambers, where clerks draft short memos on
most.

With the mounting workload in the 1970s, the role of law
clerks in the screening process changed again. In 1972, at the
suggestion of Lewis Powell, a majority of the Court's members began to pool their clerks, dividing up all filings and having a single clerk's certiorari memo then circulate to all those
participating in the "cert. pool." Six justices—Powell, White,
Blackmun, Rehnquist, O'Connor, and Burger—now share the
memos prepared by their pool of clerks. When the memos
from the cert. pool are circulated, Rehnquist has told, each

justice typically has one of his or her clerks go over each memo and make a recommendation on whether the case should be granted or denied.

Those justices who objected to the establishment of the cert. pool and who refuse to join nevertheless find it necessary to have their clerks prepare memos on the most important of those one hundred or more filings that come in each week. Brennan has described his use of clerks this way: Although "I try not to delegate any of the screening function to my law clerks and to do the complete task myself," he reports,

I make exceptions during the summer recess when their initial screening of petitions is invaluable training for next Term's new law clerks. And I also must make some few exceptions during the Term on occasions when opinion work must take precedence. When law clerks do screening, they prepare a memorandum of not more than a page or two in each case, noting whether the case is properly before the Court, what federal issues are presented, how they were decided by the courts below, and summarizing the positions of the parties pro and con the grant of the case.[75]

Stevens, who does not participate in the cert. pool either, has a somewhat different practice. "I have found it necessary to delegate a great deal of responsibility in the review of certiorari petitions to my clerks," Stevens has said. "They examine them all and select a small minority that they believe I should read myself. As a result, I do not even look at the papers in over 80 percent of the cases that are filed."[76] Stevens's two clerks write memos on only those petitions they deem important. He reviewed those and reads the lower-court opinions on all cases to be discussed at conference. For Stevens, the preliminary screening of cases consumes about a day and a half per week.

After the justices vote in conference to hear a case, each usually assigns that case to a clerk. The clerk then researches

the background and prepares a "bench memo." Bench memos
outline pertinent facts and issues, propose possible questions
to be put to participating attorneys during oral arguments,
and address the merits of the cases.[77] The clerk stays with the
case as long as the justice does, helping with research and
draft opinions. The nature of the work at this stage varies with
the justice and the case, but it includes research, a hand in
drafting the opinion and in commenting on other justices'
responses to it, and the subsequent checking of citations and
proofreading of the final version. Justices may also tell their
clerks to draft concurring and dissenting opinions, while they
themselves concentrate on the opinions they are assigned to
write for the Court. As each term draws to a close and the
justices feel the pressure of completing their opinions by the
end of June or the first week of July, clerks perhaps inevitably
assume an even greater role in the opinion-writing process.[78]

Has too much responsibility been delegated to law clerks?
Do they substantively influence the justices' voting and the
final disposition of cases? After thirty-six years on the bench,
Douglas claimed that during the Burger Court circumstances
were such that "many law clerks did much of the work of the
justices."[79] Rehnquist has provided one perspective on the
function of law clerks: "I don't think people are shocked any
longer to learn that an appellate judge receives a draft of a
proposed opinion from a law clerk." He adds, however,

I think they would be shocked, and properly shocked, to learn that
an appellate judge simply "signed off" on such a draft without fully
understanding its imput and in all probability making some changes
in it. The line between having law clerks help one with one's work,
and supervising subordinates in the performance of *their* work, may
be a hazy one, but it is at the heart . . . [of] the fundamental concept
of "judging."[80]

Some twenty-five years earlier, Rehnquist, who clerked
for two years with Robert Jackson, had charged that law clerks—
who he also claimed tend to be more "liberal" than the jus-

tices for whom they work—have a substantive influence on the justices when preparing both certiorari memos and first drafts of opinions.[81] The degree to which law clerks substantively influence justices' voting and opinion writing is difficult to gauge, and it certainly varies from justice to justice. With the increasing caseload, justices have perhaps inevitably come to rely more heavily on their law clerks' recommendations when voting in conference. Yet, even when Rehnquist served as a clerk and when the caseload was less than a third of its present size, justices no doubt voted overwhelmingly along the lines recommended by their law clerks. Vinson, for one, tallied the number of times he differed with his clerks. There were differences in less than 5 percent of the cases.[82]

CASE SELECTION: CHIEF JUSTICE VINSON AND HIS CLERKS' RECOMMENDATIONS

Term	Number of Cases Disposed	Number of Times Chief Justice Vinson's Vote Diverged from Law Clerks' Recommendation
1947	1331	38 (2.8%)
1948	1434	53 (3.6%)
1949	1308	52 (3.9%)
1950	1216	51 (4.1%)
1952	1286	46 (3.5%)

Clerks would look very powerful indeed if they were not transients in the Court. Clerks, as Alexander Bickel once noted, "are in no respect any kind of a powerful kitchen cabinet."[83] As a clerk, Rehnquist, for instance, was unable to dissuade Justice Jackson from eventually going along with the decision in the landmark school desegregation ruling in *Brown v. Board of Education* (1954). In a memorandum entitled "A Random Thought on the Segregation Cases," Rehnquist charged that if the Court struck down segregated schools it would do so by reading "its own sociological views into the Constitution," just as a majority of the Court had read its own economic philos-

ophy into the Constitution when it struck down most of the
early New Deal legislation. Later, at his confirmation hearing
in 1971, Rehnquist claimed that the memo was written at
Jackson's request and reflected the justice's views rather than
his own. But the content and the style of the memo (as well
as other evidence) indicate that it was Rehnquist's own han-
diwork. Rehnquist wrote in the conclusion of the memo, "I
realize that it is an unpopular and unhumanitarian position,
but I think *Plessy v. Ferguson* was right and should be reaffirmed. If the Fourteenth Amendment did not enact Spenser's *Social Statics*, it just as surely did not enact Myrdal's
American Dilemma."*[84] Rehnquist remains a staunch strict

---

* *Social Statics* (1866), by the English philosopher Herbert Spenser, profoundly influenced late-nineteenth-century American legal, political, and
economic thought by popularizing Charles Darwin's evolutionary theory of
the "survival of the fittest" and by inspiring the movement of Social Dar-
winism. The Court was not immune from the intellectual currents of its
time. A majority legitimated laissez-faire capitalism by striking down economic regulation under the guise of a "liberty of contract," which it invented
and inserted into the Fourteenth Amendment's prohibition against any state
depriving a person of "life, liberty, or property, without due process of
law." When *Lochner v. New York* (1905) overturned a New York statute
regulating the number of hours that bakers could work, the dissenting Justice Holmes charged that the Court had become a "super legislature" by
impermissibly reading into the Constitution a "liberty of contract" in order
to enforce its own conservative social-economic theory. As Holmes put it,
"The Fourteenth Amendment does not enact Mr. Herbert Spenser's *Social
Statics.*" Later, when enforcing the Fourteenth Amendment in the landmark school segregation ruling in *Brown v. Board of Education* (1954), the
Warren Court cited seven social science studies in support of overturning
the racial doctrine of "separate but equal facilities." Among those studies
showing the adverse social and psychological effects of racial segregation
was the Swedish economist and sociologist Gunner Myrdal's book *An
American Dilemma* (1944), the premier work on race relations in America.
The Court's mention of *An American Dilemma* intensified the antagonism
of powerful southerners, such as the South Carolina governor and former
Supreme Court justice James F. Byrnes and the Mississippi senator James
O. Eastland. They and others attacked the Court for citing the work of
"foreign sociologists," bad social science research, and, most of all, for drawing
on social science in the first place, rather than simply sticking to the text
and historical context of the Constitution.

constructionist, maintaining that the Court goes awry when it ventures beyond what he considers to be the meaning of the language and historical context of constitutional provisions.

As part of the institutionalization of the Court, law clerks have assumed a greater role in conducting the business of the Court. Their role in the justices' screening process is now considerably greater than it was in the past. At the stage of opinion writing, the substantive influence of law clerks varies from justice to justice, and from time to time in each chamber, as well as from case to case. No less important, the greater numbers of law clerks and of delegated responsibilities contribute to the steady increase in the volume of concurring and dissenting opinions written each year and to the justices' production of longer and more heavily footnoted opinions.

The Legal Office—A Tenth Little Law Firm

Brandeis, who spoke proudly of the justices' doing their own work, would have abhorred the Legal Office. In the 1970s, the Burger Court hired two legal officers, or staff counsel. A growing caseload was only one reason for creating this tenth little law firm. Burger and Powell, among others, also feel that because law clerks are transients, they need more permanent and specialized help.

Staff counsel serve at least four or more years. They advise the Clerk, the administrative staff, and the justices' clerks on procedure and jurisdiction. They recommend action on special motions and applications, such as requests for stays of execution and expedited proceedings. For example, in *United States v. Nixon* (1974), in the heat of the Watergate crisis, the Legal Office advised the Court to expedite the case, ordering the President to turn over secret White House tapes before the court of appeals had ruled on his claim of executive privilege. At the time, Congress had not finished investigating the Watergate break-in and the possibility of impeaching the President for conspiracy and obstruction of justice.[85] In addition, the Legal Office handles cases that come on original jurisdiction under Article III of the Constitution. Those cases tend to carry over from one year to the next and involve, for example, complex land and water disputes. Staff counsel may also occasionally assist justices with their circuit duties and with the Court's periodic revision of its rules. In addition, they may advise the justices on personal legal matters. And they serve as liaison to the Department of Justice when disgruntled individuals file nuisance suits against individual justices. Blackmun, for one, has been the target of many such fruitless suits because of his opinion in *Roe v. Wade.*[86]

Administrative Staff and Political Struggles

The days of unassisted justices are long past. Within the chambers, the justices and their clerks and secretaries do all their work. But the court as an institution embraces five officers outside the chambers: the Clerk, the Reporter of Decisions, the Marshal, the Librarian, and the Administrative Assistant to the Chief Justice. After they moved into the marble temple, their offices gradually became more professional and acquired larger separate staffs. These developments have tended to further the bureaucratization of the contemporary Court. More employees handle the Court's caseload and manage its administration. There is a greater division of labor and delegation of responsibility within the Court and an increasingly specialized and professional staff.

THE CLERK OF THE COURT

The Office of the Clerk is central to the Court's administration. It has also traditionally served as the primary liaison with attorneys practicing in the Court.

For most of the Court's history, the Clerk earned no salary. Instead he pocketed filing fees and attorneys' admission fees. Thus, even at the turn of this century, the Clerk's income often exceeded that of the justices. In 1883, the Court cut off the Clerk's access to filing fees at $6,000 a year. The Clerk still took in all admission fees. In 1921, Taft became chief justice and the Clerk died. With the change in the office, Taft lobbied for legislation that put the office in his hands. The Clerk became a salaried employee, paid out of fees but receiving a salary fixed by the justices.[87]

The Clerks' early financial independence often made them players in the Court's internal politics. From the very first, justices were lobbied by those seeking the position.[88] After their appointment, Clerks often rendered personal favors to the justices. In the last century, for example, they secured lodgings for the justices—occasionally with considerable diplomacy, as when the aging and feeble Justice Robert Grier proposed living in the Capitol itself. At other times, the Clerk became involved in rather bitter conflicts with the justices and other officers. One of the more astonishing incidents arose when the Clerk, at Chief Justice Taney's request, refused to give Justice Benjamin Curtis a copy of the final written opinion in *Dred Scott* so that he could prepare his dissent from the Court's decision. Curtis was furious, but the Clerk and Taney stood firm.[89]

Over the years, the responsibilities and size of the Clerk's office became greater and more crucial to the conducting of the Court's business. The office continues to collect filing and admission fees; to receive and record all motions, petitions, jurisdictional statements, briefs, and other documents; and to circulate those necessary items to each chamber. The Clerk establishes the Court's argument calendar; approximately 180 cases are heard each term at the rate of one hour each, 4 cases a day, three days a week, for two weeks out of every month, from the first of October through April. In addition to managing the docket and answering correspondence and notifying attorneys of the Court's decisions, the office prepares and maintains the order list of cases granted or denied review, and formal judgments, as well as the *Supreme Court Journal* (containing the minutes of its sessions).

In 1975, the Clerk's office acquired a computer system. The system automatically notifies counsel in over 95 percent of all cases of the disposition of their filings; produces conference and order lists; and prints out the majority of simple Court orders and opinions. Justices Brennan and Marshall have it programmed to print automatically all dissents from denial of certiorari when a capital punishment case is denied review. The Clerk may also conduct limited case searches and statistical computations with the system.

THE REPORTER OF DECISIONS

For the first quarter century of the Court, there was no official Reporter of Decisions, and not until 1835 were the justices' opinions given to the Clerk. In 1816, the Court officially appointed a Reporter, Henry Wheaton, an action that preceded congressional authorization by almost a year. Early Reporters, following the English custom, worked at their own expense and for their own profit and prestige. For most of the nineteenth century, the Reporter could practice law before the Court or serve as a judge in a lower court. In publishing the Court's decisions, the Reporter could advertise his legal services as well. Until the chief justiceship of Taft, the Reporter continued to engage in this semiprivate enterprise and supplemented his salary by negotiating contracts with publishers and by selling to the public the *United States Reports* (containing the final opinions of the Court). In 1922, Congress established the present arrangement: the Reporter's salary is fixed by the justices and paid by the government, and the Government Printing Office publishes the *United States Reports*.[90]

The practices of early Reporters engendered numerous controversies over the reporting of decisions. When Richard

Peters succeeded Henry Wheaton in 1827, for instance, he updated and revised the entire series of prior Court decisions, omitting a good deal of Wheaton's headnotes (which summarize the opinions) and other matter that Wheaton had included. Wheaton was furious and sued Peters. The latter countered with the agrument, rather novel at the time, that "the opinions of the Court are public property." The Court eventually held in *Wheaton v. Peters* (1834) that its opinions were indeed in the public domain but that Wheaton's notations were private property subject to copyright. Though Peters won, he had other problems. In 1831, he published the decision in *Cherokee Nation*—denying Indians the right to sue under the Court's original jurisdiction—as a separate pamphlet along with, in his words, "Mr. Wirt's great argument in behalf of the Cherokees, which had been taken down by stenographers employed for that purpose."[91] This displeased Jacksonian populists—and Justice Henry Baldwin, in particular. A decade later he had his revenge. In the absence of Justice Joseph Story, a close friend of the Reporter, the Court voted four to three to fire Peters and hire Benjamin Howard, a Jacksonian.[92] Given the status of the Reporter in the nineteenth century, it is not surprising that there were other such instances of patronage and ideological divisions within the Court over the selection and tenure of its Reporter.[93]

The responsibilities of writing headnotes or syllabi, making editorial suggestions, and supervising the publication of the Court's opinions invite controversy. Though Justice Gray wrote headnotes for his opinions, most justices do not bother. Headnotes are now considered the work of the Reporter and not part of the Court's decision.[94] Still, besides being useful for attorneys and the press, headnotes have tangible and symbolic importance.

There is perhaps no better illustration of the consequence of a headnote than in *Santa Clara County v. Southern Pacific Railroad Company* (1886). There, after consulting Chief Jus-

tice Waite, the Reporter at his own discretion decided to note
in an otherwise uninteresting tax case that the Court considered corporations "legal persons" entitled to protection under
the Fourteenth Amendment.[95] Corporations, like individual
citizens, could thereafter challenge the constitutionality of
congressional and state legislation impinging on their interests. With decisions like this in the late nineteenth and early
twentieth centuries, the Court encouraged and protected the
interests of business and fortified the basis of American capitalism.

Justice Stone later objected to the Reporter's notation in
the *Gold Clause* cases (1935) that the chief justice's opinion
was "the opinion of the Court" instead of "the majority's opinion," since only four justices subscribed to it.[96] A bare majority of the Court approved FDR's elimination of the gold
standard and devaluation of the dollar, which conservatives
hotly contested but which the administration deemed essential to the early New Deal program for recovery from the economic depression. A conservative, Stone thought that there
was at least symbolic importance in emphasizing that only five
members of the Court agreed to the ruling.

Editing was especially difficult when justices wrote their
opinions by hand. When asked to decipher one of his opinions, Justice Stephen Field replied, "How the Hell should I
know!"[97] The Court's word-processing system is now integrated with the printing and publishing of decisions, and the
Reporter has a staff of eleven. Still, editing approximately four
hundred opinions each term takes time and painstaking care.
As each term closes, the work becomes relentless and mistakes happen. In 1983, one opinion referred to a second that
had not yet been announced.[98] Without careful attention even
to the statement of facts in a case, mistakes may become part
of a permanent record and distort the Court's decision.[99]

The Reporter's editorial changes must be approved by the
author of an opinion. Changes in an opinion for the Court and

requests for special considerations in the reporting of an opinion must be approved by a majority of the justices. Frankfurter, for instance, unsuccessfully sought to have his dissenting opinion on the denial of certiorari in *Maryland v. Baltimore Radio Show* (1950) printed with other opinions for the Court, rather than with memorandum decisions on cases denied review, in the *United States Reports*. But the brethren saw no reason to indulge Frankfurter's whim and depart from the usual practice in the printing of decisions.[100]

THE MARSHAL

For most of the first century, order in the courtroom was preserved by U.S. marshals. Congress created the Office of the Marshal of the Supreme Court in 1867. Like other Court employees, the Marshal tended to get his job either through personal friendship with the justices or through previous employment in some other capacity at the Court. The first Marshal, Richard Parson, was an intimate friend of Chief Justice Chase. Like others, Thomas Waggaman, the Marshal from 1938 to 1952, first came to the Court as a page, in 1911. More-professional criteria have now replaced personal patronage. The eighth and current Marshal is a former Secret Service agent assigned to the White House and the Executive Office Building.[101]

The Marshal has more to do than keep order in the courtroom and time oral arguments. He oversees building maintenance and security and serves as business and payroll manager. The Office of the Marshal now manages over 180 employees—messengers, carpenters, police, workmen, a nurse, a physiotherapist, a barber, a seamstress, and cafeteria workers.

THE LIBRARIAN

The Court acquired its first, small library, run by the Clerk, in 1832. The Marshal's office took over in 1884.[102] Until Congress created the Office of the Librarian, in 1948, the Court promoted pages or hired relatives of other employees as library staff, and not until the late 1970s did the Librarian have credentials as a law librarian.

The library has a staff of twenty-three and a collection of over 250,000 volumes of reports, congressional hearings, books, treatises, journals, and periodicals. In addition, the library has several computer-based research systems including Lexis, containing Supreme Court and lower-court rulings; Juris, a data base developed by the Department of Justice; Scorpio, the Library of Congress data base for books and periodicals; Legis, the House of Representatives data base, permitting searches of pending legislation; and the *New York Times* Information Bank. Within the library, five research lawyer-librarians assist the justices with legislative histories, surveys of state laws, computer searches of legal and nonlegal literature, and statistical information.

The Chief Justice and the Administrative Assistant

The chief justice is more than primus inter pares—first among equals—in terms of administrative responsibilities within the Court and for the federal judiciary. Since the chief justiceship of Taft, the responsibilities and demands for leadership have grown enormously. By statute and custom, the chief justice is the executive officer of the Court. Over fifty statutes confer additional administrative duties, ranging from serving as chairman of the Judicial Conference and of the Board of the Federal Judicial Center to supervising the Administrative Office of the U.S. Courts and serving as chancellor of the Smithsonian Institution.[103]

Unlike Taft and Hughes, Chief Justice Stone felt overwhelmed by the duties. He wrote President Harry Truman just two months before he died,

Few are aware that neither my predecessor, nor I in more than twenty years since I have been a Justice of the Supreme Court, have been able to meet the daily demands upon us without working nights and holidays and Sunday. The administrative duties of the Chief Justice have increased, and many other duties have been imposed on him by acts of Congress which my predecessors were not called on to perform. [104]

As the senior associate justice, Black temporarily assumed the responsibilities when Stone died suddenly. He later reconciled himself and others to the fact that he was not promoted to chief justice by noting, "The administrative work of the Chief Justice is a very heavy burden, and while I could perform it if I were compelled to do so, it is not the kind of task which adds glamour to the position."[105]

Stone had told Truman that the duties of a chief justice, unlike those of executive-branch officials, could not be delegated. His successor, Fred Vinson, however, immediately increased the number of his law clerks and appointed an administrative assistant or executive officer to deal with internal administrative matters and to work with the Administrative Office of the U.S. Courts. This prompted a number of the justices to refer to his chamber as "Vinson, Ltd." But Vinson's staff, like that of Earl Warren later, remained rather small, at least by comparison with Warren Burger's.

"Perhaps the most lonesome day" in his life, Warren once recalled, was when he arrived at the Court and discovered the small size of his staff:

[O]n Monday morning, I walked in about ten o'clock in the morning, and the Court didn't convene then until noon, and so I walked into the office of the Chief Justice and there was Mrs. [Margaret McHugh] who had been the secretary for Chief Justice Vinson . . . and there were three law clerks, . . . [and] two messengers. . . . And that was my staff, that's all there was, and here I came on four days notice, with no preparation and no knowledge of [the cases] in the Court at that time . . . to make the adjustment to the Supreme Court from [the governorship of California], was really an adjustment. [106]

Warren had less interest in judicial administration than would his successor. Throughout his chief justiceship, he delegated administrative matters to his secretary and the director of the Administrative Office of the U.S. Courts (which at that time was located in the Court).

Burger's interest in judicial administration and efficiency antedated his appointment.[107] Shortly after he arrived, he pushed for technological and managerial improvements both in the Court and in lower federal courts. In his view, a "sort of overhaul [was] needed up and down the line."[108] Without changes at the Court in particular, he thought, its work would by the 1980s "progressively deteriorate . . . in quality so [much] that its historic role [could] not be performed adequately."[109] He brought photocopying machines and computers to the Court. He also asked Congress to create an office of administrative assistant and to reexamine the Court's jurisdiction. Unlike his two predecessors, Burger joined the Court eager to reform the American judiciary and legal practice, and he wanted the personnel to implement his proposals. Like Taft's, Burger's extrajudicial activism led to direct and indirect lobbying—primarily through the American Bar Association—of congressmen in support of his proposals.

Burger got his Administrative Assistant in 1972, after Congress created a fifth legal officer of the Court. The duties and qualifications were not legislated, and the Administrative Assistant serves at the pleasure of the chief justice. Burger wanted someone to handle day-to-day administration and act as a liaison with judicial and legal committees, organizations, and interest groups outside the Court. The office received a cool reception from justices who saw it as "empire-building" and from other officers of the Court who felt it diminished their access to the chief. Burger wanted an individual with "high administrative and managerial talents, but also a lawyer of substantial experience or a Judge."[110] But when he filled the position in 1972, he chose a nonlawyer, Mark Cannon,

Chief Justice Warren Burger in his chambers with the first Administrative Assistant to the Chief Justice, Mark Cannon. *(Yoichi Okamoto)*

then director of the Institute of Public Administration in New York City and widely experienced in public management and in congressional-executive relations.

The office grew to include a special assistant or research associate, four secretaries, a judicial-fellows program—in which administrators, lawyers, judges, and academics were selected to work for one year at the Court—and an internship program for undergraduates and law students. The Administrative Assistant, however, never became the Court's chief executive officer. Instead, he has promoted Burger's agenda for judicial reform.[111] More specifically, the Administrative Assistant has (1) served as a confidential aide; (2) provided research assistance in drafting speeches and addresses (notably the chief justice's annual Year-End Report on the Judiciary); (3) overseen managerial and technological improvements, including the professionalization of staff and the creation of new offices in the Court; (4) served as a liaison with other judicial organizations and groups and with Congress and the executive branch; and, finally, (5) helped to publicize and promote Burger's concerns about the operation of federal and state judiciaries.

The Office of the Administrative Assistant is but one example of Burger's effort to manage the Court and the growing caseload. Those efforts have included new personnel (both more people and a greater diversity of people); new technology; and new, specialized offices (Legal Office, Personnel and Organizational Development Office, Curator's Office, and Data Systems Division), as well as an enlarged secretarial pool and Public Information Office.

In historical perspective, Burger brought Taft's marble temple into the world of modern technology and managerial practices.

Managing the Caseload

Throughout the Court's history, justices have complained of "relentless schedules" and "unremitting toil." The caseload has stimulated institutional reform, procedural change, and the evolution of internal norms and practices.

AN INCREASING CASELOAD

The Court's docket has grown phenomenally. The following chart illustrates the increase in filings, in total docket, and in number of cases disposed of each term.[112] Sometimes rulings of the Court swell the docket. For example, decisions on the constitutional rights of indigents significantly contributed to an increase in filings. But, by and large, the docket reflects the course of legislation and broad socioeconomic and political change.

During the first half of the nineteenth century, the caseload grew largely because of population growth, territorial expansion, and the incremental development of federal regulation. The Civil War and Reconstruction, both great sources of legal conflict, and the late-nineteenth-century business boom dramatically swelled the docket. No less important, Congress greatly expanded the jurisdiction of all federal courts. In particular, federal jurisdiction reached out to include civil rights, habeas corpus appeals, questions of federal law decided by state courts, and all suits over $500 arising under the Constitution or federal legislation.[113]

By the 1870s, the Court was confronting a growing backlog of cases. In response, Congress first raised the jurisdictional amount in diversity cases (cases between citizens of different states) to $2,000. In the 1891 Evarts Act, Congress provided immediate (if not long-lasting) relief by creating circuit courts of appeals. These courts were given final jurisdiction over most appeals, with the exception of certain civil cases

DOCKET AND FILINGS, 1800–1984

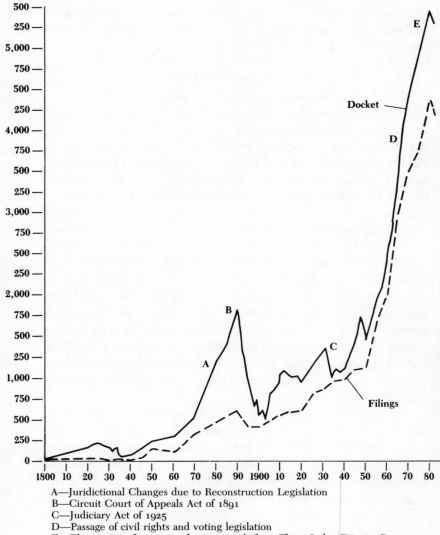

A—Juridictional Changes due to Reconstruction Legislation
B—Circuit Court of Appeals Act of 1891
C—Judiciary Act of 1925
D—Passage of civil rights and voting legislation
E—Elimination of most mandatory appeals from Three-Judge District Courts

and cases involving capital or otherwise infamous crimes. The courts of appeals had final say in admiralty and diversity suits, criminal prosecutions, and violations of revenue and patent law. The act preserved access to the Court by providing, instead of mandatory rights of appeal, for petitions for writs of certiorari, which the Court could refuse to grant. The act thus for the first time gave the Court the power of discretionary review.

In the early twentieth century, the Court's docket grew again, in part because of further population increases. Economic changes and World War I brought a rash of disputes over war contracts and suits against the government. A large measure of the Court's congested docket was nonetheless due to expanding congressional legislation and regulation. Congress inflated the Court's docket by enlarging the opportunities both for government and for special-interest groups to appeal directly to the Court. Mandatory review was extended, for instance, to government appeals from dismissals of criminal prosecutions. Individuals and businesses challenging administrative decisions under antitrust and interstate commerce laws, the Federal Employer's Liability Act (FELA), and injunctions issued by three-judge courts were also given the right of appeal to the Court.

The Court once again could not stay abreast of its caseload. Congress initially responded piecemeal. It slightly enlarged the Court's discretionary jurisdiction by eliminating mandatory rights of appeal in narrow though important areas, such as under the FELA. Then, as a result of a campaign waged by Chief Justice Taft for further relief for the Court, Congress passed the "Judges' Bill," or the Judiciary Act of February 13, 1925, which basically established the jurisdiction of the modern Court.[114] That act replaced mandatory review of appeals with discretionary review of petitions for writs of certiorari. The act enabled the Court largely to set its own agenda and to decide only cases of national importance.[115]

Since World War II, the Court's business has increased yet again. As in the past, Congress provided incremental relief by eliminating most of the remaining provisions for mandatory review of appeals, particularly those from three-judge courts. The following Table summarizes the principal legislation that altered the Court's jurisdiction and extended its power of discretionary review, enabling it to gain control over its docket.

MAJOR LEGISLATION AFFECTING THE JURISDICTION AND
BUSINESS OF THE SUPREME COURT*

Legislation	Commentary
Judiciary Act of 1789	Provided basic appellate jurisdiction; a 3-tier judiciary system staffed by justices and district court judges; required circuit riding
Acts of 1793, 1801, 1802, and 1803	Provided rotation system for circuit riding, then eliminated the responsibilities, only to have Jeffersonians reinstate circuit-riding duties
Act of 1807	Added 7th circuit and justice
Act of 1837	Divided country into 9 circuits and brought number of justices to 9 (Court's jurisdiction was also expanded to include appeals from new states and territories in 1825, 1828, and 1848)
Acts of 1855 and 1863	California added as 10th circuit, and 10th justice
Acts of 1866, 1867, 1869, and 1871	Expanded federal jurisdiction over civil rights; reorganized country into 9 circuits and reduced number of justices to 7, and later fixed the number at 9; and expanded jurisdiction over habeas corpus and state court decisions
Act of 1875	Greatly expanded jurisdiction over civil disputes, and given review of writs of error, and granted full federal question review from state courts

Legislation	Commentary
Act of 1887	Curbed access by raising amount of dispute in diversity cases; and provided writ of error in all capital cases
Circuit Court of Appeals Act of 1891	Established 9 circuit courts, and judgeships; broadened review of criminal cases and provided for limited discretionary review via writs of certiorari
Act of 1892	Provided for in forma pauperis filings
Act of 1893	Created District of Columbia Circuit
Acts of 1903 and 1907	Provided direct appeal under antitrust and interstate commerce acts; granted government right of direct appeal in dismissals of criminal prosecutions
Acts of 1910, 1911, and 1913	Altered federal injunctive power; established 3-judge courts because of abuses by single judges in enjoining state economic regulation; and later extended the jurisdiction of 3-judge courts and direct appeals to Court
Acts of 1914, 1915, and 1916	Jurisdiction over some state cases made discretionary and eliminated right to review in bankruptcy, trademark, and FELA
Judiciary Act of 1925	Greatly extended the Court's discretionary jurisdiction by replacing mandatory appeals with petitions for certiorari
Act of 1928	Appeals became the sole method of mandatory appellate review
Act of 1939	Expanded review of decisions by Court of Claims over both law and fact
Act of 1948	Judicial code revised, codified, and enacted into law; 11th circuit established
Act of 1950 (Hobbes Act)	Eliminated 3-judge court requirement in certain areas
Voting Rights Act of 1965	Provided direct appeal over decisions of 3-judge courts in area of voting rights
Acts of 1970, 1971, 1974, 1975, and 1976	Reorganized District of Columbia courts; expanded Court's discretionary review;

Legislation	Commentary
	repealed direct government appeals under Act of 1907; eliminated direct appeals in antitrust and ICC cases; further cut back jurisdiction and direct appeals from 3-judge courts, with the exception of areas of voting rights and reapportionment
Federal Courts Improvement Act of 1982	Created Court of Appeals for the Federal Circuit, by joining the Court of Claims with the Court of Customs and Patent Appeals

*Excluded, necessarily, is the vast amount of legislation expanding the administrative state and providing opportunities for challenging law and policy in federal courts.

ALTERNATIVE INSTITUTIONAL RESPONSES

In historical perspective, the process of institutionalization paralleled the growth of the caseload. There are basically three ways in which the Court has responded to a rising caseload and workload.

First, a *bureaucratic response:* the Court may make managerial and technological changes. In the late nineteenth century, for example, the Court's terms were lengthened, the time allowed for oral arguments was shortened, and the justices gradually acquired staff. In this century and especially in the last twenty years, the justices hired larger and more professional staffs and bought modern office equipment.

The bureaucratic response may prove counterproductive in a collegial institution like the Court. One problem is that caseload is not equivalent to workload. Filings and cases are not fungible; some take a great deal more time than others. Another problem is that larger staffs and the delegation of work force justices to spend more time supervising their chambers. Consequently, the nature of the justices' workload may change but need not diminish. At an institution like the Court, Justice Douglas remarked, "[d]elegation of work merely increases the length of the week—unless the Justice is to be a rubber stamp for the clerks."[116] The justices, moreover, have less opportunity and inclination to talk and try to reach accommodations with each other. Stevens has said that they are already "too busy to decide whether there [is] anything [they] can do about the problem of being too busy."[117] The present pattern of formal written communications among the chambers, in turn, encourages even greater reliance on dictaphones, secretaries, law clerks, and staff counsel for the preparation of draft opinions. Justices accordingly spend more time reading and revising and have, Burger has said, less "time and freshness of mind for private study and reflection . . . [and] fruitful interchange . . . indispensable to thoughtful, unhurried decision."[118] Further bureaucratic tendencies might also diminish the quality of the Court's work and perpetuate the recent trend toward the summary decision of more cases— that is, without full briefing and oral argument—and toward longer and more numerous separate opinions.

A second response to the burgeoning docket is the introduction of *jurisdictional* changes. Such changes include a further enlarging of the Court's power of discretionary review and the creating of new lower appellate courts so that the justices may decide only those cases of national importance which can adequately be considered in any given term. The Court must decide cases arising under its original jurisdiction, as is specified in Article III of the Constitution. But over 95 percent of all filings now come under appellate jurisdiction, which Congress provides and may change. Since the Judiciary Act of 1925, Congress has incrementally enlarged the Court's discretionary jurisdiction, allowing the justices to deny review to more cases. In Justice White's words, "the power to deny cases helps to keep us current."[119] All present members of the Court agree that Congress should eliminate remaining provisions for mandatory appellate review.[120] This would give the Court virtually complete discretionary jurisdiction, with the exception of those few cases coming under its original jurisdiction. However, such a jurisdictional change would not nec-

essarily reduce the Court's caseload; it might only affect the
justices' workload and process of deciding what to decide.

The contemporary Court's docket is now so large, in the
view of Burger, that Congress should consider establishing a
national intermediate appellate court, located between the
courts of appeals and the Supreme Court. Such a national
intermediate appellate court would either screen and decide
cases or have cases referred to it by the Court.

In 1971, Burger initially appointed a committee, chaired
by the Harvard law professor Paul Freund, to study the Court's
caseload and to make recommendations for reform. The Freund
report proposed the establishment of a national court of appeals.
The court would screen all filings, other than those on original
jurisdiction, and refer some four hundred each year to the
Supreme Court and deny without appeal the rest (in terms of
the present docket, around forty-five hundred cases a year).
The Court could then decide which of those cases merit consideration and either deny or remand the remaining cases back
to the national court of appeals for decision.[121] The Freund
report was widely criticized, most notably by retired Chief
Justice Warren and Justices Douglas and Brennan.[122] They
argued that whereas the Constitution provides for only "one
Supreme Court," the Freund proposal would block many cases,
issues, and factual circumstances from ever coming to the
attention of the Court. Thus, a national court of appeals would
function as the court of last resort in most cases, ostensibly in
violation of the Constitution. Douglas and Brennan further
contended that they were not overworked but underworked.
The latter now agrees that the Court has a workload problem,
but he still profoundly objects to the creation of a court that
would screen cases and diminish the court's power to set its
own agenda. O'Connor does not think that the proposal would
help much. By contrast, Stevens and Rehnquist have endorsed
the idea as a way to reduce both the caseload and the workload of the Court.[123] Stewart also likes the proposal because

of its "simplicity and approachability" for those seeking review of lower-court rulings.

In 1972, Congress established the Commission on Revision of the Federal Court Appellate System, chaired by Senator Roman Hruska. When its final report was released in 1975, the Hruska Commission also recommended a national court of appeals, but one that instead of screening cases would hear cases referred to it by the Court or transferred over by courts of appeals.[124] Although this proposal received more support than Freund's did, it too invited criticism. A central concern in regard to the Hruska proposal is that such a court would neither reduce the Supreme Court's caseload (except where cases are transferred by other courts of appeals) nor substantially reduce the Court's workload. Indeed, the Court's workload might actually increase since filings would still have to be screened and the justices would have to decide not merely whether to grant or deny a case but also whether a case merited reference to the national court of appeals for decision.

In 1983 and 1985, Burger again cautioned, "Only fundamental changes in structure and jurisdiction will provide a solution that will maintain the historic posture of the Supreme Court, will ensure 'proper time for reflection,' preserve the traditional quality of decisions, and avoid a breakdown of the system—or of some of the justices."[125] He also lobbied Congress to establish a temporary, five-year experimental intermediate tribunal, staffed by judges drawn from the various courts of appeals. The tribunal would decide cases involving circuit conflicts—that is, cases where two or more courts of appeals have ruled differently on the same issue—and any other cases referred to it by the Court or transferred over by courts of appeals. Rehnquist, O'Connor, White, and Powell endorsed the idea.

Burger's latest proposal has the attraction of being experimental and combining elements of both the Freund and the Hruska recommendations. Congress held hearings on it, but the Department of Justice after an initial favorable response refused to endorse the creation of such a court. [126] Other justices and numerous federal appellate court judges, moreover, opposed and lobbied against the proposal. [127] Stevens wrote Congressman Kastenmeier that there were too few intercircuit-conflict cases to merit creation of such a court. He also pointed out that most of these cases are decided by the Court because of the constitutional and statutory issues presented, not because of a conflict among the circuits, and that there were alternative ways of securing national uniformity in the law and judiciary. [128] Stevens further maintained that the Court's present workload problems arise because the justices lack self-restraint and simply grant review to too many cases. In addition, a proposal like that of the Hruska Commission would not necessarily reduce either the caseload or the workload, since the justices still would have to agree on which cases should be referred, denied, or decided and to write opinions for those cases granted full consideration.

A final and third institutional response relates to the Court's internal *procedures and processes:* formal procedural rules and informal processes and practices in the screening and disposing of cases may be modified by the justices. The Court has often changed formal requirements for accepting cases, raised filing fees, and imposed penalties for filing "frivolous" cases, for example. It has also altered internal processes and practices of judicial review. Such changes in procedure and process will be examined in the next chapter, on how the Court decides what to decide.

Meanwhile, it bears emphasizing that none of these alternative responses to the Court's growing caseload are mutually exclusive. All of the members of the Burger Court agree that a workload problem exists, but they disagree about its causes and solutions. As the business of the Court increases, some combination of responses will prove necessary, but will also further change life in the marble temple.

FOUR

Deciding What to Decide

I'LL TAKE my case all the way to the Supreme Court." People say that when they feel they have been treated unjustly and want a fair hearing. But few actually do take their cases all the way to the Court, and even fewer are granted a hearing. Clarence Earl Gideon was one who succeeded in getting his case accepted by the Court. Gideon, a fifty-one-year-old rambler, in and out of jails for most of his life, was convicted of breaking and entering into the Bay Harbor Poolroom in Panama City, Florida. At his trial, he claimed he was too poor to afford an attorney and requested that one be provided. The judge refused, but Gideon persisted. While serving a five-year sentence for petty larceny in the Florida State Prison in 1961, he mailed a petition, printed childishly on lined paper obtained from a prison guard. His petition led to the landmark ruling in *Gideon v. Wainwright* (1963) that indigents have a right to counsel in all felony cases.

Gideon was exceptional, for the overwhelming number of all petitions are denied. Less than 10 percent of the cases on the Court's docket are decided, and only half of those are given full consideration and eventually decided by written opinion. Out of the more than 4,000 cases that now arrive each term, only 150–200 get the Court's full attention. Chief Justice Burger and other justices complain that even that number is too large for them to consider adequately and efficiently. Unlike other federal judges, however, the justices have virtually complete discretion to screen out of the many cases they receive the few they will decide. By deciding what to decide, the Court can stay abreast of its caseload. The cornerstone of the modern Court's operation, as the second Justice John Harlan remarked, "is the control it possesses over the amount and character of its business."[1]

The power to decide what to decide also enables the Court to set its own agenda. Like other courts, the Court must await issues brought by lawsuits. One hundred and fifty years ago, the court's docket did not include issues of personal privacy raised by the possibility of electronic surveillance and computer data banks, for instance, or controversies over abortion and the patentability of organic life-forms. As technology develops and society changes, courts respond. Law evolves (more or less quickly) in response to social change. Unlike any other court, however, the Supreme Court, as its caseload changed and grew, got the power to pick which issues it would decide. The Court now functions like a roving commission, or legislative body, in responding to social forces.

Gideon's petition provided a vehicle for the Warren Court to change the course of American law. Gideon was wrong in claiming that the Court had said that the poor have a right to a court-appointed attorney. He did not know that he was asking the Court to reverse itself. The Sixth Amendment provides simply that in criminal cases the accused has the right "to have the Assistance of Counsel for his defense." The guarantee applied only in federal, not in state, courts; and it did not require that the government provide attorneys for indigent defendants. The Court had first addressed the issue of a right to counsel in *Powell v. Alabama* (1932). Seven black youths—the Scottsboro boys, as they were called—were convicted of raping a white girl by an all-white jury in a small southern town. Under these circumstances, the Court ruled, without the benefit of counsel "the defendants, young, ignorant, illiterate [and] surrounded by hostile sentiment," were denied a fair hearing. Six years later, in *Johnson v. Zerbst* (1938), Hugo Black wrote for a bare majority that the Sixth Amendment requires counsel for indigents in all federal criminal cases. A majority of the Court nonetheless refused to apply that ruling to indigents in state courts. In *Betts v. Brady* (1942), the Court held that only in "special circumstances," like those in the Scottsboro case, was counsel required. Black, along with William Douglas and Frank Murphy, dissented. Anticipating his eventual opinion for the Court in *Gideon* that overturned *Betts*, Black insisted that no one should be "deprived of counsel merely because of his poverty." He added, "Any other practice seems to me to defeat the promise of our democratic society to provide equal justice under the law."

Gideon was not known to the justices, nor was he part of a special-interest group seeking legal reform. Yet, he "was part of a current history," as the Pulitzer Prize winner Anthony Lewis observed; "there were working for him forces in law and society larger than he could understand."[2] Constitutional law is a constantly changing dialogue between the Court and the country. *Betts*'s special-circumstances rule stood for two decades, but it was increasingly criticized by Black and others. Only three members of the Court that decided *Betts* remained when Gideon's petition was granted: two of the dissenters, Black and Douglas; and Felix Frankfurter, who was eighty years old, ill, and in his last year on the bench. They had been joined by Tom Clark and Eisenhower's appointees— Warren, Harlan, Brennan, Whittaker, and Stewart. By the time *Gideon* was decided, Frankfurter had retired and Whittaker was disabled. They had been replaced by Kennedy's appointees—Arthur Goldberg and Byron White.

Gideon fit the agenda of a majority of the Warren Court.

In cases like Gideon's, their "liberal jurisprudence" revolutionized criminal law by extending the guarantees of the Bill of Rights to the poor and others in state as well as in federal courts. By contrast, members of the Burger Court select cases in order to cut back, if not reverse, the direction of Warren Court policy-making. The Warren Court, in *Douglas v. California* (1963), for example, extended the ruling in *Gideon* to require counsel for indigents appealing their convictions. But in *Ross v. Moffitt* (1974), over the dissents of Douglas, Brennan, and Marshall, the Burger Court held that indigents have a right to counsel only on their first appeal to a state supreme court or the U.S. Supreme Court. The Burger Court also cut back on *Gideon* by holding in *Argersinger v. Hamlin* (1972) that counsel is required only when there is a possibility of a defendant's imprisonment and by then holding in *Scott v. Illinois* (1979) that it is required only when a defendant is actually imprisoned for committing a felony.

Each Court, with its unique combination of justices, sets its own agenda. Justices, of course, differ on what cases they think should be decided. "There is an ideological division on the Court," Justice Rehnquist has admitted, "and each of us has some cases we would like to see granted, and on the contrary some of the other members would not like to see them granted."[3] Justices compete for influence in setting the Court's agenda. That competition flows from the jurisdictional rules and doctrines governing access to the Court's power.

Access to Justice

Jurisdiction is power over access to justice and the exercise of judicial review. The Court's jurisdiction derives from three sources: (1) Article III of the Constitution, which defines the Court's original jurisdiction; (2) congressional legislation, providing appellate jurisdiction; and (3) the Court's own interpretation of one and two together with its own rules for accepting cases.

Article III of the Constitution provides that the judicial power extends to all federal questions—that is, "all Cases, in Law and Equity, arising under this Constitution, the Laws of the United States, and Treaties." The Court also has original jurisdiction over specific kinds of "cases or controversies": those affecting ambassadors, other public ministers, and consuls; disputes to which the United States is a party; between two or more states; between a state and a citizen of another state; and between a state (or its citizens) and foreign countries. The Court today has only about ten cases each term coming on original jurisdiction. Most involve states suing each other over land and water rights, and they tend to be rather complex and carried over for several terms before they are finally decided.

Congress establishes (and may change) the appellate jurisdiction of the federal judiciary, including the Supreme Court.[4] Most cases used to come as direct appeals, requiring obligatory review. But as the caseload increased, Congress expanded the Court's discretionary jurisdiction by replacing appeals with petitions for certiorari, which the court may in its discretion grant or deny. Before the Judiciary Act of 1925, which broadened the Court's discretionary jurisdiction, appeals amounted to 80 percent of the docket and petitions for certiorari less than 20 percent. Today, approximately 95 percent of the docket comes on certiorari.

Although most cases now come as certiorari petitions or appeals, Congress provides that appellate courts may submit a writ of certification to the Court, requesting the justices to clarify or "make more certain" a point of federal law. The Court receives only a handful of such cases each term. Congress also gave the Court the power to issue certain extraordinary writs, or orders. In a few cases, the Court may issue writs of mandamus and prohibition, ordering lower courts or public officials to either do something or refrain from some action. In

AVENUES OF APPEAL: THE TWO MAIN ROUTES
TO THE SUPREME COURT

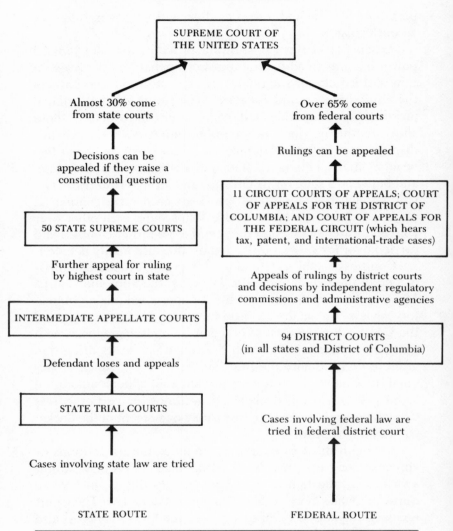

Note: In addition, some cases come directly to the Supreme Court from trial courts when they involve reapportionment or civil rights disputes. Appeals from the Court of Military Appeals also go directly to the Supreme Court. A few cases come on "original jurisdiction" and involve disputes between state governments.

addition, the Court has the power to grant writs of *habeas corpus* ("produce the body"), enabling it to review cases by prisoners who claim that their constitutional rights have been violated and that they are unlawfully imprisoned.

Congress also established the practice of giving poor citizens, like Gideon, the right to file without the payment of fees.[5] When filing an appeal or petition for certiorari, indigents may file an affidavit requesting that they be allowed to proceed *in forma pauperis* ("in the manner of a pauper"), without the usual filing fees and forms. Gideon's first petition, for example, was returned because he failed to include a statement that he was an indigent and unable to pay the cost of filing his petition. The Court sets both the rules governing filing fees and the form that appeals, certiorari petitions, and other documents must take. Except for indigents, the Court now requires $200 for filing any case and another $100 if a case is granted oral argument. Indigents are exempt as well from the Court's rules specifying particular colors and lengths of paper for various kinds of filings. All certiorari petitions, for instance, must have a white color, whereas opposing briefs are light orange. Any document filed by the federal government has a gray cover. No petition or appeal may exceed thirty pages; for those few cases granted oral argument, briefs on the merits of cases are limited to fifty pages.

The Constitution and Congress thus stipulate the kinds of cases and controversies the Court may consider. Yet, as Chief Justice Hughes candidly remarked, "We are under the Constitution, but the Constitution is what the judges say it is."[6] The Court has developed its own doctrines for denying review to a large number of cases and for setting its own agenda. These doctrines depend, in one justice's words, upon "our sense of self-restraint."[7]

JURISDICTIONAL DOCTRINES AND POLICIES

Each "case or controversy" has, Earl Warren observed,

an iceberg quality, containing beneath [the] surface simplicity, sub-merged complexities which go to the very heart of our constitutional form of government. Embodied in the words "cases" and "contro-versies" are two complementary but somewhat different limitations. In part those words limit the business of federal courts to questions presented in an adversary context and in a form historically viewed as capable of resolution through the judicial process. And in part those words define the role assigned to the judiciary in a tripartite allocation of power to assure that the federal courts will not intrude into areas committed to the other branches of government. Justici-ability is a term of art employed to give expression to this dual lim-itation placed upon federal courts by the case and controversy doctrine.[8]

In other words, the Court considers first whether it had juris-diction over a "case or controversy" and then whether that dispute is justiciable, capable of judicial resolution. Justices thus may (or may not) deny a case if it (1) lacks adverseness; (2) is brought by parties who lack "standing to sue"; or poses issues that either (3) are not "ripe" or (4) have become "moot"; or (5) involves a "political question."

Adverseness and Advisory Opinions • The Court generally maintains that litigants must be real and adverse in seeking a decision that will resolve their dispute and not some hypo-thetical issue. The requirement of real and adverse parties means that the Court will not decide "friendly suits," (in which the parties do not have adverse interests in the outcome of a case). Nor will the Court give "advisory opinions" on issues not raised in an actual lawsuit. The Jay Court denied two requests for advisory opinions: one, in 1790, by Secretary of the Treasury Alexander Hamilton for advice on the national government's power to assume state Revolutionary War debts, and another, in 1793, by Secretary of State Thomas Jefferson for an interpretation of certain treaties and international law. Chief Justice Jay held that it would be improper for the Court to judge such matters, because the President might call on cabinet heads for advice. The Court continues to maintain that it is inappropriate "to give opinions in the nature of advice concerning legislative action, a function never conferred upon it by the Constitution and against the exercise of which this court has steadily set its face from the beginning."[9]

Historically, justices have nevertheless extrajudicially advised attorneys, congressmen, and Presidents. They occasionally even accuse each other of including in opinions *dicta* (statements of personal opinion or philosophy not necessary to the decision handed down)—an inclusion that is tantamount to "giving legal advice."[10] The Court, furthermore, upheld the constitutionality of the Declaratory Judgment Act, authorizing federal courts to declare, or make clear, rights and legal relationships even before a law has taken effect, though only in "cases of actual controversy."[11]

The requirement of adverseness and the prohibition against advisory opinions from time to time admit of exceptions. When both parties in a suit agree on how an issue should be decided but need a judicial ruling, the Court will approve a special counsel or *amicus curiae* ("friend of the court") to argue the other side and assure opposition. This occurred in the 1983 one-house veto case, *Immigration and Naturalization Service v. Chadha.* Jagdish Rai Chadha came to the United States on a nonimmigrant student visa, but remained after it expired. The Immigration and Naturalization Service (INS) moved to deport him, but the attorney general suspended deportation and, as required, reported his decision to Congress. Congress then passed a resolution vetoing the suspension of Chadha's deportation. The INS, the Department of Justice, and Chadha all agreed that Congress's action was unconstitutional. The Court of Appeals for the Ninth Circuit, which initially heard the case, requested Congress to submit amicus briefs arguing the opposite.

Standing to Sue • Standing, like adverseness, is a threshold requirement for getting into court. "Generalizations about standing to sue," Douglas discouragingly but candidly put it, "are largely worthless as such."[12] Nonetheless, the basic requirement is that an individual show injury to a legally protected interest or right and demonstrate that other opportunities for defending that claim (before an administrative tribunal or a lower court) have been exhausted. The claim of an injury "must be of a personal and not official nature" and of "some specialized interest of [the individual's] own to vindicate, apart from political concerns which belong to it."[13] The interest must be real as opposed to speculative or hypothetical.

The injuries and legal interests that were claimed traditionally turned on a showing of personal or proprietary damage. Typically, plaintiffs had suffered some "pocketbook" or monetary injury. In the last twenty years, however, individuals have sought standing in order to represent nonmonetary injuries and "the public interest."

The law of standing is a combination of judge-made law and congressional legislation, as interpreted by the Court. The Warren Court era substantially lowered the threshold for standing and permitted more litigation of public policy issues. In *Frothingham v. Mellon* (1923), the Taft Court had denied individual taxpayers standing to challenge the constitutionality of federal legislation. Mrs. Frothingham, a taxpayer, attacked a congressional appropriation to the states for a maternal and infant care program. She claimed that Congress exceeded its power and intruded on "the reserved rights of the states" under the Tenth Amendment. The Taft Court avoided confronting the merits of the claim by denying standing. It did so on the ground that an individual taxpayer's interest in the financing of federal programs is "comparatively minute and indeterminable," when viewed in light of all taxpayers. Frothingham's injury was neither direct nor immediate, and the issue raised was basically "political, not judicial."[14] The government relied on the ruling in *Frothingham* to provide an absolute barrier to subsequent taxpayer suits.

The Warren Court repudiated that view in *Flast v. Cohen* (1968). *Flast* involved a taxpayer's challenge, under the First Amendment establishment clause, of the appropriation of funds for private religious schools in the Elementary and Secondary Education Act of 1965. Here, the Warren Court found that Mrs. Flast, unlike Mrs. Frothingham, had standing. The Court ruled that she had a "personal stake in the outcome," which assured concrete adverseness and litigation that would illuminate the constitutional issues presented. In so doing, the Warren Court created standing where there is a logical relationship between a taxpayer's status and the challenged legislative statute as well as a connection between that status and the "precise nature of the constitutional infringement alleged." The Warren Court's two-pronged test invited more taxpayer lawsuits.

The Burger Court tightened the requirements for standing in some cases, but relaxed it in others. In 1972, in two closely divided decisions, the Burger Court denied standing to a group challenging military surveillance of lawful political protests in public places and to the Sierra Club when challenging the construction of a ski resort in Mineral King National Park. In both cases a bare majority found that the groups failed to show a "personal stake in the outcome" of the litigation. [15] The following year, however, the Burger Court granted standing to a group of law students attacking a proposed surcharge on railroad freight. The students contended that the surcharge would discourage the recycling of bottles and cans and thus contribute to environmental pollution. In *United States v. Students Challenging Regulatory Agency Procedures (SCRAP)* (1973), the Burger Court granted standing, observing,

Aesthetic and environmental well-being, like economic well-being, are important ingredients of the quality of life in our society, and the fact that particular environmental interests are shared by the many rather than the few does not make them less deserving of legal protection through the judicial process.

Plaintiffs must still claim a personal injury, but they can now act as surrogates for special-interest groups. The personal injuries claimed thus embrace a public injury. Congress at the same time expanded the principle even more by providing that any individual "adversely affected or aggrieved" may challenge administrative decisions. Health, safety, and environmental legislation passed in the 1970s mandated such "citizen suits" and right to judicial review of regulatory action. Even when legislation does not provide for the "citizen suits," individuals may claim personal injuries, or a "private cause of action," to gain access to the courts and to force agency compliance with the law.

The Burger Court has restricted standing requirements in two ways. First, it has refused to recognize new interests and injuries in granting standing. In one 1973 case, an unwed mother sought enforcement of child support under the Texas penal code. The local prosecutor refused to enforce the statute against fathers of illegitimate children. A majority of the Burger Court ruled that she had no recognizable injury, no standing, since she could not prove that payments stopped because the statute was unenforced. White and Douglas, in dissent, argued that unwed mothers and illegitimate children were thus rendered nonpersons: "Texas prosecutes fathers of legitimate children on the complaint of the mother asserting nonsupport and refuses to entertain like complaints from the mother of an illegitimate child. [We] see no basis for saying that the latter mother has no standing to demand that the discrimination be ended, one way or another."[16] In a later ruling in *Paul v. Davis* (1976), a majority of the Burger Court rejected a claim of injury to personal reputation by an individual who objected to the circulation of a flier to local merchants that carried his photograph along with that of other alleged "Active Shoplifters." Rehnquist dismissed the claim out of hand.

However, Brennan in dissent responded, "The Court by mere fiat and with no analysis wholly excludes personal interest in reputation from the ambit of 'life, liberty, or property' under the Fifth and Fourteenth Amendments, thus rendering due process concerns *never* applicable to the official stigmatization however arbitrary." Both of these cases illustrate the judicial politics involved in the law of standing, and the importance of legal definitions of interests and injuries.

The second way the Burger Court has tried to dilute *Flast* is to say that standing is not a citizen's right but instead a set of prudential rules. In *Warth v. Seldin* (1975), the majority denied review to a group claiming that zoning laws excluded persons of low income from living in a township outside Rochester, New York. In a dissenting opinion joined by White and Marshall, Brennan charged that the majority had denied standing simply because it unfavorably viewed the merits of the case:

While the Court gives lip service to the principle, often repeated in recent years, that "standing in no way depends on the merits of the plaintiff's contention that particular conduct is illegal," . . . in fact the opinion, which tosses out of court almost every conceivable kind of plaintiff who could be injured by the activity claimed to be unconstitutional can be explained only by an indefensible hostility to the claim on the merits.

Ripeness and Mootness • With these doctrines the Court wields a double-edged sword. A plaintiff may discover that a case is dismissed because it was brought too early or because the issues are moot and the case was brought too late. A case is usually rejected as not ripe if the injury claimed has not yet occurred or if other avenues of appeal have not yet been exhausted. Alternatively, a case may be dismissed if pertinent facts or law change so that there is no longer real adverseness or an actual case or controversy. The issue becomes moot since "there is no subject matter on which the judgement of the court can operate," and hence a ruling would not prove "conclusive" and final. [17]

In practice, both doctrines bend to the Court's will. In *United Public Workers v. Mitchell* (1947), the majority dismissed as too speculative the claim of some federal employees. The employees claimed that they would lose their jobs and forfeit their First Amendment rights of free speech and assembly, if the Civil Service Commission enforced the Hatch Act provisions against civil servants taking "any active part in political management or in political campaigns." In the majority's view, such a "hypothetical threat" is not enough: no injury, no ripeness. In the view of the dissenting justices Douglas and Black, by contrast,

> to require these employees first to suffer the hardship of a discharge is not only to make them incur a penalty; it makes inadequate, if not wholly illusory, any legal remedy which they might have. Men who must sacrifice their means of livelihood in order to test their jobs must either pursue prolonged and expensive litigation as unemployed persons or pull up their roots, change their life careers and seek employment in other fields.

The requirement of ripeness permits the Court to avoid or delay deciding certain issues. Between 1943 and 1965, the Court refused standing to individuals attacking the constitutionality of a late-nineteenth-century Connecticut statute. The law prohibited virtually all single and married individuals from using contraceptives and physicians from giving advice about their use. In *Tileston v. Ullman* (1943), a doctor sued, charging that the statute prevented him from giving information to patients. But the Court ruled that he had no real interest or personal injury, since he had not been arrested.

Over a decade later, in *Poe v. Ullman* (1961), a doctor and a patient were likewise denied standing on the ground that the law had not been enforced for eighty years, even though the state had begun to close birth-control clinics. Finally, after two individuals were found guilty of prescribing contraceptives to a married couple, the Warren Court in *Griswold v. Connecticut* (1965) struck down what Stewart called Connecticut's "uncommonly silly law." The ruling was limited to the privacy and marital decisions of couples. Consequently, in *Eisenstadt v. Baird* (1972), in order to gain standing to claim that single individuals also have a right to acquire and use contraceptives, a doctor arranged to be arrested after delivering a public lecture on contraceptives and handing out samples to single women in the audience. The Burger Court accepted the case and ruled that single women also have the right to acquire and use contraceptives.

A finding of mootness likewise enables the Court to avoid, if not escape, deciding controversial political issues. *DeFunis v. Odegaard* (1974), for example, involved a white student who was denied admission to the University of Washington Law School. The student claimed that the school's affirmative-action program discriminated against him and allowed the entrance of minorities with lower Law School Admission Test scores. After the trial judge's ruling in his favor, he was admitted into law school, but by the time his case reached the Supreme Court he was completing his final year and assured of graduation. Over four dissenters, the majority held that the case was moot. Yet, as the dissenters predicted, the issue would not go away. Within four years, the Burger Court reconsidered the issue of reverse discrimination in university affirmative-action programs in *Regents of the University of California v. Bakke* (1978). In *Bakke,* Powell held not only that quota systems for minorities in college admissions are unconstitutional but also that the Constitution is not "color blind" and that affirmative-action programs are permissible in order to achieve a diverse student body in colleges and universities.

The issue of mootness presented no serious problem when the Burger Court tackled abortion in *Roe v. Wade* (1973). Here, we saw, a Texas criminal statute prohibiting abortions, except when necessary to save a mother's life, was attacked as infringing on a woman's right of privacy recognized in *Griswold*. In defending the law, the state attorney general argued that the plaintiff was a single woman whose pregnancy had terminated by the time the case reached the Court and that hence her claim was moot. Blackmun, writing for the Court, rejected that view:

[W]hen, as here, pregnancy is a significant fact in the litigation, the normal 266-day human gestation period is so short that the pregnancy will come to term before the usual appellate process is complete. If that termination makes a case moot, pregnancy litigation seldom will survive much beyond the trial stage, and appellate review will be effectively denied. Our law should not be that rigid. Pregnancy often comes more than once to the same woman, and in the general population, if man is to survive, it will always be with us. Pregnancy provides a classic justification for a conclusion of nonmootness. It truly could be "capable of repetition, yet evading review."

Political Questions • Even when the Court has jurisdiction over a properly framed suit, it may decline to rule because it decides that a case raises a political question that should be resolved by other political branches. Like other jurisdictional doctrines, the political-question doctrine means what the justices say it means.

The doctrine has its origin in the following observation by Chief Justice Marshall in *Marbury v. Madison* (1803): "The province of the Court, is, solely, to decide on the rights of individuals. . . . Questions in the nature political, or which are, by the constitution and laws, submitted to the executive can never be made in this Court." Yet, as Alexis de Tocqueville noted in the 1830s, "Scarcely any political question arises in the United States that is not resolved, sooner or later, into a judicial question."[18] Litigation that reaches the Court is political, and the justices for political reasons decide what and how to decide cases on their docket.

The Taney Court first developed the doctrine in *Luther v. Borden* (1849). There, the Court was called on to decide whether Rhode Island had a "republican form of government," as guaranteed by Article IV of the Constitution. Taney reasoned that Article I gave Congress and not the Court "the right to decide." Subsequent rulings elaborated other reasons for the doctrine besides deference to separation of powers. The Court may lack information and resources needed for a ruling. In some areas, as in foreign policy and international relations, the Court lacks both adequate standards for resolving disputes and the means to enforce its decisions.

For many decades, the Court relied on the doctrine to avoid entering the "political thicket" of state representation and apportionment.[19] Yet, blacks and other minorities in urban areas were often denied equal voting rights. The Court finally responded and reversed itself in *Baker v. Carr* (1962). The Court reasserted its power to decide what is and is not a "political question" when it held that disputes over state representation and apportionment are within its jurisdiction and justiciable. The Warren Court thus forced state and local governments to provide equal voting rights and established the principle of "one man, one vote."

The doctrine's logic is circular. "Political questions are matters not soluble by the judicial process; matters not soluble by the judicial process are political questions. As an early dictionary explained," the political scientist John Roche has said, " violins are small cellos, and cellos are large violins."[20] Still, as the Columbia Law professor Louis Henkin has pointed out, even when denying review because of a political question, "the court does not refuse judicial review; it exercises it. It is not dismissing the case or the issue as nonjusticiable; it adjudicates it. It is not refusing to pass on the power of the political branches; it passes upon it, only to affirm that they had the power which had been challenged and that nothing in the Constitution prohibited the particular exercise of it."[21]

Stare Decisis and Other Policies • The justices occasionally also rely on other self-denying policies to avoid reaching issues. They may, for example, invoke what has been called the doctrine of *strict necessity,* and thereupon formulate and decide only the narrowest possible issue.

The doctrine of *stare decisis* ("let the prior decision stand") is also not a mechanical formula. It is, rather, a judicial policy that promotes "the certainty, uniformity, and stability of the law." Even the conservative justice George Sutherland recognized that members of the Court "are not infallible, and when convinced that a prior decision was not originally based on, or that conditions have so changed as to render the decision no longer in accordance with, sound reason, [they] should not hesitate to say so."[22] "*Stare decisis* is usually the wise policy," Brandeis remarked, "because in most matters it is more important that the applicable rule of law be settled than that it be settled right."[23] On constitutional matters, however, Douglas among others has emphasized, "*stare decisis*—that is, established law—was really no sure guideline because what did . . . the judges who sat there in 1875 know about, say, electronic surveillance? They didn't know anything about it."[24]

In sum, stare decisis and the precedential value of the Court's jurisdictional doctrines and policies, as Justice Jackson quipped, "are accepted only at their current valuation and have a mortality rate as high as their authors."[25]

FORMAL RULES AND PRACTICES

Except for government attorneys and members of the practicing bar, few people pay any attention to the technical rules of the Court. Yet, the rules are an exercise of political power and determine the nation's access to justice. They govern the admission and activities of attorneys in filing appeals, petitions, and motions and in conducting oral arguments. They stipulate the fees, forms, and length of filings. Most important, they explain the Court's formal grounds for granting and disposing of cases.

In order to expedite the process of deciding what to decide, the Court periodically revises its rules. For example, even after the Judiciary Act of 1925 expanded the Court's discretionary jurisdiction, the justices still felt burdened by mandatory appeals. Accordingly, in 1928 the Court required the filing of a jurisdictional statement, explaining the circumstances of an appeal, the questions presented, and the reasons why the Court should grant review. The requirement, as Justice Stone explained, "enabled us to dispose of many questions without bringing counsel to argue them, but it has also helped to enlighten counsel as to the nature of our jurisdiction and the burden which always rests on an appellant to establish jurisdiction."[26] The requirement also allowed the justices to screen appeals just as it screened petitions for certiorari. As the Clerk of the Court in 1945 remarked,

Most attorneys are well aware of the fact that the Court may and does exercise its discretion in passing on applications for certiorari but insofar as appeals are concerned they harbor the mistaken impression that review is obligatory and that where they have an appeal "as of right" they are entitled to oral argument on the merits. On the contrary, at least fifty percent of the appeals are dismissed or the judgments affirmed upon consideration of the jurisdictional statements, before records are printed and without oral arguments. Jurisdictional statements and petitions for certiorari now stand on practically the same footing. . . .[27]

The vast majority of filings, regardless of whether they are obligatory appeals or discretionary petitions, can now be quickly scanned.

One of the reasons for granting certiorari that the Court's rules gives is that "a federal court of appeals has rendered a decision in conflict with the decision of another federal court

of appeals on the same matter." This rule is especially advantageous for the federal government. The Department of Justice has a relitigation policy. If it receives an adverse ruling
from a circuit court of appeals, it will relitigate the issue in
other circuits in order to obtain favorable decisions and generate a conflict among the circuits, which then may be brought
to the Court. One function of the Court, in Chief Justice Vinson's words, has become the resolution of "conflicts of opinion
on federal questions that have arisen among lower courts."[28]
Yet, each term the Court denies review to between fifty and
sixty such conflicts. In 1983, Warren Burger even proposed
the creation of a special tribunal to handle these kinds of cases
and thereby to reduce the Court's workload.[29]

The rule for granting circuit conflicts, however, does not
control the justices' actual practice of granting certiorari. In
1981, the Burger Court granted oral argument to 184 cases.
But only 47 (25 percent) involved an alleged conflict among
the circuits, and only 28 (16 percent) of the Court's final opinions resolved circuit conflicts. The number of alleged conflicts
is undoubtedly somewhat larger, since included here is only
that small number of cases accepted for oral argument.[30] Still,
these figures are significant because the government and individuals often allege circuit conflicts simply in an effort to get
their cases accepted. The figures show that most conflicts are
"tolerable" and need not be immediately decided. That is, as
Justice Harlan explains, when "the conflict may be resolved
as a result of future cases in the Courts of Appeals, or where
the impact of the conflict is narrowly confined and is not apt
to have continuing future consequences."[31]

Justices often feel that conflicts should percolate in the
circuits before they take them. Sometimes, a majority may
want to avoid or delay addressing an issue that has created a
conflict among the circuits. For instance, over the dissent of
Burger and White, a majority of the Court denied review of a
clear circuit conflict involving the question whether private

hospitals, funded largely by the government, may refuse to perform elective abortions.[32] At other times, the Court grants review, regardless of any circuit conflict, simply because of the constitutional issues raised. The Burger Court thus granted *Michael M. v. Superior Court* (1980). There, circuit courts were divided over an important issue of constitutional law: whether statutory rape laws applying to males but not females violate the Fourteenth Amendment's equal-protection clause. Rehnquist, writing for the majority, upheld the laws because "the risk of pregnancy itself constitutes a substantial deterrence to young females. No similar natural sanctions deter males. A criminal sanction imposed solely on males thus serves to 'equalize' the deterrents on the sexes."

Most crucial in granting certiorari is simply the majority's agreement on the importance of the issue presented. This fact is underscored by the justices' screening process. The Burger Court relies primarily on law clerks' memos when granting certiorari. But these memos only summarize the facts, questions, and arguments presented. On that basis, they recommend whether a case should be granted or denied. Clerks' memos do not fully explore whether an alleged conflict is "real," "tolerable," or "square" and must be decided. The workload usually precludes such an examination until a case has already been granted and set for oral argument.

That the Court's rules for granting or denying cases do not dictate judicial behavior should not be surprising. But we should not conclude that justices do not take the rules seriously. In 1980, when the Burger Court revised its rules, it repeatedly warned that documents should "be as short as possible." In 1984, a majority then refused to permit an attorney to submit an appendix to a brief that exceeded the length allowed under the rules.[33] Burger, Rehnquist, and O'Connor have also denied the waiver of fees for individuals filing in forma pauperis and sought to impose penalties for the filing of cases they consider frivolous.[34]

Setting the Agenda

The justices' interpretations of their jurisdiction and rules govern access to the Court. But the justices also need flexible procedures for screening cases and deciding what to decide. The Court is a collegial institution in which all nine justices have an equal vote, and so justices need room for compromise. Attempts at streamlining the process and imposing strict procedures can get in the way of compromise and sharply divide the justices.

Justice Frankfurter's unsuccessful efforts to persuade his brethren to adopt formal rules for conducting their deliberations illustrates the dynamics of the Court. A persistent meddler, every year from 1951 until his last term on the bench, in 1961, Frankfurter circulated a memorandum (often the same each year but with minor editorial changes) proposing formal procedural rules for conducting the Court's deliberative process.[35] Always a hyper-self-conscious law professor, he became increasingly concerned with a fact of life in the Court that Justice Brandeis initially pointed out to him in 1923, while Frankfurter was still a professor at Harvard. "Nothing is decided without consideration," Brandeis had told him, "but hardly anything is decided with adequate consideration. . . . [Y]ou must constantly bear in mind the large part played by personal considerations and inadequacy of consideration."[36] Once on the bench, Frankfurter campaigned for procedures *he* thought would ensure "adequate consideration" of the Court's business. He succeeded only in distancing himself from Chief Justice Warren and the others.[37] In particular, Douglas protested,

If we unanimously adopted rules on such matters we would be plagued by them, bogged down, and interminably delayed. If we were not unanimous, the rules would be ineffective. I, for one, could not agree to give anyone any more control over when I vote than over how I vote.[38]

Likewise, Black opposed the adoption of formal rules. "I am satisfied with our present flexible procedures," he wrote Frankfurter, adding, "The majority, I suppose, could not by mechanical rules bind individual Justices as to the exercise of their discretion."[39]

The current Court now wrestles with a similar problem as a result of changes in the process of screening cases. One reaction has been a rise in the number of dissents from the denial of review of cases that justices feel are not properly screened or fully considered.

SCREENING CASES

When any appeal or certiorari petition arrives at the Court, it immediately goes to the Clerk's office. There, staff determine whether it satisfies requirements regarding form, length, and fees and, if the filing is from an indigent, whether there is an affidavit stating that the petitioner is too poor to pay fees. All unpaid cases are assigned a number, in the order they arrive, and placed on what is called the Miscellaneous Docket. Paid cases are also assigned a number, but placed on the Appellate Docket. The Clerk then notifies the other party, or respondent, in each case that they must file a brief in response within thirty days. After receiving briefs from respondents, the Clerk circulates to the justices' chambers a list of cases ready for consideration and a set of briefs for each case.

For much of the Court's history, every justice was responsible for reviewing each case. The justices did not work by panels or delegate responsibility for screening cases to others. That is no longer true.

Changes in the screening of cases began because of the increasing number of unpaid petitions (as is indicated in the Chart).[40] Each justice traditionally received copies of the briefs in all paid cases. But, beginning with the Taft Court (1921–1930), justices deferred to the chief justice and his law clerks' recommendations on whether unpaid cases should be granted. When the number was still manageable in the 1930s, Chief

PAID AND UNPAID FILINGS, 1935–1984

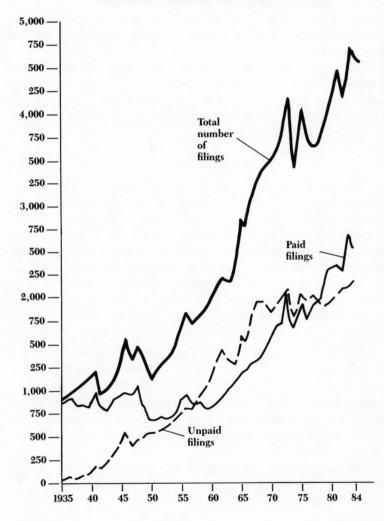

Justice Hughes examined all unpaid petitions and orally reported his findings at conference. Only exceptional cases were distributed to other justices. Yet, as Frankfurter noted, Hughes's concern for indigents was such that it "made him the leader of the legal aid movement." Stone initially continued the practice, but in conference, rather than briefly stating his views, he read his law clerks' memos on each petition. "After two or three Stone terms a spontaneous feeling developed among [the justices] that instead of having Stone merely read the memorandum, full as it was, by his law clerk, it would be better to have multiple copies made of it for circulation among the brethren prior to conference."[41] During his last two years, Stone had copies of his clerks' memos sent to all the justices. At conference, the justices discussed only those Stone or others placed on a "take-up list," appended to the regular conference list that included appeals and other paid cases. Vinson and Warren continued this practice, except that gradually petitions in death penalty and other extraordinary cases were routinely circulated to all justices and discussed at conference. Only those unpaid cases thought to be important by a chief justice, or by another justice, were discussed at conference. All other unpaid cases were placed on a "Dead List" and formally denied at conference.

When Burger arrived at the Court, in the summer of 1969, the number of unpaid cases constituted almost half of the total docket. He immediately sought congressional approval for nine additional law clerks but succeeded in obtaining only three. These three "general" law clerks, along with one of the chief's, wrote memos on all unpaid cases. Their memos were photocopied (on the Court's newly acquired and, at the time, only copier) and sent around to the other justices. This "inordinate burden" on the chief justice's chambers, however, was not one that Burger was "willing to bear, along with an average of at least 20 hours a week on administrative duties."[42]

During his first term, Burger had the National Archives

and Records Service (NARS) study the paperwork involved in processing the caseload and estimate the cost-effectiveness of alternative practices. At conference, Burger proposed three alternatives: (1) a revolving panel of senior judges to act as "Special Masters" who would review all unpaid cases and recommend a few for the justices' consideration; (2) divide all the unpaid cases among the justices, with each examining one-ninth; and (3) copy and circulate all unpaid cases, along with paid cases, to each chamber. There was vehement opposition to the first proposal. The justices refused to give up control over their docket and agenda setting. The second alternative also met opposition, and NARS estimated that it would be the most expensive and would greatly increase the workload of each chamber. The conference settled on the third option, having all unpaid cases circulated to each chamber. The

Justice William Rehnquist discussing cases with his law clerks in his chambers. (*Yoichi Okamoto*)

increased workload would be offset by the addition of one law clerk for each justice.[43]

Subsequently, in 1972, at the suggestion of Powell, the "cert. pool" was established. Six of the justices now share their collective law clerks' memos on all paid and unpaid cases. Those justices not joining the pool—Brennan, Marshall, Douglas, and, later, Stevens—receive copies of unpaid cases along with other filings. Brennan examines each case himself, when he has time to do so. Stevens has his clerks screen all the cases and write memos on only those they deem important enough for him to consider.

Until the appointment of Burger, the justices thus deferred the screening of unpaid cases to the chief justice. Since the creation of the cert. pool, all chambers share responsibility for the screening of filings, though the Legal Office now initially takes capital punishment and extraordinary motions. The responsibility for screening paid and unpaid cases has been delegated by a majority of the Burger Court to their twenty-three collective law clerks.

The expanded role of law clerks in screening cases is significant and problematic. Although bright, the clerks are much less experienced than the justices. As Harlan noted, "Frequently the question whether a case is 'certworthy' is more a matter of 'feel' than of precisely ascertainable rules."[44]

The problems of relying too much on clerks is apparent at the beginning of each term. The term runs from October to the end of June, but filings come in year-round. Until justices delegated to their clerks the responsibility of screening filings, bags of petitions and appeals were sent out by the Clerk throughout the summer to the justices wherever they were vacationing; this was done when Hughes spent his summers in Jasper Park, Canada, Stone retreated to the Isle au Haute, and Douglas made his annual trek to Goose Prairie, in the Pacific Northwest. The justices now initiate their clerks, who come aboard in July, by having them write memos on the filings that arrive in the summer. The justices review these memos before their conference at the beginning of the term. Yet, these memos are written by clerks who have little experience with the Court's rules and norms. [45]

Law clerks in their initial two or three months at the Court screen about one-fifth of the cases for a term. The number of filings has grown so much that the Court now has a docket of about two thousand cases before it even starts its term. As the caseload increased, the justices' initial conference grew longer and carried over for several days during the first week of each term. [46] The Burger Court found it necessary to begin meeting the last week of September, prior to its formal opening on the first Monday in October. During this week-long conference in 1983, the justices disposed of over nine hundred cases, discussing fewer than two hundred. Before the start of its term, the Court has thus already disposed of approximately one-fifth of its entire docket. Over four-fifths of those cases are screened out by law clerks and never collectively discussed and considered by the justices.

CONFERENCE DISCUSSIONS

The justices meet alone in conference to decide which cases to accept and to discuss the merits of those few cases on which they hear oral arguments. Throughout the term, during the weeks in which the Court hears oral arguments, it holds conferences on Wednesday afternoons to take up the four cases argued on Monday, and then on Fridays to discuss new filings and the eight cases on which it heard oral argument on Tuesday and Wednesday. In May and June, when the Court does not hear oral arguments, conferences are held on Thursdays, from ten in the morning until four or four-thirty in the afternoon, with the justices breaking for a forty-five-minute lunch around twelve-thirty. A majority may vote to hold a special session during the summer months, when extraordinarily urgent cases arise—such as the 1953 stay of execution of the

Rosenbergs, who had been convicted of espionage, and President Nixon's claim of "executive privilege" in *United States v. Nixon* (1974) during the Watergate episode.

Summoned by a buzzer five minutes before the hour, the justices meet in the conference room, located directly behind the courtroom itself and next to the chief justice's chambers. The oak-paneled room is lined with *United States Reports* (containing the Court's decisions). Over the mantel of an exquisite fireplace at one end hangs a portrait of Chief Justice Marshall. Next to the fireplace stands a large rectangular table, where the justices sit. The chief justice sits at the one end and the senior associate justice at the other. Along the right-hand side of the chief justice, next to the fireplace, sit Marshall, Blackmun, and White; on the left-hand side, Powell, Rehnquist, Stevens, and O'Connor, the most junior justice. The seating of the justices has traditionally been on the basis of seniority. But variations occur because of individual justices' preferences. In the late nineteenth century, for instance, Justice Rufus Peckham grew accustomed to the seat at the foot of the table; on Joseph McKenna's appointment, he refused to move one seat up and thus retained the junior justice's place. Sitting closest to the outside double door, the junior justice by tradition receives and sends messages that come and go by way of knocks on the door—a tradition that led Tom Clark to comment wryly, "For five years I was the highest paid doorkeeper in the world."[47]

Two conference lists are circulated to each chamber by noon on the Wednesday before the Friday conference. They structure conference discussion and enable the justices to get through their caseload. On the first list—Special List I, or the Discuss List—are jurisdictional statements, petitions for certiorari, and motions that are ready and worth discussing. The Discuss List typically includes between forty and fifty cases for each conference. Attached is a second list—Special List II, or what was called the Dead List—containing those cases considered unworthy of discussion. Any justice may request that a case be put on the Discuss List, and only after the chief's conference secretary has heard from all chambers do the lists become final. About 70 percent of the cases on the conference lists are automatically denied without discussion, and most of those that do make the Discuss List are denied as well. [48] The conference lists are an important technique for saving time and focusing attention on the few cases deemed worthy of consideration. Still, as Earl Warren observed, "It may be fairly said that a majority of the time of our conferences is devoted to this purpose." [49]

Each conference begins with the customary shaking of hands, which reminded Justice James Byrnes of "the usual instruction of the referee in the prize ring, 'Shake hands, go to your corner and come out fighting.' "[50] A typical conference, Burger tells visitors to the Court, "opens with a discussion of the applications for review . . . and then we move to a consideration of which opinions are ready for announcement; and from that we go to a discussion of the argued cases."[51] The chief justice begins discussions. Burger usually reads from his law clerk's memos and states his view of whether a case should be granted or denied. Discussion then passes from one justice to another in order of their seniority.

Chief justices have significant opportunities for structuring and influencing conference discussions. But they vary in their skills, style, and ideological orientations. Hughes is widely considered to be the greatest chief justice in this century. "Warren was closer to Hughes than any others." And in Douglas's view, "Burger was close to Vinson. Stone was somewhere in between."[52]

Hughes's photographic memory, authoritative demeanor, and personal charisma made him a respected task and social leader. At conference, Hughes strove to limit discussion by giving crisp three-and-a-half-minute summaries of each filing. His "machine gun style" was largely successful. Owen Roberts recalled that "so complete were his summaries that in many cases nothing needed to be added by any of his associates."[53] But Stone, a former Columbia law professor always interested in a searching examination of every issue, took a different view. He found it annoying that Hughes conducted conferences "much like a drill sergeant."[54] When Stone was elevated to the post of chief justice, he encouraged lengthy discussions, at the cost of prolonging conferences and carrying

The conference room in the Supreme Court. During a break for lunch, the chief justice's secretary arranges docket books and other materials. (*Supreme Court Historical Society*)

unfinished business over to special conferences later in the week. Personally inclined to debate every point, Stone was not disposed to cut short the debates that erupted from disagreements between Black and Frankfurter or Jackson. As a result, under Stone, Douglas observed, the justices were "almost in a continuous Conference." Vinson was not as intellectually equipped or as interested in the law as Stone. But he was more business minded, though Douglas claimed that "he would filibuster for hours to have his way on a case."

Earl Warren was more of a politician, a big bear of a man with great personal charm. "We all loved him," Stewart has fondly recalled. But when Warren first arrived, he was totally unprepared and unfamiliar with Court ways. Frankfurter immediately tried to bring him under his sphere of influence and to some extent succeeded in the first couple of terms. By the end of the 1956 term, however, Warren had grown wary of Frankfurter, and thereafter the latter became an increasingly overbearing pest. Warren developed a warm working relationship with Brennan. They had a practice of meeting in Brennan's chambers on Thursday afternoons to discuss the cases that would be taken up at the Friday conference. Warren still had some problems stifling Frankfurter, who irritated all by trying to dominate conference discussions. Yet, Warren gradually came into his own at conference. Though not a legal scholar, he showed that he was more than a skilled politician and that he had more intellectual ability than many critics gave him credit for. Warren drew on his experiences as a former attorney general and governor of California and grew intellectually with his role as chief justice.

Burger tends to be more like Vinson. Outside of the area of criminal procedure, he does not have a "legal mind" or a "taste for the law." He is more interested (and his great accomplishments lie) in the area of judicial administration. With considerable personal charm and a good sense of humor, but also a temper, Burger does about all he can to promote collegial relations within the Court. But, like Vinson, he is basically managerial in his approach, believing that the Court can adequately decide only around one hundred cases each term. At conference, Burger likewise tends to rely heavily on his clerks' memos when opening conference discussions of cases. He claims to make a conscious attempt not to mention every point raised in a case, in order to let the others pick up on those points and contribute to the discussion. Burger's discussion of cases at conference, however, leaves some of the justices feeling that he is "the least prepared member of the Court." Yet, his lack of precision at conference allows him to join a perceived majority and later to assign the opinion, and thereby to continue to influence the outcome.

There is a good deal of give-and-take in conference, and, as Justice White has noted, "by the time that everyone has had his say, the vote is usually quite clear; but, if not, it will be formally taken."[55] The justices once voted in ascending order of seniority. Clark, for one, gave the following rationale for this manner of voting: "Ever since Chief Justice Marshall's day the formal vote begins with the junior Justice and moves up through the ranks of seniority, the Chief Justice voting last. Hence the juniors are not influenced by the vote of their elders."[56] A quaint rationale, but the procedure has not been followed since Hughes was chief justice. The caseload is now so heavy that there is no longer time for each justice to discuss, and deliberate over what the others have said, and then vote on each case. The justices come prepared to vote when explaining how they view each case. As Black emphasized, it is "a fiction that everybody always waits for the youngest man to express himself, or vote, as they say. Well that's fiction."[57] Likewise, Blackman now affirms, "we vote by seniority, as you know, despite [the fact] that some texts say we vote by juniority."[58]

Conference discussions can become heated. Following one such conference, Rehnquist wrote his brethren, "I had a feeling that at the very close of today's Conference we may have fitted Matthew Arnold's closing lines in 'Dover Beach' wherein he refers to those 'Swept with confused alarms of Struggle and flight Where ignorant armies clash by night.' "[59] Confusion thus occasionally resulted over who voted how and which justices later switch votes.[60]

Immediately after conference, the chief justice traditionally had the task of reporting the votes to the Clerk. Burger delegated this task to a junior justice, initially to Rehnquist and then to O'Connor. This was done in part because Burger occasionally made mistakes recording conference votes. All the justices have a large docket book in which they may note votes and discussions for their personal records. But the junior justice now tells the Clerk which cases have been granted oral arguments and which have been denied. The Clerk then notifies both sides in a case granted review that they have thirty days to file briefs on merits and supporting documents. Once all briefs (forty copies of each) are submitted, the Clerk schedules the case for oral argument.

Given the volume of the Court's business, and the justices' ideological differences, unanimity in case selection is remarkably high. Unanimity is a rather consistent pattern in case selection, regardless of the Court's composition. During the chief justiceships of Vinson and Warren, the political scientist Marie Provine found, on the basis of a study of Harold Burton's docket books for the period (1947–1957), 82 percent of all cases were unanimously disposed; and of these, 79 percent were denied and 3 percent were granted review.[61] During that period, the Court disposed of approximately fifteen hundred cases each term.

The Burger Court now disposes of almost three times that number each term. An examination of Brennan's docket book for the 1973 term nevertheless reveals comparable unanimity. Almost 79 percent of all petitions and appeals were initially unanimously decided. Some 72 percent of the denials of certiorari were unanimous. But the number of petitions unanimously granted dropped by half, to less than 2 percent. The extent of unanimous case selection within the Burger Court is illustrated below:[62]

DISPOSITION IN CASE SELECTION, 1973 TERM

Disposition	Unanimous (%)	Divided (%)	Total Number (%)
Denied petition	2,797 (71.93)	558 (14.35)	3,355 (86.28)
Granted petition	58 (1.49)	155 (3.98)	213 (5.47)
Appeal accepted	15 (0.38)	32 (0.82)	47 (1.2)
Appeal affirmed	18 (0.46)	31 (0.79)	49 (1.25)
Appeal dismissed	148 (3.80)	22 (0.55)	170 (4.35)
Miscellaneous	33 (0.84)	21 (0.54)	54 (1.38)
TOTAL	3,069 (78.90)	819 (21.03)	3,888

The vast majority of unanimously denied cases sit on the Dead List and are never discussed at conference. The percentage of unanimous denials would have been higher (reaching 83 percent), had it not been for a large number of cases—decided along with the major ruling in *Miller v. California* (1973)—in which Douglas cast a single dissent. He vehemently opposed the Burger Court's view that local (rather than national) community standards should determine what is obscene and pornographic.

THE RULE OF FOUR AND WHAT IT MEANS

When Congress gave the Court discretionary jurisdiction in the Judiciary Act of 1925, by substituting petitions for certiorari for mandatory appeals, the justices developed the informal rule of four to decide which petitions they would grant. During conference, at least four justices must agree that a case warrants oral argument and consideration by the full Court.

The rule of four evolved in a flexible, collegial manner.

Exceptions were often made to the rule of four when the case-load was lighter than it is today. Influential justices and persuasive arguments occasionally won cases a hearing on fewer than four votes.[63] Even during the 1930s, under Chief Justice Hughes, the rule was rather liberally applied. As he explained, "certiorari is always granted if four justices think it should be, and not infrequently, when 3, or even 2, justices strongly urge the grant."[64] Justice Reed once pleaded with Hughes,

Won't you consider further the soundness of the suggestions made yesterday in Conference that three votes should be sufficient to bring up Bethlehem [*United States v. Bethlehem Steel Corporation* (1940)]? There is really no absolute rule that four votes are necessary when a full Court sits. Certainly when there are only six justices sitting, it seems that three should be sufficient to justify a hearing on the merits.[65]

To pressure the chief justice further, Reed emphasized the agreement with his view of two others, Frankfurter and Douglas, who often were at odds with each other. On another occasion, when a petition in a capital punishment case was denied, Frankfurter appealed to emotion: "On any view, these petitioners are worthless creatures. But the fact that worthless creatures may invoke the protection of the Constitution is not the least of the glories of our country."[66] Yet another time, Douglas adopted a different tactic. He agreed to supply the necessary fourth vote if the other three justices would limit their grant of a case to one of several issues presented.[67]

After a conference vote denying a case, three justices may still find or persuade another to vote to grant the case at the next conference.[68] But that rarely happens now. The rule of four operates in a fraction of cases because of the increasing caseload. Whereas in 1941 the Court acted on 951 petitions, that number doubled by 1961; it doubled again, with a total of 4,066 petitions, by 1981.[69] Stevens estimated, on the basis of the docket books of Harold Burton, that during the Vinson

Court, in 1946–1947, over 25 percent of the cases granted had the support of no more than four justices. Brennan's docket book for 1973 reveals that 19 percent of the cases accepted for oral argument received less than a majority vote. Of those cases granted, 80 percent were on the basis of five or more of the justices, and only 27 percent as the result of a bare majority.

The rather consistent pattern of unanimous case selection, and the small number of petitions granted upon the rule of four, raises several important questions about the Court's agenda setting. What explains the patterns of unanimity in case selection, despite the changing composition of the Court? Since the rule of four operates in a small number of cases, is it useful any longer? Finally, since only about 2 percent of all petitions are granted on less than a majority vote, what is the meaning of a denial of certiorari?

Agreement by a majority or more on case selection reflects the interplay of a number of factors. Most important, institutional norms promote a shared conception of the role of the Court as a tribunal for resolving only issues of national importance. With the increasing business of the Court, the justices have come to accept the following view, first expressed by Chief Justice Taft:

No litigant is entitled to more than two chances, namely, to the original trial and to a review, and the intermediate courts of review are provided for that purpose. When a case goes beyond that, it is not primarily to preserve the rights of the litigants. The Supreme Court's function is for the purpose of expounding and stabilizing principles of law for the benefit of the people of the country, passing upon constitutional questions and other important questions of law for the public benefit.[70]

Justices agree that the overwhelming proportion of cases are "frivolous" and that there is a limited number of cases to which they may give full consideration. "As a rule of thumb," White, among others on the current Court, has said, "the Court should not be expected to produce more than 150 opinions per term in argued cases."[71]

These factors tend to overshadow ideological divisions in case selection. Ideological differences appear less pronounced in voting on case selection than in voting on the merits of cases disposed by written opinions. The selection process may appear as "the first battleground on the merits,"[72] but principally for those justices at either end of the Court's ideological spectrum. In 1973, for example, Douglas voted against the prevailing position in case selection more than half the time. He voted in opposition 485 times, compared with 135 and 124 votes cast by Brennan and Rehnquist, who represent the two most extreme ideological positions within the Court. If Powell is excepted, the justices averaged 105 votes against the prevailing position in case selection. It is not surprising to find that the most ideologically opposed members disagreed most frequently on case selection and that Powell was least often (70 times) in disagreement on case selection, underscoring his reputation as a team player and pragmatist. In regard to voting alignments, a similar pattern appears. Douglas and Brennan voted together most often (35 percent of the time), whereas Burger went along with Rehnquist in 21 percent of the cases.

The caseload and institutional norms push toward a limiting of the operation of the rule of four. But the rule remains useful, particularly if there is a bloc of justices who share the same ideological orientation. In 1983, Burger proposed that Congress establish a special tribunal to which one-fourth to one-third of the cases on which the Court now hears oral argument might be referred (and thereby relieve the justices' workload). Stevens countered by proposing that the Court abandon the rule of four and grant petitions only on a majority vote.[73] Stevens estimated that that would eliminate as many as one-fourth of the cases now granted. In 1973, 19 percent of the cases granted were on the basis of four votes, but that percentage has risen in recent years. Stevens's docket books for 1979–1981 show that between 23 and 30 percent of the cases accepted for oral argument rest on only four votes. Often the four votes to grant cases come from justices who participate in the cert. pool and who share the same ideological orientation—Burger, Rehnquist, O'Connor, and Powell or White. The rule of four thus enables a bloc of justices to work together in picking cases they want the Court to rule on.

"What is the significance of this Court's denial of certiorari? That question is asked again and again," Stevens has lamented; "it is a question that is likely to arise whenever a dissenting opinion argues that certiorari should have been granted."[74] Denial of certiorari purportedly "imparts no expression of opinion upon the merits of the case."[75] The Court, however, is "not quite of one mind on the subject," as Jackson observed. "Some say denial means nothing, others say it means nothing much. Realistically, the first position is untenable and the second is unintelligible."[76]

Justice Frankfurter explained the orthodox view that "a denial no wise implies agreement" on the merits of a case: "It simply means that fewer than four members of the Court deemed it desirable to review a decision of the lower court as a matter of 'sound judicial discretion.' Pertinent considerations of judicial policy here come into play."[77] A case could be denied, Brennan has likewise explained, on the grounds that

the issue was either not ripe enough or too moribund for adjudication; that the question had better wait for the perspective of time or that time would bury the question or, for one reason or another, it was desirable to wait and see; or that the constitutional issue was entangled with nonconstitutional issues that raised doubt whether the constitutional issue could be effectively isolated; or for various other reasons not related to the merits.[78]

Justices may have any number of reasons for denying certiorari. But as Jackson observed, "Because no one knows all that a denial means, does it mean that it means nothing?"[79] A denial cannot mean "nothing much." The Court does not grant certiorari to review the facts of cases. Do denials thus convey approval of the lower-court ruling? In *Brown v. Allen* (1953), involving federal courts' jurisdiction over habeas corpus appeals from state courts, three justices indicated that when issues are repetitiously raised, denials should be understood as affirming the lower court's ruling. Yet, if a grant or a denial is based on the justices' view of the merits of a case, then a paradox results in voting on case selection. Since only four justices may grant a case, a minority binds the majority to deciding the merits of a case that they do not think need to be considered. In all other respects, the Court operates by majority vote. "Even though a minority may bring a case here for oral argument," Frankfurter contended, "that does not mean that the majority has given up its right to vote on the ultimate disposition of the case as conscience dictates."[80] Frankfurter made a practice of refusing to vote on the merits of some cases that he thought the Court had improperly granted.[81] If Frankfurter's practice were widely accepted, the rule of four would be superfluous. As Douglas objected, "If four can grant and the opposing five dismiss, then the four cannot get a decision of the case on the merits. The integrity of the four vote rule would then be impaired."[82]

Because the Court declines to take a case, it does not follow that "[i]t means nothing else."[83] The denial of certiorari cannot be considered meaningless, for a number of reasons. Brennan's docket book shows that 98 percent of the cases granted or denied are on the basis of a vote of a majority or more. Stevens's proposal for replacing the rule of four by a majority vote would thus simply acknowledge what already occurs in practice. Adoption of a rule of five, even more than the present voting pattern, of course, would legitimize the view that denials amount to passing on the merits of cases. Denials inevitably send signals as to which and what kind of cases "do not present questions of sufficient gravity."[84]

That justices pass on the merits when screening cases is inescapable in view of the growing number of dissents and dissenting opinions from the denial of certiorari. In the 1940s and 1950s, dissents were relatively rare. They gradually increased with the caseload of the Warren and Burger Courts. The two most pro-review justices, Black and Douglas, began noting their dissents from denial of certiorari. "Gradually the practice spread to a few other Justices," Douglas has written, "and finally I ended up in the sixties noting my vote in all cases where dismissals or denials were contrary to my convictions."[85] The growth in number of dissents appears staggering: there were 237 dissents in 1969, 469 in 1970, and 625 in 1973. Even after Douglas resigned, the number of dissents remained high. In 1978, for example, there were 413 total dissenting votes, coming from every justice, except Stevens, who in his first years on the Court opposed the practice. In more than half of them, the justices indicated their view that the lower-court decision was wrong and should have been reversed.[86] The most ideologically opposed justices are likely to write opinions dissenting from denials. In 1980–1981, Rehnquist wrote 32 percent of the dissents from denials, and Brennan wrote 22 percent. All justices joined in one or more dissents from the denial of cases.

Why don't the justices simply explain what they are doing, why they are denying review? They don't, because the power to deny review enables the Court to dispose of its caseload, and to explain each denial would increase the justices' workload. As Justice Stone put it, "to state a reason which would be accurately expressed and would satisfy the members of the Court, would require an amount of time and energy that is simply impossible to give."[87] A denial without explanation also gives the justices greater flexibility in agenda setting. They may take up an issue in a later case without feeling bound by their earlier denial.

Because denials are usually not explained, there may be
no way of knowing how a majority views the merits of particular cases. Members of the Burger Court have dissented from
the denial of a large number of cases dealing with obscenity
and capital punishment. Their dissents illustrate the difficulties of determining the meaning of a denial of certiorari.

After a bare majority of the Burger Court redefined the
standards for obscenity and pornography in *Miller v. California* (1973), Brennan and Marshall dissented from the denial
of later similar cases. Stevens, in an unusual concurring opinion to the denial of one such case, explained the futility of
granting cases in which a majority of the Court has already
expressed its view of the merits:

For there is no reason to believe that the majority of the Court
which decided *Miller v. California* . . . is any less adamant than the
minority. Accordingly, regardless of how I might vote on the merits
after full argument, it would be pointless to grant certiorari in case
after case of this character only to have *Miller* reaffirmed time after
time. . . . [U]ntil a valid reason for voting to grant one of these
petitions is put forward, I shall continue to vote to deny. In the
interest of conserving scarce law library space, I shall not repeat this
explanation every time I cast such a vote.[88]

Brennan and Marshall also oppose the Burger Court's
upholding of the constitutionality of capital punishment, and
they consistently express their dissenting position when such
cases are denied review. In 1981, however, Rehnquist dissented from the denial of one such petition. Thereupon, Stevens again issued a concurring opinion in support of the denial.
He explained that the Court had ninety such petitions on its
docket and that it would be imprudent for the Court to grant
all, since over half of the oral argument calendar would be
used up.[89]

Not all capital punishment cases raise issues or factual situations on which a majority has already ruled. In 1983, the
Burger Court denied review of the death penalty imposed on

a black man who was sentenced by an all-white jury after the prosecution had used its peremptory challenges to remove all blacks from the jury. Noting that this was the third time such a petition had been denied, Marshall objected to his "Colleagues' inclination to delay until a consensus emerges on how best to deal with misuse of peremptory challenges." He insisted "that for the Court to indulge that inclination on this occasion is inappropriate and ill-advised."[90] As Marshall has indicated, sometimes cases are denied because a majority has not yet agreed on the merits. Alternatively, in another capital punishment case denied review in 1984, Stevens accused Burger, Rehnquist, and O'Connor of dissenting because they wanted to grant a case in order to reach issues other than those actually presented by the petition.[91]

Denial of certiorari is an important technique for managing the Court's caseload. But its meaning in particular cases may be far from clear. The Court has few fixed rules, and even the rule of four is not "an absolutely inflexible rule."[92] In 1980, in two capital punishment cases, *four* justices issued dissenting opinions from the denial of review of both cases. Each justice indicated that, but for one more vote, they would have granted the case, vacated the ruling below, and remanded the case to the lower court.[93]

Although enabling the Court to manage its business, denials invite confusion and the suspicion, as Justice Jackson once observed, "that this Court no longer respects impersonal rules of law but is guided in these matters by personal impression which from time to time may be shared by a majority of the justices."

DECIDING CASES WITHOUT FULL CONSIDERATION

The distinction between mandatory and discretionary review of appeals and certiorari petitions has largely disappeared in the Court's process of deciding what to decide. Less than 20 percent of all appeals are now granted oral argument and full consideration. In 1981, the Court disposed of 241 appeals but granted oral argument in only 48. It summarily decided the other 193 (without hearing oral arguments and full consideration). The Court simply dismissed them for want of jurisdiction or for failure to present a substantial federal question, or it ordered the lower-court ruling affirmed or reversed.

More than half of the cases decided on merits, regardless of whether they come as certiorari petitions or appeals, are now summarily decided.[94] In the 1981 term, 5,311 cases were on the docket. Review was denied to 3,841 petitions for certiorari and 96 motions for extraordinary remedies. Another 28 cases were withdrawn by consent of the parties, as was permitted under Rule 53. The Court decided the merits of 468 cases, carrying the remaining 878 cases over to the next term. Less than 9 percent of the docket was thus considered and decided on merits. About half of those cases (184, or not quite 4 percent of the docket) were granted oral argument and full consideration. The other half were summarily decided.

When disposing of the merits of cases, the justices have a number of options available. They may either affirm or reverse the lower-court decision. But over 40 percent of the appeals are simply dismissed for lack of jurisdiction or for failure to pose a substantial federal question. In their summary disposition of appeals, justices typically distinguish between those coming from state courts and those coming from federal courts. They believe that it is better to dismiss an appeal than to affirm a state court. Yet, they should dismiss appeals from federal courts only when they are "practically frivolous" and either affirm or reverse the court of appeals ruling.[95] Even when an appeal presents a constitutional issue and must be decided, the Burger Court explained in *Hicks v. Miranda* (1975), a case involving a theater owner's effort to get a declaratory judgment that a California obscenity statute was unconstitutional, it did not feel obligated to grant the case full consideration.

The Burger Court feels required to deal only with the merits of appeals, and so it summarily decides most. Sometimes it will consider a case both as an appeal and as a petition for certiorari. In 1981, some 13 percent of the cases decided were dismissed as appeals and denied as certiorari petitions. At other times, a case may be granted but after consideration dismissed as improvidently granted. In over 45 percent of the petitions granted, the Court vacated the lower-court ruling and remanded the case for further consideration in light of other relevant rulings.

DISPOSITION OF CASES ON MERITS, 1981 TERM

Disposition	Original	Appeals	Certiorari	Number of Cases
Granted, vacated, and remanded		18	85	103
Dismissed for want of jurisdiction or lack of substantial federal question		99	1	100
Reversed and remanded		16	55	71
Affirmed	1	34	36	71
Dismissed and denied	2	61		63
Reversed		10	31	41
Dismissed as improvidently granted			6	6
Affirmed in part and reversed or vacated		1	6	7
Reversed in part and remanded		2	1	3
Affirmed and remanded			2	2
Decree and judgment entered	1			1
Total Cases Decided on Merits	*4*	*241*	*223*	*468*

As the caseload grew, the number of summary decisions increased. The number granted, vacated, and remanded without further explanation, for instance, was very small during the 1940s. In the 1950s and 1960s, the number rose to about fifty, and in the 1970s it frequently exceeded eighty per term.[96]

A large number of summary dispositions of appeals are unanimous. In 1980, about 41 percent of the appeals were

unanimously considered to have been improperly brought to
the Court. Like certiorari petitions, most appeals are thought
to be insubstantial and frivolous. In a 1982 letter to Congressman Robert Kastenmeier urging the elimination of the Court's
remaining mandatory appellate jurisdiction, the justices
explained,

It is impossible for the Court to give plenary consideration to all the
mandatory appeals it receives; to have done so, for example, during
the 1980 Term would have required at least 9 additional weeks of
oral argument or a seventy-five percent increase in the argument
calendar. To handle the volume of appeals presently being received,
the Court must dispose of many cases summarily, often without
written opinion.[97]

Summarily decided cases enable the Court to cut down on
its workload. But they also engender confusion among the lower
courts. Summary decisions take the form of rather cryptic orders
or per curiam (unsigned) opinions. Like denials of certiorari
petitions, they invite confusion over how the Court views the
merits of a case and the lower-court ruling. The problem is
one of the Court's own making. The Court holds that summarily decided cases do not have the same precedential weight
as plenary decisions but that they are nonetheless binding on
lower courts "until such time as the Court informs [them] that
[they] are not."[98]

Another problem is that some cases deserving of full consideration are now summarily decided by the Burger Court.
"No specter of increasing caseload can possibly justify today's
summary disposition of this case," Brennan charged in a 1975
decision, holding that a Tennessee statute forbidding "crimes
against nature" was not unconstitutionally vague, as was claimed
by an individual convicted of having forcibly performed cun-
nilingus.[99] Stewart sounded the refrain the next term: "While
our heavy caseload necessarily leads us sometimes to dispose
of cases summarily, it must never lead us to dispose of any

case irresponsibly. Yet I fear precisely that has happened here."[100] These are the words of dissenters in cases they thought merited full consideration, but where they were outvoted by a majority who simply did not want to bother with hearing oral arguments and giving the cases full consideration. In *Goldwater v. Carter* (1979), for example, the Burger Court issued an order vacating the lower-court decision in a dispute between several congressmen and the President over the termination of a defense treaty with Taiwan. Blackmun and White viewed the decision as "indefensible" in failing to "set the case for oral argument and giv[ing] it the plenary consideration it so obviously deserved." Later that term, Stevens, Brennan, and Marshall dissented in *Snepp v. United States* (1980), which they thought raised important First Amendment issues. In *Snepp,* a majority of the Burger Court summarily decided that a former CIA agent had to submit all future writings for prepublication review by the CIA. He also forfeited all profits earned from his book about the CIA, *Decent Interval,* because he had not submitted it to the agency for prepublication approval.

Agenda for Policy-making—Who Benefits, Who Loses?

The power to decide what to decide entails more than merely selecting a manageable number of cases for oral argument and full consideration. The Court also sets its own substantive agenda.

The Court did not always have the power to set its own agenda, nor did its docket include the kinds of major issues of public policy that arrive today. During its first decade, the Court had little important business. Over 40 percent consisted in admiralty and prize cases. About 50 percent raised issues of common law, and the remaining 10 percent dealt with matters like equity, including one probate case.[101] Not until the chief justiceship of John Marshall did the Court assert its power of judicial review. Still only a tiny fraction of its business raised important issues of public policy. By the late nineteenth century, the Court's business had gradually changed in response to developments in American society. The number of admiralty cases, for instance, had by 1882 dwindled to less than 4 percent of the total. Almost 40 percent of the decisions handed down still dealt with either disputes at common law or questions of jurisdiction and procedure in federal courts. Over 43 percent of the Court's business, however, involved interpreting congressional statutes. Less than 4 percent of the cases raised issues of constitutional law. The decline in admiralty and common law litigation, and the increase in statutory interpretation, reflected the impact of the Industrial Revolution and the growing governmental regulation of social and economic relations. In this century, the trend has continued. In 1980, 47 percent of the cases decided by opinion involved matters of constitutional law. Another 38 percent dealt with the interpretation of congressional statutes. The remaining 15 percent resolved issues of administrative law, taxation, patents, and claims. The table on page 205 illustrates the changing nature of the Court's business.[102]

The current Court's power to pick the cases it wants from a very large docket enables it to assume the role of a superlegislature. The overwhelming number of cases on the docket involve indigents' claims and issues of criminal procedure. Yet, as is indicated below, few are selected and decided on merits. Cases raising other issues of constitutional law have a better chance of being selected; so do cases involving statutory, administrative, and regulatory matters. These are all areas in which the government has an interest in legitimating its policies. The Court thus functions like a roving commission, selecting and deciding only issues of national importance for the governmental process.

The Court directly and indirectly encourages interest groups

THE BUSINESS OF THE SUPREME COURT, OCTOBER TERMS, 1825–1980

Subject of Court Opinions	1825	1875	1925	1930	1935	1945	1955	1960	1965	1970	1975	1980
Admiralty	2	5	8	2	1	3	1	0	0	0	0	0
Antitrust	0	0	2	5	3	2	2	0	8	3	3	0
Bankruptcy	0	13	9	1	9	7	1	0	5	3	0	0
Bill of Rights (civil liberties; except rights of accused)	0	2	3	3	3	9	6	22	15	30	8	22
Commerce clause												
1) Constitutionality *and* construction of Federal legislation, regulation, and administrative action	0	0	31	17	13	28	28	42	13	20	31	50
2) Constitutionality of state regulation	0	2	2	4	11	4	1	5	8	5	27	7
Common law	10	81	11	5	3	3	0	0	0	0	0	0
Misc. statutory interpretation	4	16	15	14	16	9	16	1	12	8	4	4
Due process												
1) Economic interests	0	0	20	8	8	3	1	0	0	0	0	2
2) Procedure of rights of accused contained in Bill of Rights	0	2	3	3	2	5	7	18	18	28	34	21
Impairment of contract	0	1	4	0	6	1	0	0	1	0	0	0
Indians	0	0	7	3	0	2	1	0	0	1	4	0
International law, war, and peace	2	5	6	0	2	12	3	0	0	0	1	0
Jurisdiction, procedure, and practice	4	30	29	21	27	27	17	11	16	8	4	2
Land legislation	0	11	3	0	3	0	0	0	0	1	0	0
Patents, copyright, and trademarks	1	8	4	12	5	2	1	1	1	1	1	1
Slaves	3	0	0	0	0	0	0	0	0	0	0	0
Other suits against the government and officials	0	12	17	1	1	2	1	1	1	1	1	0
Suits by states	0	0	8	6	5	0	2	5	5	5	16	10
Taxation (federal and state)	0	5	27	59	40	19	7	8	5	3	4	7

CASE DISPOSITION BY SUBJECT, 1981 TERM

Subject Matter	Decided on Merits (%) [No. of Opinions]	Paid Cases Denied (%)	Ifp Cases Denied (%)	Dismissed Rule 53 (%)	Number of Cases
Taxation	14 (18.9) [8]	56 (73.6)	6 (7.8)	0	76
Patents and claims	3 (10) [1]	25 (83.3)	2 (6.6)	0	30
Administrative	9 (16.6) [9]	35 (64.8)	9 (16.6)	1 (1.8)	54
Statutory	97 (15.1) [60]	457 (71.5)	80 (12.5)	5 (0.8)	639
Criminal law	95 (4.1) [27]	586 (25.7)	1,595 (69.9)	4 (0.17)	2,280
Constitutional	210 (56) [52]	79 (21)	72 (19.2)	14 (3.7)	375
Civil law	34 (3.5) [2]	726 (78.9)	158 (17.1)	1 (0.1)	919
Miscellaneous	6 (10) [4]	1 (1.5)	50 (83.3)	3 (5)	60
Total	*468 (10.5) [163]*	*1,965 (44.4)*	*1,972 (44.4)*	*28 (0.6)*	*4,433*

and the government to litigate issues of public policy. The Court selects and decides "only those cases which present questions whose resolution will have immediate importance far beyond the particular facts and parties involved." Attorneys whose cases are accepted by the Court "are, in a sense, prosecuting or defending class actions;" as Chief Justice Vinson emphasized, "you represent your clients, but [more crucially] tremendously important principles, upon which are based the plans, hopes and aspirations of a great many people throughout the country."[103]

For the poor, minorities, and interest groups, as the Warren Court observed in *NAACP v. Button* (1963), "under the conditions of modern government, litigation may well be the sole practicable avenue open to a minority to petition for redress of grievances."[104] Interest-group litigation, however, is by no means confined to the poor and minorities. Pointing to the successes of the American Civil Liberties Union (ACLU), Lewis Powell, shortly before his appointment to the Court, urged the Chamber of Commerce of the United States to consider that "the judiciary may be the most important instrument for social, economic and political change."[105]

Interest groups from the entire political spectrum look to the Court to decide issues of public policy: from business organizations and corporations in the late nineteenth century to the Jehovah's Witnesses in the 1930s; the ACLU and NAACP in the 1950s and 1960s; "liberal" women's rights groups and consumer and environmental protection groups, such as the National Organization for Women (NOW), Common Cause, "Nader's Raiders," the Sierra Club, the Environmental Defense Fund, and the Natural Resources Defense Council; as well as a growing number of conservative "public interest" law firms like the Pacific Legal Foundation, the Mountain States Legal Foundation, and the Washington Legal Foundation. "This is government by lawsuit," Justice Jackson declared. "These constitutional lawsuits are the stuff of power politics in America."[106]

Interest-group activities and "public-interest" law firms offer a number of advantages for litigating policy disputes. They command greater financial resources than the average individual. A single suit may settle a large number of claims, and the issues are not as likely to be compromised or settled out of court. Interest-group law firms typically specialize in particular kinds of lawsuits. They are therefore able to litigate more skillfully and over a longer period of time. There are also tactical opportunities. Litigants may be chosen to bring "test cases," and those cases may be coordinated with other litigation and the activities of other organizations. In addition, interest groups may enter litigation as third parties by filing amicus curiae briefs, which are no longer neutral or friendly, but partisan. In the reverse discrimination case of *Regents of the University of California v. Bakke* (1978), 120 organizations joined 58 amicus briefs filed before the Court: 83 for the University of California, 32 for Bakke, and 5 urging the Court not to accept the case.

The Court may directly invite third-party litigation, as it did in *NAACP v. Button*. Its rulings also indirectly encourage or discourage groups from coming to the Court. The ACLU,

example, won 90 percent of the cases it appealed in 1968–
1969, the last year Warren presided over the Court. By contrast, in 1974–1975, the ACLU's win rate plunged below 50
percent. With the prospect of adverse rulings, the ACLU and
other "liberal" public-interest law firms have been more
reluctant to take their cases to the Burger Court.

Do justices select cases because they are brought by particular interest groups? There is no evidence that they do and
considerable evidence that they do not. Some political scien-
tists hypothesize that justices select cases on the basis of certain "cues" in the filings.[107] According to "cue theory," justices
disproportionately grant cases in which one or more of the
following "cues" are present: (1) a civil liberties issue, (2) disagreement in lower courts, and (3) the involvement of the
federal government as the petitioner. Studies of Burton's docket
books for 1947–1957 and of samples drawn from the petitions
granted and denied during 1967–1968 and 1976–1977, however, indicate that the strongest correlation between any of
these "cues" and the acceptance of a case is the participation
of the federal government. Although justices' attitudes toward
upperdogs (the government and corporations) or underdogs
(individuals and minorities) may predispose their voting on
whether to grant a case,[108] the overwhelming number of filings are unanimously denied. Institutional norms promote a
shared conception of the work appropriate for the Court.[109]
Besides, the justices tend not to look for "cues" to reduce
their workload but simply to rely on their clerks to screen
cases.

The government has a distinct advantage in getting cases
accepted, but its higher rate of success is not surprising. Since
the creation of the office in 1870, the solicitor general of the
United States assumed responsibility for representing the
federal government. From the Court's perspective, the solicitor general performs an invaluable service. He screens all
prospective federal appeals and petitions and decides which
should be taken to the Court. Unlike any other petitioner,

the solicitor general has the opportunity of selectir̦
large number of cases around the country and appe̲ъ̳̲g
those likely to win Court approval. Since he typically argues
all government cases before the Court, the solicitor general
has intimate knowledge of the justices and has been characterized as the Court's "ninth-and-a-half" member. Given these
tactical advantages, the government's applications for review
are usually granted. Between 1977 and 1981, some 70 percent
of the government's cases were granted each year, whereas
less than 6 percent of all others were. The government also
participates in about one-half of all cases decided on merits,
and in 70 percent of these the Court decides in favor of the
government's position.[110]

By contrast, indigents like Gideon are unlikely to have
their cases given full consideration. With the increasing number of unpaid cases, the percentage of those granted declined
sharply. During the Vinson and Warren Courts, the number
dropped from around 9 percent to less than 3 percent, and
then to about 1 percent during the Burger Court. The decline
is due to a number of factors. First and foremost is simply the
reality that the more filings, the larger the number of those
considered "frivolous." "The claims made are often fantastic,
surpassing credulity," Douglas observed. Although "98 or 99%
of them are frivolous," he added, "[w]e read them all because
they produce classic situations like *Gideon* and *Miranda* and
so on."[111] But most members of the Burger Court no longer
individually consider indigents' petitions. Rather, they rely
on their law clerks' recommendations. Moreover, a majority
of the Burger Court, unlike the Warren Court, is unsympa-
thetic to claims brought by indigents.

Review Denied, Justice Denied?

The Burger Court decides less than 10 percent of the cases
on its docket. It gives full consideration to only 4 or 5 percent

each year. Is this not a matter of review denied, justice denied?

Hugo Black has provided a partial response to that question:

I don't think it can fairly be said that we give no consideration to all who apply. I think we do. You can't decide the case, you can't write long opinions, but when we meet, we take up the cases that are on our docket that have been brought up since we adjourned. Frequently I'll mark up at the top [of a petition] "Denied—not of sufficient importance." "No dispute among the circuits," or something else. And I'll go in and vote to deny it. Well, I've considered it to that extent. And every judge does that same thing in [our] conference.[112]

As Black indicates, every case is given some consideration, though now more often by law clerks than by the justices. No case, of course, is entitled to unlimited review.

No less crucial, the justices generally agree that the vast majority of filings are frivolous. Testifying before Congress in 1937, Chief Justice Hughes observed,

I think that it is safe to say that almost 60 percent of the applications for certiorari are wholly without merit and ought never to have been made. There are probably about 20 percent or so in addition which have a fair degree of plausibility, but which fail to survive critical examination. The remainder, falling short, I believe, of 20 percent, show substantial grounds and are granted.[113]

Even prior to the expansion of the Court's discretionary jurisdiction, Justice John Clarke in 1922 was surprised "at the great number of cases finding their way into court which are of entirely negligible importance, whether considered from the point of view of the principles of law or of the property involved in them. That impression has been intensified as time has passed, for their number constantly increases."[114] Justices as ideologically opposed as Douglas and Harlan agree that less "than nine-tenths of the unpaid petitions [are] so insubstantial that they never should have been filed" and that "more than one-half of all appeals are so untenable that they never should have been filed." In Rehnquist's words, "a lot of the filings are junk."[115]

But what are "frivolous" cases? Clarence Brummett, for one, repeatedly asked the Court to assist him in a war of extermination he vowed to wage against Turkey.[116] Brennan has given further illustrations of the kinds of frivolous cases that arrive at the Court:

Are Negroes in fact Indians and therefore entitled to Indians' exemptions from federal income taxes? Are the federal income tax laws unconstitutional insofar as they do not provide a deduction for depletion of the human body? Is the 16th Amendment unconstitutional as violative of the 14th Amendment? and . . . Does a ban on drivers turning right on a red light constitute an unreasonable burden on interstate commerce?[117]

The largest category of "frivolous" cases comes from "jailhouse lawyers" like Gideon. From his prison cell, the Reverend Clovis Green, founder of the Church of the New Song and the Human Awareness Universal Life Church, alone filed an estimated seven hundred cases in federal and state courts during the 1970s.[118]

Which cases appear "frivolous" and which merit the Court's attention, of course, depends on the justices. In *Cohen v. California* (1971), for example, the Court overturned as inconsistent with the First Amendment the criminal conviction of a man who wore in a courthouse a jacket bearing the words "Fuck the Draft." The Court established the important First Amendment principle that four-letter words are not obscene per se and may symbolically express political ideas as well. But, in a circulated and unpublished dissent, Burger protested

that this Court's limited resources of time should be devoted to such a case as this. It is a measure of a lack of a sense of priorities. . . . It is nothing short of absurd nonsense that juvenile delinquents and

their emotionally unstable outbursts should command the attention
of this Court. The appeal should be dismissed for failure to present
a substantial federal question. [119]

Whether justice is denied depends on who sits on the Court
and the process of deciding what to decide. In Douglas's words,
"The electronics industry—resourceful as it is—will never
produce a machine to handle these problems. They require
at times the economist's understanding, the poet's insight, the
executive's experience, the political scientist's understanding,
the historian's perspective."[120]

FIVE

Deciding Cases and Writing Opinions

THE COURT grants a full hearing to less than 180 of the more than 5,000 cases on the docket each term. Deciding the merits of those few cases taxes the individual powers of the justices and their capacity for compromise. All members of the Burger Court agree that they are overworked because they take too many cases. But they cannot agree on what to do about this situation.

When cases are granted full consideration, attorneys for each side submit briefs setting forth their arguments and how they think the case should be decided. The Clerk of the Court circulates the briefs to each chamber and sets a date for the attorneys to argue their views orally before the justices. After hearing oral arguments, the justices in private conference vote on how to decide the issues presented in a case.

Cases are decided by majority rule on the basis of a tally of the justices' votes. But conference votes by no means end the work or resolve conflicts. Votes are tentative until an opinion announcing the Court's decision is handed down. After conference, a justice assigned to write the Court's opinion must

circulate drafts to all the other justices for their comments and
then usually revise the opinion before delivering it in open
Court. Justices are free to switch their votes and to write separate opinions concurring in or dissenting from the Court's
decision. They thus continue after conference to compete for
influence on the final decision and opinion.

"The business of the Court," Potter Stewart has said, "is
to give institutional opinions for its decisions."[1] The Court's
opinion serves to communicate an institutional decision. It
should also convey the politically symbolic values of certainty,
stability, and impartiality in the law. In most cases, justices
therefore try to persuade as many others as possible to join an
opinion. Sometimes when the justices cannot agree on an
opinion for their decision, or in minor cases, an unsigned (per
curiam) opinion is handed down.

In extraordinary cases all the justices may sign an opinion
to emphasize their agreement. This happened in *Cooper v.
Aaron* (1958), when the Warren Court reaffirmed the unanimous ruling in *Brown v. Board of Education* (1954) and refused
to permit delays in school desegregation in Little Rock,
Arkansas. Brennan initially prepared a draft of the opinion,
but then all nine justices gathered around a table and rewrote
portions of the opinion. The justices' collective drafting of
Cooper v. Aaron was exceptional, though reminiscent of the
nineteenth-century opinion-writing practice. The justices also
took the unusual step of noting in the opinion that three—
Brennan, Stewart, and Whitaker—were not on the Court when
the landmark ruling in *Brown* was handed down but that they
would have joined the unanimous decision if they had been.
All nine justices then signed the Court's opinion in order to
emphasize their unanimity and because Frankfurter insisted
on adding a concurring opinion. This departure from the usual
practice of having one justice sign the opinion was strongly
opposed by Douglas. But all agreed to depart in this way so
that Frankfurter's concurring opinion "would not be accepted

as any dilution or interpretation of the views expressed in the Court's joint opinion."[2]

What is significant about opinions for the Court is that they are not statements of a particular justice's jurisprudence. Rather, they are negotiated documents forged from ideological divisions within the Court. On rare occasions, the justice delivering the Court's opinion may add his own separate concurring opinion.[3] But, traditionally, justices have sought compromise, if not pride of authorship, because the Court's opinion must serve as an institutional justification for a collective decision.

The unanimous ruling in *United States v. Nixon* (1974) provides a good, even if extreme, example of the justices working toward an institutional decision and opinion. The case against President Richard Nixon grew out of the scandal of Watergate that began in the summer of 1972. By the time the case reached the Court, a major constitutional crisis loomed over the country.

The Watergate complex in Washington housed the headquarters of the national Democratic party. On the night of June 17, 1972, five men broke in to plant bugging devices so they could monitor the Democratic party's campaign plans for the fall presidential election. The plumbers, as they were called, were caught by some off-duty policemen. On the next day, it was learned that one of them, E. Howard Hunt, a former agent for the Central Intelligence Agency (CIA), worked for Nixon's reelection committee. Within two weeks Nixon's former attorney general, John Mitchell, resigned as chairman of the Committee for the Re-election of the President.

Nixon and his associates managed to cover up involvement in the break-in and won reelection in November 1972. But reporters and congressional committees continued to search for links between the break-in and the White House. Judge John Sirica presided over the trial of the five burglars and pressed for a full disclosure of White House involvement. These investigations led to further cover-ups.

A year later, the Nixon administration was implicated in the break-in and the cover-up. To give the impression of cleaning house, Nixon dismissed his chief aides, H. R. Haldeman and John Ehrlichman; his counsel, John Dean; and Mitchell's replacement as attorney general, Richard Kleindienst. In the spring of 1973, however, the Senate Select Committee on Presidential Activities of 1972, chaired by North Carolina's Senator Sam Ervin, began its investigations, carried over national television. Nixon's former counsel, John Dean, became the star witness, revealing much of the President's involvement in the cover-up. A surprise witness and former Haldeman deputy, Alexander Butterfield, then disclosed that Nixon had installed listening devices in order to tape conversations in the Oval Office. The possibility of evidence in the tapes showing Nixon's direct involvement in the cover-up deepened the Watergate crisis.

The Senate committee and a special prosecutor, Archibald Cox, appointed to investigate illegal activities of the White House, immediately sought a small number of the tapes. Nixon refused to relinquish them. He claimed an executive privilege to withhold information that might damage national security interests. The President's attorney, Charles Alan Wright of the University of Texas School of Law, denied that Congress or the special prosecutor could force the release of the tapes. Congress, contended Wright, could impeach Nixon but not compel him to produce the tapes. Congress was not yet willing to go that far. Its investigations, however, had already revealed that the Nixon administration had engaged in a wide range of illegal activities. It turned out that Nixon had approved "hush money" for Hunt and had had the CIA pressure the FBI to curtail its investigation of Watergate. The Watergate break-in was part of a larger domestic-spying operation. White House plumbers broke into the office of Daniel Ellsberg's psychiatrist. They did so with the aim of finding information with which to discredit him. Ellsberg had angered the Nixon administration by giving the *New York Times* a top-secret report, the so-called Pentagon Papers, detailing America's involvement in the Vietnam War. Other government officials, senators, newspaper reporters, and antiwar protesters were subject to illegal wiretaps and surveillance by the Nixon administration.

The special prosecutor subpoenaed Nixon's attorneys to hand over the tapes. When Nixon again refused, Sirica ordered the release of the tapes. Nixon would still not comply. Cox appealed to the Court of Appeals for the District of Columbia Circuit, whose judges urged that some compromise be found. When none could be reached, the court ruled that Nixon had to surrender the tapes.

After the court of appeals ruling, Nixon announced his own compromise. On Friday, October 19, 1973, he offered to provide summaries of relevant conversations. Cox found the deal unacceptable. Nixon then ordered the "Saturday Night Massacre." His chief of staff, Alexander Haig, told Attorney General Elliot Richardson to fire the special prosecutor. Instead, Richardson resigned. So did the Deputy Attorney General, William Ruckelshaus. Finally, Solicitor General Robert Bork became acting attorney general, and he fired Cox. The Saturday Night Massacre unleashed a wave of public anger. Within four days, Nixon was forced to tell Sirica that nine tapes would be forthcoming.

The public outcry against Nixon would not subside, nor did the release of the nine tapes end the controversy. It was soon discovered that an eighteen-and-a-half minute segment of the first conversation after the break-in between Nixon and Haldeman had been erased. That and other revelations by mid-November 1973 prodded the House of Representatives to establish a committee to investigate the possibility of impeachment. Three months later, in February 1974, the House directed its Judiciary Committee to begin hearings on impeachment.

Nixon continued to refuse to give additional tapes to the

Judiciary Committee and Leon Jaworski, who had replaced
Cox as special prosecutor. Then, on March 1, 1974, the federal grand jury investigating Watergate indicted top White
House aides. The grand jury also secretly named Nixon as an
unindicted co-conspirator and asked that the information against
him be turned over to the House Judiciary Committee.

The Judiciary Committee subpoenaed the release of all
documents and tapes related to Watergate. Nixon remained
adamant about his right to decide what to release. Jaworski
countered by asking Sirica to enforce the subpoena for sixty-
four tapes. When Nixon would not yield, Jaworski appealed
directly to the Supreme Court.

In his appeal, Jaworski asked that the case be granted and
expedited, because of the constitutional issues at stake and so
that the trial of Mitchell and the other conspirators might proceed. On May 31, 1974, the Court announced it would hear
the appeal in *United States v. Nixon*. At conference, Justice
Rehnquist, a former assistant attorney general in the Nixon
administration, had disqualified himself from participating. He
did so not because of the case at hand but because of his
"close professional association with three of the named
defendants" in the criminal prosecution of Mitchell and the
others.[4] Blackmun and White wanted to deny certiorari and
an expedited hearing, but they were outvoted and later changed
their minds.

Before the Court received the briefs on the merits of the
case, on June 21, Nixon had surrendered the transcripts—but
not the tapes—of some of his conversations. Although incom-
plete, the transcripts proved damaging to the President. Public opposition steadily mounted. The House Judiciary
Committee moved toward recommending the impeachment
of Nixon for obstructing justice, misusing government agencies, and defying his constitutional duty "to see that the laws
be faithfully executed."

The Court heard oral arguments on July 8, 1974. The fundamental issue, Jaworski argued, was "Who is to be the arbi-

ter of what the Constitution says?" Nixon's claim of executive privilege in withholding the tapes, Jaworski insisted, placed the President above the law. Douglas pointed out that nowhere in the Constitution is the President granted such a privilege. But Burger twice interrupted to point out that courts had recognized a privilege of executives to withhold information in certain circumstances. Jaworski conceded that much. He did not deny that the Constitution might provide "for such a thing as executive privilege." What Jaworski denied was that Nixon, or any President, had the power to claim an absolute, unreviewable privilege. If he had that power, the President, not the Court, would be the supreme interpreter of the Constitution.

After Jaworski argued for an hour, it was time for Nixon's attorney, James St. Clair, to respond. As in his brief, St. Clair asked that the case be dismissed. He argued that there was a "fusion" between the criminal prosecution of Mitchell and the others, on the one hand, and the impeachment proceedings against Nixon, on the other. Information used at the trial of the Watergate conspirators would be turned over to Congress for use against the President. That, he claimed, violated the principle of separation of powers. Moreover, St. Clair pressed Nixon's view that the President should decide as a political matter what should be made available to the House Judiciary Committee. The dispute, he unsuccessfully urged, "is essentially a political dispute. It is a dispute that this Court ought not be drawn into."[5]

When the justices later discussed *Nixon* in conference, all agreed that the Court had jurisdiction, that the case did not raise a "political question," and that the case should be decided as soon as possible.[6] All agreed, furthermore, that Nixon's claim of executive privilege could not withstand scrutiny. They nonetheless differed in their deference to the President. Those differences had to be reconciled during the opinion-writing process.

Given unanimity on the outcome, and the symbolism and

tactical advantages of drafting the Court's opinion, Burger took the case for himself. But what followed in the weeks after conference was truly a process of collective deliberation and drafting. It soon became clear that Burger was too deferential to the President, who had appointed him for his strict constructionism and advocacy of judicial self-restraint. An exchange of memoranda suggesting possible treatment of various sections of the opinion circulated from chamber to chamber. "My effort to accommodate everyone by sending out 'first drafts' is not working out," Burger wrote and at one point was driven to respond, "I do not contemplate sending out any more material until it is *ready*."[7]

The importance of the case compelled the justices to try to arrive at an opinion acceptable to all. The case had been heard at the end of the term, and by then the Court had already handed down most of its decisions. The justices had more time to devote to the case than they might otherwise have had. Blackmun worked on the statement of facts. Douglas offered suggestions on issues of standing and jurisdiction. Brennan worked on issues of justiciability and intrabranch disputes, while White focused on issues involving the power to subpoena the President. Powell and Stewart tried to sharpen the treatment of the merits of the claim of executive privilege to establish unequivocally that any such privilege is neither absolute nor unreviewable.

In the evenings and over the weekend, the justices met "in the interest of a cooperative effort" to find common ground. "After individually going over the circulation," Stewart explained, "we collected our joint and several specific suggestions and met with the Chief Justice in order to convey these suggestions to him."[8] When submitting another revision of a section to Burger, Powell wrote Brennan, "I have tried to move fairly close to your original memo on this point, as I understand it and what you said at conference."[9]

In such circumstances, when there is an implicit agreement on the importance of achieving a unanimous opinion for the Court, the spirit of cooperation prevails. At the same time, threats of a concurring or dissenting opinion carry more weight. Burger's initial draft appeared not merely deferential but weak in treating the authority and power of judicial review. According to Burger, judicial review and executive privilege are on the same constitutional footing—neither is specifically mentioned in the Constitution, but both derive legitimacy from the operation of government. Stewart offered revisions, which White supported in a memo to Burger, stating,

Because I am one of those who thinks that the Constitution on its face provides for judicial review; especially if construed in the light of what those who drafted it said at the time or later. I always wince when it is inferred that the Court created the power or even when it is said that the "power of judicial review [was] first announced in *Marbury v. Madison.*" See page 4 of your draft. But perhaps this is only personal idiosyncrasy.

"Perhaps none of these matters is of earthshaking importance," White continued, "but it is likely that I shall write separately if your draft becomes the opinion of the Court."[10]

What emerged as a unanimous opinion was the result of negotiations and compromises among the justices. In the end, various justices had assumed a major role in drafting different sections of the final opinion. Blackmun's work became incorporated in the statement of facts. The first section, on matters of jurisdiction, reflected Douglas's work. The second, on justiciability, was a compromised version of drafts by Burger and Brennan. The third, dealing with subpoenaing the President, drew on White's early work. Powell, Stewart, and Brennan had a hand in drafting various parts of the final section, on judicial review of claims to executive privilege.

Before the decision was to come down, Brennan suggested that all the justices sign the final opinion, as was done in *Cooper v. Aaron,* because of their cooperative drafting.

But Burger insisted on delivering the opinion. The others agreed since he had accommodated their views and since landmark and unanimous rulings have historically been handed down by the chief justice. In addition, some no doubt relished the irony in having forced Burger to accept their revisions, and then having Burger deliver the Court's ruling against the President who had appointed him.

On July 24, 1974, just sixteen days after hearing oral arguments, the Court handed down its ruling. In the thirty-one-page opinion delivered by Burger, the Court rejected Nixon's claim of executive privilege as inconsistent with "the fundamental demands of due process of law in the fair administration of justice." The announcement was dramatic and devastating for the President. Later that day, the House Judiciary Committee began televised debates on the exact wording of its articles of impeachment. Two weeks later, on August 8, 1974, Nixon resigned.

The unanimous decision and opinion in *United States v. Nixon* was exceptional. The justices have worked together to reach an institutional decision and opinion in this way only two or three times in the last thirty years. The trend is now toward less consensus on the Court's rulings. The justices are increasingly divided over their decisions. Individual opinions have become more highly prized than institutional opinions. The Court now functions more like a legislative body relying simply on a tally of the votes to decide cases than like a collegial body working toward collective decisions and opinions.

The Role of Oral Argument

For those outside the Court, the role of oral argument in deciding cases is vague, if not bewildering. Visitors at the Court must often stand in line for an hour or more before they are seated in the courtroom to hear oral arguments. They are then given only three or four minutes to listen and watch attorneys argue cases, before they are ushered out. Only by special request, and subject to available seats, may members of the public hear entire arguments in a case. There are reserved seats for the press, so they may hear all oral arguments.

The importance of oral argument, Chief Justice Hughes observed, lies in the fact that often "the impression that a judge has at the close of a full oral argument accords with the conviction which controls his final vote."[11] The justices hold conference and take their initial, often decisive, vote on cases within a day or two after hearing arguments. Oral arguments come at a crucial time. They focus the minds of the justices and present the possibility for fresh perspectives on a case. "Often my idea of how a case shapes up is changed by oral argument," Brennan has noted. "I have had too many occasions when my judgment or a decision has turned on what happened in oral argument."[12] The fact is, Powell has said, "that the quality of advocacy—the research, briefing and oral argument of the close and difficult cases—does contribute significantly to the development of precedents."[13]

The role of oral argument was more prominent in the business of the Court in the nineteenth century. Virtually unlimited time for oral argument was once allowed. In the important case of *Gibbons v. Ogden* (1824), the Court heard twenty hours of oral arguments over five days. In *Gibbons*, the Marshall Court held that Congress's power over interstate commerce limits the power of states to regulate commerce and transportation within their borders. By contrast, it gave only two hours to *Dames & Moore v. Regan* (1981). Yet, *Dames & Moore*, as Rehnquist has pointed out, was "a similarly important commercial case."[14] There, the Burger Court upheld President Jimmy Carter's agreement with Iran securing the release of fifty-two American hostages, but also canceling attachments of Iranian assets and transferring the claims of businesses against Iran from courts in the United States to an international tribunal. Those two hours of oral argument in *Dames & Moore* were an exception to the present practice. Cases are now given only one hour, unless time is extended.

The Court began cutting back on time for oral arguments in 1848. The 1848 rule allowed eight hours per case—two hours for two counsel on each side. In 1871, the Court cut the amount of time in half, permitting two hours for each side. Subsequently, in 1911, each side got an hour and a half; in 1925, though, time was limited to one hour per side. Finally, in 1970, Burger persuaded the Court to limit arguments to thirty minutes per side.

The Court's current argument calendar permits the hearing of approximately 180 cases each year. For fourteen weeks each term, from the first Monday in October until the end of April, the Court hears arguments from ten to twelve and from one to three on Monday, Tuesday, and Wednesday about every two weeks. Although the amount of time per case was substantially reduced by the Burger Court, more cases are heard now than thirty years ago. At the turn of the century, the Court heard between 170 and 190 cases. After the Judiciary Act of 1925 enlarged the Court's power to deny cases review, the number of cases accepted for oral argument dropped. During the chief justiceship of Vinson, the Court heard an average of 137 cases each term, and during that of Warren about 138. But, by cutting back on the time allowed for oral arguments, the Burger Court increased the number of cases it could hear to between 160 and 180 each term.

Oral argument usually takes place about four months after a case has been accepted. The major exception is in cases granted after February. By then, the Court's calendar typically has already been filled, so the case is put over to the beginning of the next term. Occasionally, in very pressing cases, the Court will advance a case for oral argument. It did so in the Little Rock School case, *Cooper v. Aaron* (1958), argued three days after the petition was filed, and in *United States v. Nixon* (1974), heard less than six weeks after being granted. In *New York Times Co. v. United States* (1971), the Nixon administration sought to suppress publication of the Pentagon

Papers, a history of America's involvement in Vietnam. And the Court moved at a "frenzied" pace to decide the case, over the protests of Burger and others. On the morning of June 24, the Court received the *New York Times*'s petition. Those of the government arrived later that day. The briefs on the merits of the case arrived just two hours before oral argument took place on June 26, 1971. Four days later, in a single-paragraph per curiam opinion, the Court upheld the First Amendment right to publish without prior restraint. But all nine justices filed separate opinions, six concurring and three dissenting, for a total of ten opinions!

The reduction in the amount of time devoted to oral arguments was only part due to an increasing caseload. No less important, the justices grew dissatisfied with the quality of advocacy.

For most of the nineteenth century, a relatively small number of attorneys, like Daniel Webster and William Wirt, argued before the Court and excelled in the art of oratory. The Court's sessions were short, and the difficulties of transportation precluded many attorneys from traveling to Washington to argue their cases. Hence, attorneys hired Washington lawyers and members of the Court's bar to make oral presentations. The Court's bar was small, and there was usually a close friendship between the justices and counsel. Daniel Webster epitomizes the best of nineteenth-century oratory and the mutual respect of the Court and its bar. At issue in one of his early cases, *Dartmouth College v. Woodward* (1819), was whether, without abridging the contract clause of the Constitution, New Hampshire could revise a college charter, granted originally by the crown of England, in order to replace a board of trustees with one more to its liking. With his sonorous and histrionic power Webster concluded his argument in a grand manner:

Sir, you may destroy this little institution. It is weak. It is in your hands! I know it is one of the lesser lights in the literary hori-

zon of the country. You may put it out. But if you do so, you must
carry through your work. You must extinguish, one after another,
all those great lights of science which, for more than a century, have
thrown their radiance over our land.

It is, Sir, as I have said, a small college and yet, there are those
who love it. . . .

Sir, I care not how others may feel, but, for myself, when I see
my Alma Mater surrounded, like Caesar in the senate-house, by
those who are reiterating stab on stab, I would not, for this right
hand, have her turn to me, and say *et tu quoque, mi fili!*[15]

Webster's oratory won the day, as it often did. He described
his feelings when later arguing *Gibbons v. Ogden* (1824) before
Chief Justice Marshall: "I think I never experienced more
intellectual pleasure arguing [a] novel question to a great man
who appreciate it and take it in; and he did take it in, as a
baby takes in its mother's milk."[16] The Court also appreciated
Webster's presence, as is evident from Justice Samuel Miller's praise of a case "argued at much length by Mr. Webster,
Mr. Sergeant and Mr. Clayton whose names are a sufficient
guarantee that the matter was well considered."[17]

As travel became easier in the late nineteenth century,
attorneys journeyed more often to Washington for the publicity of arguing cases before the highest court in the land. But
their lack of experience became all too evident. The quality
of advocacy declined. Oral presentations seemed to Justice
John Clarke to "stretch out as if to the crack of doom."[18] Holmes
used the time to write letters, confessing, "[W]e don't shut
up bores, one has to listen to discourses dragging slowly along
after one has seen the point and made up one's mind. That is
what is happening now and I take the chance to write as I sit
with my brethren. I hope I shall be supposed to be taking
notes."[19] Once Frankfurter passed a note to Black asking, "You
are more indulgent of poor advocacy than I am—so please tell
me why a lawyer having limited time wastes 10 minutes before
he comes to the point 'on which the case turns'?"[20]

More recently, an assistant attorney general spent thirteen minutes telling the Court what the state was *not* appealing, whereupon Burger pressed him to get "to the heart of your case." The attorney sat down, saving a few minutes for his later rebuttal.[21] But outstanding advocates still appear before the Court. The Washington lawyer William Coleman was cool and urbane when he gave his arguments as a "friend of the court" in the controversial case *Bob Jones University v. United States* (1983), denying tax exemptions for private schools that discriminate on racial grounds. His style was conversational to the point that when Byron White interrupted him, he merely nodded that he would get to this question after finishing his discussion with Stevens about another issue.

Even before time was limited to thirty minutes per side, a number of justices agreed that the best arguments were those presented in half an hour. In Frankfurter's words, "A number of lawyers think it is a constitutional duty to use an hour when they have got it."[22] Burger and others on the Court continue to complain about the quality of oral argument.

Oral argument remains the only opportunity for attorneys to communicate directly with the justices. Two basic factors appear to control the relative importance of oral argument. As Wiley Rutledge observed, "One is brevity. The other is the preparation with which the judge comes to it."[23]

The justices have enforced their interest in brevity in several ways. Chief Justice White invented what was called the summary docket: if an appeal could not be dismissed but the Court did not deem a case worth full argument time, each side was allowed thirty minutes. Taft had a practice of announcing, "The Court does not care to hear the respondent," if the appellate or petitioner failed to sustain his contention in opening argument.[24] A rigorous enforcer of rules governing oral arguments, Hughes reportedly called time on a lawyer in the middle of the word "if." But the Court is "more liberal now," claims Burger. "We allow a lawyer to finish the

sentence that is unfolding when the red light goes on, provided, of course, the sentence is not too long." However, when
the Court revised its rules in 1980, the justices underscored
their admonishment: *"The Court looks with disfavor on any
oral argument that is read from a prepared text."*

Central to preparation and delivery is a bird's-eye view of
the case, the issues and facts, and the reasoning behind legal
developments. Crisp, concise, and conversational presentations are what the justices want. An attorney must never forget, in Rehnquist's words, that "[H]e is not, after all, presenting
his case to some abstract, platonic embodiment of appellate
judges as a class, but . . . [to] nine flesh and blood men and
women." Oral argument is definitely not a "brief with ges-
tures."[25]

Justices differ in their own preparation. Douglas insisted
that "oral arguments win or lose a case," but Warren found
them "not highly persuasive."[26] Most justices now come prepared with "bench memos" drafted by their law clerks. Bench
memos identify central facts, issues, and possible questions.
By contrast, Holmes rarely found oral argument influential. If
not writing letters, he took catnaps while on the bench. He
relied primarily on lower-court records and briefs. Both
Frankfurter and Douglas claimed never to read briefs before
oral arguments, but once they were on the bench their styles
and strategies varied markedly. Frankfurter consumed large
segments of time with questions, exasperating counsel and
other justices. Frankfurter once interrupted a lawyer ninety-
three times during a 120-minute oral argument.[27] During one
such interrogation, Douglas intervened to help counsel with
a useful answer. Thereupon, Frankfurter asked the attorney,
"I thought *you* were arguing the case?" The attorney responded,
"I am but I can use all of the help I can get."[28] In 1979, a
lawyer urging the Court to approve plans for school desegregation in Columbus, Ohio, found himself in a similar crossfire
between Rehnquist and Marshall. Battered by Rehnquist's

questions and with little else to say, the lawyer finally sat down pleading, "We ask this Court to send *Brown* to Columbus."[29]

Justices also vary in their style and approach to the questioning of attorneys during oral arguments. O'Connor, Rehnquist, and Stevens are aggressive and relentless. Marshall often sits back listening and saying nothing, but then he'll suddenly fire a battery of involved questions. An often confused attorney will reply, only to receive some comical remark from Marshall, such as "Why didn't you tell me that five minutes ago," which invariably draws laughter from spectators.

Conference on Merits

The justices hold a private conference on Wednesday afternoons to discuss the merits of the four cases heard on Monday, and then another on Friday to discuss the eight cases they heard on Tuesday and Wednesday. Conference discussions are secret, except for revelations in justices' opinions, off-the-bench communications, or, when available, private papers. "The integrity of decision making would be impaired seriously if we had to reach our judgments in the atmosphere of an ongoing town meeting," Powell has asserted. "There must be candid discussion, a willingness to consider arguments advanced by other Justices, and a continuing examination and reexamination of one's own views."[30]

Since the content of conference discussions is not revealed, their importance apart from the voting on cases is difficult to determine. But the significance of conference discussions has certainly changed with the increasing caseload. "Our tasks involve deliberation, reflection and mediation," Douglas has observed.[31] Those tasks no longer take place at conference; they now revolve around the activities in and among each chamber before and after conference.

Conference discussions do not play the role that they once

did. When the docket was smaller, in the nineteenth century, conferences were integral to the justices' collective delibera- tions. Cases were discussed in detail and differences ham- mered out. The justices not only decided how to dispose of cases but also reached agreement on an institutional opinion for the Court. As the caseload grew, conferences became largely symbolic of past collective deliberations. They now serve only to discover consensus. There is no longer time for justices to reach agreement and compromise on opinions for the Court.

With the limited time available, Douglas has commented, "[c]onference discussion sometimes changes one's view of a case, but usually not."[32] When examining the Court's work- load in the late 1950s, the Harvard Law School professor Henry Hart estimated that the justices heard oral arguments about 140 hours and deliberated in conference about 132 hours each term.[33] The Court's docket included around 2,000 cases, meaning that each case could have been given an average of three to four minutes at conference. A large number, how- ever, were never brought up for discussion. If we can assume (on the basis of the discussion of the Court's screening process in Chapter 4) that at least 65 percent of the cases are not dis- cussed, each remaining case could have been given at most eleven minutes. Assuming further (and unrealistically) that the Court devoted entire conferences to only those cases argued and decided on merits (around 125 cases at the time), each case would have received an average of sixty-three minutes or almost seven minutes of conference discussion per justice.

The docket is now over twice as large (around 5,300 cases). But the justices spend only slightly more time in conference and have a little less time to discuss each case. The Court hears oral argument on more cases (180) in less time (about 150 hours) and spends a little more time in conference (about 156 hours) each term.[34] Yet, at least 70 percent of all cases now never make the Discuss List. The placement of more cases on the Dead List leaves each of the remaining cases eligible for six minutes of conference consideration, compared with the eleven minutes thirty years ago. Each justice has less than a minute to discuss each case on the Discuss List. Assuming further (and again unrealistically) that entire conferences were devoted only to the discussion of cases on which the Court heard oral arguments, then each case would receive up to fifty-two minutes, compared with over an hour's time in the 1950s. But the justices now hold short conferences (for about an hour and a half) on Wednesdays during the weeks when they hear oral arguments. At those conferences they vote on the four cases on which they heard arguments on Monday. Each of those cases is given an average of twenty-two minutes of discussion. If we assume that the justices devote about half of their regular Friday conferences to discussing the merits of the cases on which they heard arguments on Tuesday and Wednesday, then each case granted full consideration would receive about twenty-nine minutes of collective deliberation. And justices may express their views on the merits of each case for an average of three minutes. In sum, the Court's caseload and conference schedule now permits an average of six minutes per pending case on the Discuss List, and about twenty-nine minutes for each case granted full consideration.

Some cases undoubtedly are discussed at greater length and even at more than one conference. But conference discussions have less significance in the Burger Court's decision making. The cost of the practice of devoting less time to collective deliberation and consensus building is more divided decisions and less agreement on the Court's rulings. Because the justices no longer have the time or inclination to agree on opinions for the Court, they file a greater number of separate opinions. The reality of cases and less collective deliberation discourages the reaching of compromises necessary for institutional opinions. Ideological and personal differences in the Burger Court are reinforced.

STRATEGIES DURING CONFERENCE

Justices vary in the weight they place on conference deliberations. They all come prepared to vote. Some, like Douglas, have little interest in discussions. Others take copious notes. Much depends on a justice's intellectual ability, self-confidence, and style. The "freshman effect" on junior justices is especially apparent at conference. Since senior justices speak first, newly appointed members tend to be somewhat circumspect and often have little to say after the others have spoken. Hughes once observed that "it takes three or four years to get the hang of it, and that so extraordinary an intellect as Brandeis said that it took him four or five years to feel that he understood the jurisdictional problems of the Court."[35]

The justices' interaction at conference has been analyzed by the political scientist David Danelski in terms of small-group behavior. He specifically examined the role of the chief justice, distinguishing between two kinds of influence—"task" and "social" leadership.[36] Task leadership relates to the managing of the workload, even at the cost of ignoring personal relations among the justices. By contrast, social leadership addresses the interpersonal relations among the justices that are crucial for a collegial body. Danelski found that some chief justices tend to be either more task or more social-leadership oriented. Few assume both roles, and some fail at both.

Though the chief justice is the titular head of the Court, it by no means follows that he has a monopoly on leadership. Taft was good-humored but, recognizing his own intellectual limitations, relied on Van Devanter for task leadership.[37] Warren, likewise socially oriented, found it useful to consult with Brennan when planning conferences. On the Burger Court, Powell has shown considerable task leadership with suggestions for expediting the processing of the Court's caseload.

Any justice may assume task or social leadership. He or

she may also assert a third kind of leadership—policy leadership. Justices demonstrate policy leadership by persuading others to vote in ways (in the short and long run) favorable to their policy goals. Some members of the Burger Court deny the possibility of such influence. "It may well be that, since the days of John Marshall, an individual Justice or Chief Justice cannot 'lead,' " Blackmun has noted. "The Court pretty much goes its own way."[38] But all three kinds of influence— task, social, and policy leadership—are intertwined and present various strategies for justices trying to affect the outcome of the Court's decisions.

On especially controversial cases, one strategy may be simply to confer but not vote. Forcing a vote may sharply divide the justices and foreclose negotiations. Warren adopted this approach with *Brown v. Board of Education* (1954). When Warren arrived at the Court, in 1953, *Brown* had already been on the docket for over a year. Oral arguments were then held in November, but he carried the case over week after week at conference. No vote was taken until the middle of February. Warren's strategy, statement of the moral issue at stake, and persistence made the ruling unanimous. Warren wanted a unanimous ruling because *Brown* would inevitably engender resistance. If *Brown* had been decided when it first arrived, the vote would probably have been six to three or five to four. Vinson was still chief justice then. Jackson's notes of conference discussions indicate that Reed would "uphold segregation as constitutional," as Vinson would have. Clark and Jackson were also inclined to let segregated schools stand. Yet, Warren persuaded all the justices to join the ruling striking down segregation. At the last minute, Warren got Jackson, who was in the hospital recovering from a heart attack, to suppress a concurring opinion he had written. Jackson had a practice of writing separate opinions, with a view to clarifying his thinking and bargaining with the others, and then withholding their publication when the Court's final ruling came along. But, as

Burton noted in his diary, Warren did a "magnificent job in getting a unanimous Court (This would have been impossible a year ago—probably 6–3 with the Chief Justice at that time one of the dissenters)."*[39]

The strategy of postponing a vote is not one open only to the chief justice. Since the chief justiceship of Vinson, the practice has been "to pass any argued case upon the request of any member of the Court."[40] Obviously, there are limits to how often this can be done if the Court is to complete its work. Vinson's experience during 1946–1950 indicates that less than 9 percent of the cases were decided "upon votes not cast at the first conference following argument."[41]

Another strategy may prove more prudent and afford a justice additional opportunities to influence others. "The practice has grown up," according to Burger, "of assigning one Justice to simply prepare a memorandum about the case, and at that time all other Justices are invited if they want to submit a memorandum; and then out of that memorandum usually a consensus is formed and someone is identified who can write an opinion that will command a majority of the Court."[42] The practice sharpens the confrontation between opposing policy preferences. This occurred, for instance, with the circulation of rival opinions in the important obscenity case *Miller v. California* (1973). Burger and Brennan directly competed for votes to support their respective draft opinions. In the end, a bare majority accepted Burger's analysis and more restrictive definition of obscenity based on local community standards of what appeals to a prurient interest in sex.[43]

A justice who decides to draft a memorandum on a case

* Although Warren managed to bring the Court's full prestige to the ruling, opposition to *Brown* was nevertheless intense and widespread, as will be further discussed in Chapter 6; and perhaps, as Stevens has said, a nonunanimous decision would have been preferable since southerners might have felt that at least some of the members of the Court understood their traditions and the inexorable problems of ending segregation.

for conference discussion gains time for refining ideas and trying to rationally persuade others. This strategy so appealed to Frankfurter that he often circulated memos on cases pending before conference and urged the others to do the same. The disadvantage of a regular practice of preconference reports is the inevitable increase in the workload. Such a practice, Douglas thought, would also "launch the Court into the law review business, multiplying our volumes, and load them with irrelevances."[44]

At conference justices may try to reason with each other. But their success depends on how much time they have and on their style as much as on the reasons they offer. Frankfurter was inclined to try to monopolize discussions, occasionally standing up and lecturing. Stewart was prompted to tell him "that he held forth for exactly fifty minutes, the length of a law school class period at Harvard."[45] Once, when Frankfurter refused to answer one of Douglas's questions, the latter protested but added, "We all know what a great burden your long discourses are. So I am not complaining."[46] In contrast, Frankfurter's ideological ally on the matter of judicial self-restraint, John Harlan, never talked at great length. He always focused on the facts he thought controlling, and frequently concluded, "Now that we have the whole case before us it is clear this is a 'peewee' but it is here and we should deal with it."[47]

Some justices use more-indirect tactics, appealing to emotions and egos rather than to reason. Jackson once observed of another that "you just can't disagree with him. You must go to war with him if you disagree."[48] Actual physical aggression, of course, is rare. However, Douglas recalled one time when Chief Justice Vinson became so perturbed that he got up from the conference table and headed around the room, shouting at Frankfurter, "No son-of-a-bitch can ever say that to Fred Vinson."[49] Personal animosities sometimes prevail.

The most extreme were those of Justice McReynolds. He was anti-Semitic, and whenever Brandeis spoke at conference, he would get up from his chair and go out of the conference room. But he would leave the door open a crack and peek in until Brandeis was through, and then he would come back and take his seat. For the most part, justices do not let professional differences become personal. They must disagree without being disagreeable.

When discussions become heated, humor may prove useful. There is the story of Holmes's interrupting one of the senior Harlan's discourses, violating the unwritten rule against interruptions. "But that just won't wash," he said, outraging Harlan. Thereupon Chief Justice Fuller quickly started a washboard motion with his hands and said, "But I just keep scrubbing away, scrubbing away."[50] During another heated debate at conference, Frankfurter and Chief Justice Stone squared off. Again, humor helped to relieve the tensions. After Stone made one of his long presentations on a case, Frankfurter snapped, "I suppose you know more than those who drafted the Constitution." To which Stone shot back, "I know some things better than those who drafted the Constitution." "Yes, wine and cheese," Frankfurter quipped, drawing an uproar of laughter from the justices.[51]

At other times, justices may more or less subtly appeal to each other's ego. Personally offended by a remark at a conference, Murphy passed a note to Black stating, "Hugo: I appreciate your sentiments because you are the bravest and keenest man on this Court."[52] By contrast, Sherman Minton thought Black a "Demagogue" after he made "one of his inflammatory outbursts at Conference."[53]

Justice Douglas contended that Frankfurter "was always a divisive influence." In particular, he claimed that Frankfurter abused Murphy for his own purposes. "Frankfurter did more [to] tear down Murphy, to ridicule him, make fun of him," Douglas maintained. "It was very sad and pathetic that he spent hours every week talking to people about Murphy, laughing behind Frank Murphy's back."[54] Frankfurter himself once told Murphy, "You have some false friends—those who flatter you and play on you for your place in history, not in tomorrow's columns, as lasting as yesterday's snow."[55] Murphy was not oblivious to Frankfurter's duplicity. As he once wrote Frankfurter, "My grievance against you grows out of 1st—1. My belief in you—2. My many acts of friendship toward you.—3. That you, too believed statements, stories . . . brought to you by unworthy characters.—4. That—as I see it—you were ungrateful and chose to undo me . . . [and] 5. That you have espoused legal views that seemed to me not only wrong but contrary to all that your early gospel stood for."[56]

Even ideological foes, like Black and Frankfurter, may nonetheless appeal to, if not retain, each other's self-esteem. Black once wrote to the latter,

> More than a quarter of a century's close association between us in the Supreme Court's exacting intellectual activities has enabled both of us, I suspect, to anticipate with reasonable accuracy the basic position both are likely to take on questions that importantly involve the public welfare and tranquility. Our differences, which have been many, have rarely been over the ultimate and desired, but rather have related to the means that were most likely to achieve the end we both envisioned. Our years together, and these differences, have but added to the respect and admiration that I had for *Professor* Frankfurter even before I knew him—his love of country, steadfast devotion to what he believed to be right, and to his wisdom.[57]

TENTATIVE VOTES

Voting presents each justice with opportunities for negotiating on which issues are finally decided and how. "*Votes* count," one of Black's colleagues reminded him in a note passed at conference. "I vote to reverse, if there were two more of my mind there would be a reversal."[58] But the justices' votes are always tentative until the day the Court hands down its decision and opinion. Before, during, and after conference, justices may use their votes in strategic ways to influence the disposition of a case. "The books on voting are never closed until the decision actually comes down," Harlan has explained. "Until then any member of the Court is perfectly free to change his vote, and it is not an unheard of occurrence for a persuasive minority opinion to eventuate as the prevailing opinion."[59]

At conference, a justice may vote with others if they appear to constitute a majority, even though he or she disagrees with their treatment of a case. The justices may then bargain and try to minimize the damage, from his or her policy perspective, of the Court's decision. Alternatively, justices may threaten dissenting opinions or try to form a voting bloc, and thereby influence the final decision and written opinion.

The utility of such voting strategies depends on how the justices line up at conference. They may prove quite useful if the initial vote is five to four or six to three. But their effectiveness also depends on institutional norms and practices.

The importance of voting strategies at conference is also conditioned by the complexity of the issues presented and by their divisiveness. Complex cases may result in confusion at conference. When the Court considered the issue of abortion in *Roe v. Wade* (1973), for example, Burger claimed that there was too much confusion at conference about how the justices stood on the issues. "At the close of discussion of this case there were, literally, not enough columns to mark up an accurate reflection of the voting," he explained afterward. Burger "therefore marked down no vote and said this was a case that would have to stand or fall on the writing, when it was done."[60]

In two other controversial cases, involving claims by the press to a First Amendment right of access to visit and interview prisoners, Burger switched his vote after conference. During the conference discussion of *Pell v. Procuiner* (1974) and *Saxbe v. Washington Post* (1974), the vote went five to four for recognizing that the press has a First Amendment right of access. But Burger later changed his mind and explained that the final outcome of the cases depended on how the opinions were written:

Chief Justice Warren Burger and Justice William O. Douglas. *(Office of Curator, Supreme Court of the United States)*

For my friend and colleagues, William O. Douglas who will always climb new mountains as long as they are there.
With best wishes
Warren E. Burger

This difficult case has few very clear cut and fixed positions but my further study over the weekend leads me to see my position as closer for those who would sustain the authority of the corrections administrators than those who would not! I would therefore reverse in 73–754, affirm in 73–918 and reverse in 73–1265.

This is another one of those cases that will depend a good deal on "how it is written." The solution to the problem must be allowed time for experimentation and I fear an "absolute" constitutional holding adverse to administrators will tend to "freeze" progress.[61]

The Court ultimately divided five to four, but held that the press does not have a First Amendment right of access to interview inmates of prisons. Like *Roe,* these examples illustrate how important postconference deliberations and communications among the chambers have become for the Court's decision making.

Opinion-Writing Process

Opinions justify or explain votes at conference. The opinion for the Court is the most important and most difficult to write because it represents a collective judgment. Writing the Court's opinion, as Holmes put it, requires that a "judge can dance the sword dance; that is he can justify an obvious result without stepping on either blade of opposing fallacies."[62] Holmes in his good-natured way often complained about the compromises he had to make when writing an opinion for the Court. "I am sorry that my moderation," he wrote Chief Justice White, "did not soften your inexorable heart—But I stand like St. Sebastian ready for your arrows."[63]

Since conference votes are tentative, the assignment, drafting, and circulation of opinions is crucial to the Court's rulings. At each stage, justices compete for influence in determining the Court's final decision and opinion.

OPINION ASSIGNMENT

The power of opinion assignment is perhaps a chief justice's "single most influential function" and, as Tom Clark has emphasized, an exercise in "judicial-political discretion."[64] By tradition, when the chief justice is in the majority, he assigns the Court's opinion. If the chief justice did not vote with the majority, then the senior associate justice who was in the majority either writes the opinion or assigns it to another.

Chief justices may keep cases for themselves. This is in the tradition of Chief Justice Marshall, but as modified by the workload and other justices' expectations of equitable opinion assignments. In unanimous decisions and landmark cases, the chief justice often self-assigns the Court's opinion. "The great cases are written," Justice John Clarke observed, "as they should be, by the Chief Justice."[65] But chief justices differ. Fuller, even against the advice of other justices, frequently "gave away" important cases;[66] Taft, by contrast, retained 34 percent, Hughes 28 percent, and Stone 11 percent of "the important cases."[67] Various considerations may lie behind a chief justice's self-assignment, such as how much time he has already invested in a case and how he finally decides to vote. Warren explained his self-assignments in two cases as follows:

> Because I prepared a memorandum in No. 15—*Yellin v. United States*—before our Conference discussion, I thought it would be advisable for me to assign the case to myself.
>
> You will recall that when we discussed No. 24—*Halliburton Oil Well Cementing Co. v. Reily*—I did not vote because I was uncertain as to what my decision would be, and Justice Black assigned the case further, I have decided to vote to reverse. I am, therefore, reassigning the case to myself.[68]

Chief justices approach opinion assignment differently. Hughes tended to write most of the Court's opinions and was "notoriously inclined to keep the 'plums' for himself." Between 1930 and 1938, Hughes wrote an average of twenty-one opinions for the Court, while other justices averaged only sixteen each term. Hughes also made all assignments immediately after conference. Typically, "assignments would arrive at each Justice's home within a half hour or so" of their return from the Court.[69] Since conference tended to drag on under Stone, he was not as prompt in his assignments. Like Hughes, however, Stone tended to take more of the opinions for himself. He averaged about nineteen, whereas other justices each wrote only about fifteen opinions for the Court every term.

The inequities in opinion assignments by Hughes and Stone angered some justices. When Vinson became chief justice, he strove to distribute opinions more equitably. The increase in the business of the Court also led Vinson to safeguard against justices' piling up of too many opinions and forcing the Court to sit for extra weeks while they were completed at the end of the term. On a large chart, he kept track of the opinions assigned, when they were completed, and which remained outstanding.[70] Vinson was remarkably successful in achieving parity in opinion assignments. All justices on the Vinson Court averaged about ten opinions for the Court every term. Warren followed that practice and achieved the same result. Warren "was the Super Chief," in Brennan's view, and "bent over backwards in assigning opinions to assure that each Justice, including himself, wrote approximately the same number of Court opinions and received a fair share of the more desirable opinions."[71] Burger has likewise sought equity in opinion writing. Between 1969 and 1981, Burger averaged 14.8 opinions for the Court each term, whereas the other justices averaged 14.4 opinions.[72]

Parity in opinion assignment now generally prevails. But the practice of immediately assigning opinions after conference, as Hughes did, or within a day or two, as Stone did, was gradually abandoned by the end of Vinson's tenure as chief justice. Warren and Burger assigned opinions after each two-week session of oral arguments and conferences. With more assignments to make at any given time, they thus acquired greater flexibility in distributing the workload. They also enhanced their own opportunities for influencing the final outcome of cases through their assignment of opinions.

Assignment of opinions is complicated in controversial cases. Occasionally, a justice assigned to write an opinion discovers that it "just won't write," and it must then be reassigned. Reassignment of opinions occurs infrequently. In the 1964 and 1973 terms, from 1 to 3 percent of the cases were reassigned. This was due to sharp divisions among the justices. When the Court first tackled the controversy over televising criminal trials, in *Estes v. Texas* (1965), for example, the justices were deeply split. Stewart's initial draft failed to command a majority. He was relegated to writing a dissenting opinion, joined by three others. Clark wrote the Court's final opinion, holding that the cameras in the courtroom were too disruptive and denied the defendant's right to a fair trial. Later, when the Burger Court reexamined the constitutionality of the death penalty in *Gregg v. Georgia* (1976), White found that "his approach to the capital cases may no longer command a majority." He accordingly gave *Gregg* and its companion cases back for reassignment. After holding a conference in early May to "clear the air," Burger reassigned the opinions to Stewart, who wrote the Court's opinion upholding capital punishment.[73]

Sometimes justices switch votes after an opinion has been assigned, and thus necessitate reassignment. The "cases of the Murdering Wives," as Frankfurter referred to them, illustrate the consequences of switching votes and the effect of changes in the Court's composition. Both cases, *Reid v. Covert* (1956) and *Kinsella v. Krueger* (1956), involved women who had allegedly killed their husbands stationed abroad in the military. They raised the issue of the constitutionality of subjecting civilians living abroad with military personnel to courts-martial under the Uniform Code of Military Justice, which

does not extend the same guarantees as those in the Bill of
Rights for criminal trials. Warren initially assigned the opinions, but Stanley Reed changed his vote. The decision went
the other way, and the opinion was reassigned to Clark. He
held that the women could be tried under military law. In the
next year, though, Sherman Minton retired and William
Brennan took his place on the bench. The Court reconsidered
the issue in *Reid v. Covert* (1957) and reversed its earlier
decision. This time, the Court enforced the protections of the
Bill of Rights.[74]

The justice assigned to write an opinion for the Court
occasionally decides that the case should go the other way.[75]
Taft once assigned himself an opinion, but wrote it reversing
the vote taken at conference. He explained to his brethren,
"I think we made a mistake in this case and have written the
opinion the other way. Hope you will agree."[76]

Dramatic instances of vote switching and opinion reassignment are rare. Changes in voting alignments usually only
increase the size of the majority.[77] The unpublished opinions
of John Harlan during his service on the Court (1955–1971)
reveal that of some sixty-one undelivered opinions only nine
were abandoned because of a reversal of a majority on the
treatment of a case. Typically, Harlan withdrew a draft of a
concurrence or a dissent because the author of the Court's
opinion accommodated his views. Harlan did so in twelve cases.
In thirteen cases, he substantially revised his own initial separate opinion in light of changes made in the opinion for the
Court. In four cases, he abandoned an initial concurrence or
dissent in favor of joining another. And in about one case each
term, Harlan suppressed an opinion because the Court was
so divided that the final vote was to issue a brief per curiam
opinion, affirming the lower-court ruling by an equally divided
Court, or to carry the case over for reargument the next term.[78]

Since justices may switch their votes and since opinions
for the Court require compromise, chief justices may assign

opinions on the basis of a "voting paradox" or, as David Danelski has explained, "assign the case to the justice whose views are closest to the dissenters on the ground that his opinion would take a middle approach upon which both majority and minority could agree."[79] Hughes apparently adopted this approach when giving Frankfurter the first flag-salute case, *Minersville School District v. Gobitis* (1940). There, a bare majority denied the Jehovah's Witnesses' claim that requiring school children to salute the American flag at the start of classes violates the First Amendment. But three years later, in a second case, the Court reversed itself. In *West Virginia Board of Education v. Barnette* (1943), the Court held that the First Amendment guarantee of freedom of religion prohibits states from compelling school children to recite the pledge of allegiance to the flag.

Some chief justices employ the strategy of assigning opinions to pivotal justices more than others do. Hughes, Vinson, and Warren tended to favor justices likely to hold on to a majority, and perhaps even win over some of the dissenters. Taft and Stone were not so inclined.[80] Assigning opinions to pivotal justices presents a chief justice with additional opportunities for influencing the Court's final ruling. Because votes are always tentative, a chief justice may vote with a majority and assign the case to a marginal justice, but later switch his vote or even write a dissenting opinion.

Chief justices may take other factors into account in assigning opinions. What kind of reaction a case is likely to engender may be important. Hughes was inclined to give "liberal" opinions to "conservative" justices in order to defuse opposition to rulings striking down early New Deal legislation. Later, when the Court decided the Texas "White Primary" case, *Smith v. Allwright* (1944), ruling that blacks may not be excluded from voting in state primary elections, Stone assigned the Court's opinion to Frankfurter. But Jackson immediately expressed his concerns about the assignment.

Frankfurter was a Vienna-born Jew, raised in New England, and a former professor at the elite Harvard Law School. Stone and Frankfurter were persuaded of the wisdom of reassigning the opinion to Reed, a native-born Protestant from Kentucky, long associated with the Democratic party. The justices thought that they might thereby diminish some of the opposition in the South to the ruling.[81]

A number of other cases illustrate that public relations may enter into a chief justice's calculations. The leading civil libertarian on the Court, Hugh Black, wrote the opinion in *Korematsu v. United States* (1944), upholding the constitutionality of the relocation of Japanese-Americans during World War II. A former attorney general experienced in law enforcement, Tom Clark, wrote the opinion in the landmark exclusionary rule case, *Mapp v. Ohio* (1961), holding that evidence obtained in violation of the Fourth Amendment's requirements for a reasonable search and seizure may not be used against criminal suspects at trial. And a former counsel for the Mayo Clinic, experienced in the law of medicine, Harry Blackmun, was assigned the abortion case *Roe v. Wade* (1973).

These examples also suggest that chief justices may look for expertise in particular areas of law. Taney gave Peter Daniel a large number of land, title, and equity cases, but few involving constitutional matters.[82] Taft was especially apt to assign opinions on the basis of expertise: Clarke and McKenna wrote patent cases; Brandeis, tax and rate opinions; and McReynolds was "the boss on Admirality," while Van Devanter and Sutherland, both from "out West," were given land and Indian disputes.[83] Burger tends to give First Amendment cases to White and Stewart and those involving federalism to Powell or Rehnquist, depending on the size of the conference vote. By contrast, Warren expressly disapproved of specialization. He thought that it both discouraged collective decision making and might make a "specialist" defensive when challenged.[84] Yet, Brennan wrote the watershed opinions on the First Amendment and became a kind of custodian of obscenity cases during the Warren Court.

The power of opinion assignment invites resentment and lobbying by the other members of the Court. Justice Murphy, for instance, was known within the Court to delegate his opinion writing largely to his clerks. Neither Stone nor Vinson had much confidence in his work. Accordingly, he received few opinions in important cases from either chief justice. Murphy once complained to Vinson, when tendering back his "sole assignment to date", "I have done my best to write an opinion acceptable to the majority who voted as I did at the conference. I have failed in this task and a majority has now voted the other way."[85] Only when Murphy's ideological ally, Hugo Black, as the senior associate, assigned opinions did he receive major cases.

"During all the years," Warren claimed, "I never had any of the Justices urge me to give them opinions to write, nor did I have anyone object to any opinion that I assigned to him or anyone else."[86] Warren's experience was exceptional, but he also often conferred with other justices before making his assignments. Black and Douglas, for instance, urged Warren to assign Brennan the landmark case on reapportionment, *Baker v. Carr* (1962). They did so because Brennan's views were closest to those of Stewart, the crucial fifth vote, and his draft would be most likely to command a majority.[87] Most chief justices find themselves lobbied, to a greater or lesser degree, when they assign opinions.[88]

WRITING AND CIRCULATING OPINIONS

Writing opinions is the justices' most difficult and time-consuming task. As Frankfurter once put it, when appealing to Brennan to suppress a proposed opinion, "psychologically speaking, voting is one thing and expressing views in support of a vote quite another."[89]

Justices differ in their styles and approaches to opinion

writing. They now more or less delegate responsibility to their clerks for assistance in the preparation of opinions (as was discussed in Chapter 3). But only after a justice is satisfied with an initial draft does the opinion go to the other justices for their reactions.

The circulation of opinions among the chambers added to the Court's workload and changed the process of opinion writing. The practice of circulating draft opinions began around the turn of the century and soon became pivotal in the Court's decision-making process. The circulation of opinions provides more opportunities for the shifting of votes and further coalition building or fragmentation within the Court. Chief Justice Marshall, with his insistence on unanimity and nightly conferences after dinner, achieved unsurpassed unanimity. Unanimity, however, was based on the reading of opinions at conferences. No drafts circulated for other justices' scrutiny. Throughout much of the nineteenth century, when the Court's sessions were shorter and the justices had no law clerks, opinions were drafted in about two weeks and then read at conference.[90] If at least a majority agreed with the main points, the opinion was approved.

In this century, the practice became that of circulating draft opinions, initially carbon copies and now two photocopies, for each justice's examination and comments. Because they gave more attention to each opinion, the justices found more to debate. The importance of circulating drafts and negotiating language in an opinion was underscored when Jackson announced from the bench, "I myself have changed my opinion after reading the opinions of the members of the Court. And I am as stubborn as most. But I sometimes wind up not voting the way I voted in conference because the reasons of the majority didn't satisfy me."[91] Similarly, Brennan noted, "I converted more than one proposed majority into a dissent before the final decision was announced. I have also, however, had the more satisfying experience of rewriting a dissent as a majority opinion for the Court." In one case, Brennan added, he "circulated 10 printed drafts before one was approved as the Court's opinion."[92]

As the amount of time spent on the considering of proposed opinions grew, so did the workload. More law clerks were needed, and they were also given a greater role in opinion writing. Though clerks are now largely responsible for drafting and commenting on opinions, they remain subordinates when it comes to negotiating opinions for the Court. There are exceptions. Frankfurter often tried to use his clerks as lobbyists within the Court. And Rutledge once found that during his absence "at the request of Justice Black two minor changes were made by [his] staff in the final draft of the opinion, but apparently that draft was not circulated to show those changes."[93] But, even if a clerk is delegated or assumes responsibility for working on an opinion, the justice ultimately must account for what is circulated.

How long does opinion writing take? In the average case, Tom Clark observed, about three weeks' work by a justice and his clerks is required before an opinion circulates. "Then the fur begins to fly."[94] The time spent preparing an opinion depends on how fast a justice works, what his style is, how much use of law clerks he makes, and how controversial the assigned case is. Holmes and Cardozo wrote opinions within days after being assigned, with little assistance from law clerks. Even into his eighties, Holmes "thirsted" for opinions. Chief Justice Hughes held back assignments from Cardozo because the justice's law clerk, Melvin Segal, complained that Cardozo would spend his weekends writing his opinions and thus he had little to do during the week. Cardozo later gave his clerk responsibility for checking citations and proofreading drafts. But Cardozo still overworked himself, and Hughes continued to hold back assignments for fear that the bachelor's health would fail.[95] By comparison, Frankfurter relied a great deal on his clerks and was still notoriously slow. As he

once said, in apologizing to his brethren for the delay in circulating a proposed opinion, "The elephant's period of gestation is, I believe, eighteen months, but a poor little hot dog
has no such excuse."[96]

A comparison of the Warren and Burger Courts during the
1964 and 1973 terms provides an indication of the amount of
time involved in writing and circulating of opinions.* In the
tradition of Holmes and Cardozo, Black and Douglas expedi-
tiously completed their opinions in about twenty-two days,
whereas others took an average of thirty-nine days. Unlike
some who acquired more law clerks, Douglas used about the
same amount of time to complete his opinions. During the
Warren Court, it took an average of thirty-five days for justices to complete their opinions, but it took Douglas only
twenty-seven. The Burger Court averaged fifty-two days, but
Douglas averaged twenty-five. Both Warren and Burger took
longer than other justices when completing their opinions,
doubtless because of their additional responsibilities as chief
justice. Warren took fifty-two days, whereas Burger takes about
eighty-two to complete his opinions.[97]

The greater amount of time now taken to complete opinions is undoubtedly due in part to the increased role of law
clerks in the opinion-writing process. At least in Rehnquist's
view, "law clerks tend to do a more elaborate job than if the
justices were doing it alone." And with the increased number
of clerks, it takes more time to circulate proposed opinions
within a justice's chambers and among those of the others.

Controversial cases also lengthen the opinion-writing pro-

* The estimates of the average number of days for opinion writing is based
on the assumption that a justice works only five days a week and devotes
the entire time to a case. Obviously, justices do not devote all their time to
writing opinions, and hence the comparison is not intended to suggest the
number of eight-hour days spent in opinion writing. Justices have other
demands on their time and more or less rely on their clerks for drafting of
opinions. Other things being equal, however, the comparison provides an
illustration of the differences in opinion writing.

cess. In the 1973 term, for example, Burger wrote opinions in two divisive cases on the law of standing, *United States v. Richardson* (1974) and *Schlesinger v. Reservists Committee to Stop the War* (1974), involving unsuccessful attempts to challenge the constitutionality of the war in Vietnam. Both cases took more than twice his usual time. Likewise, Powell's opinion in a landmark libel case, *Gertz v. Robert Welch, Inc.* (1974), took well over twice the time that his other opinions did. After Powell was assigned the case, it was another 220 days before *Gertz* came down. Elmer Gertz was a Chicago lawyer hired to sue a policeman by a family whose son had been killed by the officer. The John Birch Society in its magazine *American*

Justice Byron White working at one of the Court's word processors in his chambers.
(Justice Byron White, American Bar Association Journal)

Opinion charged that Gertz was a "Leninist" and "Communist-fronter" and that the lawsuit against the policeman was part of a nationwide communist conspiracy to discredit law enforcement. Gertz sued Robert Welch, publisher of the magazine, for libel. For a bare majority, Powell held that private individuals do not have to show "actual malice" on the part of publishers in order to win libel awards; as public officials and figures must do under *New York Times Co. v. Sullivan* (1964). Instead, private individuals need show only that a publisher was negligent in printing false and defamatory statements.

The interplay of professional and psychological pressures on a justice writing the Court's opinion is a complex but crucial part of the Court's decision making. When the practice, in the 1920s and 1930s, was to return comments within twenty-four hours after receipt of a draft, the pressures were especially great. There are no time limits now, but the pressures persist, especially during the last two months of a term, when the justices concentrate on opinion writing.[98] Burger has recalled how late one term Black insisted on changes in one of Brennan's opinions and the latter became very curt on the telephone with his esteemed friend, whereupon Black came into Brennan's chamber and told him, "This place can be a pressure cooker and it can beat the strongest of men. You should get out of here and forget it for a few days." Brennan did.[99]

Whether drafting or commenting on a proposed opinion, justices differ when trying to influence each other. They look for emotional appeals, sometimes personal threats. Justice Clark thought that Warren was the greatest chief justice in the history of the Court and sought his approval of a revised opinion. But he received this disturbing response: "Tom: Nuts. E.W."[100] Shortly after coming to the Court, Brennan wrote Black, "I welcome, as always every and any comment you will be good enough to make on anything I ever write—whether we vote together at the time or not."[101] On the back of Stone's draft opinion in *United States v. Darby* (1941), Douglas wrote, "I heartily agree. This has the master's touch." "This is grand plum pudding," Frankfurter added. "There are so many luscious plums in it that its invidious to select."[102]

Douglas could be a real charmer—if he wanted to be— when appealing for modifications in proposed opinions. "I would stand on my head to join with you in your opinion," he told James Byrnes, though continuing, "I finally concluded, however, that I cannot." His strategy was that of the "Yes, but game." This is evident in his response to one of Reed's drafts: "I like your opinion in No. 18 very much. You have done an excellent job in a difficult field. And I want to join you in it. *But*—"[103] He then set forth the changes that would have to be made.

By contrast, the style of McReynolds was abrupt—sometimes rude—and usually left little room for negotiation. "This statement makes me sick," he once observed.[104] Frankfurter's approach also could be irritating. He was not above making personal attacks. To threaten his ideological foe Hugo Black, Frankfurter circulated but did not publish the following concurring opinion:

> I greatly sympathize with the essential purpose of my brother (former Senator) Black's dissent. His roundabout and turgid legal phraseology is a *cris de coeur.* "Would I were back in the Senate," he seems to say, "so that I could put on the statute books what really ought to be there. But here I am, cast by Fate into a den of judges devoid of the habits of legislators, simple fellows who have a crippling feeling that they must enforce the laws as Congress wrote them and not as they ought to have been written. . . ."[105]

Frankfurter nonetheless usually tempered his criticisms by making fun of his own academic proclivities: "What does trouble me is that you do not disclose what you are really doing." He wrote Douglas, "As you know, I am no poker player and naturally, therefore, I do not believe in poker playing in the disposition of cases. Or has professing for twenty-five years disabled me from understanding the need for these involutions?"[106]

More typically when commenting on circulated drafts, justices appeal to professionalism and jurisprudential concerns. Even McReynolds, perhaps at the prompting of Taft, once appealed to Stone's basic conservatism: "All of us get into a fog now and then, as I know so well from my own experience. Won't you 'Stop, Look, and Listen'?"[107] Such appeals may carry subtly or explicitly the threat of a concurring or dissenting opinion. Stone, in one instance, candidly told Frankfurter, "If you wish to write [the opinion] placing the case on the ground which I think tenable and desirable, I shall cheerfully join you. If not, I will add a few observations for myself."[108]

Justices may suggest minor editorial or major substantive changes. Before joining one of Arthur Goldberg's opinions, Harlan requested that the word "desegregation" be substituted for "integration" throughout the opinion. As he explained, " 'Integration' brings blood to Southerners' eyes for they think that 'desegregation' means just that—'integration.' I do not think that we ought to use the word in our opinions."[109] Likewise, Stewart strongly objected to some of the language in Abe Fortas's proposed opinion in *Tinker v. Des Moines School District* (1969), which upheld the right of students to wear black armbands in protest of the government's involvement in Vietnam. "At the risk of appearing eccentric," Stewart wrote, "I shall not join any opinion that speaks of what is going on in Vietnam as a 'war' [since Congress never formally declared a war in Vietnam]."[110] Frankfurter was more caustic when he wrote Reed that "all talk about 'jurisdictional facts' and 'constitutional facts' seems to be rubbish—worse than rubbish misleading irrevelances." He further explained;

For all I know you probably think me very persnickety or, at least, academic in fussing about your reference to "constitutional facts" and *Crowell v. Benson*. Well, the fact is that I am academic and I have no excuse for being on this Court unless I remain so. By which I mean that Harvard paid me a high salary for the opportunity of understanding the problems covered by the phrase "judicial review." . . . The fact of the matter is that probably the deepest source of error and darkness in the law is the loose use of language reflecting too often a disregard of the history of doctrines.[111]

Editorial suggestions may also be directed at a justice's use of precedents and basic conceptualization. Douglas, for instance, sent Brennan a letter outlining fourteen changes he thought necessary in the proposed opinion for the watershed reapportionment decision in *Baker v. Carr* (1962).[112] Likewise, Brennan sent a twenty-one-page list of revisions on Earl Warren's initial draft of *Miranda v. Arizona* (1966), which upheld the right of criminal suspects to remain silent at the time of police questioning. At the outset, Brennan expressed his feeling of guilt "about the extent of the suggestions." But he emphasized the importance of careful drafting. Brennan explained, "[T]his will be one of the most important opinions of our time and I know that you will want the fullest expression of my views."[113]

Occasionally, proposed changes led to a recasting of the entire opinion. Douglas was assigned the Court's opinion in *Griswold v. Connecticut* (1965), in which he announced the creation of a constitutional right of privacy based on the "penumbras" of various guarantees of the Bill of Rights. His initial draft, however, did not develop this theory. Rather, Douglas sought to justify the decision on the basis of earlier cases recognizing a First Amendment right of associational privacy. The analogy and precedents, he admitted, "do not decide this case." "Marriage does not fit precisely any of the categories of First Amendment rights. But it is a form of association as vital in the life of a man or a woman as any other, and perhaps more so." Both Black and Brennan strongly objected to Douglas's extravagant reliance on First Amendment precedents. In a three-page letter, Brennan detailed an alternative approach, as the following excerpt indicates:

I have read your draft opinion in *Griswold v. Connecticut*, and, while I agree with a great deal of it, I should like to suggest a substantial change in emphasis for your consideration. It goes without saying, of course, that your rejection of any approach based on *Lochner v. New York* is absolutely right. [In *Lochner*, a majority read into the Fourteenth Amendment a "liberty of contract" in order to strike down economic legislation. Although the Court later abandoned the doctrine of a "liberty of contract," *Lochner* continues to symbolize the original sin of constitutional interpretation—that is, the Court's creation and enforcement of unenumerated rights.] And I agree that the association of husband and wife is not mentioned in the Bill of Rights, and that that is the obstacle we must hurdle to effect a reversal in this case.

But I hesitate to bring the husband-wife relationship within the right to association we have constructed in the First Amendment context. . . . In the First Amendment context, in situations like *NAACP v. Alabama*, privacy is necessary to protect the capacity of an association for fruitful advocacy. In the present context, it seems to me that we are really interested in the privacy of married couples quite apart from any interest in advocacy. . . . Instead of expanding the First Amendment right of association to include marriage, why not say that what has been done for the First Amendment can also be done for some of the other fundamental guarantees of the Bill of Rights? In other words, where fundamentals are concerned, the Bill of Rights guarantees are but expressions or examples of those rights, and do not preclude applications or extensions of those rights to situations unanticipated by the Framers.

The restriction on the dissemination and use of contraceptives, Brennan explained,

would, on this reasoning, run afoul of a right to privacy created out of the Fourth Amendment and the self-incrimination clause of the Fifth, together with the Third, in much the same way as the right of association has been created out of the First. Taken together, those amendments indicate a fundamental concern with the sanctity of the home and the right of the individual to be alone.

"With this change of emphasis," Brennan concluded, the opinion "would be most attractive to me because it would require less departure from the specific guarantees and because I think there is a better chance it will command a Court." Douglas subsequently revised his opinion and based the right of privacy on the penumbras of the First, Third, Fourth, Fifth, and Ninth amendments.[114]

In order to accommodate the views of others, the author

Justice William J. Brennan, Jr., in his chambers. *(Supreme Court Historical Society)*

of an opinion for the Court must negotiate language and bargain over substance. "The ground you recommend was not the one on which I voted 'no'—But I think that, as a matter of policy, you are clearly right; and I am engaged in redrafting the opinion on that line," Brandeis wrote to the respected craftsman Van Devanter, adding, "May I trouble you to formulate the rule of law, which you think should be established?"[115]

At times, justices may not feel that a case is worth fighting over. "Probably bad—but only a small baby. Let it go," Sutherland noted on the back of one of Stone's drafts. Hughes was a bit more graphic when responding to another proposed opinion: "I choke a little at swallowing your analysis, still I do not think it would serve any useful purpose to expose my views."[116] Similarly, Pierce Butler agreed to go along with one of Stone's opinions, though noting, "I voted to reverse. While this sustains your conclusion to affirm, I still think reversal would be better. But I shall in silence acquiesce. Dissents seldom aid in the right development or statement of the law. They often do harm. For myself I say: 'Lead us not into temptation.' "[117]

Justices sometimes join an opinion with which they disagree, perhaps with the hope that in some later case other justices will reciprocate and not threaten a dissenting vote or opinion. This tactic was not lost on Stone, who explained to Frankfurter, in language reminiscent of Butler's twenty years earlier; "I voted the other way in this case but I shall acquiesce in the decision unless some of my brethren see the light and point out that you cracked the law in order to satisfy your moral scruples."[118] Disturbed by one of Holmes's draft opinions, Joseph McKenna wrote, "It may be that there is some defect in my mental processes for I can't appreciate the reasoning. But I will not dissent alone."[119] Another of Holmes's circulated opinions prompted Mahlon Pitney to respond, "Cannot agree, but will say nothing."[120]

In major cases, compromise becomes more difficult. In 1967, for instance, the Court agreed to decide two important cases, *Marchetti v. United States* and *Grosso v. United States*. Both raised the issue of whether requiring gamblers to register with the Internal Revenue Service and pay an occupational tax on their gambling earnings violates the Fifth Amendment privilege against self-incrimination. By registering with the IRS, a gambler becomes open to state and federal prosecution for engaging in organized gambling and thus incriminates himself.

Harlan's first draft met with opposition from Brennan and Douglas. Initially, Brennan sought accommodation:

I think your conclusion is fully supported without that part of your Part III. . . . I expect, however, that you'd rather not omit that portion. Could you stop at Part III at page 10, and make a new section IV beginning with the [next] full paragraph. . . . If so, I could file a concurrence stating that I join the judgment of reversal for the reasons expressed in Parts I, II, IV and V of your opinion.

Douglas, however, immediately circulated a concurrence for *Marchetti* and a dissenting opinion for *Grosso*. Although Brennan preferred these drafts, he thought it wiser to try to mediate the growing dispute within the majority. "Is there anything about Parts I, II, IV and V which you can't join?" Brennan gently pushed Douglas, emphasizing that "it might be helpful on this prickly problem if we could join as much as possible of what John has written." Black, the senior associate who assigned the opinion, agreed. But he told Harlan; "With my constitutional beliefs I could not possibly agree with any part of subdivision III of your opinion except the next to the last sentence in the last paragraph."

After thinking it over for two days, Harlan offered a compromise:

Because of the fact that you, Bill Douglas and Bill Brennan feel so strongly that Part III of my opinion in this case contains implications that were never intended on my part—namely that the taxing power may in some circumstances override the protections afforded by the Fifth Amendment privilege—I have decided to delete that section of my opinion, and am recirculating accordingly.

With his revised draft of *Marchetti*, Harlan was able to hang on to a bare majority, but found himself completely alone on his *Grosso* draft.

Discouraged by the growing dissension, Harlan wrote Black;

I am faced with the unusual experience of having to withdraw from the opinion which I prepared for the Court in this case under your assignment. I intend to propose at next Thursday's Conference that this case, and also No. 181, *Grosso v. United States*, be set for reargument next Term, as suggested by Brother White in his separate opinion, dissenting in *Marchetti*, and concurring in the Judgment in *Grosso*.

The proposal was accepted, and the case was reargued the next term. Tempers cooled, and Harlan further modified his approach; this eventually enabled him to command a majority on both opinions. In the end, only Chief Justice Warren dissented from the ruling striking down the statute as a violation of the Fifth Amendment.[121]

More than a willingness to negotiate is sometimes required. Judicial temperament and diplomacy are also crucial, as is illustrated by the deliberations behind the landmark decision inaugurating the reapportionment revolution. *Baker v. Carr* (1962) raised two central issues: first, whether the malapportionment of a state legislature is a "political question" for which courts have no remedy; second, the merits of the claim that individuals have a right to equal votes and equal representation. With potentially broad political consequences, the case was divisive, being carried over and reargued for a term. The extreme positions within the Court remained firm, but the center tended to be soft. Allies on judicial self-restraint, Frankfurter and Harlan were committed to their view, expressed in *Colegrove v. Green* (1946), that the "Court ought not to enter this political thicket." At conference, Clark and Whittaker supported their view that the case presented a nonjusticiable political question. By contrast, Warren, Black, Douglas, and Brennan thought that the issue was justiciable. They were prepared to address the merits of the case. The pivotal and youngest justice, Potter Stewart, considered the issue justiciable. But he adamantly refused to address the merits of the case. He would vote to reverse the lower-court ruling that the issue was a political question only if the decision was limited to holding that the lower court had jurisdiction to decide the dispute. Stewart did not want the Court to decide the merits of the case.

Assigned the task of drafting the opinion, Brennan had to hold on to Stewart's vote and dissuade Black and Douglas from writing opinions on the merits that would threaten the loss of the crucial fifth vote. After circulating his draft and incorporating suggested changes, he optimistically wrote Black, "Potter Stewart was satisfied with all of the changes. The Chief also is agreed. It, therefore, looks as though we have a court agreed upon this as circulated."[122] It appeared that the decision would come down on the original five-to-four vote.

Clark, however, had been pondering the fact that in this case the population ratio for the urban and rural districts in the state was more than nineteen to one. As he put it, "city slickers" had "too long deprive[d the citizens] of a constitutional form of government."[123] Clark concluded that citizens denied equal voting power had no political recourse; their only recourse was to the federal judiciary. Clark wrote an opinion abandoning Frankfurter and going beyond the majority to address the merits of the claim.

Brennan faced the dilemma of how to bring in Clark without losing Stewart, and thereby enlarge the consensus. Further negotiations were necessary but limited. Brennan wrote his brethren;

The changes represent the maximum to which Potter will sub-
scribe. We discussed much more elaborate changes which would
have taken over a substantial part of Tom Clark's opinion. Potter felt
that if they were made it would be necessary for him to dissent from
that much of the revised opinion. I therefore decided it was best
not to press for the changes but to hope that Tom will be willing to
join the Court opinion but say he would go further as per his separate opinion.[124]

Even though there were five votes for deciding the merits, the final opinion in *Baker v. Carr* was limited to the jurisdictional question. Douglas refrained from addressing the
merits in his concurring opinion. Stewart joined with an opinion emphasizing the limited nature of the ruling. Clark filed
an opinion explaining his view of the merits. Whittaker withdrew from the case, retiring from the Court two weeks later
because of poor health. Only Frankfurter and Harlan were
left dissenting.

The Value of Judicial Opinions

Published opinions for the Court are the residue of conflicts and compromises among the justices. But they also reflect
changing institutional norms. In historical perspective, changes
in judicial norms have affected trends in opinion writing, the
value of judicial opinions, and the Court's contributions to
public law and policy.

OPINIONS FOR THE COURT

During the nineteenth century and down through the chief
justiceship of Hughes, there were few separate, concurring,
or dissenting opinions from the opinion for the Court's decision. In the last forty years, however, there has occurred a
dramatic increase in the total number of opinions issued each
term, as is depicted in the chart on page 263.[125]

Individual opinions now predominate over institutional

OPINION WRITING, 1800–1984

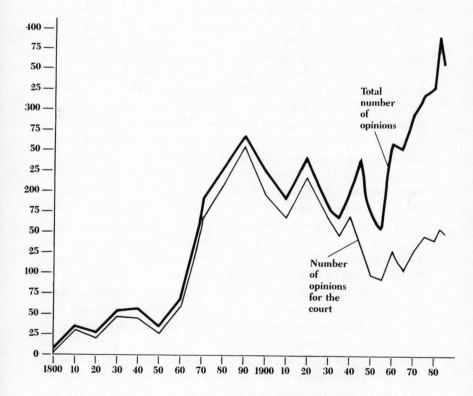

opinions for the Court. In keeping with the greater caseload, the Burger Court disposes of more cases each term by signed opinion than did the Warren Court, though of about the same number as did the Hughes and Stone Courts. In the last years of the Hughes Court (1937–1940), the justices produced about 144 institutional opinions each term and issued another 35 separate, concurring, or dissenting opinions. By contrast, the Burger Court from 1969 to 1980 averaged 138 institutional opinions and issued another 43 separate opinions, 45 concurring opinions, and 105 dissenting opinions—for a total of 331 opinions each term. When we compare the Burger Court's practice with that of forty years ago, we find ten times the number of concurring opinions, four times more dissenting opinions, and seven times the number of separate opinions in which the justices explain their personal views and why they partially concur in and / or dissent from the Court's opinion. The chart on page 265 illustrates these trends.

The justices now care less about reaching a consensus on opinions for the Court. Whereas unanimity remains high on case selection (around 80 percent, as was discussed in Chapter 4), unanimity on opinions for the Court drops to around 30 percent. Even though the business of the Court is to give institutional opinions, Stewart has observed, "that view has come be that of a minority of the justices."[126]

Traditional norms supporting institutional opinions have been, eroded. There are now more divided decisions and opinions. Their number has grown markedly. Between 1900 and 1930, the percentage of divided decisions ranged from less than 10 percent to a high of 17 percent each term. During the chief justiceships of Hughes and Stone, it steadily climbed to over 60 percent each term.[127] Since the Vinson Court, the proportion of divided decisions has ranged between 60 and 70 percent every term. The number of dissenting votes cast each term has also almost doubled since the Vinson Court, from about 160 to 290 during the Burger Court.

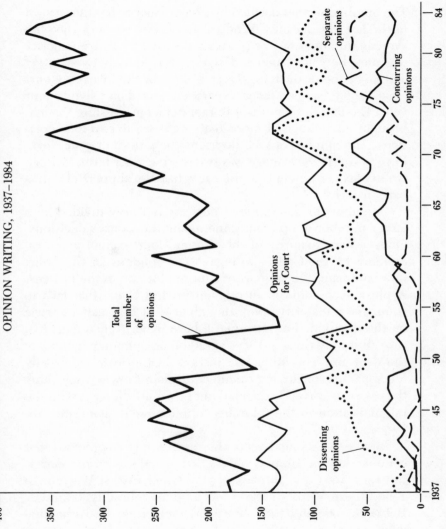

OPINION WRITING, 1937–1984

The justices are now more interested in the mere tally of votes than in arriving at an institutional decision and opinion. The number of cases decided by a bare majority has thus grown in the last few decades. Whereas between 1801 and 1900 the average number of cases per term decided by a bare majority was one, between 1900 and 1937 it was four, between 1937 and 1955 about fourteen. During most of the Warren Court (1956–1969), sixteen cases a year were based on a five-to-four vote. The first three years of Burger's chief justiceship, though, brought an average of more than eighteen five-to-four decisions. The number of such decisions continues to remain high: in 1979–1981, the average was twenty-seven per term; in 1983, twenty-six (17 percent) of the cases had the support of only a bare majority.[128]

Members of the Burger Court are not only divided on a larger number of opinions announcing the Court's decisions. Often a bare majority of the Burger Court cannot agree on opinions for the Court's rulings. More opinions for the Court now command the support of a mere plurality of the justices. A plurality opinion is an opinion for the Court that fails to command a majority, even though at least five justices agree on the decision. For example, a bare majority may decide a case. But only three justices agree on an opinion announcing the decision. The other two justices in the majority usually file separate concurring opinions, explaining why they think the case was correctly decided but how they disagree with the rationalization in the (plurality) opinion announcing the ruling.

Between 1800 and 1900, there were only 10 opinions that commanded the support of less than a majority of the Court. Between 1901 and the last year of Chief Justice Warren, in 1969, there were 51 cases decided by plurality opinions. Between 1969 and 1984, however, the Burger Court handed down 111 plurality opinions, more plurality opinions than were rendered in the entire previous history of the Court.[129]

These trends reflect basic changes in judicial behavior and the value of institutional and individual opinions. Individual opinions are now more highly prized than opinions for the Court. As consensus declines, the Court's rulings and policy-making appear more fragmented, less stable, and less predictable.

SEPARATE, CONCURRING, AND DISSENTING OPINIONS

The tension between institutional and individual opinions is part of a deeper conflict in judicial behavior between the norms of interdependence and independence. "I defend the right of any justice to file anything he wants," Douglas observed.[130] Yet, the proliferation of individual opinions comes at the cost of consensus on the Court's policy-making.

In contrast to the author of an opinion for the Court, a justice writing separate, concurring, or dissenting opinions does not carry the burden of massing other justices. But in extraordinary circumstances a separate opinion may be necessary, the only practical way of obtaining a ruling for the Court. That is what happened in *Regents of the University of California v. Bakke* (1978).

In *Bakke,* the Burger Court addressed the controversy over reverse discrimination and the permissibility of quota systems and affirmative-action programs for minorities in higher education. Alan Bakke, a white male, was denied admission to the medical school at the University of California at Davis. There were only one hundred openings each year, and sixteen of them were reserved for minority students. Bakke was twice denied admission, even though minorities who had lower grade-point averages and scores on the Medical College Admission Test were admitted. Bakke decided to challenge the admission policy for minorities.

Powell's separate opinion announced the Court's ruling in *Bakke,* upholding affirmative-action programs (but not quota systems like that at Davis) and admitting Bakke to the medical

school. But the only part of his opinion joined by another justice was a one-paragraph statement of the facts. Powell delivered the Court's ruling because the other justices were
unwilling to bend on their positions. The justices were divided
four to four on the issues.

Burger, Rehnquist, and Stewart accepted the view of Stevens that the Court need not address the question of whether
affirmative-action programs violate the Constitution. They
would have struck down quota systems as an impermissible
racial classification under Title VI of the Civil Rights Act of
1964 and admitted Bakke.

White, Marshall, and Blackmun sided with Brennan in
maintaining that affirmative-action programs are constitutionally permissible remedies for past racial discrimination. They
would not have admitted Bakke.

Powell was able to gather the votes, but not the justices'
support for his opinion, from each bloc on each of the two key
issues. His opinion declared that quota systems were invalid
and that Bakke should be admitted, relying on the four votes
of the Stevens bloc. At the same time, Powell upheld affirmative-action programs in universities and thereby won the
vote of the Brennan bloc. Powell, however, refused to accept
Brennan's view that past racial discrimination justified the
ruling. Instead, Powell ruled that affirmative-action programs
are permissible because under the First Amendment universities need a diverse student body to ensure academic freedom and the educational process. Powell's pragmatic
rationalization for the controversial decision thus had the support of no other justice.

Justices usually write separate concurring opinions to
explain how the Court's decision could have been otherwise
rationalized. Some are defensible, in Stevens's view, because
a compromised opinion would be meaningless. Concurring
opinions may be required because of a "greater institutional
interest in the forthrightness of differing justices' views."[131]

Although agreeing with the result reached in an opinion by Nathan Clifford, for example, Joseph Bradley was dissatisfied with the treatment of the merits of the case. Bradley explained, "I think I had better, in a few sentences, expressing my conclusion [write] separately instead of our trying to make up a compromise opinion which would mean nothing, and fail to be a frank exposition of our views."[132]

Even though agreeing with the Court's opinion, justices sometimes write concurring opinions for egocentric or political reasons. Angering Warren, Black, and Brennan, and over the strong opposition of Douglas, Frankfurter insisted in *Cooper v. Aaron* (1958), the Little Rock school desegregation case, on publishing a concurring opinion. Because many southern lawyers and law professors had been his students at Harvard Law School, Frankfurter insisted that it was important for him to lecture them on the soundness of the Court's decision not to permit delays in school desegregation. At other times, justices try to send "signals" to lower courts about the direction of Supreme Court policy-making. Such concurring opinions, in the view of Stevens, are objectionable because they amount to "advisory opinions."

Concurring opinions were rare for most of the nineteenth and early twentieth centuries. They are no longer uncommon. Every member of the Burger Court now writes anywhere from four to twelve concurrences each term. Marshall and Rehnquist tend to write the fewest (about four a year), whereas Blackmun and Stevens average about twelve.

Ideological differences do not appear to have any bearing on whether justices publish concurrences. Advocates of judicial self-restraint and activism are just as likely to publish concurring opinions. "Centralists," like Powell, Stewart, and White, may tend to write a few more, since their votes are often pivotal to the Court's decisions.

Such factors as personal style and use of law clerks appear more important in determining whether justices write a large number of concurrences. Burger as a matter of practice tries not to write concurrences. He does so only to "nail down" points that the majority has not fully stated or been willing to accept. Like White and Marshall, Burger consistently writes a small number, about five or six, every year. But the number of concurrences written by some others on the Burger Court has more than doubled in the last decade. The average number of concurrences by Rehnquist and Powell rose, respectively, from 3.2 and 7.6 in 1971–1975 to 6.5 and 13.5 during 1976–1981. Blackmun also tends to write more than he did when he first joined the Court. In 1970–1975 Blackmun averaged about six, but by 1976–1981 he was writing more than sixteen each term. With the exception of Burger, the justices who acquired more law clerks during the period tended to issue more concurrences. What was once true of dissents may now be true about concurrences: "Associate Justices are remembered chiefly by their dissenting opinions, in which they wrote their views without restraint," Justice Clarke observed. [133]

Dissenting opinions are more understandable and defensible. Dissenting opinions, in the view of Hughes, who rarely wrote dissents, appeal "to the brooding spirit of the law, to the intelligence of a future day, when a later decision may possibly correct the error into which the dissenting judge believes the Court to have been betrayed." [134] Harlan's dissent from the doctrine of "separate but equal" in *Plessy v. Ferguson* (1896) was eventually vindicated in *Brown v. Board of Education* (1954). Dissents may also appeal for more-immediate legislative action: James Iredell's dissent in *Chisholm v. Georgia* (1793) invited the adoption of the Eleventh Amendment, overturning the Court's decision; and the dissenters' arguments in *Dred Scott v. Sandford* (1857) lent support to the passage of the Thirteenth, Fourteenth, and Fifteenth amendments after the Civil War.

A dissenting opinion is a way of undercutting the Court's

decision and opinion. The threat of a dissent may thus be useful for a justice trying to persuade the majority to narrow its holding or tone down the language of its opinion. Brandeis, who often dissented, complained, "The Court does not heed dissents sufficiently."[135] Yet, he himself at times "suppressed dissents for tactical reasons." "I think this case is wrongly decided," he wrote Holmes. "But you have restricted the opinion so closely to the facts of this case, that I am inclined to think it will do less harm to let it pass unnoticed by dissent."[136] By contrast, Brennan issued a dissent from a 1983 reapportionment case, *Brown v. Thomson,* precisely because he wanted to underscore the limited precedential value of the ruling: "Although I disagree with today's holding, it is worth stressing how extraordinarily narrow it is, and how empty of likely precedential value."

There is a crucial difference between threatening a dissent and having it published. A number of considerations enter into a decision to publish a dissent. A revised opinion struck Justice Pitney as "still indefensible." "But the revision of the opinion," he wrote William Day, "has eliminated some errors of statement, construction, and reasoning that would have wrought far-reaching mischief in the general administration of the law. In view of this, possibly [it would be] better to submit in silence, consoling ourselves that the injustice to the individual defendant in error will, in all human probability, be rectified upon a new trial."[137]

Threats of dissents now carry less force. Although in the nineteenth and early twentieth centuries, justices might threaten (and bargain with) a dissent, they usually withheld publication. "I should now, as is my custom, when I have the misfortune to differ from this Court," Chief Justice Marshall observed, "acquiesce silently in its opinion."[138]

Lower dissent rates in the nineteenth century do not reflect more agreement within the Court.[139] Instead, institutional decisions were more highly prized. Taft, who suppressed more than two hundred dissents during his service on the high bench, wrote, "I don't approve of dissentings generally, for I think in many cases where I differ from the majority, it is more important to stand by the Court and give its judgment weight than merely to record my individual dissent where it is better to have the law certain than to have it settled either way."[140]

COMPARISON OF DISSENT RATES

Justice	Number of Dissenting Opinions	Average Per Term
"THE GREAT DISSENTERS"		
W. Johnson, 1804–1834	30	1.0
J. Catron, 1837–1865	26	0.9
N. Clifford, 1858–1881	60	2.6
J. Harlan, 1877–1911	119	3.5
O. Holmes, 1902–1932	72	2.4
L. Brandeis, 1916–1939	65	2.9
H. Stone, 1925–1946	93	4.6
H. Black, 1937–1971	310	9.1
F. Frankfurter, 1939–1962	251	10.9
J. Harlan, 1955–1971	242	15.1
THE BURGER COURT		
W. Douglas, 1969–1974	231	38.5
J. Stevens, 1975–1984	205	20.5
W. Brennan, Jr., 1969–1984	281	17.5
W. Rehnquist, 1971–1984	219	15.6
T. Marshall, 1969–1984	241	15.0
P. Stewart, 1969–1980	130	10.8
B. White, 1969–1984	171	10.6
H. Blackmun, 1971–1984	145	10.3
L. Powell, Jr., 1971–1984	144	10.2
S. O'Connor, 1981–1984	31	7.7
W. Burger, 1969–1984	106	6.6

Published dissents are a manifestation of "institutional disobedience."[141] But justices differ in how far they carry that disobedience. Holmes and Brandeis were among "the great dissenters." Yet, Holmes was "reluctant to [dissent] again after he had once had his say on a subject."[142] Likewise, Tom Clark would dissent once from the Court's rulings with which he disagreed, and thereafter in similar cases silently acquiesce.[143] In contrast, Black and Douglas noted every dissent and frequently issued a dissenting opinion, even when they had previously made clear their disagreements with the majority. In Black's words, "Dissents keep the boys on their toes." For Black, a dissenter is an advocate. He once told Blackmun, "That's the way to do it, Harry—strike for the jugular, strike for the jugular."[144]

As the publishing of dissenting opinions gradually spread, the practice became an acceptable form of institutional disobedience. The change in judicial norms is evident from a comparison of current rates of dissenting opinions with those of "the great dissenters," those who wrote a disproportionate number of dissents during earlier periods of the Court's history.

Institutional and Individual Opinions

At the swearing-in of Warren Burger, retiring Chief Justice Warren reflected, "I hope the Court will never agree on all things. If it ever agrees on all things, I am sure that its virility will have been sapped because it is composed of nine independent men who have no one to be responsible to except their own consciences. It is not likely ever, with human nature, as it is, for nine men to agree always on the most important and controversial things of life."[145] Later, Burger similarly observed that "divisions are a source of strength, not weakness."[146]

But the devaluation of opinions for the Court and the greater premium placed on individual opinions affect the implementation of Supreme Court policy-making. Even Black, who had no qualms about threatening or filing separate opinions, recognized the importance of institutional opinions. Black wrote Tom Clark about one of his proposed opinions,

I have no idea what troubles you about my treatment of the [case].
. . . It is rather bad I think to have less than a majority for a court
opinion. Consequently, I would be glad to see if your objections,
whatever they are can be met. I feel so strongly that one should
have a court opinion that I would be willing to have the case reassigned if that would help.[147]

By contrast, Frankfurter came to value individual expression
more than the compromises and cooperation essential to
achieving institutional opinions. "Unanimity is an appealing
abstraction," Frankfurter concluded, but "a single Court
statement on important constitutional issues and other aspects
of public law is bound to smother differences that in the interests of candor and of the best interest of the Court ought to
be expressed."[148]

A number of realities lie behind the changing norms and
patterns of institutional and individual opinions. Personal and
ideological differences contribute to changes in judicial behavior
and policy-making. But the contemporary Court's virtually
complete discretionary jurisdiction also enables it to select
primarily cases of national importance for public law and policy. The Court now decides principally major questions of
constitutional and statutory interpretation. These are areas in
which the justices are most likely to disagree and to be least
inclined to compromise. Constitutional interpretation, in
Frankfurter's words, "is not at all a science, but applied politics,"[149] and thus proves especially divisive. Cases granted oral
argument and decided by opinion are also the most thor-
oughly researched and considered cases. They are the ones to
which the justices devote the most of their time, and hence
those on which they have most clarified their own thinking
and differences.

The increasing caseload may also contribute to changes in
norms of opinion writing. The "proliferation of concurring
opinions and even some dissenting opinions is a result of these
pressures" of a greater workload, Burger has claimed, "and

the consequent lack of time to try to hammer out differences."[150] Justices once spent more time in conference discussing each case and were more inclined to try to reach compromises. There is now less direct communication and more formal, written exchanges among the justices. There are more law clerks and a greater tendency to assign them responsibility for drafting concurring and dissenting opinions. Justices in turn are less willing to withdraw concurring or dissenting opinions because of the time their clerks devoted to them. As one justice put it, even though his concerns had been accommodated in the majority's opinion, "it would break [his] law clerk's heart" to suppress his concurring opinion.

Accompanying the trend toward more separate opinions has been "the ascendency of the law-review type of opinion" and an "increased length of opinions."[151] Opinions have become not merely more numerous but also longer. Opinions in 1938 averaged about eight pages, by 1970 slightly more than nine pages, and by the 1980s eleven pages. That increase may seem small, but the justices are now writing almost twice as many opinions each term as they did fifty years ago.[152]

Less agreement and more numerous and longer opinions invite uncertainty and confusion about the Court's rulings, interpretation of law, and policy-making. As individual opinions have come to predominate, they have also become more idiosyncratic: "It is a genuine misfortune to have the Court's treatment of the subject be a virtual Tower of Babel, from which no definite principles can be clearly drawn," Rehnquist lamented in his dissent in *Metromedia v. City of San Diego* (1981), adding, "I regret even more keenly my contribution to this judicial clamor, but find that none of the views expressed in the other opinions written in the case came close enough to mine to warrant the necessary compromise to obtain a Court opinion."

SIX

The Court and American Life

"W HY DOES the Supreme Court pass the school desegregation case?" asked one of Chief Justice Vinson's law clerks in 1952. *Brown v. Board of Education of Topeka, Kansas* had arrived on the Court's docket in 1951, but it was carried over for oral argument the next term and then consolidated with four other cases and reargued in December 1953. The landmark ruling did not come down until May 17, 1954. "Well," Justice Frankfurter explained, "we're holding it for the election"—1952 was a presidential election year. "You're holding it for the election?" The clerk persisted in disbelief. "I thought the Supreme Court was supposed to decide cases without regard to elections." "When you have a major social political issue of this magnitude," timing and public reactions are important considerations, and, Frankfurter continued, "we do not think this is the time to decide it."[1] Similarly, Tom Clark has recalled that the Court awaited, over Douglas's dissent, additional cases from the District of Columbia and other regions, so as "to get a national coverage, rather than a sectional one." Such political considerations are by no means unique. "We often delay adjudication. It's not a question of evading at all," Clark concluded. "It's just the practicalities of life—common sense."[2]

Denied the power of the sword or the purse, the Court must cultivate its institutional prestige. The power of the Court lies in the pervasiveness of its rulings and ultimately rests with other political institutions and public opinion. As an independent force, the Court has no chance to resolve great issues of public policy. *Dred Scott v. Sandford* (1857) and *Brown v. Board of Education* (1954) illustrate the limitations of Supreme Court policy-making. The "great folly," as Senator Henry Cabot Lodge characterized *Dred Scott,* was not the Court's interpretation of the Constitution or the unpersuasive moral position that blacks were not persons under the Constitution. Rather, "the attempt of the Court to settle the slavery question by judicial decision was simple madness." As Lodge explained,

Slavery involved not only the great moral issue of the right of one man to hold another in bondage and to buy and sell him but it involved also the foundations of a social fabric covering half the country and caused men to feel so deeply that it finally brought them beyond the question of nullification to a point where the life of the Union was at stake and a decision could only be reached by war.[3]

A hundred years later, political struggles within the country and, notably, presidential and congressional leadership in enforcing the Court's school desegregation ruling saved the moral appeal of *Brown* from becoming another "great folly."

Because the Court's decisions are not self-executing, public reactions inevitably weigh on the minds of the justices. Justice Stone, for one, was furious at Chief Justice Hughes's rush to hand down *Powell v. Alabama* (1932). Picketers protested the Scottsboro boys' conviction and death sentence. Stone attributed the Court's rush to judgment to Hughes's "wish to put a stop to the [public] demonstrations around the Court."[4] Opposition to the school desegregation ruling in *Brown* led to bitter, sometimes violent confrontations. In Lit-

tle Rock, Arkansas, Governor Orval Faubus encouraged disobedience by southern segregationists. The federal National
Guard had to be called out to maintain order. The school board
in Little Rock unsuccessfully pleaded, in *Cooper v. Aaron*
(1958), for the Court's postponement of the implementation
of *Brown*'s mandate. In the midst of the controversy, Frankfurter worried that Chief Justice Warren's attitude had become
"more like that of a fighting politician than that of a judicial
statesman." In such confrontations between the Court and the
country, "the transcending issue," Frankfurter reminded the
brethren, remains that of preserving "the Supreme Court as
the authoritative organ of what the Constitution requires."[5]
When the justices move too far or too fast in their interpretation of the Constitution, they threaten public acceptance of
the Court's legitimacy.

The political struggles of the Court (and among the justices) continue after the writing of opinions and final votes.
Announcements of decisions trigger diverse reactions from the
media, interest groups, lower courts, Congress, the President, and the general public. Their reactions may enhance or
thwart compliance and reinforce or undermine the Court's
prestige. Opinion days thus may reveal something of the
political struggles that might otherwise remain hidden within
the marble temple. They may also mark the beginning of larger
political struggles for influence in the country.

Opinion Days

The justices announce their decisions in the courtroom,
typically crowded with reporters, anxious attorneys, and curi-
ous spectators. When several decisions are to be handed down,
the justices delivering the Court's opinions make their
announcements in reverse order of seniority. Authors of concurring or dissenting opinions are free to give their views orally

as well. Before 1857, decisions were announced on any day the Court was in session. Thereafter the practice was to announce decisions only on Mondays, but in 1965 the Court reverted to its earlier practice. In 1971, the Court further broke with the late-nineteenth-century tradition of "Decision Mondays." On Mondays, the Court now generally releases only orders and summary decisions and admits new attorneys to its bar. In those weeks when the justices hear oral arguments (October through April), the Court usually announces opinions on Tuesdays and Wednesdays, and then on any day of the week during the rest of the term (May, June, and, often, the first week of July). By tradition, there is no prior announcement as to when cases will be handed down.

In 1971, Burger persuaded the justices to abandon the practice of reading their full opinions, which often included most, if not all, footnotes. The practice was simply too time-consuming. The announcement of the decision in the *Passenger Cases* (*Smith v. Turner,* 1849) was typical of the Court's early practice. The Court held that states could not tax passengers arriving on ships from abroad, since that was interstate commerce subject to regulation by Congress. But more than seven hours passed by the time all nine justices had read aloud their separate opinions. The practice became even more burdensome with the growing caseload and number of opinions issued each term. Although some justices gradually departed from the practice of reading their opinions, the proliferation of opinions handed down forced Earl Warren to try to ride herd on his brethren's announcements. Even as late as Warren's last term, in 1968–1969, entire days were devoted to the delivery of opinions and admission of attorneys.[6] Burger managed to persuade the others, over the strong objections of Black, to make only brief summary announcements. Justices now announce most opinions in two to four minutes, merely stating the result in each case.

The erosion of the practice of reading the full text of opinions was only partly due to its time-consuming nature. The practice sometimes occasioned outbursts and caustic exchanges among the justices, publicly dramatizing the struggles within the Court. Once, when vigorously dissenting, McReynolds hit the bench with his fist, exclaiming, "The Constitution is gone!" and then explained why he thought so. Frankfurter tended to monopolize opinion days, just as he liked to dominate oral arguments and conference discussions. In one instance, after he had ad-libbed at length when delivering the Court's opinion, Chief Justice Stone snidely remarked, "By God, Felix, if you had put all that stuff in the opinion, never in my life would I have agreed to it."[7] On another occasion, in a relatively minor case, Frankfurter took nearly fifteen minutes to attack the majority's ruling as nonsense. His sharp criticism prompted Chief Justice Warren, who had not even written an opinion in the case, to offer a rebuttal in open Court. Warren then turned to Frankfurter and invited him to respond. Not to be outdone, the latter told the courtroom, "The Chief Justice urges me to comment on what he said, but of course I won't. I have another case."[8]

Extemporaneous exchanges are less common now, with the prevalence of summary announcements. At the conclusion of the 1984 term, though, Stevens took the opportunity to read aloud his dissent from the Court's five-to-four ruling in *Hudson v. Palmer* (1984) that prison inmates have no Fourth Amendment privacy rights against the inspection and destruction of their personal papers by prison guards. Given the large number of opinions handed down that day, he did so in order to draw attention to a case that might not otherwise have appeared "newsworthy."

Communicating Decisions to the Media

"Sir, we write the opinions, we don't explain them." That was the response of New Jersey State Supreme Court Chief

Justice Arthur Vanderbilt to a reporter's request that he explain a passage in an opinion. Members of the Supreme Court generally agree with that motto. Opinions, Brennan has observed, "must stand on their own merits without embellishment or comment from the judges who write or join them."[9] Reporters nonetheless complain about the secrecy surrounding the Court's decision making, while justices complain that their decisions are distorted by the media.

Justices do appreciate that compliance with their decisions depends on public understanding of their opinions. Sometimes they are particularly sensitive to this consideration. Chief Justice Hughes, for instance, permitted President Roosevelt to run a telephone line from the White House to the Court in order to learn immediately the Court's decision in the *Gold Clause* cases (1935). This decision was vital to the New Deal in upholding FDR's removal of the gold standard and the devaluation of the dollar. In Frankfurter's view, Hughes "established the very bad precedent of pandering to journalist impatience" by pushing for quick decisions and brief opinions.[10] When *Brown v. Board of Education* was decided, Warren insisted that "the opinions should be short, readable by the lay public, non-rhetorical, unemotional and, above all, non-accusatory."[11]

Media coverage of the Court has grown in the last thirty years. In the 1930s, less than half a dozen reporters covered the Court on a regular basis. During Hughes's chief justiceship, a "Press Office" was established in the Office of the Marshal. The single "press officer"—a former reporter—would announce those cases on the Court's conference list and those set for oral argument. Later, in the 1940s, he began distributing an edited list of the cases. Reporters had six small cubicles on the ground floor, just below the courtroom, where they received copies of opinions sent down through a pneumatic tube.[12] By the late 1950s, there were full-time reporters from the United Press International (UPI), the Associated Press

(AP), a few major newspapers, and a couple of more specialized legal periodicals, such as *U.S. Law Week*. In the last two decades, the number of reporters steadily increased to about thirty. All three major television networks, along with Cable News Network, now have regular reporters at the Court.

Despite the growing media attention, the justices remain somewhat indifferent to the problems of journalists who try to make the Court's decisions understandable for the public. Inevitably at odds with the Court's traditions, journalists have become more antagonistic and frustrated by their limited access to the justices. Shortly after coming to the Court, Burger was confronted with a petition of grievances by the corps of reporters covering the court. They presented "an outline of some problems which [they perceived to be] of mutual concern to the Court and to the press" and suggested changes "so that the public may be better informed about the Court." Not all of the demands appeared reasonable from the Court's perspective. The Court was unreceptive to demands for reasons why justices sometimes disqualify themselves from cases and for "access to the staff of the justices." The Court also rejected a proposed press privilege of having—"on a confidential basis"—advance notification and copies of the opinions to be handed down.[13]

But changes have been made, though not without opposition from some justices. On opinion days, journalists now receive copies of the headnotes—prepared by the Reporter of Decisions and summarizing the main points of a decision. Justice Black disapproved on the ground that "the press will understand the opinions better."[14] The Court also now has an expanded Public Information Office. The office serves primarily reporters (not members of the general public, whose inquiries are typically handled by the offices of the Clerk, Marshal, or Curator) and provides space for a "press room" with sixteen assigned cubicles. The Public Information Officer makes available all filings and briefs for cases on the docket, the Court's conference lists and final opinions, as well as speeches made by the justices. Reporters thus may follow cases from the time of filing to acceptance for oral argument, and then listen to oral arguments and the delivery of decisions as well as immediately read the final published opinions. Even so, the media's access to the justices remains limited. Although Stevens and a couple of other justices favor recording oral arguments before the Court, Burger remains opposed to the presence of cameras in the courtroom. No cameras are permitted in the courtroom when the Court is in session.

In light of these changes, Burger feels that "except for its decision conferences, the Supreme Court literally operates 'in a goldfish bowl.' "[15] But reporters feel differently. They do not have the kind of access to the Court that they do to Congress, the President, and the executive branch. To them the secrecy within the marble temple is disturbing, though others are less troubled by it. "It is more valuable to have a Justice on the record [in a printed opinion] saying what he or she means than hearing some Hill aide anonymously explain the actions of a senator or congressman." The *Washington Post* reporter Fred Barbash has remarked, "No other institution explains itself at such length, such frightening length."[16]

Some of the difficulties of covering the Court are inherent in the business of journalism—press deadlines, the problems of condensing complex decisions into a 180-second "news slot," and, possibly, even the training of reporters. The Court has tried to address even such practical matters. For example, in opening the session at ten in the morning rather than at noon, the Warren Court provided a couple of extra hours so as to relieve some of the pressures of reporters' deadlines. "Decision Mondays" were also abandoned in response to complaints that the "massing of opinions" on a single day made conscientious reporting virtually impossible. Reporters continue to complain that the Court hands down too many of its major decisions during the last week of the term.

The public learns through the media something about only a few of the Court's rulings each term. Usually, only the most controversial rulings by the Court are reported. Prime-time television coverage invariably remains limited and inadequate. "You have to present television news as a nice package," the CBS reporter Fred Graham has noted, and an "interesting and attractive" test often determines which cases get air time.[17]

Within a short period of time, both print and broadcast reporters must condense often complex and lengthy opinions in an understandable way for the public. Only about half of the reporters who cover the Court have law degrees. Not surprisingly, they disagree about the importance of formal legal education. "Lawyer-reporters tend to use less jargon," claims NBC's Carl Stern. "Non-lawyers fear to stray from the literal words used by the Court." By contrast, the veteran reporter Lyle Denniston has maintained, "A law degree inhibits one's ability to cover the Court." Law schools, he has insisted, "train you to have too much respect for authority" and "teach you to believe that things are done better the higher you go."[18]

Regardless of whether reporters have a legal background, the interpreting of opinions remains difficult. Some decisions are "literally impossible to decipher," the *New York Times* reporter Linda Greenhouse has noted. Of one case, *Guardians Association v. Civil Service Commission* (1983), involving a "first hired, last fired" reverse-discrimination dispute, she recalled, "All I could tell my readers is that the Court has done 'X.' I could not tell them why. One wire service hailed the decision as a great civil liberties victory, while the other wire service called the decision a great civil rights defeat."[19]

Some problems in communicating decisions are of the Court's own making. Since opinions for the Court must meet the approval of a majority of the justices, ambiguity results from the negotiations and compromises necessary to reach agreement. Hughes, for instance, met opposition to one of his

opinions because of "the insertion of the word 'reasonable' in
certain places," even though he "put in the word out of abun-
dant caution" to qualify the Court's holding. Since it was not
"worth while to have a division in the Court over its use in
the present case," he omitted the word from the opinion.[20]
Ambiguities may also be prudent. They leave problems open
for later cases, and the Court preserves its policy-making
options. For example, reporters, school boards, and citizens
celebrated or cursed *Brown v. Board of Education* for mandating integration rather than merely ending segregation. But
justices like Stanley Reed had no doubt about that "big distinction." They would never have gone along with a ruling
mandating integration. As Warren later emphasized, the justices "decided only that the practice of segregating children
in public schools solely because of their race was unconstitutional. This left other questions to be answered"—answered
in later cases, after the justices had gauged public reactions
and further deliberated among themselves.[21]

Misunderstanding also results when opinions include
extraneous matter, statements of personal philosophy, and other
forms of obiter dicta—words entirely unnecessary for the
decision of the case. These problems are exacerbated by longer,
more heavily footnoted opinions. The justices are particularly
confusing when they divide five to four and issue numerous
concurring and dissenting opinions.

Justice Stewart's opinion in *Gannett Co. v. DePasquale*
(1979) illustrates these problems. His opinion not only invited
sharp criticism from the four dissenters but also caused confusion in the press and lower courts. The case involved a
reporter's claim of a right of access, under the First Amendment and the Sixth Amendment's provision for "public trials,"
to cover a preliminary hearing on the suppression of allegedly
involuntary confessions and certain physical evidence. The trial
judge closed the hearing at the defendants' request because
adverse pretrial publicity might jeopardize a fair trial.

In holding that there is no right to attend pretrial proceedings, Stewart refused to address the First Amendment claim and rejected the claim that the Sixth Amendment embodies a right of the public to attend criminal trials. But because he stated twelve times that there is no right of access to either pretrials or trials, his opinion reached issues not raised by the case and invited confusion. Burger's concurring opinion therefore underscored that the case dealt only with pretrial hearings. Although Powell agreed with the treatment of the Sixth Amendment claim, his concurrence emphasized the importance of First Amendment interests of the press. Rehnquist continued the dialogue with his concurrence. He claimed that "the public does not have *any* Sixth Amendment right of access to such proceedings" and rebuffed the position on the First Amendment advanced by Powell, Brennan, and Marshall. This Court, Rehnquist asserted, "repeatedly has held that there is no First Amendment right of access in the public or the press to judicial or other governmental proceedings." Blackmun's opinion, for the four dissenters, contended that the Sixth Amendment establishes a public's right of access to trials and pretrial hearings.

Burger, Powell, Brennan, Marshall, and Stevens later sought publicly to clarify and defend the ruling. Their extrajudicial explanations merely exacerbated the confusion. Reporters found the decision "cloudy," "confused," "mushy," and a "muddle." As the media lawyer James Goodale summed it up, "*Gannett* Means What It Says: But Who Knows What It Says?"[22]

Implementing Rulings and Achieving Compliance

The ambiguity of *Gannett* had considerable effect on judicial proceedings. In the following year, defendants, prosecutors, witnessess, and judges sought to close proceedings in no fewer than 13 federal courts and 259 state courts. Closure was sought in 214 pretrial proceedings and in 47 trials as well as in 11 posttrial proceedings. The tradition of open judicial proceedings in criminal cases was significantly undermined. The press and public were excluded from more than half of those pretrial hearings, and judges closed 33 trials and 5 posttrial arraignments.[23]

The Court sought to address the confusion in *Richmond Newspapers, Inc. v. Virginia* (1980). In another plurality opinion, Burger held that the First and Sixth amendments run together to create a presumption of open trials. His opinion nonetheless failed to command a majority, and uncertainty continued. Two years later, in *Globe Newspapers Co. v. Superior Court* (1982), Brennan massed a majority. Over the dissents of Burger, Rehnquist, and Stevens, Brennan proclaimed a broad First Amendment right of access to criminal trials. *Globe* struck down a statute excluding the press and public from criminal trials during the testimony of rape victims who are minors. Rarely, if ever, may trials now be closed.

Gannett illustrates that conflicts among the justices and ambiguous rulings make compliance virtually impossible. At best, lawyers and lower courts may use closely divided opinions to anticipate the Court's future rulings.

When deciding major issues of public law and policy, justices must consider strategies for getting public acceptance of their rulings. When striking down the doctrine of "separate but equal" facilities in 1954 in *Brown v. Board of Education (Brown I)*, for instance, the Warren Court waited a year before issuing, in *Brown II*, its mandate for "all deliberate speed" in ending racial segregation in public education.

Resistance to the social policy announced in *Brown I* was expected. A rigid timetable for desegregation would only intensify opposition. During oral arguments on *Brown II*, devoted to the question of what kind of decree the Court should issue to enforce *Brown*, Warren confronted the hard fact of southern resistance. The attorney for South Carolina, S. Emory

Rogers, pressed for an open-ended decree—one that would not specify when and how desegregation should take place. He boldly proclaimed;

Mr. Chief Justice, to say we will conform depends on the decree handed down. I am frank to tell you, right now [in] our district I do not think that we will send—[that] the white people of the district will send their children to the Negro schools. It would be unfair to tell the Court that we are going to do that. I do not think it is. But I do think that something can be worked out. We hope so.

"It is not a question of attitude," Warren shot back, "it is a question of conforming to the decree." Their heated exchange continued as follows:

CHIEF JUSTICE WARREN: But you are not willing to say here that there would be an honest attempt to conform to this decree, if we did leave it to the district court [to implement]?

MR. ROGERS: No, I am not. Let us get the word "honest" out of there.

CHIEF JUSTICE WARREN: No, leave it in.

MR. ROGERS: No, because I would have to tell you that right now we would not conform—we would not send our white children to the Negro schools.[24]

The exchange reinforced Warren's view "that reasonable attempts to start the integration process is [sic] all the court can expect in view of the scope of the problem, and that an order to immediately admit all negroes in white schools would be an absurdity because impossible to obey in many areas. Thus, while total immediate integration might be a reasonable order for Kansas, it would be unreasonable for Virginia, and the district judge might decide that a grade a year or three grades a year is reasonable compliance in Virginia."[25] Six law clerks were assigned to prepare a segregation research report. They summarized available studies, discussed how school districts in different regions could be desegregated, and projected the effects and reactions to various desegregation plans.

The Court's problem, as one of Reed's law clerks put it, was to frame a decree "so as to allow such divergent results without making it so broad that evasion is encouraged."[26] The clerks agreed that there should be a simple decree but disagreed on whether there should be guidelines for its implementation. One clerk opposed any guidelines. The others thought that their absence "smacks of indecisiveness, and gives the extremists more time to operate." The problem was how precise a guideline should be established. What would constitute "good faith" compliance? "Although we think a 12-year gradual desegregation plan permissible," they confessed, "we are not certain that the opinion should explicitly sanction it."[27]

At conference, Warren repeated these concerns. Black and Minton thought that a simple degree, without an opinion, was enough. As Black explained, "the less we say the better off we are." The others disagreed. A short, simple opinion seemed advisable for reaffirming *Brown I* and providing guidance for dealing with the inevitable problems of compliance. Harlan wanted *Brown II* expressly to recognize that school desegregation was a local problem to be solved by local authorities. The others also insisted on making clear that school boards and lower courts had flexibility in ending segregation. In Burton's view, "neither this Court nor district courts should act as a school board or formulate the program" for desegregation.

Agreement emerged that the Court should issue a short opinion-decree. In a memorandum, Warren summarized the main points of agreement. The opinion should simply state that *Brown I* held radically segregated public schools to be unconstitutional. *Brown II* should acknowledge that the ruling creates various administrative problems, but emphasize that "local school authorities have the primary responsibility for assessing and solving these problems; [and] the courts will have to consider these problems in determining whether the efforts of local school authorities" are in good-faith compliance. The cases, he concluded, should be remanded to the lower courts "for such proceedings and decree necessary and proper to carry out this Court's decision." The justices agreed, and along these lines Warren drafted the Court's short opinion-decree.[28]

The phrase "all deliberate speed" was borrowed from Holmes's opinion in *Virginia v. West Virginia* (1911), a case dealing with how much of the state's public debt, and when, Virginia ought to receive at the time West Virginia broke off and became a state. It was inserted in the final opinion at the suggestion of Frankfurter. Forced integration might lead to a lowering of educational standards. Immediate, court-ordered desegregation, Frankfurter warned, "would make a mockery of the Constitutional adjudication designed to vindicate a claim to equal treatment to achieve 'integrated' but lower educational standards." The Court, he insisted, "does its duty if it gets effectively under way the righting of a wrong. When the wrong is deeply rooted state policy the court does its duty if it decrees measures that reverse the direction of the unconstitutional policy so as to uproot it 'with all deliberate speed.' "[29] As much an apology for not setting precise guidelines as a recognition of the limitations of judicial power, the phrase symbolized the Court's bold moral appeal to the country.

Ten years later, after school closings, massive resistance, and continuing litigation, Black complained, "There has been entirely too much deliberation and not enough speed" in complying with *Brown*. "The time for mere 'deliberate speed' has run out."[30] *Brown*'s moral appeal amounted to little more than an invitation for delay. At the beginning of the school year in 1964, President Johnson was apprised of the piecemeal progress and continuing resistance:

Arkansas: Desegregation expanded in schools in Little Rock and Fort Smith. About 870 Negroes reported in previously white schools, compared to 390 last year. Twenty-one districts desegregated, compared to 13 last year.

Florida: Four counties integrated, bringing to 21 the number admitting Negroes (State has 67 counties). No trouble. Estimated 8,000 Negroes attending all-white schools.

Mississippi: Biloxi—Seventeen Negro children attended integrated classes in four previously all-white elementary schools, after 10 years of angry resistance. *Canton*—Nineteen Negro students attempted to enroll in the all-white high school but left quietly when rejected by school officials. Civil rights workers said earlier they would not oppose school officials if the youngsters were turned away, but would follow with court action later.

Virginia: Virginia will have 25 newly-desegregated districts this year—including Prince Edward County [which had previously closed rather than desegregate its schools]—making 80 of 128 in the State with some integration. About 6,000 Negroes are attending once-white schools. [31]

With no federal leadership, implementation of *Brown* was deliberately slow and uneven. Ruby Martin, an attorney for the U.S. Commission on Civil Rights in the early 1960s, has recalled that "the work of the lawyers from 1954 to 1964 resulted in two percent of the Negro kids in the Southern states attending schools with white students."[32] The Department of Justice had little role in ending school segregation before the passage of the Civil Rights Act of 1964. The department had participated in a few school desegregation cases but ordinarily only by filing *amici* briefs. The Civil Rights Division within the department was created after Congress passed the Civil Rights Act of 1957, which expanded federal jurisdiction over voting rights and which was the first such legislation in eighty-seven years. But the division had virtually no authority, expertise, or resources to enforce *Brown* until the passage of the 1964 act. The litigation strategy during the Kennedy administration sought to secure voting rights for blacks and thereby "encourage the inevitable integration but never at the cost of disturbing the social equilibrium."[33]

Even after the Department of Justice assumed a role in enforcing school desegregation, it initially gave little attention to areas outside of the South or to problems other than ending de jure segregation—segregation enforced by laws prohibiting the integration of public schools. The department paid almost no attention to de facto segregation, due to socioeconomic conditions such as housing patterns, in the North and the West. President Johnson's special assistant Joseph Califano was advised by the attorney general, "There are no current federal programs directly related to the problem of *de facto* school segregation. Title VI of the Civil Rights Act is of doubtful applicability." Attorney General Nicholas de B. Katzenbach admitted, "[O]ne of our difficulties is that we don't know enough about *de facto* segregation."[34] The Department of Health, Education, and Welfare (HEW) was subsequently given responsibility for the federal government's role in ending segregated schools. It had authority to issue guidelines and review plans for integration. More important, HEW had the power to cut off federal funding if school districts refused to submit to or comply with desegregation plans.

By the mid-1960s, the Departments of Justice and HEW had assumed leadership in implementing *Brown*. But it took time to build records and evidence of segregation in northern and western school districts and to challenge local authorities in the courts. Not until the summer of 1968 did the outgoing Johnson admininstration initiate the first school desegregation cases in the North and the West and try to achieve the national coverage that the Court envisioned in *Brown*.[35]

In 1969, Black impatiently observed "there is no longer the slightest excuse, reason, or justification for further postponement of the time when every public school system in the United States will be a unitary one."[36] In *Alexander v. Holmes County Board of Education* (1969), the Burger Court agreed on a brief per curiam opinion holding that the Fifth Circuit Court of Appeals should deny further requests for delay from southern school districts. In its opinion, the Court observed that the "standard allowing 'all deliberate speed' for desegregation is no longer constitutionally permissible." *Alexander* sent a message to the Nixon administration that "the obligation of every school district is to terminate dual school systems at once and to operate now and hereafter only unitary schools."[37]

The message in *Alexander*, like that in *Brown*, was still ambiguous. Justice Marshall could not win unanimity on finally setting a "cut-off" date for school desegregation. Black threatened a dissenting opinion noting that "all deliberate speed," as Frankfurter understood when suggesting the Holmesian phrase, connotes delay, not speed. Black concluded that the Court's emphasis on "all deliberate speed" had been a "self-inflicted wound." "The duty of this Court and of the others," he implored, "is too simple to require perpetual litigation and deliberation. That duty is to extirpate all racial discrimination from our system of public schools NOW." On the Court less than four months, Burger vigorously opposed setting any final cut-off date for desegregation. Brennan sought consensus, but the justices could not agree on a more precise order than that of proceeding with desegregation plans "here and now." *Alexander*, White lamented in an unpublished memo, "neither says the order is to be entered now, within six months or even with deliberate speed." "Hugo," he added, "is convinced that a mistake was made in 1954–1955 with respect to the deliberate speed formula. I am beginning to understand how mistakes like that happen. Nevertheless, I join, expecting the Court of Appeals to make sure that the shortcomings of this order never come to light."[38]

The shortcomings of *Alexander* came to light when the court of appeals delayed yet again. The Court, in *Carter v. West Feliciana Parish School Board* (1970), scolded about the continued failure to proceed with desegregation. This time, Burger, Rehnquist, and Stewart voiced their disagreement and insistence on maintaining a flexible approach to implementation. The fifth circuit, they said, "is far more familiar than we with the various situations of these several school districts, some large, some small, some rural and some metropolitan, and has exhibited responsibility and fidelity to the objectives of our holdings in school desegregation cases."

Twenty years after *Brown*, some schools remained segregated. David Mathews, secretary of the Department of Health, Education, and Welfare, reported to President Ford the results of a survey of half of the nation's primary and secondary public schools, enrolling 91 percent of all students: 42 percent had an "appreciable percentage" of minority students, 16 percent had undertaken desegregation plans, while 26 percent had not, and 7 percent of the school districts remained racially segregated.[39]

For over three decades, problems of implementing and achieving compliance with *Brown* persisted. Litigation by civil rights groups forced change, but it was piecemeal, costly, and modest. The judiciary alone could not achieve desegregation. Evasion and resistance were encouraged by the reluctance of presidents and Congress to enforce the mandate. Refusing publicly to endorse *Brown*, Eisenhower would not take steps to enforce the decision until violence erupted in Little Rock, Arkansas. He then did so "*not* to enforce integration but to prevent opposition by violence to orders of a court."[40] Later, the Kennedy and Johnson administrations lacked congressional authorization and resources to take major initiatives in enforcing school desegregation. Not until 1964, when Congress passed the Civil Rights Act, did the executive branch have such authorization.

Enforcement and implementation required the cooperation and coordination of all three branches. Little progress could be made, as Assistant Attorney General Pollack has explained, "where historically there had been slavery and a long tradition of discrimination [until] all three branches of the federal government [could] be lined up in support of a movement forward or a requirement for change."[41] The elec-

tion of Nixon in 1968 then brought changes both in the policies of the executive branch and in the composition of the
Court. The simplicity and flexibility of *Brown,* moreover,
invited evasion. It produced a continuing struggle over measures, such as gerrymandering school district lines and busing
in the 1970s and 1980s, because the mandate itself had evolved
from one of ending segregation to one of securing integration
in public schools.

"By itself," the political scientist Robert Dahl observed,
"the Court is almost powerless to affect the course of national
policy."[42] *Brown* dramatically altered the course of American
life, but it also reflected the justices' awareness that their
decisions are not self-executing. The rulings from *Brown* to
Alexander were unanimous but ambiguous. The ambiguity in
the desegregation rulings, unlike that in cases like *Gannett,*
was the price of achieving unanimity. Unanimity appeared
necessary if the Court was to preserve its institutional prestige while pursuing revolutionary change in social policy. Justices sacrificed their own policy preferences for more precise
guidelines, while the Court tolerated lengthy delays in recognition of the costs of open defiance and the pressures of
public opinion.

PUBLIC OPINION

Public opinion serves to curb the Court when it threatens
to go too far or too fast in its rulings. The Court has usually
been in step with major political movements, except during
transitional periods or critical elections.[43] It would nevertheless be wrong to conclude, along with Peter Finley Dunne's
fictional Mr. Dooley, that "th' supreme court follows th' ilic-
tion returns."[44] To be sure, the battle over FDR's "Court-
packing" plan and the Court's "switch-in-time-that-saved-nine"
in 1937 gives that impression. Public opinion supported the
New Deal, but turned against FDR after his landslide reelection in 1936 when he proposed to "pack the Court" by

increasing its size from nine to fifteen. In a series of five-to-four and six-to-three decisions in 1935–1936, the Court had struck down virtually every important measure of FDR's New Deal program. But in the spring of 1937, while the Senate Judiciary Committee considered FDR's proposal, the Court abruptly handed down three five-to-four rulings upholding major pieces of New Deal legislation. Shortly afterward, FDR's close personal friend and soon-to-be nominee for the Court, Felix Frankfurter, wrote Justice Stone confessing that he was "not wholly happy in thinking that Mr. Dooley should, in the course of history turn out to have been one of the most distinguished legal philosophers."[45] Frankfurter, of course, knew that justices do not simply follow the election returns. The influence of public opinion is more subtle and complex.

Life in the marble temple is not immune from shifts in public opinion. But justices deny being directly influenced by public opinion. The Court's prestige rests on preserving the public's view that justices base their decisions on interpretations of the law, rather than on their personal policy preferences. Yet, complete indifference to public opinion would be the height of judicial arrogance. Even one so devoted to the law as Frankfurter was not above appealing to the forces of public opinion. When the Warren Court debated the landmark reapportionment case, Frankfurter asked Stewart—who had the pivotal vote—to consider that *Baker v. Carr* could

bring the Court in conflict with political forces and exacerbate political feeling widely throughout the Nation on a larger scale, though not so pathologically, as the Segregation cases have stirred. The latter . . . resulted in merely regional feeling against the Court, with the feeling of most of the country strongly in sympathy with the Court. But if one is right about the widely scattered assailable apportionment disparities, . . . clash and tension between Court and country and politicians will assert themselves within a far wider area than the Segregation cases have aroused.

Baker v. Carr, Frankfurter feared, would turn the whole country against the Court. But, after there was a clear majority for the overturning of laws that denied equal voting rights, Douglas pushed for an early announcement of the decision with the comment "This is an election year."[46]

Most of the Court's decisions do not attract widespread public attention. Most people find it remote and confusing or identify only with its institutional symbols. The public perceives the Court as a temple of law rather than of politics—impartial and removed from the pressures of special, partisan interests.[47] Issues like school desegregation, school prayer, and abortion focus public attention and may mobilize public support or opposition for the Court. But those issues are also the most divisive in the country. Public opinion therefore tends to be diffuse and indirectly expressed by public officials and elected representatives.

Constituents and Publics

Less concerned about public opinion than are elected public officials, justices are sensitive to the attitudes of the Court's immediate constituents: the solicitor general, the attorney general, and the Department of Justice, counsel for federal agencies, states' attorneys general, and the legal profession. Their responses to the Court's rulings shape public understanding and determine the extent of compliance.

The solicitor general, attorney general, and agency counsel interpret the Court's decisions and advise the White House and agencies on compliance. Justices may find a favorable or unfavorable reception from the executive branch. Immediately after *Alexander*, for instance, Nixon directed his staff to begin work on how to combat the Court's implicit sanctioning of busing and on eventual approval of court-ordered busing in *Swann v. Charlotte-Mecklenburg Board of Education* (1971). The solicitor general decides which and what kinds of cases to take to the Court. In selecting cases, he tries to offer the Court (or a majority) opportunities for pursuing their policy goals and those of the President.

The attorney general, cabinet heads, and agency counsel

may likewise extend or thwart the Court's policies. They do so through their advisory opinions, litigation strategies, and development of agency policy and programs. During the Ford administration and the continuing controversy over busing, for instance, the Department of Justice tried to achieve retrenchment from court-ordered busing by its selection of cases and relitigation of busing issues. At the same time, White House counsel and HEW sought ways to avoid busing and to "depoliticize" the controversy.[48]

The reactions of the fifty state attorneys general are no less important. They have a pivotal role in advising governors, mayors, police chiefs, and others in their states. Their responses tend to reflect state and local reactions to the Court's rulings. Regional differences were evident in responses to the 1962 and 1963 school prayer decisions. The Court struck down a state-composed prayer in *Engel v. Vitale* (1962) and the reciting of the Lord's Prayer in public schools in *Abington School District v. Schempp* (1963). Long-standing practices of school prayer in the East and the South were not to be easily relinquished. Voluntary school prayer, silent meditation, and "the objective study of the Bible and of religion" were viewed as still permissible. Where school prayer received support in state constitutions or legislation, state and local officials denied the legitimacy of the Court's decrees and refused to obey.

Local and regional opposition to rulings like those on school desegregation and prayer does not emerge in a vacuum. Opposition tends to reflect broader national political debates. Southern resistance to *Brown* was encouraged in 1957 by 101 U.S. senators and representatives who signed the "Southern Manifesto," challenging the authority of the Court and declaring,

We pledge ourselves to use all lawful means to bring about a reversal of this decision [*Brown v. Board of Education*] which is contrary to the Constitution and to prevent the use of force in its implementation.

In this trying period, as we seek to right this wrong, we appeal to our people not to be provoked by the agitators and trouble makers invading our states and to scrupulously refrain from disorder and lawlessness.[49]

Congressional and presidential responses to the school prayer rulings similarly have tended to legitimize opposition to the Court's decisions. Within three days after *Engel,* more than fifty proposed constitutional amendments to override or limit the decision were introduced in Congress. Two decades later, the number had swelled into the hundreds. Both the House of Representatives and the Senate at various times voted in favor of constitutional amendments but failed to achieve their enactment. Congress did pass appropriations bills for the Department of Education specifying that no funds "shall be used to prevent the implementation of programs of voluntary prayer and meditation in the public schools." In 1982, Reagan asked Congress to pass the following constitutional amendment:

Nothing in this Constitution shall be construed to prohibit individual or group prayer in public schools or other public institutions. No person shall be required by the United States or by any State to participate in prayer.[50]

Over twenty years after *Engel,* compliance remained uneven. Twenty-two states had laws calling for silent or voluntary prayers at the beginning of the school day in public schools. Arizona, Connecticut, and Rhode Island permitted classes to begin with a moment of silent meditation. But, in *Wallace v. Jaffree* (1985), the Court reaffirmed its earlier rulings. Over the dissent of Burger, White, and Rehnquist, the Court struck down an Alabama law requiring each school day to begin with a moment of silent prayer or meditation. The majority held that states may not require silent prayer, though meditation may be allowed so long as states do not expressly try to promote religion in the classroom. *Wallace v. Jaffree* intensified opposition and congressional and presidential attempts to thwart, if not reverse, the Court's rulings on school prayer.

When the Court attempts to forge major changes, its rulings galvanize special-interest groups. *Brown* sent a signal to groups like the NAACP and the ACLU to use the judicial process to achieve what they could not through the political process. The school prayer and abortion decisions, likewise, fragmented the Court's public. Polarized by the Court's decisions and often divided over its authority to decide major issues of public policy, special-interest groups fuel political struggles at all levels of government.

The justices do consider the anticipated reactions of the immediate audience of the Court's rulings. One example is that of Chief Justice Warren in *Miranda v. Arizona* (1966), which held that police must read suspects their Fifth and Sixth Amendment rights to remain silent and to consult and have an attorney present during police questioning.

When working on *Miranda,* Warren recalled a controversy involving a law professor's seminar for Minneapolis-area police and Minnesota's state attorney general (and later senator and Vice-President) Walter Mondale. At the seminar, police were told how to adhere to the Court's decisions and still maintain past interrogation practices. "For instance, you're supposed to arraign a prisoner before a magistrate without unreasonable delay," the law professor advised. "But if the magistrate goes hunting for the weekend on a Friday afternoon at 3:00 p.m., you can arrange to arrest your suspect at 3:30. That way you've got the whole weekend." Mondale took the law professor to task. At a news conference, he responded, "Some persons claim the Supreme Court has gone too far. Others claim to know how constitutional protections may be avoided by tricky indirection. Both viewpoints are wrong— this [seminar] was called to assist us in better fulfilling our sworn duty to uphold the Constitution. It was not called to second guess the Supreme Court." Warren knew full well that not all state attorneys general and police supported the Court's rulings on criminal procedure. He therefore strove to outline in *Miranda* a code for police procedures governing the interrogation of criminal suspects that police could not easily evade. There was considerable antagonism toward the *Miranda* warnings, but they became widely accepted in police practice.[51]

Policy considerations, such as the cost of compliance, may also persuade the justices to limit the scope and application of their decisions. In another controversial decision, *Mapp v. Ohio* (1961), the Warren Court reversed an earlier holding in *Wolf v. Colorado* (1949). In *Wolf*, the Court had held that the Fourth Amendment's prohibition against "unreasonable searches and seizures" applied to the states and the national government. But the Court refused also to extend to the states the Fourth Amendment's exclusionary rule, forbidding the use at trial of evidence obtained in violation of requirements for a proper search and seizure. *Mapp* reversed *Wolf* by holding that the exclusionary rule applies in state as well as in federal courts. The decision raised the possibility that all convictions secured in state courts before 1961 on the basis of illegally obtained evidence would be challenged and new trials demanded.

The Court's decisions have traditionally applied retroactively, permitting individuals to have retrials. In *Linkletter v. Walker* (1965), however, the Court refused to apply *Mapp* retroactively. Justice Clark reasoned that the exclusionary rule was designed to deter police misconduct and that retrials "would tax the administration of justice to the utmost." The Burger Court subsequently developed what became known as its "ambulatory-retroactively doctrine" in other areas of criminal law as well. "That doctrine," Harlan explained, "was the product of the Court's disquietude with the impacts of its fast-moving pace in constitutional innovation in the criminal field." But he also objected that the doctrine merely rationalizes the Court's freedom "to act, in effect, like a legislature, making its new constitutional rules wholly or partially retroactive or only prospective as it deems wise."[52]

The Court has no direct means of mobilizing support for its rulings. Justices may appeal, as Frankfurter unsuccessfully did during the Little Rock school desegregation crisis in *Cooper v. Aaron,* to the legal profession for understanding and assistance. He felt compelled to do so because many of his former students at Harvard Law School were leading members of the southern bar and because the ex-justice (and former governor of South Carolina) James Byrnes had called on the country to curb the Court. Byrnes had published an attack on *Brown* and an article written by one of Frankfurter's favorite former law clerks, Alexander Bickel. As a clerk, Bickel had prepared a lengthy research report on school desegregation when the Court first considered *Brown.* Later, when back at Harvard, Bickel revised and published it in the *Harvard Law Review.* Given Byrnes's attack, Frankfurter personally felt the need to lecture southern lawyers on the legitimacy of the Court's ruling in *Brown.*[53]

Justices usually maintain close relationships with members of the legal profession, which provides the justices with a natural constituency. A former president of the American Bar Association (ABA), Lewis Powell has urged bar associations to lobby for congressional legislation to limit the availability of criminal appeals.[54] Burger has repeatedly appealed to the ABA to promote and lobby Congress for improvements in the administration of justice. Mobilizing the ABA depends on the issue and on ideological compatibility. Whereas Burger enjoys the support of most of the leadership of the ABA, his predecessor resigned as a member and refused to attend any meetings of the association. Warren did so because the ABA castigated the Court for its desegregation and "pro-Red" rulings. The ABA contributed to the hysteria of the McCarthy era and lent credibility to campaigns, like that of the John

Birch Society, to "Impeach Earl Warren." The ABA does not represent the views of all members or of the legal profession as a whole, but its resources and prestige are useful political weapons for or against the Court.

The Court is an instrument of political power, but the justices remain dependent on the attitudes and actions of their immediate constituents, elected officials, and the dynamics of pressure-group politics and public opinion. Implementation and compliance largely depend on lower courts, Congress, and the President.

COMPETITION AND COMPLIANCE IN LOWER COURTS

The Court's "bare bones" opinion-decree in *Brown II* maximized flexibility. "Local passions aroused by [*Brown I*] would thereby be absorbed or tempered," Frankfurter insisted. But, he pointed out, "local conflicts would be left on the doorsteps of local judges." The Court left the job of achieving compliance to the lower courts. Unloading "responsibility upon lower courts most subject to community pressures without any guidelines for them except our decision of unconstitutionality," Frankfurter prophetically observed, "would result in drawn-out, indefinite delay without even colorable compliance."[55]

Lower-court judges bore the social and psychological burdens of opposition to *Brown.* For many southern judges, social ostracism became a fact of life. As the political scientist Jack Peltason describes in his book *Fifty-eight Lonely Men: Southern Federal Judges and School Desegregation,*

The District judge is very much a part of the life of the South. He must eventually leave his chambers and when he does he attends a Rotary lunch or stops at the club to drink with men outraged by what they consider "judicial tyranny." A judge who makes rulings adverse to segregation is not likely to be honored by testimonial dinners, or to read flattering editorials in the local press, or to partake in the fellowship at the club.

There were also less gentle and subtle pressures on judges.
They were forced "to discontinue the public listing of their
telephone number to avoid anonymous and obscene telephone calls made round the clock. Their mail [was] loaded
with threatening letters. Some [were] forced to seek police
protection for themselves and their families."[56] Others, like
Judge J. Skelly Wright in Louisiana, were denied elevation
from district to circuit courts. Their rulings angered southern
senators, who invoked "senatorial courtesy" to veto their
appointments.

When trial judges decide wide-ranging disputes over
desegregation or the environment, community pressures may
confront them with hard choices. The more responsive to local
community values judges are the more threatened their legitimacy as dispassionate enforcers of national law. The plight of
the federal district court judge Miles Lord in the controversy
over Reserve Mining Company is extreme but illustrative. Lord
went to war with his community over the daily dumping of
67,000 tons of taconite (a low-grade iron ore) into Lake Superior. Lord was immersed in the problems of assessing the car-
cinogenic risk entailed by the mining of taconite. He became
outraged by the reluctance of local political officials to inter-
vene. They feared economic loss to the community if Reserve
Mining closed. During the trial, he likened himself to Moses
in the wilderness and expressed his frustration:

> Now it's very difficult to be a lone and lonesome federal judge
> at a time like this, because it affects the lives of many people. Many
> people who are working versus many people who may be dying. . . .
> I personally question the wisdom, and I make this observation
> to you, of even having a Minnesota judge sit on this [case], and
> particularly question the wisdom of having a local judge . . . sit on
> such a case, because the pressures are just too much.[57]

Impatient with the diversionary tactics of attorneys for Reserve
Mining, Lord called and examined his own expert witnesses.

He offered his own testimony and charged that witnesses for Reserve Mining could not be trusted. Lord was eventually removed from the case. The Eighth Circuit Court of Appeals observed, "Judge Lord seems to have shed the robe of a judge and to have assumed the mantle of the advocate. The court thus becomes lawyer, witness and judge in the same proceeding and abandons the great virtue of a fair and conscientious judge—impartiality."[58]

Circuit court of appeals judges are, to an extent, geographically removed from local community pressure. Still, the decentralized structure of the federal judiciary encourages them to apply the Court's decisions in ways that accommodate regional and local values. Federal appellate judges fashion a law of the circuit. Among the circuits, the political scientist J. Woodford Howard has found, "[i]nformal norms are national in scope but regionally enforced."[59] Unlike southern circuit judges after *Brown,* for instance, northern appellate court judges ordered massive busing and redistricting of school lines in order to achieve integration. Appellate court judges thus regionalize public law and policy.

Compliance with the Court's decisions by lower courts is invariably uneven. They may extend or limit decisions in anticipation of later rulings by the high court. Following the watershed ruling on privacy in *Griswold v. Connecticut* (1965), lower courts interpreted the newfound constitutional right of privacy as striking down a wide range of laws, from those limiting the length of male employees' and students' hair, to ones forbidding certain sexual acts between consenting adults and the use of marijuana, to ones requiring psychological tests of applicants for government jobs, and to ones governing access to financial and medical records. The Court reversed or would not approve the extension of the right of privacy in many of these areas.

A simple model of compliance is not very useful: decisions handed down by the Court are not necessarily or readily applied by lower courts. Ambiguity and plurality or five-to-four decisions invite lower courts to pursue their own policy goals. Crucial language in an opinion may be treated like dicta. Differences between the facts on which the Court ruled and the circumstances of a case at hand may be emphasized so as to distinguish or reach a result opposite to the Court's decision. Lower courts, for example, interpreted *Abington School District v. Schempp*, which struck down compulsory reciting of the Lord's Prayer in public schools, as permitting voluntary and nondenominational prayer in public schools. Likewise, Texas courts refused to extend the ruling in *Norris v. Alabama* (1935), forbidding racial discrimination against blacks in jury selection. They did not forbid the exclusion of Mexicans from juries until *Hernandez v. Texas* (1954) directly ordered them to do so. Lower courts may thus effectively delay implementation and compliance.

Open defiance is infrequent but not unprecedented. In *Jaffree v. Board of School Commissioners* (1983), a federal district court judge in Alabama directly challenged the legitimacy of the Court. Here, the judge upheld the daily recitation of the Lord's Prayer in public schools and expressly rejected the Court's twenty-year-old rulings in *Engel* and *Abington* that the First Amendment's ban on the establishment of church and state applies to the states and that compulsory school prayer violates the establishment clause. A majority of the Court rebuffed the lower court when it decided an appeal of the ruling and struck down the "moment of silence" law in *Wallace v. Jaffree* (1985).

Federal and state judges frequently express their disagreements and criticisms of the Court at judicial conferences, at bar association meetings, and in legal publications and correspondence. The Conference of State Chief Justices in 1958 went so far as to pass a resolution condemning the Warren Court for its erosion of federalism and its tendency "to adopt the role of policymaker without proper judicial restraint."[60] The Warren Court's rulings in cases like *Gideon*, *Mapp*, and *Miranda* revolutionized criminal procedure by holding that the rights of the accused guaranteed in the Bill of Rights apply in state no less than in federal courts. The Warren Court thus drew intense criticism from state judges. That criticism is exemplified by the reaction to *Katz v. United States* (1967). *Katz* held that the Fourth Amendment "protects people, not places" and that police must obtain a search warrant before tapping telephone lines, even those of a public telephone booth. Writing to Harlan, one of the most conservative members of the Court at the time, Georgia State Supreme Court Chief Justice William Duckworth castigated the ruling and expressed the views of many critics of the Warren Court:

By such nearsighted decisions you victimize the innocent public and force them to endure crime, solely because some individual officer personally violated rights of the criminal. . . . If your court would recognize that State courts are capable of honestly and intelligently enforcing criminal laws—and by experience know more than most of you about how to do it within the Constitution, the flood-tide of crime would abate. No honest judge can or will deny that the Constitution is the Supreme Law. But Justices of the Supreme Court, although given the final word, are not superior in qualification, dedication and honor in deciding cases.[61]

Surprised by the frankness of the criticism, Harlan responded that "the great debates that have been taking place, both within and without the judiciary [are] the product of the extraordinary era in which we are living and not of any change in the basic point of view of the federal judiciary."[62]

Opposition and defiance by federal and state judges reflect their own policy preferences and the political currents of the time. When the Warren Court handed down *Mapp v. Ohio* (1961), the California State attorney general (and later state supreme court justice) Stanley Mosk told Justice Douglas, "Thank the good Lord for *Mapp v. Ohio*." He explained that a bare majority of the California State Supreme Court had just interpreted their state constitution to incorporate the exclusionary rule. Their decision was attacked by the press and local politicans. Mosk explained that, "with the system of elective judges they have in California, pressure on the trial courts was very, very great not to apply [the decision] or to find there were more exceptions to it, or in others, try to get around it." *Mapp*, Douglas reported to his brethren, took "the pressure off the local judges to create exceptions and to follow the exclusionary rule and all its ramifications."[63]

Whether state judges oppose or comply with the Court's leadership depends on their political views and the direction of the Court's policy-making. During the Warren Court revolutions in school desegregation, criminal procedure, and reapportionment, state judges like Georgia's Chief Justice Duckworth complained about the nationalization of public law and policy. The autonomy of state judges appeared eroded by the Warren Court's rulings that they respect and apply basic guarantees of the Bill of Rights. *Miranda*'s safeguards against coerced confessions, for example, established a minimal-threshold requirement that all fifty states had to respect. State courts could guarantee more procedural safeguards than the Court, but they could not grant fewer.

In the 1970s and 1980s, the direction of the Court's policy-making gradually changed reflecting the views of Burger and other appointees of Nixon and Reagan. Although not outright reversing Warren Court rulings, the Burger Court refused further extensions and achieved retrenchment in some areas. More-liberal state supreme courts accordingly refused to follow rulings of the Burger Court. "Why should we always be the tail being wagged by the Federal dog?" asked New Hampshire State Supreme Court Justice Charles Douglas and other state judges. "Liberal state courts have taken the doctrines of federalism and states' rights, heretofore associated with [conservatives] like George C. Wallace," California's Justice Stanley Mosk has explained, "and adapted them to give citizens more rights under their state constitutions rather than to oppress them." Such developments in state constitutional law, in the view of Brennan, are a sign of "the strength of our federal system." By contrast, Burger, Rehnquist, Powell, O'Connor, and White have sought to bring state courts into line by reversing decisions vindicating broader constitutional rights than they approved.[64]

CONGRESSIONAL ACTION AND REACTION

Legislators frequently "have gone after the Supreme Court because it doesn't cost anything," Attorney General Katzenbach once observed.[65] On the floor of the Senate or the House of Representatives, rhetoric is cheaper than building coalitions. The views of constituents also constrain congressional action. As a senator from Texas in the 1950s, Lyndon Johnson expressed his reservations about the wisdom of *Brown v. Board of Education*. But, when responding to his constituents, LBJ was more antagonistic and responsive to their views. "Unfortunately," he wrote to one of them, "the edict was handed down by men many miles removed from our part of the country and in most cases men who had no first-hand knowledge of conditions in the South and Southwest." He assured another, "[T]he people of Texas can depend on me to stand firmly against forced integration."[66]

Major confrontations between Congress and the Court have occurred a number of times. With the election of Thomas Jefferson in 1800, Republicans gained control of Congress. The defeated President John Adams and the outgoing Federalists in Congress passed the Judiciary Act of 1801, creating new circuit court judgeships and stipulating that when the next vacancy on the Court occurred it should go unfilled. That attempt to maintain influence in the judiciary was quickly countered. In 1802, the Republican Congress repealed the act of 1801, abolishing the judgeships and returning the num-

ber of justices to six. Congress also postponed the Court's next
term in order to preclude it from immediately hearing a challenge, in *Stuart v. Laird* (1803), to its repealing legislation.
When the Court decided *Stuart*, it upheld Congress's power
to repeal the Judiciary Act of 1801. The Jeffersonian Republicans then impeached Justice Samuel Chase for expounding
Federalist doctrine. Though the Senate acquitted him, it would
not confirm nominees for federal judgeships unless they were
Republicans.

The Marshall Court approved the expansion of national
governmental power, but in response Congress in the 1820s
and 1830s threatened to remove the Court's jurisdiction over
disputes involving states' rights. After the Civil War, Congress succeeded in repealing the Court's jurisdiction over certain denials of writs of habeas corpus—orders commanding
that a prisoner be brought before a judge and that cause be
shown for his imprisonment. In *Ex parte McCardle* (1869),
the Court upheld the repeal of its jurisdiction and thus avoided
deciding a controversial case attacking the constitutionality of
Reconstruction legislation.

At the turn of the century, Progressives in Congress
unsuccessfully sought to pressure the Court—dominated at
the time by advocates of laissez-faire social and economic policy. They proposed requiring a two-thirds vote by the justices
when striking down federal statutes, and permitting Congress
to overrule the Court's decisions by a two-thirds majority. The
confrontation escalated with the Court's invalidation of the
early New Deal program in the 1930s. Although Congress
refused to go along with FDR's Court-packing plan, it passed
legislation allowing justices to retire, after ten years of service
at age seventy, with full rather than half salary. Congress thus
made retirement more financially attractive and gave FDR
opportunities to appoint justices who shared his political philosophy. Later, the Warren Court faced almost persistent
attempts to curb its jurisdiction and reverse specific deci-

sions. And the Burger Court's rulings on abortion continue to generate proposals to curb the Court's jurisdiction and overturn or modify its decisions.

Congress may put pressure on the Court in a number of ways. The Senate may try to influence judicial appointments and may impeach justices. More often, Congress uses institutional and jurisdictional changes as weapons against the Court.

Congress has tried to pressure the Court when setting its terms and size and when authorizing appropriations for salaries, law clerks, secretaries, and office technology. Only once, in 1802 when repealing the Judiciary Act of 1801 and abolishing a session for a year, did Congress actually set the Court's term in order to delay and influence a particular decision.

The size of the Court is not preordained, and changes generally reflect attempts to control the Court. The Jeffersonian Republicans' quick repeal of the act passed by the Federalists in 1801, reducing the number of justices, was the first of several attempts to influence the Court. Presidents James Madison, James Monroe, and John Quincy Adams all claimed that the country's geographical expansion warranted enlarging the size of the Court. But Congress refused to do so until the last day of Andrew Jackson's term, in 1837. During the Civil War, the number of justices increased to ten, ostensibly because of the creation of a tenth circuit in the West. This gave Abraham Lincoln his fourth appointment and a chance to secure a pro-Union majority on the bench. Antagonism toward President Andrew Johnson's Reconstruction policies led to a reduction from ten to seven justices. After General Ulysses S. Grant was elected President, Congress again authorized nine justices—the number that has prevailed. In the nineteenth century, at least, Congress rather successfully denied Presidents additional appointments in order to preserve the Court's policies and increased the number of justices so as to change the ideological composition of the Court.

Although Article III of the Constitution forbids reducing

justices' salaries, Congress may withhold salary increases as punishment, especially in times of high inflation. In 1964, when authorizing the first pay increase in almost a decade for federal employees, Congress gave the justices $3,000 less than other top-level employees. Members of Congress did so as a way of expressing their disapproval of Warren Court rulings on reapportionment. Representative (and later Senate leader) Robert Dole, a Kansas Republican, even proposed that for the justices "the effective date of the pay increase if adopted by this House, would be the date the Supreme Court reverses" its reapportionment decisions.[67]

More direct attacks are possible. Under Article III, Congress is authorized "to make exceptions" to the appellate jurisdiction of the Court. That authorization has been viewed as a way of denying the Court review of certain kinds of cases. But Congress succeeded only once, with the 1868 repeal of jurisdiction over writs of habeas corpus, which the Court upheld in *Ex parte McCardle* (1869).[68]

Court-curbing legislation is not a very effective weapon. Rather than limiting judicial review, Congress has given the Court the power to set its own agenda and decide major issues of public law and policy—precisely the kinds of issues that Congress then seeks to deny the Court review. The Court has also suggested that it would not approve repeals of its jurisdiction that were merely attempts to dictate how particular kinds of cases should be decided.[69] Most proposals to curb the Court, of course, are simply that. During the McCarthy era, for instance, the Republican senator William Jenner spearheaded a drive to forbid review of cases challenging legislative committees investigating un-American activities. Another unsuccessful attempt was made in 1968 to amend the Omnibus Crime Control and Safe Streets Act so as to prevent the Court from reviewing state criminal cases raising *Miranda* issues. In 1979, Senator Jesse Helms of North Carolina succeeded in persuading the Senate to pass, by a vote of fifty-one to forty, an amendment eliminating federal court jurisdiction over school prayer cases, but the House of Representatives never considered the bill.[70] Given the overwhelming failure of Court-curbing attempts, the political scientist C. Herman Pritchett has pointed out, "Congress can no longer claim with good conscience the authority granted by Article III, Section 2, and every time proposals to exercise such authority are rejected," he adds, "the Court's control over its appellate jurisdiction is correspondingly strengthened."[71]

Congress has had somewhat greater success in reversing the Court by constitutional amendment. Congress must pass a constitutional amendment, which three-fourths of the states must then ratify. The process is cumbersome, and thousands of amendments to overrule the Court have failed. But four decisions have been overturned by constitutional amendment. *Chisholm v. Georgia* (1793), holding that citizens of one state could sue another state in federal courts, was reversed by the Eleventh Amendment, guaranteeing sovereign immunity for states from suits by citizens of another state. The Thirteenth and Fourteenth amendments, abolishing slavery and making blacks citizens of the United States, technically overturned the ruling in *Dred Scott v. Sandford* (1857) that blacks were not persons under the Constitution. With the ratification in 1913 of the Sixteenth Amendment, Congress reversed *Pollock v. Farmers' Loan and Trust Co.* (1895), which had invalidated a federal income tax. In 1970, an amendment to the Voting Rights Act of 1965 lowered the voting age to eighteen years for all elections. Though signing the act into law, Nixon had Attorney General John Mitchell challenge the validity of lowering the voting age by simple legislation rather than by constitutional amendment. Within six months, in *Oregon v. Mitchell* (1970), a bare majority of the Burger Court held that Congress exceeded its power by lowering the voting age for state and local elections. Less than a year later, the Twenty-sixth Amendment was ratified, extending the franchise to eighteen-year-olds in all elections.

More successful than Court-curbing and Constitution-amending efforts are congressional enactments and rewriting of legislation in response the Court's rulings. For example, the Court held in *Pennsylvania v. Wheeling and Belmont Bridge Co.* (1852) that a bridge built across the Ohio River obstructed interstate commerce and violated a congressionally approved state compact. Congress immediately passed a statute declaring that the bridge did not obstruct interstate commerce.

Congressional reversals usually relate to nonstatutory matters involving administrative policies. In *Zurcher v. The Sanford Daily* (1978), however, the Burger Court held that there was no constitutional prohibition against police searching newsrooms for "mere evidence," photographs, of a crime. Congress basically reversed that holding by passing the Privacy Protection Act of 1980, prohibiting unannounced searches of newsrooms and requiring that such evidence be obtained by a subpoena.

Congressional reversals of the Court's statutory interpretations are less frequent. Congress is usually constrained by the lobbying efforts of beneficiaries of the Court's rulings. Out of over two hundred cases in which the Court construed statutes governing antitrust and labor relations, a bare 12 percent generated a congressional attempt at reversal, and in only 4 percent was legislation passed that overturned rulings of the Court.[72]

The Court may invite Congress to reverse its rulings when legislation appears ambiguous. Burger suggested as much in *Tennessee Valley Authority v. Hill* (1978), when holding that a TVA dam could not be put into operation, because it would destroy the only habitat of a tiny fish—the snail darter—protected under the Endangered Species Act of 1973. Congress subsequently modified the act by authorizing a special board to decide whether to allow federally funded public works projects when they threaten an endangered species.

When Congress redrafts legislation, the Court occasionally refuses to yield. During the Vietnam War, the Warren Court ruled in *United States v. Seeger* (1965) that the Selective Service Act's exemption from military service for "reason of religious training or belief" applied to conscientious objectors who did not necesarily believe in a Supreme Being but who had strong moral and philosophical beliefs. Congress rewrote the statute to make clear that the religious exemption applied only to those who objected to war on the basis of traditional religious beliefs in a Supreme Being. In *Welsh v. United States* (1970), the Court nevertheless granted Elliott Welsh II draft exemption because of his philosophical beliefs. The Court ruled that those beliefs may be held with the same "strength of more traditional religious convictions."

Congress cannot overturn the Court's interpretations of the Constitution by mere legislation. But Congress can enhance or thwart compliance with the Court's rulings. After the Warren Court's landmark decision in *Gideon v. Wainwright* (1963) that indigents have a right to counsel, Congress provided attorneys for indigents charged with federal offenses. By contrast, in the Crime Control and Safe Streets Act of 1968, Congress permitted federal courts to use evidence obtained from suspects who had not been read their *Miranda* rights, if their testimony appeared voluntary on the basis of the "totality of the circumstances" surrounding their interrogation. Congress thus attempted to return to a pre-*Miranda* standard for police questioning of criminal suspects. In 1977, Congress passed the so-called Hyde Amendment, sponsored by Representative Henry Hyde, a Republican from Illinois, and supported by President Jimmy Carter and HEW Secretary Joseph Califano. The amendment registered well-organized opposition to *Roe v. Wade* and to federal funding of abortions. In 1976, estimates of the number of Medicaid-funded abortions ranged as high as 300,000 per year.[73] The Hyde Amendment to appropriations bills for HEW limited the availability of elective abortions for indigent women, by barring Medicaid coverage of abortions except where the life of the mother would be endangered if the fetus were carried full term.

Congress may also openly defy the Court's rulings. When holding, in *Immigration and Naturalization Service v. Chadha* (1983), that Congress may not delegate decision-making authority to agencies and still retain the power of vetoing decisions with which it disagrees, the Court invalidated over two hundred provisions for one-house vetoes of administrative actions. Congress responded by deleting or substituting joint resolutions for one-house veto provisions. But, in the year following *Chadha*, Congress also passed no fewer than thirty new provisions for legislative vetoes.

Congress indubitably has the power to delay and undercut implementation of the Court's rulings. For example, Congress delayed implementation of *Brown* by not authorizing the executive branch to enforce the decision prior to the Civil Rights Act of 1964. Then, by cutting back on appropriations for the Departments of Justice and HEW during the Nixon and Ford administrations, Congress registered increasing opposition to busing and further attempts at achieving integrated public schools. "What the Congress gave in Title VI of the 1964 Civil Rights Acts," Joseph Califano observed, "it took away in part through the annual HEW appropriations bills by forbidding the use of any funds to bus school children."[74]

On major issues of public policy, Congress is likely to prevail or, at least, temper the impact of the Court's rulings. In a study of the Court's invalidation of legislation between 1790 and 1957, Robert Dahl found that Congress ultimately prevailed 70 percent of the time. Congress was able to do so by reenacting legislation and because of changes in the composition and direction of the Court.[75] The Court, Dahl concluded, generally serves to legitimate dominant national political coalitions. But the Court forges public policy not only when invalidating federal legislation but also by overturning state and local laws and practices.[76] The continuing controversies over decisions striking down state laws on school desegregation, school prayer, and abortion are a measure of the Court's influence on American life.

Campaign Politics and Presidential Leadership

Charged with the responsibility of taking "care that the laws be faithfully executed," the President is the chief executive officer under the Constitution. As the only nationally elected public official, the President represents the views of the dominant national political coalition. A President's obligation faithfully to execute the laws, including decisions of the Court, may thus collide with his own perceived electorial mandate.

The Court has often been the focus of presidential campaigns and power struggles. But Presidents seldom openly defy particular decisions by the Court. Presidential defiance is, perhaps, symbolized by the following famous remark attributed to Andrew Jackson: "John Marshall has made his decision, now let him enforce it." Jackson's refusal to enforce the decision in *Worcester v. Georgia* (1832), which denied state courts jurisdiction over crimes committed on Indian lands, in fact simply left enforcement problems up to the courts and legislatures. During the Civil War, however, Lincoln ordered his military commanders to refuse to obey writs of habeas corpus issued by Chief Justice Taney. On less dramatic occasions, Presidents have also instructed their attorneys general to refuse to comply with other court orders. Carter's attorney general Griffin Bell, for one, was found in contempt of court for refusing to provide a list of informers to a judge presiding over a civil rights suit brought by the Socialist Workers Party.

In major confrontations, Presidents generally yield to the Court. Nixon complied with the ruling in *New York Times Co. v. United States*, which struck down, as a prior restraint on freedom of the press, an injunction against the publication of the Pentagon Papers—a top-secret report detailing the history of America's involvement in Vietnam. Then, in 1974, he submitted to the Court's decision in *United States v. Nixon*, ordering the release of White House tape recordings pertinent to the trial of his former attorney general John Mitchell and other presidential assistants for conspiracy and obstruction of justice.

Although Presidents seldom directly defy the Court, their reluctance to enforce rulings may thwart implementation. Eisenhower's reaction to the school desegregation decision was quite similar to Jackson's earlier one. *Brown* was "a hot potato handed to [him] by the judiciary," Attorney General Herbert Brownell has recalled. "After the Court decision [the President] realized that it then became his job as head of the executive branch of government to enforce it. And he went about doing that in what he thought was the right way—it was a long-term way."[77] Eisenhower told his brother, "You keep harping on the Constitution, I should like to point out that the meaning of the Constitution is what the Supreme Court says it is."[78] Eisenhower would not assume leadership for enforcing *Brown*. He disapproved of the Court's bold attempt to mandate a change in the way of life of many Americans. "Laws are rarely effective unless they represent the will of the majority," and, he reasoned, *Brown* removed the "cloak of legality to segregation in all its forms," which the Court itself had given in *Plessy v. Ferguson* (1896), when proclaiming the doctrine of "separate but equal" in public transportation. "After three score years of living under these patterns," Eisenhower concluded, "it was impossible to expect complete and instant reversal of conduct by mere decision of the Supreme Court."[79]

Styles and strategies of political leadership vary, but presidential persuasion can significantly influence compliance with the Court's rulings. By the late 1960s, considerable progress had been made toward ending segregated public schools. This was due largely to the leadership of Presidents Kennedy and Johnson. In the 1968 presidential campaign, though, Nixon won the southern vote with antibusing pledges and promises to take a "middle-of-the-road" approach to school desegregation. After his election, he observed, "[T]here are those who want instant integration and those who want segregation forever. I believe that we need to have a middle course between these two extremes."[80] Surprised by the unanimous decision in *Alexander v. Holmes County School Board* (1969), he became the first President to disagree publicly with one of the Court's rulings on school desegregation. *Alexander* did not deter Nixon from keeping his campaign promises. His strategy was to return the problems of compliance to the courts by curtailing the Department of Justice's prosecution of school districts that refused to desegregate and to cut back on the funding and jurisdiction of HEW for enforcing integration.

In both the short and the long run, Presidents may undercut Supreme Court policy-making. By issuing contradictory directives to federal agencies and by assigning low priority to enforcement by the Department of Justice, they may limit the Court's decisions. Although most of the early New Deal program was invalidated by the Court, after 1937 FDR persuaded Congress to reenact major provisions of his social and economic policies. Presidents may also make broad moral appeals in response to the Court's rulings, and those appeals may transcend their limited time in office. The Court put school desegregation and abortion on the national agenda. But Kennedy's appeal for civil rights captivated a generation and encouraged public acceptance of the Court's rulings. Similarly, Reagan's opposition to abortion serves to legitimate resistance to the Court's decisions.

Presidential influence over the Court in the long run remains contingent on appointments to the Court. Vacancies occur at the rate of one every twenty-two months. Four Presidents—including Jimmy Carter—had no opportunities to

appoint members of the Court. There is no guarantee how a
justice will vote or that his other vote will prove sufficient in
limiting or reversing past rulings with which a President disagrees. But through their appointments Presidents may leave
their mark on Supreme Court policy-making and possibly align
the Court and the country or precipitate later confrontations.

The Supreme Court and American Life

"The powers exercised by this Court are inherently oligarchic," Frankfurter once observed when pointing out that
"[t]he Court is not saved from being oligarchic because it pro-
fesses to act in the service of humane ends."[81] Judicial review
is antidemocratic. But the Court's power stems from its duty
to give authoritative meaning to the Constitution, and rests
with the persuasive forces of reason, institutional prestige, the
cooperation of other political institutions, and, ultimately,
public opinion. The country, in a sense, saves the justices
from being an oligarchy by curbing the Court when it goes
too far or too fast with its policy-making. Violent opposition
and resistance, however, threaten not merely the Court's
prestige but the very idea of a government under law.

Some Court watchers, and occasionally even the justices,
warn of "an imperial judiciary" and a "government by the
judiciary."[82] For much of the Court's history, though, the work
of the justices has not involved major issues of public policy.
In most areas of public law and policy, the fact that the Court
decides an issue is more important than what it decides. Relatively few of the many issues of domestic and foreign policy
that arise in government reach the Court. When the Court
does decide major questions of public policy, it does so by
bringing political controversies within the language, structure, and spirit of the Constitution. By deciding only immediate cases, the Court infuses constitutional meaning into the

resolution of the larger surrounding political controversies. But by itself the Court cannot lay those controversies to rest.

The Court can profoundly influence American life. As a guardian of the Constitution, the Court sometimes invites controversy by challenging majoritarian sentiments to respect the rights of minorities and the principles of a representative democracy. The Court's influence is usually more subtle and indirect, varying over time and from one policy issue to another. In the end, the Court's influence on American life cannot be measured precisely, because its policy-making is inextricably bound up with that of other political institutions. Major confrontations in constitutional politics, like those over school desegregation, school prayer, and abortion, are determined as much by what is possible in a system of free government and in a pluralistic society as by what the Court says about the meaning of the Constitution. At its best, the Court appeals to the country to respect the substantive value choices of human dignity and self-governance embedded in our written Constitution.

Appendix

MEMBERS OF THE SUPREME COURT OF THE
UNITED STATES

	Appointing President	Dates of Service
CHIEF JUSTICES		
Jay, John	Washington	1789 – 1795
Rutledge, John	Washington	1795 – 1795
Ellsworth, Oliver	Washington	1796 – 1800
Marshall, John	Adams, J.	1801 – 1835
Taney, Roger Brooke	Jackson	1836 – 1864
Chase, Salmon Portland	Lincoln	1864 – 1873
Waite, Morrison Remick	Grant	1874 – 1888
Fuller, Melville Weston	Cleveland	1888 – 1910
White, Edward Douglass	Taft	1910 – 1921
Taft, William Howard	Harding	1921 – 1930
Hughes, Charles Evans	Hoover	1930 – 1941
Stone, Harlan Fiske	Roosevelt, F.	1941 – 1946
Vinson, Frederick Moore	Truman	1946 – 1953
Warren, Earl	Eisenhower	1953 – 1969
Burger, Warren Earl	Nixon	1969–
ASSOCIATE JUSTICES		
Rutledge, John	Washington	1790 – 1791
Cushing, William	Washington	1790 – 1810

	Appointing President	Dates of Service
Wilson, James	Washington	1789 – 1798
Blair, John	Washington	1790 – 1796
Iredell, James	Washington	1790 – 1799
Johnson, Thomas	Washington	1792 – 1793
Paterson, William	Washington	1793 – 1806
Chase, Samuel	Washington	1796 – 1811
Washington, Bushrod	Adams, J.	1799 – 1829
Moore, Alfred	Adams, J.	1800 – 1804
Johnson, William	Jefferson	1804 – 1834
Livingston, Henry Brockholst	Jefferson	1807 – 1823
Todd, Thomas	Jefferson	1807 – 1826
Duvall, Gabriel	Madison	1811 –.1835
Story, Joseph	Madison	1812 – 1845
Thompson, Smith	Monroe	1823 – 1843
Trimble, Robert	Adams, J. Q.	1826 – 1828
McLean, John	Jackson	1830 – 1861
Baldwin, Henry	Jackson	1830 – 1844
Wayne, James Moore	Jackson	1835 – 1867
Barbour, Philip Pendleton	Jackson	1836 – 1841
Catron, John	Van Buren	1837 – 1865
McKinley, John	Van Buren	1838 – 1852
Daniel, Peter Vivian	Van Buren	1842 – 1860
Nelson, Samuel	Tyler	1845 – 1872
Woodbury, Levi	Polk	1845 – 1851
Grier, Robert Cooper	Polk	1846 – 1870
Curtis, Benjamin Robbins	Fillmore	1851 – 1857
Campbell, John Archibald	Pierce	1853 – 1861
Clifford, Nathan	Buchanan	1858 – 1881
Swayne, Noah Haynes	Lincoln	1862 – 1881
Miller, Samuel Freeman	Lincoln	1862 – 1890
Davis, David	Lincoln	1862 – 1877
Field, Stephen Johnson	Lincoln	1863 – 1897
Strong, William	Grant	1870 – 1880
Bradley, Joseph P.	Grant	1870 – 1892
Hunt, Ward	Grant	1873 – 1882
Harlan, John Marshall	Hayes	1877 – 1911
Woods, William Burnham	Hayes	1881 – 1887
Matthews, Stanley	Garfield	1881 – 1889

	Appointing President	Dates of Service
Gray, Horace	Arthur	1882 – 1902
Blatchford, Samuel	Arthur	1882 – 1893
Lamar, Lucius Quintus C.	Cleveland	1888 – 1893
Brewer, David Josiah	Harrison	1890 – 1910
Brown, Henry Billings	Harrison	1891 – 1906
Shiras, George, Jr.	Harrison	1892 – 1903
Jackson, Howell Edmunds	Harrison	1893 – 1895
White, Edward Douglass	Cleveland	1894 – 1910
Peckham, Rufus Wheeler	Cleveland	1896 – 1909
McKenna, Joseph	McKinley	1898 – 1925
Holmes, Oliver Wendell	Roosevelt, T.	1902 – 1932
Day, William Rufus	Roosevelt, T.	1903 – 1922
Moody, William Henry	Roosevelt, T.	1906 – 1910
Lurton, Horace Harmon	Taft	1910 – 1914
Hughes, Charles Evans	Taft	1910 – 1916
Van Devanter, Willis	Taft	1911 – 1937
Lamar, Joseph Rucker	Taft	1911 – 1916
Pitney, Mahlon	Taft	1912 – 1922
McReynolds, James Clark	Wilson	1914 – 1941
Brandeis, Louis Dembitz	Wilson	1916 – 1939
Clarke, John Hessin	Wilson	1916 – 1922
Sutherland, George	Harding	1911 – 1938
Butler, Pierce	Harding	1923 – 1939
Sanford, Edward Terry	Harding	1923 – 1930
Stone, Harlan Fiske	Coolidge	1925 – 1941
Roberts, Owen Josephus	Hoover	1930 – 1945
Cardozo, Benjamin Nathan	Hoover	1932 – 1938
Black, Hugo Lafayette	Roosevelt, F.	1937 – 1971
Reed, Stanley Forman	Roosevelt, F.	1938 – 1957
Frankfurter, Felix	Roosevelt, F.	1939 – 1962
Douglas, William Orville	Roosevelt, F.	1939 – 1975
Murphy, Frank	Roosevelt, F.	1940 – 1949
Byrnes, James Francis	Roosevelt, F.	1941 – 1942
Jackson, Robert Houghwout	Roosevelt, F.	1941 – 1954
Rutledge, Wiley Blount	Roosevelt, F.	1943 – 1949
Burton, Harold Hitz	Truman	1945 – 1958
Clark, Thomas Campbell	Truman	1949 – 1967
Minton, Sherman	Truman	1949 – 1956

	Appointing President	Dates of Service
Harlan, John Marshall	Eisenhower	1955 – 1971
Brennan, William Joseph, Jr.	Eisenhower	1956 –
Whittaker, Charles Evans	Eisenhower	1957 – 1962
Stewart, Potter	Eisenhower	1958 – 1981
White, Byron Raymond	Kennedy	1962 –
Goldberg, Arthur Joseph	Kennedy	1962 – 1965
Fortas, Abe	Johnson, L.	1965 – 1969
Marshall, Thurgood	Johnson, L.	1967 –
Blackmun, Harry A.	Nixon	1970 –
Powell, Lewis Franklin, Jr.	Nixon	1972 –
Rehnquist, William Hubbs	Nixon	1972 –
Stevens, John Paul	Ford	1975 –
O'Connor, Sandra Day	Reagan	1981 –

Notes

ABBREVIATIONS FOR PRIMARY SOURCES

BHLUM	Bentley Historical Library, University of Michigan, Ann Arbor, Michigan
BLUC	Bancroft Library, Oral History Project, University of California, Berkeley, California
CLE	Clemson University, Cooper Library, Clemson, South Carolina
CU	Columbia University, Butler Library, New York, New York
CUOHP	Columbia University, Oral History Project, New York, New York
CWM	College of William and Mary, Williamsburg, Virginia
EPL	Dwight David Eisenhower Presidential Library, Abilene, Kansas
FPL	Gerald R. Ford Presidential Library, Ann Arbor, Michigan
HI	Hoover Institution on War, Revolution, and Peace, Stanford, California
HLS	Harvard Law School, Manuscripts Room, Cambridge, Massachusetts
HPL	Herbert Hoover Presidential Library, West Branch, Iowa
JPL	Lyndon Baines Johnson Presidential Library, Austin, Texas
KPL	John F. Kennedy Presidential Library, Waltham, Massachusetts
LC	Library of Congress, Manuscripts Division, Washington, D.C.
MHL	Minnesota Historical Library, St. Paul, Minnesota
MLPU	Seeley G. Mudd Library, Princeton University, Princeton, New Jersey
NARS	National Archives and Records Service, Washington, D.C.
RPL	Franklin D. Roosevelt Presidential Library, Hyde Park, New York
SC	Supreme Court of the United States, Washington, D.C.
TPL	Harry S. Truman Presidential Library, Independence, Missouri
UK	University of Kentucky, Special Collections Library, Lexington, Kentucky
UT	University of Texas, Manuscripts, Law School Library, Austin, Texas
UV	University of Virginia, Alderman Library, Charlottesville, Virginia
YA	Yale University Library, New Haven, Connecticut
YU	Yeshiva University, Cardozo School of Law, New York, New York

ONE

A *Struggle for Power*

1. Quoted by L. Shearer, "Intelligence Report," *Parade* magazine (January 23, 1983).
2. Docket Book, William J. Brennan, Jr., Papers, Box 417, LC.
3. The discussion of the oral arguments in *Roe v. Wade* is based on recordings of the arguments, available at NARS, and transcripts (which do not contain the names of the justices asking the questions) in *Landmark Briefs and Arguments of the Supreme Court of the United States*, ed. P. Kurland and G. Casper (Arlington, Va.: University Publications of America, 1974). On the basis of the author's experience, a judgment was made as to which justices were asking what questions, but all quotations are from the transcripts of the oral argument.
4. Docket Book, Brennan Papers, Box 420A, LC.
5. Memos, December 18 and 20, 1971, Brennan Papers, Box 281, LC.
6. Memos, May 18 and 19, 1972, from Douglas and Brennan, and Memos to Conference, May 18 and 25, 1972, from Blackmun, Brennan Papers, Box 281, LC.
7. Memorandum to the Conference, May 31, 1972, Brennan Papers, Box 281, LC.
8. Memo to Blackmun, May 31, 1972, Brennan Papers, Box 281, LC.
9. Memorandum for Conference, June 1, 1972, Brennan Papers, Box 281, LC.
10. Memo to Chief Justice Burger, June 1, 1972, Brennan Papers, Box 281, LC.
11. Memo to Blackmun, January 4, 1973, Brennan Papers, Box 281, LC.
12. Memorandum to the Conference, January 16, 1973 Brennan Papers, Box 281, LC.
13. Quoted in *New York Times* A1, A20 (January 23, 1973).
14. Quoted ibid., at A20.
15. See, e.g., J. H. Ely, "The Wages of Crying Wolf: A Comment on *Roe v. Wade*," 82 *Yale Law Journal* 920 (1973).
16. See D. M. O'Brien, *Privacy, Law, and Public Policy* (New York: Praeger, 1979).
17. Senate Committee on the Judiciary, *Constitutional Amendments Relating to Abortion: Hearings before the Subcommittee on the Constitution*, 97th Cong., 1st sess., vol. 1, at 90 (Washington, D.C.: GPO, 1983).
18. U.S. Bureau of the Census, *Statistical Abstract of the United States, 1985 Edition* (Washington, D.C.: GPO, 1985).
19. See C. A. Johnson and J. Bond, "Coercive and Noncoercive Abortion Deterrence Policies: A Comparative State Analysis," 2 *Law and Policy Quarterly* 106 (1980).
20. See, e.g., *Planned Parenthood v. Danforth*, 428 U.S. 52 (1976) (written consent of woman, after doctor's explanation of dangers of abortion, permissible; but spousal consent unconstitutional if husband is allowed to prohibit abortion); *Bellotti v. Baird*, 443 U.S. 622 (1979) (parental veto of minor's abortion unconstitutional); *H.L. v. Matheson*, 450 U.S. 398 (1981) (upheld requirements that parents be notified of minor's decision to have an abortion); *Bigelow v. Virginia*, 421 U.S. 809 (1975) (states may not ban advertisements for abortion clinics); *Poelker v. Doe*, 432 U.S. 519 (1977) (upholding city's policy of refusing nontherapeutic abortions in public hospitals); *Beal v. Poe*, 432 U.S. 438 (1977), and *Maher v. Roe*, 432 U.S. 464 (1977) (upholding restrictions on the funding of nontherapeu-

tic abortions); *Harris v. McRae*, 448 U.S. 297 (1980) (upholding Hyde Amendment, which forbids funding of nontherapeutic abortions under Medicaid programs).

21. See K. Lewis and T. Carr, *Abortion: Judicial and Legislative Central, Issue Brief* (Washington, D.C.: Congressional Research Service, August 3, 1984).

22. J. Davis, *General Social Surveys, 1972–1982: Cumulative Codebook* (Chicago: National Opinion Research Center, 1982); and "Public Opinion About Abortion: An Annotated Bibliography," in Senate Committee on the Judiciary, supra note 17, at 965.

23. Table is based on a list of cases in *The Constitution of the United States of America: Analysis and Interpretation* 1595–97 (Washington, D.C.: Library of Congress, 1973), and supplementary materials provided by the Congressional Research Service, Library of Congress, and by Henry J. Abraham. A list of federal statutes declared unconstitutional through 1984 may be found in H. Abraham, *The Judicial Process*, table 9 (New York: Oxford University Press, 5th ed., 1986).

TWO

The Cult of the Role

1. W. Rehnquist, "Presidential Appointments to the Supreme Court" (Lecture, University of Minnesota, October 9, 1984) (copy on file with the author).

2. Memorandum to the President, January 6, 1965, John Macy Papers, Box 726, "Judgeships File," JPL.

3. Oral History Interview with Justice Frankfurter, at 52–53, KPL. See also Letter, May 15, 1964, Charles Wyzanski Papers, Box 1, File 26, HLS.

4. Letter to Alexander Bickel, March 18, 1963, Felix Frankfurter Papers, Box 206, HLS.

5. Letter, November 17, 1975, White House Central Files—Federal Government (WHCF-FG), Box 51, FPL.

6. H. Abraham, "A Bench Happily Filled: Some Historical Reflections on the Supreme Court Appointment Process," 66 *Judicature* 282, 286 (1983).

7. *Jacobellis v. Ohio*, 378 U.S. 184, 197 (1964).

8. Based on an updating of data collected in A. Blaustein and R. Mersky, *The First One Hundred Justices* 20–21 (Hamden, Conn.: Archon, 1978).

9. Letter, October 9, 1928, Harlan F. Stone Papers, Box 24, LC.

10. Ibid.

11. Robert Kennedy Oral History Interview, at 620–21, KPL.

12. Memorandum, May 18, 1967, WHCF-FG, Box 535, JPL.

13. Letter, November 13, 1975, WHCF-FG, Box 51, FPL.

14. Letter to Henry Stimson, February 17, 1932, quoted in letter from H. Gotlieb to Frankfurter, October 23, 1961, WHCF-FG, Box 194, KPL.

15. Letter, February 20, 1932, White House Central Files (WHCF), Box 878, HPL.

16. See I. Carmen, "The President, Politics and the Power of Appointments: Hoover's Nomination of Mr. Justice Cardozo," 55 *Virginia Law Review* 616 (1969).

17. WHCF, Box 193, HPL. (The undated note from Justice Stone appears in a file of endorsements of Hughes for chief justice. Justice Stone may have also suggested Cardozo for the chief justiceship, but the note, with President Hoover's notations, appears to have been intended for filling Justice Sanford's vacancy.) See also Benjamin Cardozo Papers, Box 11, CU and YU.

18. See materials on the Parker Nomination, WHCF, Boxes 192 and 193, HPL; and Stone Papers, Box 17, LC.

19. Homer Cummings Diaries, UV; and White House Central Files—President's Secretary's Files (WHCF-PSF), Box 231, TPL.

20. See L. Berkson, S. Beller, and M. Grimaldi, *Judicial Selection in the United States: A Compendium of Provisions* (Chicago: American Judicature Society, 1980); and V. Flango and C. Ducat, "What Difference Does Method of Judicial Selection Make?" 5 *Justice System Journal* 25 (1979).

21. See James Eastland Oral History Interview, at 14–15, JPL; and Kennedy Interview, at 603–7, KPL.

22. Quoted in "Here Come the Judges," *Time* 112 (December 11, 1978), and "'Merit Selection Chances Improve," *Congressional Quarterly Weekly* 393, 394 (February 18, 1978). See also S. Goldman, "Carter's Judicial Appointments: A Lasting Legacy," 64 *Judicature* 344 (1981).

23. Kennedy Interview, at 603, KPL. See also WHCF-FG, Boxes 505 and 530, KPL.

24. W. Mitchell, "Appointment of Federal Judges," 17 *American Bar Association Journal* 569 (1931). See also William Mitchell Papers, Box 7, MHS; and WHCF, Box 441, HPL.

25. Letter, October 17, 1975, WHCF-FG, Box 50; Letter from Baroody, November 19, 1975, WHCF-FG, Box 51; Telephone Logs, WHCF-FG, Box 17, FPL.

26. See ABA, *Standing Committee on Federal Judiciary: What It Is and How It Works* (ABA, 1983). See also E. Slotnick, "The ABA Standing Committee on Federal Judiciary: A Contemporary Assessment," 66 *Judicature* 349 (1983); and White House Central Files—General Files (WHCF-GF), Box 67, EPL.

27. Leon Jaworski Oral History Interview, at 15, JPL.

28. Ramsey Clark Oral History Interview, at 8, JPL.

29. See P. Smith, "Powell Says He Lobbied Member of ABA Panel for Wilkinson," *Washington Post* A4 (March 13, 1984).

30. Letter to Thomas Reed Powell, October 15, 1928, Stone Papers, Box 24, LC.

31. Records of the Department of Justice, Harold Burton Files, NARS; William O. Douglas Interview with Walter Murphy, MLPU; Tom C. Clark Oral History Interview, TPL; and White House Central Files—Confidential Files (WHCF-CF), Box 5, TPL.

32. See, generally, D. Danelski, *A Supreme Court Justice Is Appointed* (New York: Random House, 1964).

33. Letter to the President, November 12, 1938, Hugo Black Papers, Box 63, LC.

34. File on Wiley Rutledge, Records of the Attorney General, Department of Justice, NARS; also, Papers as President, President's Secretary's Files (PSF), Box 186, RPL.

35. Douglas Interview, at 86–89, MLPU.

36. See R. Evans, Jr., and R. Novak, *Nixon in the White House* 159–71 (New York: Random House, 1971).

37. See, e.g., Memos to the President on Lower Court Appointments, WHCF-FG, Box 505; Larry Temple Papers, Box 1; Barefoot Sanders Papers, Box 1; and John Macy Oral History Interview, Tape 3, at 13, JPL.

38. Letters, November 22, 1954, and September 10, 1941, Wyzanski Papers, Box 1, Files 13 and 18, HLS.

39. L. R. Wilfry to the President, October 31, 1910, Edward White Papers, LC.

40. See Memorandum for the Attorney General, November 27, 1942, and Comparative List Showing Religion of Judges Appointed during the Periods of 1922–1933 and 1933–1942, Francis Biddle Papers, Box 2, RPL.

41. Note on telephone conversation with Attorney General Brownell, September 9, 1956, Dwight David Eisenhower (DDE) Diaries, Box 11, EPL.
42. Quoted in Memorandum on Confirmation of Justice Louis Brandeis, WHCF, Fortas / Thornberry Series, Chron. File, JPL. See, generally, A. T. Mason, *Brandeis: A Free Man's Life* (New York: Viking Press, 1946).
43. Kennedy Interview, at 319, KPL.
44. Memorandum for the President, Supreme Court Vacancy, Ramsey Clark Papers, "Judgeships File," JPL.
45. Letter to the President, July 19, 1965, WHCF-FG, Box 535, JPL.
46. Letter from Paul Carrington, March 13, 1967, to Joseph Califano, Records of Department of Justice, NARS.
47. Thurgood Marshall Oral History Interview, at 7, JPL.
48. Letter, June 13, 1967, John Macy Papers, Box 365, Marshall File, JPL.
49. Kennedy Interview, at 614–15, KPL.
50. Douglas Interview, at 155, MLPU.
51. Letter, June 21, 1965, WHCF-FG, Box 535, JPL.
52. Macy Interview, at 31–33, JPL.
53. White House Central Files—Office Files (WHCF-OF), 41A, Box 212, TPL.
54. Macy Papers, Box 726, JPL.
55. R. Nixon, *RN: The Memories of Richard Nixon* 423 (New York: Grosset & Dunlap, 1978).
56. Materials in WHCF-FG 51, FPL.
57. Letter to Thomas Reed Powell, October 15, 1928, Stone Papers, Box 24, LC.
58. "The Black Controversy," Robert Jackson Papers, LC.
59. Statement Appended to Letter to Virginia Hamilton, April 7, 1968, Black Papers, Box 31, LC. (I am grateful to Professor Howard Ball for directing me to this note.) See also materials in Black Papers, Box 234, LC; and Cummings diary, UV.
60. Cummings Diaries, UV; Stanley Reed Interview, 3–35, CUOHP; and Stanley Reed Papers, Boxes 282 and 370, UK.
61. Cummings Diaries, UV.
62. Henry Morganthau Diaries, vol. 69, p. 308, RPL; and G. Kanin, "Trips to Felix," *Atlantic Monthly* 55, 60 (1964).
63. Interview Session, Justice Felix Frankfurter and Gerald Gunther, Felix Frankfurter Papers, Box 201, HLS; and Cummings Diaries, UV.
64. Papers as President, PSF, Box 77, RPL.
65. Douglas Interview, at 2–15; MLPU. See also President Roosevelt's correspondence with Senator Schwellenbach, Papers as President, PSF, Box 186, RPL.
66. Cummings Diaries, UV.
67. Robert Jackson Interview, at 779, CUOHP; and Robert Jackson Papers, LC.
68. On Hughes's appointment, compare M. Pusey, *Charles Evans Hughes*, vol. 2, at 651 (New York: Macmillan, 1951), with F. B. Wiener, "Justice Hughes' Appointment—The Cotton Story Re-examined," *Yearbook of the Supreme Court Historical Society* 78 (1981). A dispute has arisen over whether President Hoover was telephoned and encouraged by his acting secretary of state, Joseph Cotton, to offer the chief justiceship to Hughes on the basis of his belief that the latter would decline the offer and thus leave President Hoover free to appoint someone else—like Learned Hand, as Cotton apparently hoped, or elevate the President's good friend Justice Stone. That dispute is unlikely to be finally resolved since the telephone logs for the period in question are missing from both the Hoover Presidential Library and the Hoover Institution on War, Revolution, and Peace,

where the papers of the President were initially stored. Apart from the conjectures in the above article and book, there is also evidence that Justices Holmes and Brandeis conferred with President Hoover before his nomination of Hughes and may have indicated their preference for the appointment of Hughes rather than for the elevation of Justice Stone. Hoover Papers, Boxes 62 and 317, HI; Mitchell Papers, Box 7, MHL; WHCF, Boxes 22 and 191, HPL; Appointment Books and Telephone Logs, HPL; Post-Presidential Series (PPS), Box 370, HPL; Felix Frankfurter Papers, Box 169, HLS; and Stone Papers, Box 13, LC.

69. Notes on "H.F.S. & C.J.' ship," Felix Frankfurter Papers, Box 172, HLS.

70. Jackson Interview, at 1086–87, CUOPH; and Robert Jackson Papers, LC.

71. Fred Vinson Papers, Box 218, UK; Reed Papers, Box 325, UK; WHCF-PSF, Boxes 221 and 231, and Office Files, Box 212, TPL; Eban Ayers Papers, 1947 Diary in Box 26, TPL; and Jackson Papers, LC.

72. Letter, June 11, 1946, reprinted in R. Ferrell, ed., *Off the Record: The Private Papers of Harry S. Truman* 90 (New York: Harper & Row, 1980).

73. Tom Clark Oral History Interview, at 16, UK.

74. William Rogers Oral History Interview, UK.

75. Douglas Interview, at 265–66, MLPU.

76. There is no doubt that Nixon and Knowland found the appointment fortunate. See Letter from Senator Knowland to the President, September 25, 1953 (the letter arrived at the White House after the appointment of Warren was announced), WHCF-OF, Box 371, EPL.

77. Herbert Brownell Oral History Interview, at 6–11, EPL; Brownell Interview, at 60–65, BLUC; and DDE Diary, Box 4, EPL.

78. October 8, 1953, DDE Diary, Box 4; and letter to Edgar Eisenhower, White House Central Files—Name Series (WHCF-NS), Box 11, EPL.

79. Bernard Shanley Papers, Box 1, EPL.

80. Letter, WHCF-NS, Box 11, EPL.

81. Nixon, supra note 55, at 419–20.

82. H. J. Abraham, *Justices and Presidents* 70 (New York: Oxford University Press, 2d ed., 1985).

83. M. Miller, *Plain Speaking: An Oral Biography of Harry S. Truman* 225–26 (New York: Berkeley, 1973).

84. Letter, July 9, 1952, WHCF-PSF, Box 118, TPL.

85. Handwritten note by the President, President's Personal Files (PPF), Box 6, TPL.

86. *McGrath v. Kristensen*, 340 U.S. 162, 172 (1950) (Jackson, J., con. op., quoting Baron Bramwell).

87. "Truman Accuses Brownell of Lying," *New York Times* A1 (November 17, 1953).

88. See Reed Papers, Box 270. UK; Vinson Papers, Box 220, UK; and Frankfurter Papers, Box 353, LC.

89. Post-Presidential, Memoirs of Philip Perlman, Box 2, TPL. Also, Ayers Papers, Box 17, TPL.

90. Quoted in Abraham, supra note 82, at 69.

91. Clark Interview, at 212–13, TPL.

92. Kennedy Interview, KPL.

93. Rehnquist, supra note 1, at 23–24.

94. See L. Tribe, *God Save This Honorable Court*, chap. 2 (New York: Random House, 1985).

95. Jackson Interview, at 1104, CUOHP; "The Black Controversy," Jackson Papers, LC; and Sidney Fine Interview with William Douglas, at 8, BHLUM.

96. Letter, February 2, 1955, Felix Frankfurter Papers, Box 1, HLS.

97. J. Lash, ed., *From the Diaries of Felix Franfurter* 155 (New York: W. W. Norton, 1974).

98. This is based on the definitive study of extrajudicial activities, by William Cibes, "Extra-Judicial Activities of Justices of the United States Supreme Court, 1790–1960" (Ph.D. diss., Princeton University, 1975) (based on public and presidential papers); and the author's own study of papers of the justices and other presidential papers.

99. For a further discussion of off-the-bench commentaries, see A. Westin, "Out of Court Commentary by United States Supreme Court Justices, 1790–1962: Of Free Speech and Judicial Lockjaw," 62 *Columbia Law Review* 633 (1962); and M. Cannon and D. M. O'Brien, eds., *Views from the Bench: The Judiciary and Constitutional Politics,* intro. (Chatham, N.J.: Chatham House, 1985).

100. Letter, August 8, 1793, reprinted in H. P. Johnson, ed., *The Correspondence and Public Papers of John Jay* 488–89 (New York: Putnam's, 1890). For other correspondence see John Jay Papers, CU.

101. A. T. Mason, *William Howard Taft: Chief Justice* (New York: Simon & Schuster, 1965).

102. Cummings Diaries, UV; Memorandum, March 1, 1943, PSF, Box 76, RPL.

103. Newton Minow Oral History Interview, at 14, UK; Vinson Papers, Box 229, UK; Ayers, Box 26, TPL.

104. Notes of telephone conversations, June 19, 1957, John Foster Dulles Papers, Box 12; and Papers as President—Ann Whitman Diary Series, EPL.

105. J. Ehrlichman, *Witness to Power: The Nixon Years* 132–33 (New York: Simon and Schuster, 1982); *Washington Post* A3 (December 11, 1981); and *Washington Post* A33 (December 18, 1981).

106. E. Warren, *The Memoirs of Chief Justice Earl Warren,* 339 (New York: Doubleday, 1977); and Justice Brennan's memo on the Landau interviews, Earl Warren Papers, Box 348, LC.

107. Senate Committee on the Judiciary, *Hearings on the Nomination of Abe Fortas of Tennessee to the Chief Justice of the United States,* 90th Cong., 2d sess., September 13, 1968, at 1303.

108. A. Lief, *Brandeis: The Personal History of an American Ideal* 409 (Harrisburg, Pa.: Telegraph Press, 1936).

109. B. Murphy, *The Brandeis / Frankfurter Connection* (New York: Oxford University Press, 1982).

110. Based on conversations with the former solicitor general and dean of Harvard Law School Erwin Griswold (1983) and the Washington lawyer-lobbyist Thomas "Tommy the Cork" Corcoran (1982).

111. Note to President, October 26, 1938, PPF, Box 4877, RPL.

112. Justice Murphy's notes on his meetings with President Roosevelt during 1940–1943 are in Eugene Gressman Papers, BHLUM; and Justice Byrnes's memorandum to the President and other White House advisers are in James F. Byrnes Papers, Box 1229, CLE. See also Alpha Files, Boxes 607, 4877, and 6389, and PSF, Box 186, RPL.

113. WHCF-PSF, Boxes 118 and 284; PPF, Box 504, TPL. Kennedy Interview and Robert Kennedy Papers, Box 16, KPL. WHCF-NS, Letter of 22 March 1966; White House-Famous Names, Letter of February 25, 1964; WHCF-FG, 535 and 505 / 9, JPL.

114. Goldberg attended less than half of the cabinet meetings held during his first two and one-half years as ambassador to the United Nations. Memoranda and

other materials in White House Central Files—Official Files of the President, Goldberg File, JPL.

115. Memo from Jim Jones to the President, November 2, 1967, White House-Notes File; Meetings Notes File, November 2, 1967; March 20 and 27, 1968, Meetings Notes Files, JPL.

116. Diary Backup, Boxes 43, 60, 63, and 66, JPL.

117. Thorston Morton Oral History Interview, at 22, JPL.

118. WHCF, Fortas / Thornberry Series, Box 1, JPL; Diary Backup, Box 45, WHCF-Name File (Douglas); and Macy Papers (Fortas File), JPL.

119. Memorandum to Temple, WHCF, Fortas / Thornberry Series, Chron. File, JPL; and Letter, September 9, 1968, Warren Christopher Papers, Box 18, JPL.

120. Clark Clifford Oral History Interview, Tape 4, at 29; Paul Porter Interview, at 28–34; Macy Interview, at 726; and Larry Temple Oral History Interview, JPL.

121. Letter, September 6, 1968; WHCF, Fortas / Thornberry Series, Chron. File, JPL.

122. Eastland, in Senate Committee on the Judiciary, *Report on the Nominations of Abe Fortas,* 90th Cong., 2d sess., at 41 (Washington, D.C.: GPO, 1968).

123. Letter, July 25, 1968, Warren Papers, Box 352, LC.

124. Letter, July 24, 1968, John M. Harlan Papers, Box 531, MLPU.

125. Letter, May 14, 1969, Harlan Papers, Box 606, MLPU; and Warren Papers, (Statement of Wolfson), Box 353, LC.

126. Letters in Willis Van Devanter Papers, Box 35, LC; and Stone Papers, LC.

127. Correspondence in PPF, File 1662, and PSF, Box 186, RPL; and Felix Frank-furter Papers, Box 170, File 12, HLS.

128. Letter to Truman, February 13, 1946, Harold Burton Papers, Box 49, LC.

129. Address, Fordham-Stein Award Dinner (October 25, 1978).

130. Letters to and from the Justices, Supreme Court of the United States Papers, NARS.

131. Quoted in C. Fairman, *Mr. Justice Miller and the Supreme Court* 404 (Cam-bridge: Harvard University Press, 1939).

132. Quoted in Mason, supra note 101, at 271.

133. See correspondence in William Day Papers, Box 29; Van Devanter Papers, Boxes 32, 33, 34, and 35, LC; and further discussion in Chapter 3.

134. Letters of April 8, 1937 (to and from Frankfurter and Stone), Felix Frankfurter Papers, Box 171, HLS; and Letter, December 21, 1939, Stone Papers, Box 13, LC; and Charles Evans Hughes Papers, LC.

135. See, generally, P. Fish, *The Politics of Federal Judicial Administration* (Prince-ton: Princeton University Press, 1973); and J. Spaniol, "Making Federal Rules: The Inside Story," 69 *American Bar Association Journal* 1645 (1983).

136. See M. Cannon and W. Cikins, "Interbranch Cooperation in Improving the Administration of Justice," 38 *Washington and Lee Law Review* 1 (1983); E. Tamm and P. Reardon, "Warren E. Burger and the Administration of Justice," *Brigham Young University Law Review* 447 (1981); and P. Fish, *The Office of Chief Justice* (Charlottesville: University of Virginia Press, 1984).

137. R. Hartmann, *Palace Politics* 60 (New York: McGraw-Hill, 1980). For a some-what different view, compare G. Ford, *A Time to Heal* 90 (New York: Harper & Row, 1979).

138. News Release, December 16, 1970, by Congressman Ford, Robert Hartmann Papers, Box 17, FPL. Also, Letter to Congressman Celler, Chairman of the Committee on the Judiciary, July 29, 1970, Hartmann Papers, Box 12, FPL.

139. Ford, in *Cong. Rec.* 91st Cong., 2d sess., 11912, 11913 (April 15, 1970).

THREE
Life in the Marble Temple

1. Undated letters to Elizabeth Woodbury, Levi Woodbury Papers, Box 7, LC.
2. B. Cardozo, *The Nature of the Judicial Process* 168 (New Haven: Yale University, Press, 1921).
3. Quoted by C. Warren, *The Supreme Court in United States History*, vol. 1, at 48 n. 1 (Boston: Little, Brown, 1922).
4. C. Fairman, *Reconstruction and Reunion, 1864–1888*, at 69 n. 138 (New York: Macmillan, 1975).
5. *American State Papers, Misc.* I, no. 32.
6. Letter to Rufus King, Dec. 19, 1793, in C. R. King, ed., *The Life and Correspondence of Rufus King*, at 126 (New York: Putnam's, 1894).
7. Quoted by G. Hazelton, *The National Capitol* 141 (New York: Taylor, 1911).
8. C. Swisher, *History of the Supreme Court of the United States: The Taney Period, 1836–64*, (New York: Macmillan, 1974).
9. This was particularly true of Justice Joseph Story, who taught at Harvard and served as president of two banks and as a consultant to a number of firms and other organizations. See Dunne, *Justice Joseph Story and the Rise of the Supreme Court*, 121–23, 66–68, on Justice John McKinley's frequent absence from Court sessions and his private legal practice.
10. The requirement of circuit riding was finally abolished by the Circuit Court of Appeals Act of March 3, 1891, Ch. 517, 26 Stat. 826. In 1793, Congress had provided a rotation system in order to cut back on the circuit riding of the justices, and in 1801 it eliminated the duties, only to reinstate the practice in 1802. Congress modified the requirements in 1803, 1837, and 1866. For discussions of the burdens of circuit riding, see S. J. Field, *Personal Reminiscences of Early Days in California* (New York: De Capo, 1968); and J. Frank, *Justice Daniel Dissenting* (Cambridge: Harvard University Press, 1964).
11. Quoted in Warren, supra note 3, vol. 1, at 460–61.
12. See 5 Peters, preceding page 1, and 724 (Justice Baldwin dissenting) (1832); and 6 Wheaton v (1821). Henry Baldwin's Papers, NARS. For a history of the rules governing briefs and records in the nineteenth century, see Morrison Waite Papers, Box 40 (Misc. File) LC.
13. See 44 Stat. 433 (1867), providing for the employment of messengers. The provision for hiring stenographic clerks for the justices is in 24 Stat. 254 (1886).
14. A. Beveridge, *The Life of John Marshall*, vol. 4, at 90 (Boston: Houghton Mifflin, 1919).
15. Letter from Marshall to Story, July 13, 1821, reprinted in 14 *Proceedings of the Massachusetts Historical Society*, 2d ser. 328 (1900–1901). See also Letter from Justice Story to Chief Justice Marshall, June 26, 1831, John Marshall Papers, CWM (original in Joseph Story Papers, Massachusetts Historical Society).
16. See Letters from Marshall to Story, May 3, 1831, July 26, 1831, October 12, 1831, and November 19, 1831, reprinted in J. Oster, *The Political and Economic Doctrines of John Marshall* 132–39 (New York: Neale, 1914). See also G. Haskins and H. Johnson, *Foundations of Power: John Marshall, 1801–1815*, 382–89 and Table I, at 652 (New York: Macmillan, 1981).
17. Philadelphia *Union*, April 24, 1819, quoted by D. Morgan, *Justice William Johnson: The First Dissenter* 173 (Columbia: University of South Carolina Press, 1954).
18. Letter to Jefferson, December 10, 1822, Thomas Jefferson Papers MS, LC, quoted

by D. Morgan, "Mr. Justice William Johnson and the Constitution," 57 *Harvard Law Review* 328, 222–24 (1944).

19. Undated letter, John McLean Papers, Box 18, LC.

20. Justices Daniel, Campbell, and Curtis strongly objected to Chief Justice Taney's refusal to let the Clerk give copies of his opinion in *Dred Scott* to other members of the Court. See Letters from Justices Daniel and Campbell, March 10 and 18, 1857, Office of the Clerk of the Supreme Court, NARS. Justice Curtis's lengthy correspondence on this matter is also reprinted in G. Curtis, ed., *Life and Writings of Benjamin Robbins Curtis*, 2 vols. (Boston: Little, Brown, 1879).

21. C. Fairman, *Mr. Justice Miller and the Supreme Court, 1862–1890*, 121 (New York: Russell & Russell, 1939). See also Fairman, supra note 4, at 67–69; and Horace Gray Papers, Box 2; John M. Harlan (the elder) Papers; and Rufus Peckham Papers, LC.

22. W. King, *Melville Weston Fuller: Chief Justice of the United States, 1888–1910*, 191–92 (New York: Macmillan, 1950).

23. "Recollections of Justice Holmes," Arthur Sutherland Papers, HLS.

24. D. Acheson, *Morning and Noon* 41 (Boston: Houghton Mifflin, 1965).

25. See, e.g., Memorandum by Howard Westwood, Harlan F. Stone Papers, Box 48, LC. For a fascinating account of Justice McReynolds, see J. Knox, "Experiences as Law Clerk to Mr. Justice James C. McReynolds of the Supreme Court of the United States" (unpublished manuscript); and James McReynolds Papers, UV.

26. F. Frankfurter, "Chief Justices I Have Known," reprinted in P. Kurland, ed., *Felix Frankfurter in the Supreme Court* 491 (Chicago: Chicago University Press, 1970).

27. Quoted by C. Wyzanski, Jr., *Whereas—A Judge's Premises* 61 (Boston: Little, Brown, 1944).

28. See, e.g., Letters from Chief Justice Taft to Joseph Guerin, December 21, 1922, and to Justice Stone, May 28, 1925, William Howard Taft Papers, LC. See also H. F. Pringle, *The Life and Times of William Howard Taft*, vol. 2, at 1075–80 (New York: Farrar and Rinehart, 1939); and A. T. Mason, *William Howard Taft: Chief Justice* (New York: Simon & Schuster, 1965).

29. Letter from Chief Justice Fuller to Representative Joseph Cannon, December 21, 1896, Melville Fuller Papers, Box 4, LC. See also Letter of February 1, 1928, reprinted in *Cong. Record* 3285–86 (April 14, 1892). Congress had several times around the turn of the century considered but failed to pass legislation for the construction of a building for the Court. Records of the Marshal's Office, NARS.

30. See Letter to Senator Reed Smoot, President of the Building Commission, June 8, 1926, signed by the chief justice and by Justices Van Devanter, Butler, Sanford, and Stone, Stone Papers, Box 81, LC.

31. See Letter from Librarian, October 12, 1947, Stone Papers, Box 83, LC.

32. W. H. Taft, "The Jurisdiction of the Supreme Court under the Act of February 25, 1925," 35 *Yale Law Journal* 1, 2 (1925).

33. For a good discussion of nineteenth-century breaches of secrecy, see Fairman, supra note 21, at 121–37.

34. See William O. Douglas Papers, Box 228 (Memoranda to the Chief Justice, January 6, 1944, and May 21, 1945), LC; and Stone Papers, Box 74 (Memorandum from Justice Douglas, January 5, 1944), LC.

35. See C. Newland, "Personal Assistants to Supreme Court Justices: The Law Clerks," 40 *Oregon Law Review* 299, 310 (1961).

36. See, e.g., L. Denniston, "Burger Boots Court Printer Accused of Leaks," *Washington Star* A1 (April 25, 1979); and "Lust Lost," *Washington Post,* A1, col. 1 (June 3, 1982).

37. See, e.g., Memorandum to Justice Douglas from the Marshal on his appointment to the Court, Douglas Papers, Box 229, LC.

38. Much of this and the subsequent discussion about the bureaucratization of the Court draws on personal observations and conversations with Mark Cannon, Administrative Assistant to the Chief Justice.

39. Waite Papers, undated note and record of vote, Box 40, LC.

40. See, e.g., Douglas Papers, Box 218, LC (Memo from Justice Rehnquist concerning the posting of opinions to be announced because "he goofed in failing to announce Bill Douglas' dissenting opinion").

41. Felix Frankfurter Papers, Box 108, File 2267, LC.

42. E. Warren, "A Conversation with Earl Warren," WGBH-TV Educational Foundation, transcript (Boston: WGBH Educational Foundation, 1972).

43. L. Powell, "What the Justices Are Saying . . ." *American Bar Association Journal* 1454, 1454 (1976).

44. See 260 U.S. X (1922); and Letter from W. H. Taft to R. Taft, October 26, 1922 (commenting, "This is a fair sample of McReynolds's personal character and the difficulty of getting along with him"), Taft Papers, LC. For Justice Black's refusal to sign a letter to Justice Roberts, see Hugo Black Papers, Box 62, LC; and Stone Papers, Box 81, LC.

45. Based on figures in House Committee on Appropriations, *The Judiciary Appropriations for 1952: Hearings before the Subcommittee,* 82d Cong., 1st sess., at 2 (Washington, D.C.: GPO, 1951); and House Committee on Appropriations, *Departments of Commerce, Justice, and State, the Judiciary, and Related Agencies Appropriations for 1984: Hearings before a Subcommittee,* 98th Cong., 1 sess., at 297 (Washington, D.C.: GPO, 1983).

46. P. Stewart, "Reflections on the Supreme Court," 8 *Litigation* 8, 12 (1982).

47. Powell, supra note 43, at 1454.

48. J. M. Harlan, Jr., "A Glimpse of the Supreme Court at Work," 11 *University of Chicago Law School Record* 1, 1 (1963).

49. Chief Justice Burger, "In Memoriam: Hugo L. Black," 92 S.Ct. 5, 75 (1972).

50. H. Blackmun, "A Justice Speaks Out: A Conversation with Harry Blackmun," Cable News Network, transcript, at 4 (December 4, 1982).

51. Quoted in "Inside the High Court," *Time* 60, 64 (November 5, 1979).

52. See prepared statements of Justices White and Blackmun, in House Committee on Appropriations, *Departments . . . : Hearings before a Subcommittee,* 94th Cong., 2d sess., at 26 (Washington, D.C.: GPO, 1976); and Statement of Justice Powell, in House Committee on Appropriations, *Departments . . . : Hearings before a Subcommittee,* 95th Cong., 2d sess., at 181 (Washington, D.C.: GPO, 1978).

53. See, e.g., William J. Brennan Papers, Box 336, LC. In 1972, Justice Rehnquist requested, and the other justices agreed, to send all draft opinions and "join letters" in duplicate. See Brennan Papers, Box 279, LC.

54. W. Rehnquist, "Are the Old Times Dead?" (Mac Swinford Lecture, University of Kentucky, September 23, 1983 (copy on file with the author).

55. This is the view of Justice Powell. See his former law clerk's discussion of Justice Powell's selection and working relations with his law clerks in J. Harvie Wilkinson III, *Serving Justice* 52–54 (New York: Charterhouse, 1974).

56. Quoted by Barrett McGurn, "Law Clerks—A Professional Elite," 1980 *Yearbook*

of the Supreme Court Historical Society 98, at 100. See also D. Meador, "Justice Black and his Law Clerks," 15 *Alabama Law Review* 57 (1962).

57. The figures and conclusions are based on a memo to the author for the law clerk orientation day (September 7, 1983), and L. J. Pendlebury, "Court's Clerks Still Prefer Firm Pactice," *Legal Times* 10 (June 27, 1983).
58. Letter of January 21, 1974, Stone Papers, Box 48, LC.
59. Memo to Clerks from Justice Burton, John M. Harlan Papers, Box 561, MLPU.
60. Benno Schmidt Interview, at 8, CUOHP.
61. D. Acheson, "Recollections of Service with the Federal Supreme Court," 18 *Alabama Lawyer* 335, 364 (1957).
62. S. Fine, *Frank Murphy: The Washington Years* 161 (Ann Arbor: University of Michigan Press, 1984). Justice Frank Murphy's Papers, at the University of Michigan contain a large number of case files in which the law clerks' handwritten draft opinion is attached to a typewritten copy with the justice's comments and changes. BHLUM.
63. Memo from Justice Rutledge to the Chief Justice, May 17, 1948; and undated note to Justice Rutledge, Wiley Rutledge Papers, Box 166, LC.
64. *United States v. Carolene Products Co.*, 304 U.S. 144, 152 n. 4 (1938). See Stone Papers, Box 67, LC. The note was initially drafted by Louis Lusky, now a Columbia law professor.
65. Stone Papers, Box 48, LC.
66. See Black Papers, Box 60, LC.
67. Douglas, *The Court Years* 173 (New York: Random House, 1980). See also John Sapieza Oral History Interview, UK; and William Oliver Oral History Interview, BLUC.
68. Howard Trienens and Newton Minow Oral History Interviews, UK. For a good example, see files on *Dennis v. United States*, Fred Vinson Papers, Box 270, UK.
69. Quoted in Letter from Frankfurter to Reed, December 3, 1941, Stanley Reed Papers, Box 171, UK.
70. Arthur Rosett Oral History Interview, UK.
71. On Warren's practice, see Schmidt Interview, at 256, CUOHP; and Martin Richman Oral History Interview, at 4–5, BLUC. The discussion of Rehnquist's practice is based on his remarks at the Jefferson Literary Society and Debating Meeting, Charlottesville, Va., September 20, 1985.
72. Arthur Rosett Interview, UK. See also Gordon Davidson Interview, UK.
73. Recalled in F. Alley Allen Interview, UK.
74. Quoted in B. Schwartz and S. Lesher, *Inside the Warren Court* 39 (New York: Doubleday, 1983). Chief Justice Warren's instructions to his clerks on the preparation of cert. memos in Ifp cases are outlined in Memorandums for the Law Clerks, at 5–7; Earl Warren Papers, Box 398, LC. See also Suggestions in the Matter of Being a Law Clerk, Robert Garner Papers, Box 1, TPL.
75. W. J. Brennan, Jr., "The National Court of Appeals: Another Dissent," 40 *University of Chicago Law Review* 473 (1973).
76. J. P. Stevens, "Some Thoughts on Judicial Restraint," 66 *Judicature* 177, 179 (1982).
77. Bench memos, it bears emphasizing, serve two purposes: first, preparing justices for oral argument; and, second, providing a preliminary outline of a justice's possible opinion, particularly when a justice plans to write an opinion in the case, either because of the subject matter or the anticipated vote on the merits at conference. Warren Papers, Box 398, LC.

78. Like other justices, Frankfurter normally worked from a memorandum written by one of his law clerks, whether drafting an opinion for the Court or a concurring or dissenting opinion. See Felix Frankfurter Papers, Box 177, Law Clerks File, HLS. See also "Notes to Law Clerks," Tom C. Clark Papers, UT; Burton's instructions to his clerks and those of Harlan in the Harlan Papers, Boxes 561 and 583, MLPU; Fred Vinson Papers, UK; and Warren Papers, Box 398, LC.
79. Douglas, supra note 67, at 175.
80. W. Rehnquist, "Remarks," Ninth Circuit Conference, Corodoano, California, July 17, 1982, printed draft delivery copy, at 24 (copy on file with the author).
81. W. Rehnquist, "Who Writes Decisions of the Supreme Court?" *U.S. News and World Report* 74 (December 13, 1957).
82. Vinson Papers, Box 217, UK. Justice Rehnquist has recalled that when he clerked, that was true for Justice Jackson as well. Interview, November 16, 1984, SC.
83. Bickel, "Supreme Court Law Clerks" (draft of manuscript in response to Rehnquist's article), Frankfurter Paper, Box 215 (Bickel File), LC. For a different view of the practices of law clerks, see "Views of a Leading Lawyer who in his day was one of the most esteemed of Mr. Justice Brandeis' law clerks," Felix Frankfurter Papers, Box 177, File 1, HLS.
84. Memo, Robert Jackson Papers, LC. For a further discussion, see R. Kluger, *Simple Justice* 606–9 (New York: Vintage, 1977).
85. See, e.g., Memorandum to Conference on *United States v. Nixon*, Brennan Papers, Box 329, LC.
86. Brennan Papers, Box 336 (Memorandum, February 27, 1975), LC.
87. See Memorandum to the Court from Chief Justice Taft, February 12, 1928, Willis Van Devanter Papers, Box 35, LC; Memorandum Respecting the Compensation of the Clerk, Douglas Papers, Box 229, LC; and "Historical Note to the Clerk's Office Personnel," Felix Frankfurter Papers, Box 182, File 11, HLS.
88. Jay to Fisher Ames, November 27, 1789, reprinted in H. Johnston, ed., *The Correspondence and Public Papers of John Jay*, vol. 3, at 379 (New York: Franklin, 1970). For similar incidents, see correspondence—especially, from Justice Duval, Taney, and Wayne—in Records of the Clerk of the Supreme Court, NARS.
89. Justice Grier's correspondence, as well as that of Justice Curtis, may be found in the Records of the Clerk of the Supreme Court, Letters to and from the Justices, NARS. See also, Benjamin Curtis Papers, LC.
90. For further discussion of this history of the Office of the Reporter, see Letter from John Marshall to Dudley Chase, February 7, 1817, reprinted in Oster, supra note 16, at 80–83; and, generally, G. Dunne, "Early Court Reporters," *Supreme Court Historical Society Yearbook* 61 (1976).
91. Quoted in Swisher, supra note 8, at 50.
92. This story is detailed in Frank, supra note 10, at 170–72.
93. See, e.g., C. P. Magrath, *Morrison R. Waite: The Triumph of Character* 254–67 (New York: Macmillan, 1963).
94. Because of controversies surrounding the writing of headnotes, the justices voted on what the Reporter should and should not include in his headnotes. See Memorandum as to Reports, February 28, 1856, Records of the Office of the Marshal, NARS. The Court formally recognized that headnotes are not part of an opinion in *United States v. Detroit Lumber Co.*, 200 U.S. 321, 337 (1906). Note, however, that in this case the Reporter thought it sufficiently important to note in a headnote that headnotes are prepared by the Reporter and not considered binding by the Court. See also C. Butler, *A Century at the Bar of the Supreme Court of the United States* 80 (New York: Putnam's, 1942).

95. For a wonderful discussion of this event and its significance, see McGrath, supra note 93, at 224–25.
96. Letter of the justice to the Reporter and response, March 10 and 16, 1936, Stone Papers, Box 81, LC. For similar objections, see Clark Papers, UT; and Melville Fuller Papers, Box 4 (Letter from Justice Field), LC. The *Gold Clause* cases are *Norman v. Baltimore & Ohio Railroad Co.*, *United States v. Banker's Trust Co.*, *Nortz v. United States*, and *Perry v. United States* (1935).
97. Quoted by C. Fairman, "What Makes a Great Justice? Mr. Justice Bradley and the Supreme Court," *Boston University Law Review* 49, 100 (1949 / 1950). For other illustrations of the problems of editing justices' opinions, see the interview with Henry Putzel, former Reporter for the Court: "Double Revolving Peripatetic Nitpicker," *Supreme Court Historical Society Yearbook* 10 (1980).
98. See F. Barbash, "That Opinion Was Here Somewhere . . ." *Washington Post* A5 (June 10, 1983).
99. See Memorandum to the Conference, Re: *Jimenez v. Weinberger* (July 15, 1975), Brennan Papers, Box 363, LC. Occasionally, other close Court watchers, like the solicitor general, will find errors in preliminary prints of opinions and suggest modifications before an opinion is published in the official *United States Reports*. See Sherman Minton Papers, Box 6, TPL.
100. Memorandum to the Justices, January 17, 1950, Douglas Papers, Box 218, LC. A similar controversy developed over the printing of the filing of Justice Frankfurter's two opinions in *Brown v. Allen* (1953). See Letter from the Reporter to the Chief Justice, February 16, 1953, Vinson Papers, Box 224, UK.
101. See B. McGurn, "The Court's Officers," *Supreme Court Historical Society Yearbook,* 87, 91 (1979).
102. The early history of the Supreme Court's library is set forth in a Memorandum by the Law Librarian of the Library of Congress, November 1, 1940, Felix Frankfurter Papers, Box 182, File 19, HLS.
103. A partial listing of these responsibilities may be found as Appendix A in D. Meador, "The Federal Judiciary and Its Future Administration," 65 *Virginia Law Review* 1055–59 (1979). See also Warren Papers, Box 658, LC.
104. Quoted by A. Mason, *Harlan Fiske Stone: Pillar of the Law* 719 (New York: Viking, 1956). In the Stone Papers, LC, there are numerous other letters expressing his astonishment at the time-consuming administrative responsibilities of the chief justiceship.
105. Letter to Judge Sherman Minton, June 14, 1946, Black Papers, Box 61, LC.
106. Warren, supra note 42, at 1–2.
107. See, e.g., W. Burger, "The Courts On Trial," 22 F.R.D. 71 (1958); "Who Will Watch the Watchmen?" 14 *American University Law Review* 1 (1964); Remarks before Young Lawyers Section of the District of Columbia Bar Association (October 31, 1967); Remarks to the Ohio Judicial Conference (September 4, 1968); and "Court Administrators: Where Do We Find Them?" (Paper delivered at ABA Convention, August 12, 1969).
108. Interview with Chief Justice Warren E. Burger, *U.S. News & World Report* 32, 43 (December 14, 1970). The changes and reforms that he initiated are examined in Edward A. Tamm and Paul Reardon, "Warren E. Burger and the Administration of Justice," 3 *Bringham Young University Law Review* 447 (1981), excerpt reprinted in M. Cannon and D. M. O'Brien, eds., *Views from the Bench: The Judiciary and Constitutional Politics* (Chatham, N.J.: Chatham House, 1985).
109. Interview, supra 108, at 42.

110. See House Committee on Appropriations, *Departments . . . Hearings before a Subcommittee*, 92d Cong., 1st sess., at 127–28 (Washington, D.C.: GPO, 1971); Judical Conference, *Report of the Proceedings* 25 (1971); and House Committee on the Judiciary, *Administrative Assistant to the Chief Justice: Hearings before Subcommittee No. 5*, 92d Cong., 1st sess. (Washington, D.C.: GPO, 1971).

111. Some of the functions of the Office of Administrative Assistant to the Chief Justice have been described by M. Cannon in "An Administrator's View of the Supreme Court," 22 *Federal Bar News* 109 (1975); and "Administrative Change and the Supreme Court," 57 *Judicature* 334 (1974).

112. Data on filings and total docket for 1800–1913 were gathered by examining the Docket Books of the Supreme Court of the United States (available at the National Archives, Washington, D.C.). Figures for the number of filings and docket for 1913–1981 are taken from Annual Reports of the Office of the Clerk, Supreme Court of the United States. Cases disposed of each term include both cases given plenary consideration and those summarily decided or otherwise disposed of. Figures for cases disposed of and carried over for the years 1800–1810, 1820, 1822–1846, 1850, 1860, 1870, 1880, and 1890 are based on the author's tabulation of cases contained in the Docket Books of the Supreme Court of the United States. Figures for 1890–1910 were taken from *Annual Reports of the Attorney General of the United States* (Washington, D.C.: GPO, 1891, 1901, 1911). David Brewer Papers, Box 13, YA. Data for 1913–1981 were taken from Statistical Sheet, Office of the Clerk, Supreme Court. This section draws on the author's article "The Supreme Court: A Co-equal Branch of Government," *Supreme Court Historical Society Yearbook* 90 (1984).

113. See F. Frankfurter and J. Landis, *The Business of the Supreme Court*, 105–10 (Cambridge: Harvard University Press, 1927).

114. See Letter of Chief Justice Taft to Justice Van Devanter, Van Devanter Papers, Box 34, LC.

115. See W. Taft, "The Jurisdiction of the Supreme Court under the Act of February 13, 1925," 35 *Yale Law Journal* (1925); Letter to Senator Copeland, December 9, 1925, reprinted in Cong. Rec. 68th Cong., 2d sess., 2916, 2920 (1925); and testimony of Chief Justice Taft and Justices Van Devanter, McReynolds, and Sutherland on the bill, in House Committee on the Judiciary, *Jurisdiction of Circuit Courts of Appeals and of the Supreme Court of the United States*, 68th Cong., 2d sess. House Report 8206, at 6–30 (Washington, D.C.: GPO, 1925). In a letter to Mr. George Rose, Justice Van Devanter discusses the drafting of the bill by a committee of justices of the Supreme Court. Van Devanter Papers (Letter of March 9, 1925), Box 19, LC. Committees of justices drafted legislation altering the Court's jurisdiction earlier as well. See correspondence among Chief Justice White and Justices Van Devanter and Day in 1911 and 1914, William Day Papers, Boxes 27 and 29, LC.

116. Douglas, supra note 67, at 175.

117. Stevens, supra note 76, at 179.

118. Chief Justice Burger, "Annual Report on the State of the Judiciary" (Address to the American Bar Association, New Orleans, February 6, 1983); quoting *Dick v. New York Life Insurance Co.*, 359 U.S. 437, 458–59 (1959) (Frankfurter, J., dis. op.).

119. Testimony of Justice White, in House Committee on Appropriations, *Departments . . . : Hearings before a Subcommittee*, 95th Cong., 1st sess., at 55 (Washington, D.C.: GPO, 1977).

120. Letter to Congressman Robert Kastenmeier, June 17, 1982, signed by all nine

justices supporting the passage of H.R. 2406.

121. *Report of the Study Group on the Caseload of the Supreme Court,* 57 F.R.D. 573–650 (1973).

122. See, e.g., E. Warren and W. Burger, "Retired Chief Justice Attacks, Chief Justice Berger Defends Freund Study Group's Composition and Proposal," 59 *American Bar Association Journal* 721 (1973); and W. Brennan, supra note 75.

123. See J. P. Stevens, "The Life Span of a Judge-Made Rule," 58 *New York University Law Review* 1 (1983).

124. Commission on Revision of the Federal Court Appellate System, *Structure and Internal Procedures: Recommendations for Change* (Washington, D.C.: CRFCAS, 1975).

125. Burger, supra note 107, and "State of the Judiciary Address," reprinted in 71 *American Bar Association Journal* 86 (1985).

126. See, e.g., "DOJ Report Favoring Creation of Intercircuit Court," *Legal Times* 38 (May 23, 1983); and Statement of Jonathan Rose, assistant attorney general Office of Legal Policy, "Concerning the Workload of the Supreme Court," before the House Committee on the Judiciary, Subcommittee on Courts, Civil Liberties, and the Administration of Justice, November 10, 1983.

127. See Statement of Judges Wilfred Feinberg and Donald Lay, on the Intercircuit Tribunal Bill, before the House Committee on the Judiciary, Subcommittee on Courts, Civil Liberties, and the Administration of Justice, September 22, 1983. See, generally, House Committee on the Judiciary, *Supreme Court Workload,* 98th Cong., 1st sess. (Washington, D.C.: GPO, 1984).

128. Letter from Justice Stevens to Congressman Kastenmeier, October 25, 1983.

FOUR

Deciding What to Decide

1. J. M. Harlan, Jr., "A Glimpse of the Supreme Court at Work," 11 *University of Chicago Law School Record* 1, 4 (1963).

2. A. Lewis, *Gideon's Trumpet* 208 (New York: Random House, 1964).

3. Testimony of Justice Rehnquist at appropriations hearings for the Supreme Court. House Committee on Appropriations, *Departments . . .: Hearings before a Subcommittee,* 96th Cong., 1st sess., at 21 (Washington, D.C.: GPO, 1980).

4. Congress may alter the jurisdiction of federal courts by changing the criteria for "federal questions" and diversity suits (where federal courts consider disputes over state law when the parties are from two different states) and raise or eliminate the dollar amount required for filing such suits. In 1980, Congress eliminated, in certain cases, the requirement of $10,000 in a dispute, but maintained a dollar amount required for bringing diversity suits. See 31 U.S.C. 1331–32 (1982).

5. 27 Stat. 252 (1892), 28 U.S.C. Sec. 1915 (1966).

6. C. E. Hughes, *Addresses of Charles Evans Hughes* 185–86 (New York: Putnam's, 1916).

7. *United States v. Butler,* 297 U.S. 1 (1936).

8. *Flast v. Cohen,* 392 U.S. 83, 94–95 (1968).

9. *Muskrat v. United States,* 219 U.S. 346, 362 (1911).

10. *Duke Power Co. v. Carolina Environmental Study Group,* 438 U.S. 59, 103 (1978) (con. op.). See also *Bellotti v. Baird,* 443 U.S. 622 (1979).

11. *Aetna Life Insurance Co. v. Haworth,* 300 U.S. 277 (1937).

12. *Data Processing Service v. Camp*, 397 U.S. 150, 151 (1970).
13. *Braxton County Court v. West Virginia*, 208 U.S. 192, 197 (1908); *Coleman v. Miller*, 307 U.S. 433, 464 (1931) (Frankfurter, J., dis. op.).
14. *Frothingham v. Mellon*, 262 U.S. 447, 487–88 (1923).
15. See, *Laird v. Tatum*, 408 U.S. 1 (1972); and *Sierra Club v. Morton*, 405 U.S. 727 (1972).
16. *Linda R. S. v. Richard D.*, 410 U.S. 614 (1973) (dis. op.).
17. *Ex parte Baez*, 177 U.S. 378 (1900).
18. A. de Tocqueville, *Democracy in America*, ed. P. Bradley, vol. 1, at 288 (New York: Vintage, 1945).
19. See *Colegrove v. Green*, 328 U.S. 549 (1946).
20. J. Roche, "Judicial Self-Restraint," 49 *American Political Science Review* 762, 768 (1955).
21. L. Henkin, "Is There a 'Political Question' Doctrine?" 85 *Yale Law Journal* 597, 606 (1976).
22. Draft of opinion, George Sutherland Papers, Box 7, LC.
23. *Burnet v. Coronado Oil*, 285 U.S. 393 (1932) (Brandeis, J., dis. op.).
24. W. O. Douglas, Interview, "CBS Reports," transcript, at 13 (New York: CBS News, September 6, 1972).
25. R. Jackson, "The Task of Maintaining Our Liberties: The Role of the Judiciary," 39 *American Bar Association Journal* 962, 962 (1953).
26. Letter to Frankfurter, March 30, 1937, Harlan F. Stone Papers, Box 13, LC. See also Letter from Clerk to Chief Justice Taft, March 27, 1928, Willis Van Devanter Papers, Box 34, LC.
27. H. Willey, "Jurisdictional Statements on Appeals to the United States Supreme Court," 31 *American Bar Association Journal* 239 (1945).
28. F. Vinson, Address before the American Bar Association, September 7, 1949, reprinted in 69 S.Ct. v, vi (1949).
29. See Commission on Revision of the Federal Court Appellate System, *Structure and Internal Procedures; Recommendations for Change* 11–19, 76–79, 91–111 (Washington, D.C.: CRFCAS, 1975). The commission's estimate was criticized as too high by G. Casper and R. Posner, *The Workload of the Supreme Court* (Chicago: American Bar Foundation, 1976). For Chief Justice Burger's proposal, see "Annual Report on the State of the Judiciary" (Address to the American Bar Association, New Orleans, February 6, 1983) (discussed in Chapter 3 and by the author in "Managing the Business of the Supreme Court," 45 *Public Administration Review* 667 [1985]).
30. The number of cases alleging circuit conflicts is based on the author's Lexis search of briefs filed in cases accepted for oral argument. The figures for the circuit conflicts decided by opinion are based on a study prepared by the staff of the chief justice. These figures may be higher than those of others because if one examines only the Court's final published opinions the number will be smaller, since justices do not always note in the text that the decision resolves a circuit conflict. Here, conflicts appearing in papers filed with the Court in argued cases were examined as well. A list of the opinions resolving circuit conflicts in 1980 and 1981 may be found in Appendix B of Mr. John Frank's testimony on the Intercircuit Tribunal Bill, before the House Committee on the Judiciary, Subcommittee on Courts, Civil Liberties, and the Administration of Justice, May 18, 1983.
31. J. Harlan, Jr., "Some Aspects of Handling a Case in the Supreme Court of the United States" (Address at Annual Dinner of the New York State Bar Associa-

tion, January 20, 1957), p. 6, SC. See also Letter to Justice Holmes, January 7, 1930, Records of the Clerk of the Supreme Court, NARS.

32. *Greco v. Orange Memorial Hospital Corporation*, 423 U.S. 1000, 1006 (1975) (dis. op.).

33. *Professional Positioners, Inc. v. T. P. Laboratories*, 103 S.Ct. 2337 (1984).

34. See *Tatum v. Regents of the University of Nebraska*, 103 S.Ct. 3084 (1984); and *Garcia v. United States*, 103 S.Ct. 3083 (1984).

35. Memorandum to the Conference by Frankfurter, 1951, 1953–1961, SC. These items are also in the John M. Harlan Papers, Boxes 499 and 587, MLPU; in the Felix Frankfurter Papers at HLS; as well as in the Tom C. Clark Papers, UT. For an excellent discussion of Frankfurter's efforts, see D. Hutchinson, "Felix Frankfurter and the Business of the Supreme Court, O.T. 1946–O.T. 1961," *The Supreme Court Review* 143, ed. P. Kurland and G. Casper (Chicago: University of Chicago Press, 1980).

36. Brandeis-Frankfurter Conversations, at 17 and 30; Felix Frankfurter Papers, Box 224, LC.

37. See, e.g., Memorandum for the Conference by Chief Justice Warren, October 7, 1957, Frankfurter Papers, Box 220, File 4051, LC.

38. Letter from Justice Douglas to Justice Frankfurter, October 13, 1960, Felix Frankfurter Papers, Box 152, Folder 9, HLS. The letter is also in the Harlan Papers, Box 49, MLPU.

39. Letter from Justice Black to Justice Frankfurter, October 13, 1960, Felix Frankfurter Papers, Box 152, Folder 9, HLS. See also Memorandum to Conference by Justice Clark, October 7, 1957, Clark Papers, UT.

40. This Chart is based on data for 1935–1971 contained in *Report of the Study Group on the Caseload of the Supreme Court*, 57 F.R.D. 573, 614 (1973). Data for 1971–1982 are compiled from the Statistical Sheets (Final), Office of the Clerk, Supreme Court. Note that cases on the Court's original docket are included in the total number of filings but do not usually appear in the number for paid and unpaid filings. Note also that at various times between 1935 and 1971 the method of assigning cases to the miscellaneous docket changed and that there thus may be some minor variations in the composition of the miscellaneous docket. The Miscellaneous Docket was created in 1945, and beginning in 1947 all petitions for certiorari in forma pauperis were transferred to that docket, and appeals in forma pauperis were likewise docketed and transferred in 1954. After the creation of the Miscellaneous Docket, a case was transferred from it to the Appellate Docket once certiorari was granted or an appeal noted. Since 1971, the Clerk of the Supreme Court reports as a category all in forma pauperis petitions.

41. Memorandum of Justice Frankfurter on In Forma Pauperis Petitions, November 1, 1954, Felix Frankfurter Papers, Box 205, Folder 5, HLS. See also Stanley Reed Papers, Memo, November 1, 1944, Box 172, UK.

42. Memorandum for the Conference, November 1, 1944, William O. Douglas Papers, Box 228, LC.

43. Memoranda from the Chief Justice and NARS Report, Hugo Black Papers, Boxes 58, and 426, LC. See also Letter to Harlan, July 15, 1970, and Memoranda to the Conference, July 16 and 30, 1970, Harlan Papers, Box 490, MLPU. At other times, justices share the law clerks assigned to retired justices. See Memorandum from Chief Justice Burger, 1974, Clark Papers, UT.

44. Quoted by T. Clark, "Internal Operations of the United States Supreme Court," 43 *Judicature* 45, 48 (1959).

45. The preceding observations are based on conversations with law clerks. Law

clerks frankly admit their lack of maturity in screening filings when they begin their year at the Court. Similar observations by former law clerks may be found in the Harlan F. Stone Papers, LC.

46. See, e.g., Letter from Hughes to Stone, October 1, 1931, Stone Papers, Box 75, LC.

47. Quoted in "The Supreme Court: How It Operates in Private Chambers outside Courtroom," *Smithsonian* magazine, special report, 1976.

48. See W. J. Brennan, Jr., "The National Court of Appeals: Another Dissent," 40 *University of Chicago Law Review* 473, 478–79 (1973).

49. E. Warren, Remarks, American Law Institute Meeting, at 7 (Washington, D.C.: American Law Institute, 1956).

50. J. F. Byrnes, *All in One Lifetime* 154 (New York: Harper, 1958).

51. W. E. Burger, "Supreme Court Film" (film shown to visitors to the Supreme Court).

52. W. O. Douglas, *The Court Years* 223, 226, and 237 (New York: Random House, 1980).

53. O. Roberts, Address, Meeting of the Association of the Bar of the City of New York and the New York County Lawyers' Association, December 12, 1946; and Robert Jackson Papers, LC.

54. Memorandum of Howard Westwood, Stone Papers, Box 48, LC. See also Memorandum of talk with HFS, March 2, 1965, Felix Frankfurter Papers, Box 171, File 14, HLS.

55. B. White, "The Work of the Supreme Court: A Nuts and Bolts Description," 54 *New York State Bar Journal* 346, 383 (1982).

56. Clark, supra note 44, at 50.

57. H. Black, "Justice Black and the Bill of Rights," CBS Special, transcript, at 5 (New York: CBS News, December 3, 1968).

58. H. Blackmun, "A Justice Speaks Out: A Conversation with Harry A. Blackmun," Cable News Network, transcript, at 4 (December 4, 1982).

59. Memo to chief justice, June 20, 1975, William J. Brennan Papers, Box 336, LC. For a similar incident, see Frankfurter's lengthy memo to Stone, December 12, 1939, Reed Papers, Box 171, UK.

60. See, e.g., Memos between the chief justice and Blackmun, October 3, 1975, Brennan Papers, Box 363, LC.

61. M. Provine, *Case Selection in the United States Supreme Court* 32 (Chicago: University of Chicago Press, 1980).

62. This table is based on a tabulation of cases and initial votes noted in Brennan's Docket Book for the 1973 term. Brennan Papers, Boxes 421–23, LC. Excluded from this table are cases coming on original jurisdiction and those dismissed at the request of the litigants under Rule 60 (now Rule 53). The total number of filings counted here was 3,888, which is slightly higher than the figure the Clerk's records show for dispositions by the Court during the term (3876). The discrepancy is due to the inclusion here of votes on motions and other items. Included in the miscellaneous category are cases postponed, held, vacated, reversed, and / or remanded with other cases on the docket.

63. See testimony of McReynolds, in *Hearings on H.R. 8206 before the Committee on the Judiciary*, 68th Cong., 2d sess., 1924.

64. C. E. Hughes, "Reason as Opposed to the Tyranny of Force" (Speech delivered to the American Law Institute, May 6, 1937), reprinted in *Vital Speeches of the Day* 458, 459 (1937).

65. Letter from Reed, October 12, 1940, Douglas Papers, Box 228 (Frankfurter File),

LC. See also his note to Burton, March 5, 1952, Harold Burton Papers, Box 336, LC.

66. Memorandum for Conference, March 11, 1943, Douglas Papers, Box 228 (Frankfurter File), LC.

67. Memorandum for Conference, April 6, 1944, Stone Papers, Box 24, LC.

68. See,Memorandum to Conference from Stevens, May 14, 1976, Brennan Papers, Box 363, LC. Conversely, the crucial fourth vote may be lost if a justice decided to deny rather than grant a case after the conference vote. See Letter from Harlan, December 13, 1965, Clark Papers, UT. See also Letter from Frankfurter to Burton, February 1, 1965, Felix Frankfurter Papers, Box 169, File 6, HLS.

69. Data for 1941–1971 are taken from *Report of the Study Group on the Caseload of the Supreme Court* (the Freund report), 57 F.R.D. 573, 615 (1973). Data for 1981, and for argued and nonargued cases in 1971, are based on the author's analysis.

70. W. H. Taft, testimony, in *Hearings before the House Committee on the Judiciary*, 67th Cong., 2d sess., at 2 (Washington, D.C., 1922).

71. White, supra note 55, at 383.

72. P. Linzer, "The Meaning of Certiorari Denials," 79 *Columbia Law Review* 1227, 1302 (1979). See also S. Brenner, "The New Certiorari Game," 41 *Journal of Politics* 649 (1979).

73. J. P. Stevens, "The Life Span of a Judge-Made Rule" (Lecture delivered at New York University School of Law, October 27, 1982), excerpt reprinted in M. Cannon and D. M. O'Brien, eds., *Views from the Bench: The Judiciary and Constitutional Politics* (Chatham, N.J.: Chatham House, 1985).

74. *Singleton v. Commissioner of Internal Revenue*, 439 U.S. 940, 942 (1978) (Stevens, J., op. respecting denial of certiorari).

75. *United States v. Carver*, 260 U.S. 482, 490 (1922).

76. *Brown v. Allen*, 344 U.S. 443, 542 (1953).

77. *Maryland v. Baltimore Radio Show*, 338 U.S. 912, 917–19 (1950).

78. W. J. Brennan, Jr., "State Court Decisions and the Supreme Court," 31 *Pennsylvania Bar Association Quarterly* 393, 402–3 (1960).

79. *Brown v. Allen*, 344 U.S. 443, 542 (1953).

80. *Rogers v. Missouri Pacific Railroad Co.*, 352 U.S. 500, 528 (1957).

81. See ibid. and *McBride v. Toledo Terminal Co.*, 354 U.S. 517, 519–20 (1957).

82. *United States v. Shannon*, 342 U.S. 288, 298 (1952).

83. *Darr v. Burford*, 339 U.S. 200, 226 (1950) (Frankfurter, J., dis. op.).

84. *Daniels v. Allen*, 344 U.S. 443, 491 (1953).

85. W. O. Douglas, *Go East Young Man* 452 (New York: Random House, 1974).

86. See Linzer, supra note 72, at 1258.

87. Letter to Frankfurter, March 30, 1937, Stone Papers, Box 13.

88. *Liles v. Oregon*, 425 U.S. 963, 963 (1976).

89. *Coleman v. Balkcom*, 451 U.S. 949, 950 (1981).

90. *Gilliard v. Mississippi*, 104 S.Ct. 40, 41 (1983) (Marshall, J., dis. op.).

91. *Texas v. Mead*, 104 S.Ct. 1318 (1984).

92. P. Stewart, "Inside the Supreme Court," *New York Times* A17, col. 2 (Oct. 1, 1979).

93. *Drake v. Zant*, and *Westbrook v. Balkcom*, 449 U.S. 999 (1980) (dissenting opinions by Justices Brennan, joined by Marshall; Stewart; and White).

94. This discussion is based on the author's examination and tabulation of records (a single index card for each case, noting jurisdiction, mode of arrival, and nature of case as well as final disposition) maintained by the Clerk of the Supreme

Court. The records typically contain a brief description of the case—e.g., tax case—and this description was used in categorizing the case. Some 151 records did not contain such a description, and the author used other records on file to categorize the case. Note also that two cases on original jurisdiction were missing from the records and not counted here.

95. Memo to Clerks from Burton, Harlan Papers, Box 561, MLPU.
96. See, A. Hellman, " 'Granted, Vacated, and Remanded'—Shedding Light on a Dark Corner of Supreme Court Practice," 67 *Judicature* 390, 391 n. 10 (1984).
97. Letter from the justices to Congressman Kastenmeier, June 17, 1982, attachment, p. 5.
98. *Hicks v. Miranda*, 422 U.S. 332, 345 (1975), quoting *Doe v. Hodgson*, 478 F.2d 537, 539, cert. denied sub. nom., *Doe v. Brennan*, 414 U.S. 1096 (1973). See also *Colorado Springs Amusements, Ltd. v. Rizzo*, 428 U.S. 913 (1976) (Brennan, J., dis. op.) (reviewing the problems of confusion created by the Court's position).
99. *Rose v. Locke*, 423 U.S. 48, 59 (1975) (per curiam) (Brennan, J., dis. op.).
100. *United States v. Jacobs*, 429 U.S. 909, 910 (1976) (Stewart, J., dis. op.).
101. J. Goebel, Jr., *Antecedents and Beginnings to 1801*, Appendix, at 804 (New York: Macmillan, 1971).
102. This table incorporates data from and updates the statistics compiled in F. Frankfurter and J. Landis, *The Business of the Supreme Court*, Table 1, at 302 (New York: Macmillan, 1927) (data for 1825, 1875, and 1925); F. Frankfurter and J. Landis, "The Business of the Supreme Court in the October Term 1930," 45 *Harvard Law Review* 271, Table 9, at 9 (1930) (data for 1930); and E. Gressman, "Much Ado about Certiorari," 52 *Georgetown Law Journal* 742, 756–57 (1964) (data for 1935, 1945, and 1955). Data for 1960, 1965, 1970, 1975, and 1980 were compiled by the author. The table aims only to illustrate trends. The classification in this and other tables necessarily invites differences of opinion as to the dominant issue in a case.
103. Vinson, supra note 28, at vi.
104. *NAACP v. Button*, 371 U.S. 415, 429–30 (1963).
105. L. Powell, *The Powell Memorandum: Attack on American Free Enterprise System* 7 (August 24, 1971) (Chamber of Commerce of the United States, Washington, D.C.).
106. R. Jackson, *The Struggle for Judicial Supremacy* 287 (New York: Knopf, 1951).
107. See J. Tanenhaus, M. Schick, M. Muraskin, and D. Rosen, "The Supreme Court's Certiorari Jurisdiction: Cue Theory," in *Judicial Decisionmaking*, ed. G. Schubert, at 111–32 (New York: Free Press, 1963); V. Armstrong and C. Johnson, "Certiorari Decisions by the Warren & Burger Courts: Is Cue Theory Time Bound?" *Polity* 141 (1983); D. M. Provine, "Deciding What to Decide: How the Supreme Court Sets Its Agenda," 64 *Judicature* 321 (1981).
108. See S. S. Ulmer, "Selecting Cases for Supreme Court Review: An Underdog Model," 72 *American Political Science Review* 902 (1978); S. S. Ulmer, W. Hintze, and L. Kirklosky, 6 *Law & Society* 637 (1972); and G. Rathjen and H. Spaeth, "Denial of Access and Ideological Preferences: An Analysis of the Voting Behavior of the Burger Court Justices, 1969–1976," *Western Political Quarterly* 70 (1983).
109. Provine, supra note 107, at 327.
110. Data taken from Jonathan Rose, assistant attorney general, Department of Justice, "The Workload of the Supreme Court," Testimony before the House Committee on the Judiciary, Subcommittee on Courts, Civil Liberties, and the

Administration of Justice, at 5–6 (November 10, 1983). Compared with the situation fifty years earlier, the government is now participating in more argued cases each term and winning slightly more as well. During 1928–1936, the government's success rate averaged 67 percent each term; between 1937 and 1944, it averaged 74 percent. Memorandum for the Attorney General by Solicitor General Stanley Reed, June 1, 1937, Felix Frankfurter Papers, Box 170, File 16, HLS; and Report to the Attorney General, June 20, 1945, Francis Biddle Papers, Box 2, RPL.

111. W. O. Douglas, Interview, "CBS Reports," transcript, at 12 (New York: CBS News, September 6, 1972).

112. Black, supra note 58, at 5.

113. Letter to Senator Burton Wheeler, reprinted in Senate Committee on the Judiciary, *Hearings on the Reorganization of the Federal Judiciary*, 75th Cong., 1st sess., 1937, Senate Report 711, at 40.

114. J. Clarke, "Observations and Reflections on Practice in the Supreme Court," 8 *American Bar Association Journal* 263, 263 (1922).

115. J. Harlan, "Manning the Dikes," 13 *Record of the New York City Bar Association* 541, 547 (1958); Douglas, supra note 111; Rehnquist, Remarks at the Jefferson Literary and Debating Society, Charlottesville, Virginia, September 20, 1985.

116. *Ex parte Brummett*, 295 U.S. 719 (1935); 299 U.S. 514 (1936); 302 U.S. 644 (1937); 303 U.S. 570 (1938); 306 U.S. 615 (1939); 309 U.S. 625 (1940); *Ex parte Brummitt*, 304 U.S. 545 (1938); 311 U.S. 614 (1940); 313 U.S. 548 (1941); and 314 U.S. 585 (1941).

117. Brennan, supra note 48.

118. See *In re Reverend Clovis Carl Green*, 669 F.2d 779, 781 (1981).

119. Memorandum to Conference, May 25, 1971, Harlan Papers, Box 434, MLPU.

120. W. O. Douglas, "The Supreme Court and Its Caseload," 45 *Cornell Law Quarterly* 401, 413–14 (1960).

FIVE

Deciding Cases and Writing Opinions

1. Interview with Stewart, February 28, 1985, SC.

2. Memorandum, William J. Brennan Papers, Box 14, LC; and Interview with Justice Brennan, September 30, 1985, SC.

3. *Abbate v. United States*, 359 U.S. 187 (1959). Brennan wrote the opinion for the Court but also added a separate concurring opinion.

4. Memorandum, May 28, 1974, Brennan Papers, Box 423, L.C.

5. Transcript of Oral Arguments. The transcript may be found in *Landmark Briefs and Arguments of the Supreme Court of the United States: Constitutional Law*, Vol. 79, ed. P. Kurland and G. Casper (Arlington, Va.: University Publications of America, 1975).

6. Docket Book, 1972 Term, Brennan Papers, Box 423, LC.

7. Memorandum to the Conference, July 14, 1974, Brennan Papers, Box 329, LC.

8. Memorandum, July 22, 1974, Brennan Papers, Box 329, LC.

9. Handwritten note to Brennan on a Letter to Burger, July 12, 1974, Brennan Papers, Box 329, LC.

10. Letter to Burger, July 18, 1974, Brennan Papers, Box 329, LC.

11. C. E. Hughes, *The Supreme Court of the United States* 61 (New York: Columbia University Press, 1928).

12. W. J. Brennan, quoted in Report of the Commission on Revision of the Federal Court Appellate System, *Structure and Internal Procedures: Recommendation for Change*, 67 F.R.D. 195, 254 (1975).

13. L. F. Powell, Remarks at Fifth Circuit Judicial Conference, May 27, 1974; unreported manuscript, quoted in R. Stern and E. Gressman, *Supreme Court Practice* 732 (Washington, D.C.: BNA, 1978).

14. W. Rehnquist, "Oral Advocacy: A Disappearing Art" (Brainerd Currie Lecture, Mercer University School of Law, October 20, 1983) ms p. 4 (on file with the author).

15. Quoted by A. Beveridge, *The Life of John Marshall*, vol. 4, at 249–50 (Boston: Houghton Mifflin, 1919).

16. Quoted by C. Warren, *The Supreme Court in United States History*, vol. 1, at 603 (Boston: Little, Brown, 1922).

17. *Bridge Proprietors v. Hoboken Co.*, 68 U.S. 116 (1863).

18. J. Clarke, "Reminiscences of the Court and the Law," 5 *Proceedings of the Fifth Annual Meeting of the California State Bar* 20 (1932).

19. Letter to Pollock, March 17, 1898, reprinted in *Holmes-Pollock Letters*, ed. M. Howe, 81 (Cambridge: Harvard University Press, 1946)

20. Undated note, Hugo Black Papers, Frankfurter File, Box 60, LC.

21. Quoted in C. White, "Courtly Manners," *American Lawyer* 32, 33 (April 1979).

22. F. Frankfurter, *Proceedings in Honor of Mr. Justice Frankfurter and Distinguished Alumni* 18 (Occasional Paper No. 3 of the Harvard Law School, 1960).

23. W. Rutledge, "The Appellate Brief," 28 *American Bar Association Journal* 251, 251 (1942).

24. See C. H. Butler, *A Century at the Bar of the Supreme Court of the United States* 88 (New York: Putnam's, 1942).

25. Rehnquist, supra note 14, at 19.

26. Quoted in the *Philadelphia Inquirer* (April 9, 1963), cited by H. Abraham, *The Judicial Process* 203 (New York: Oxford University Press, 4th ed., 1980); and "Seminar with Mr. Chief Justice Warren," University of Virginia Legal Forum, at 9 (April 25, 1973).

27. Reported by J. Frank, *The Marble Palace* 105 (New York: Knopf, 1958).

28. Reported by A. Lewis in "The Justices' Supreme Job," *New York Times Magazine* (June 11, 1961), as quoted by Abraham, supra note 26, at 203 (emphasis added).

29. Quoted by C. White, "Courtly Manners," *American Lawyer* 30 (June 1979).

30. L. F. Powell, "What Really Goes On at the Court," printed in M. Cannon and D. O'Brien, eds., *Views from the Bench: The Judiciary and Constitutional Politics* (Chatham, N.J.: Chatham House, 1985).

31. Memo from Justice Douglas to Conference, October 23, 1961, Black Papers, Box 60, LC.

32. W. O. Douglas, *The Court Years* 34 (New York: Random House, 1980).

33. H. Hart, Jr., "Foreword: The Time Chart of the Justices," 73 *Harvard Law Review* 84 (1959). See also Henry M. Hart Papers, HLS. Hart's estimate of the number of hours devoted to conference was slightly high. During the 1949–1952 terms, the justices in fact met an average 119 hours per term. Earl Warren Papers, Box 660, LC.

34. The estimated amount of conference time is based on the assumption that the justices hold twenty-six regular conferences, running for about five hours each, and that they meet on Wednesdays for an hour and a half every week in which they hear oral arguments.

35. Letter from Frankfurter to Burton, Harold Burton Papers, Box 101, LC.

36. D. Danelski, "The Influence of the Chief Justice in the Decisional Process," in W. Murphy and C. H. Pritchett, eds., *Courts, Judges, and Politics* 568 (New York: Random House, 4th ed., 1986).

37. A. T. Mason, *William Howard Taft: Chief Justice* 220–21 (New York: Simon & Schuster, 1965).

38. Letter to the author from Blackmun, November 8, 1984.

39. E. Warren, "A Conversation with Earl Warren," WGBH-TV Educational foundation, transcript, at 12 (Boston: WGBH Educational Foundation, 1972). Warren Papers, Box 571 and, Docket Book in, Box 367, LC; Robert Jackson Papers, LC; and *Diary*, Burton Papers, Box 3, LC. For an excellent further discussion, see D. Hutchinson, "Unanimity and Desegregation: Decisionmaking in the Supreme Court, 1948–1958," 68 *Georgetown Law Journal* 1 (1979).

40. Warren to Conference, October 7, 1957, Black Papers, Box 320, LC. See also Tom Clark Memo to Conference, October 7, 1957, Tom C. Clark Papers, UT.

41. Vinson to Frankfurter, October 11, 1951, William O. Douglas Papers, Box 224, LC.

42. Burger, "Supreme Court Film," transcript, at p. 12 (film shown to visitors to the Supreme Court).

43. Brennan Papers, Box 283, LC. See also letter from Chief Justice Taft, April 22, 1927, Willis Van Devanter Papers, Box 34, LC.

44. Douglas Memorandum to Conference, Black Papers, Box 60, LC. See also Justice Frankfurter's Memorandum on *Baker v. Carr*, Clark Papers, UT.

45. Quoted by D. Dorin, "Social Leadership, Humor, and Supreme Court Decisionmaking," 66 *Judicature* 462 (1983). See also Tom C. Clark Oral History Interview, at 50, UK.

46. Memorandum for Frankfurter, Clark Papers, UT.

47. Quoted by W. Burger, "In Memoriam: John M. Harlan," 92A S. Ct 5, 44 (1972).

48. Quoted by E. Gerhart, *America's Advocate: Robert H. Jackson* 274 (New York: Bobbs-Merrill, 1958).

49. Note to Clark, May 3, 1968, Clark Papers, UT. Justice Douglas later told the story in his autobiography, supra note 32, at 226.

50. The story is told in W. King, *Melville Weston Fuller: Chief Justice of the United States* 290 (New York: Macmillan, 1950).

51. Conference Notes, Frank Murphy Papers, Box 69, File 32, BHLUM.

52. Undated note, Black Papers, Box 61, LC.

53. Undated note, Felix Frankfurter Papers, Box 170, File 9, HLS.

54. Sidney Fine Interview with William O. Douglas, October 24, 1964, BHLUM.

55. Letter to Murphy, February 10, 1947, Felix Frankfurter Papers, Box 170, File 14, HLS.

56. Note from Murphy, Felix Frankfurter Papers, Box 170, File 13, HLS.

57. Letter, Black Papers, Box 60, LC.

58. Unsigned note, January 4, 1941, Black Papers, Box 261, LC.

59. J. Harlan, "A Glimpse of the Supreme Court at Work," 11 *University of Chicago Law School Record* 1, 7 (1963).

60. Memo from Burger, December 20, 1971, Brennan Papers, Box 281, LC.

61. Memo to Conference, Brennan Papers, Box 306, LC.

62. Quoted by A. T. Mason, Review of *The Holmes-Einstein Letters*, in *New York Review of Books* 60 (November 22, 1964).

63. Oliver W. Holmes Papers, Box 42, File 35, HLS.

64. Tom C. Clark Oral History Interview, at 5, UK.

65. Quoted by J. McLean, *William Rufus Day* (Baltimore: Johns Hopkins Press, 1946).

66. See W. King, *Melville Weston Fuller* 332–35 (New York: Macmillan, 1950).
67. See Danelski, supra note 36. Obviously, what "important constitutional cases" are a matter of debate, and so the figures are only rough approximations of each chief justice's practice.
68. Memorandum, April 4, 1963, Brennan Papers, Box 83, LC. For a similar memorandum by Vinson, see Memo, November 29, 1949, Douglas Papers, Box 218, LC.
69. Memorandum of Howard Westwood, Stone Papers, Box 48, LC.
70. "Chief Justice Vinson and His Law Clerks," 49 *Northwestern University Law Review* 26, 31 (1954). The charts are in the Vinson Papers, Box 217, UK.
71. W. J. Brennan, "Chief Justice Warren," 88 *Harvard Law Review* 1, 2, 5 (1974).
72. Based on data collected each term by the Clerk of the Supreme Court, Sheet: Number of Printed Opinions and Memorandum, SC.
73. Memoranda, Brennan Papers, Box 401; and Black Papers, 420, LC.
74. Docket Book, October Term 1955, Black Papers, Box 279, LC; Memo from Reed, May 14, 1956, Felix Frankfurter Papers, Box 220, File 4651, LC; and Memo from Frankfurter, June 6, 1956, Frankfurter papers, Box 94, File 4, LC; and Clark Papers, October Term 1956, UT; John M. Harlan Papers, Boxes 490, 493, and 588, MLPU; and Stanley Reed Papers, Boxes 51, 163 and 176, UK; and Warren Papers, Boxes 428 and 434, LC.
75. See Memorandum, May 27, 1948, Douglas Papers, Box 217, LC.
76. Quoted by A. McCormack, "A Law Clerk's Recollections," 46 *Columbia Law Review* 710, 712 (1946). For another, though less successful, switch of position when writing the Court's opinion, see Memo on *Bryan v. United States* (1950), Sherman Minton Papers, Box 1, TPL.
77. See S. Brenner, "Fluidity on the United States Supreme Court: A Reexamination," 24 *American Journal of Political Science* 526 (1980); and S. Brenner, "Fluidity on the Supreme Court: 1956–1967," 26 *American Journal of Political Science* 388 (1982).
78. In another seven cases, Harlan circulated opinions as to why they should be granted or otherwise disposed of than as voted at the initial conference. After a subsequent change in the conference vote, these opinions were not filed. Harlan papers, Boxes 4, 18, 37, 55, 76, 101, 131, 154, 185, 214, 272, 295, 326, 369, and 407, MLPU.
79. Danelski, supra note 36, at 503. See also W. Murphy, *Elements of Judicial Strategy* (Chicago: University of Chicago Press, 1964).
80. Studies of the opinion assignment practices of chief justices vary in their data base and, to some extent, in their conclusions. See Danelski, supra note 36; S. Ulmer, "The Use of Power in the Supreme Court: The Opinion Assignments of Earl Warren, 1953–1960," 19 *Journal of Public Law* 49 (1970); W. McLauchlan, "Ideology and Conflict in Supreme Court Opinion Assignment, 1946–1962," 25 *Western Political Quarterly* 16 (1972); D. W. Rhode and H. Spaeth, *Supreme Court Decision Making* (San Francisco: W. H. Freeman, 1976); and S. Brenner, "Strategic Choice and Opinion Assignment on the U.S. Supreme Court: A Reexamination," 35 *Western Political Quarterly* 204 (1982).
81. The story is ably told by A. T. Mason, *Harlan Fiske Stone* 614–15 (New York: Viking, 1956).
82. See J. Frank, *Justice Daniel Dissenting* 181–83 (Cambridge: Harvard University Press, 1964).
83. See A. T. Mason, *William Howard Taft* 206–8 (New York: Simon & Schuster, 1965). On occasion, however, Taft did make assignments for expressly political reasons. He explained his assignment of one First Amendment case to Justice

Pierce Butler as follows: "He is the only one to whom I can properly give it. He was appointed by Harding and not by Wilson, and I rather think we ought to have somebody other than an appointee of Wilson to consider and decide the case." Letter to Justice Van Devanter, July 9, 1926, Van Devanter Papers, Box 35, LC.

84. See D. Atkinson, "Opinion Writing on the Supreme Court, 1949–1956: The Views of Justice Sherman Minton," 49 *Temple Law Quarterly* 105 (1975).

85. Letter to Vinson, November 13, 1947, Douglas Papers, Box 217, LC.

86. Quoted by A. Lewis in "A Talk with Warren on Crime, the Court, the Country," *New York Times Magazine* 130 (October 19, 1969), as quoted by Abraham, supra note 26, at 210.

87. Walter Murphy Interview with Douglas, at 148, MLPU.

88. Waite's Papers contain numerous examples of justices complaining about opinion assignments, as do other papers of the justices with regard to Vinson and Burger. See, e.g., Morrison Waite Papers, Box 40, Files for the 1878, 1879, and 1883 Terms, LC; Melville Fuller Papers, Boxes 4 and 6, LC; Frankfurter Papers, Box 108, File 2268, LC; and Vinson Papers, Box 215, UK; Douglas Papers and Brennan Papers, LC.

89. Letter to Brennan, RE: No. 30, Felix Frankfurter Papers, Box 169, File 5, HLS.

90. See Letters from Gray to Fuller on the problems of reading opinions aloud at conference. Fuller Papers, Box 5, LC.

91. Quoted in A. Westin, *The Anatomy of a Constitutional Law Case* 123–24 (New York: Macmillan, 1958).

92. W. J. Brennan, Jr., "State Court Decisions and the Supreme Court," 31 *Pennsylvania Bar Association Quarterly* 393, 405 (160).

93. Memorandum, April 23, 1948, Douglas Papers, Box 217, LC.

94. T. Clark, "Internal Operation of the United States Supreme Court," 43 *Judicature* 45, 51 (1959).

95. Conversation with Paul Freund. And see Douglas, "Mr. Justice Cardozo," 588 *Michigan Law Review* 549 (1960).

96. Memo, Douglas Papers, Box 228, LC.

97. The comparison is based on the assignment lists, noting date of assignment and announcement, in the Brennan Papers, Boxes 130 and 306, LC. The only opinions counted here are those for the Court. For a further discussion, see Memorandum from Chief Justice Warren, October 7, 1957, Frankfurter Papers, Box 220, File 4051, LC; Warren Papers, Boxes 125 and 127, LC. Rehnquist's remarks were made during his talk at the Jefferson Literary and Debating Society, Charlottesville, Virginia, September 20, 1985.

98. See, e.g., Letter to Justice Byrnes, November 1, 1941, Stone Papers, Box 79, LC.

99. Burger, "In Memoriam: Hugo L. Black," 92 S.Ct. 5, 78 (1972).

100. Clark Papers, UT. See also Oral History Interview with Tom Clark, JPL.

101. Undated note, Black Papers, Box 58, LC.

102. Quoted by Murphy, supra note 79, at 51.

103. Memos to Byrnes and Reed, 1941, Douglas Papers, Box 228, LC.

104. Quoted by M. Pusey, *Charles Evans Hughes*, vol. 2, at 671 (New York: Macmillan, 1951).

105. Harlan F. Stone Papers, Box 75, LC.

106. Letter December 20, 1940, Black Papers, Box 261, LC.

107. Quoted by A. T. Mason, *The Supreme Court from Taft to Burger* 65 (Baton Rouge: Louisiana University Press, 3d ed., 1979).

108. Quoted by Mason, supra note 81, at 501.
109. Note, May 20, 1963, Harlan Papers, Box 538, MLPU.
110. Note, January 2, 1969, Harlan Papers, Box 338, MLPU; Abe Fortas Papers, YA.
111. Letter to Reed, December 2, 1941, Douglas Papers, Box 128, LC.
112. Letter to Brennan, January 29, 1962, Brennan Papers, Box 145, LC.
113. Letter to Warren, May 11, 1966, Brennan Papers, Box 145, LC. See also Memo, September 13, 1966, Warren Papers, Box 348; and Warren Papers, Boxes 616 and 617, LC.
114. Letter of April 24, 1965, Brennan Papers, Box 130, LC. For the conference discussion, see Brennan Papers, Box 411; and Warren Papers, Box 267, LC. Douglas's first draft is in Brennan Papers, Box 130, LC.
115. Letter of May 19, 1926, Van Devanter papers, LC; reprinted in M. Urofsky and D. Levy, eds., *Letters of Justice Louis D. Brandeis*, vol. 5, at 128 (New York: SUNY, 1978).
116. Quoted by Murphy, supra note 79, at 53. Likewise, Sutherland wrote Holmes, "I voted 'yes' and would prefer that result. I am inclined to acquiesce and will." Holmes Papers, "Opinion Book 1926," HLS. For other instances, see Louis Brandeis Papers, HLS.
117. Quoted by Murphy, supra note 79, at 52. On another occasion, Justice Butler indicated his preference for the opposite result but decided to acquiesce "unless someone initiates opposition." Note to Justice Holmes, "Opinion Book 1926," HLS.
118. Memo, January 25, 1945, Stone Papers, Box 75, LC.
119. Note on draft opinion, Holmes Papers, "Opinion Book 1919," HLS.
120. Response on draft of *Beaumont v. Prieto*, Holmes Papers, "Opinion Book 1918," HLS.
121. Letter to Harlan, March 23, 1967; Memo to Conference, March 26, 1967; Letter to Douglas, April 6, 1967; Letter, April 4, 1967; Letter, April 6, 1967; Letter, May 2, 1967; Brennan Papers, Box 157, LC. See also, Harlan Papers, Box 297, MLPU; and Abe Fortas Papers, YA.
122. Letter to Black, January 31, 1962, Brennan Papers, Box 68, LC.
123. Letter to Frankfurter, February 3, 1962, Clark Papers, UT.
124. Memorandum, March 10, 1962, Brennan Papers, Box 68, LC.
125. Opinions refers to the number of opinions for the Court disposing of one or more cases on merits. Prior to 1801, the Supreme Court maintained the practice of issuing its opinions seriatim. Here, each case disposed of in such a manner is counted as only one opinion. This practice was largely abandoned shortly before John Marshall became chief justice. The figures for the number of opinions for the terms 1791–1800 are taken from J. Goebel, Jr., *History of the Supreme Court of the United States (1790–1800)*, Table XII, at 811 (New York: Macmillan, 1971). The number for those terms between 1800 and 1815 are taken from G. Haskins and H. A. Johnson, *Foundations of Power: John Marshall (1801–1815)*, Table 2, at 653 (New York: Macmillan, 1981). The numbers for the 1810, 1820, 1830, 1840, 1850, 1860, 1870, 1890, 1900, and 1910 terms are based on an analysis of decisions in *United States Reports* for those years. Excluded from those figures are short per curiam or memorandum orders denying review or not reaching the merits of a case or otherwise disposing of a case. Data for the October terms 1913–1981 are taken from Statistical Sheet, Office of the Clerk, SC.

Total number of opinions refers to both signed and per curiam opinions for the Court and dissenting, concurring, or separate opinions in cases given plenary consideration. Excluded, for example, are dissenting opinions from the denial of a petition for certiorari. Data for 1801–1814 are taken from Haskins and Johnson, *Foundations*. Figures for the 1800, 1810, 1820, 1830, 1840, 1850, 1860, 1870, 1880, 1890, 1900, and 1910 terms are based on an examination and tabulation by the author of opinions in *United States Reports* for those years. Figures for the October terms 1913–1981 are taken from the Annual Statement of Number of Printed Opinions, Office of the Clerk, Supreme Court, with the exception of the 1924–1936 terms, for which the number of total opinions was taken from the *Harvard Law Review's Annual Survey* of those terms.

Cases disposed of during term include both those given plenary consideration and those summarily decided or otherwise disposed of. Figures for cases disposed of and carried over for the years 1791–1810, 1820, 1822–1846, 1850, 1860, 1870, 1880, and 1890 are based on the author's tabulation of cases contained in the Docket Books of the Supreme Court of the United States (available at the National Archives, Washington, D.C.). Figures for the terms between 1890 and 1910 are taken from the *Annual Reports of the Attorney General of the United States* (Washington, D.C.: GPO, 1891, 1901, 1911). Figures for October terms 1913–1981 are taken from Statistical Sheet, Office of the Clerk, Supreme Court.

126. Interview with Stewart, February 28, 1985, SC.
127. See C. H. Pritchett, "The Roosevelt Court: Votes and Values," 42 *American Political Science Review* 54 (1948)
128. "A List of Supreme Court Cases Decided by a Majority of One" (Mimeograph, July 9, 1935; April 26, 1937; Washington, D.C.: Library of Congress) and "Five to Four Decisions of the United States Supreme Court" (Mimeograph, 1945; Washington, D.C.: Library of Congress). For the 1945–1971 terms, see Note, "Five–Four Decisions of the United States Supreme Court: Resurrection of the Extraordinary Majority," 7 *Suffolk University Law Review* 807, Appendix C, at 916 (1973). In the 1979, 1980, and 1981 terms the number of five–four decisions has ranged from twenty-eight to twenty-one to thirty-two. Based on the author's tabulations.
129. For plurality decisions before the 1969 term, see J. F. Davis and W. Reynolds, "Juridical Cripples: Plurality Opinions in the Supreme Court," 1974 *Duke Law Journal* 59. For the 1969–1979 terms, see Note, "Plurality Decisions and Judicial Decisionmaking," 94 *Harvard Law Review* 1127, Appendix, at 1147 (1981). Plurality decisions in the 1980–1984 terms were tabulated by the author.
130. Memorandum to Conference, October 28, 1961, Black Papers, Box 60, LC.
131. Interview with Stevens, April 5, 1985, SC.
132. Letter, April 20, 1874, Records of the Clerk of the Supreme Court, NARS.
133. Quoted by McLean, supra note 65, at 60.
134. Hughes, supra note 11, at 68.
135. Frankfurter-Brandeis Conversations, Frankfurter Papers, Box 224, File 4101, LC. The original transcript of these conversations is in the Brandeis Papers, Box 114, HLS.
136. Quoted in A. Bickel, *The Unpublished Opinions of Mr. Justice Brandeis* 18 (Chicago: University of Chicago Press, 1967).
137. Letter, December 8, 1915, Day Papers, Box 30, LC.
138. *Bank of the United States v. Dandridge*, 25 U.S. 64, 90 (1827). See also letters from Justice Story to the Reporter in 1818, telling of his agreement with the Court's opinion and providing a copy of a dissenting opinion that he sup-

pressed. W. W. Story, *Life and Letters of Joseph Story*, vol. 1, 303–8 (Boston: Little, Brown, 1851).

139. Holmes's "Opinion Books" contain numerous examples of justices acquiescing in a unanimous decision even though as many as three or more disagreed with the ruling. See, e.g., Letter from Justice Brown to Holmes, April 25, 1899, in which he says, "The opinion was not quite so unanimous as it appears to be. There were three members of the Court who . . . threatened to dissent, but they finally acquiesced in the result." Holmes Papers, Box 45, File 24, HLS.

140. Quoted by Mason, supra note 37, at 61 and 223.

141. J. Campbell III, "The Spirit of Dissent," 66 *Judicature* 305 (1983).

142. L. Brandeis, quoted by Bickel, supra note 136, at 18.

143. See D. Dorin, " 'Seize the Time': Justice Tom Clark's Role in *Mapp v. Ohio*," in V. Swigert, ed., *Law and the Legal Process* 21 (Beverly Hills, Calif.: Sage, 1982).

144. Quoted by Burger, "In Memoriam: Hugo L. Black," 92 S.Ct. 5, 79 (1972).

145. 89 S.Ct. 20 (1969).

146. Burger, "The Chief Justice Talks about the Court," *Reader's Digest* 2, 4 (February 1973).

147. Undated Conference Note, Clark papers, UT.

148. Memorandum for Conference, November 5, 1959, Harlan Papers, Box 486, MLPU.

149. F. Frankfurter, "The Zeitgeist and the Judiciary," in A. MacLeish and E. Prichard, Jr., eds., *Law and Politics* (New York: Harcourt, Brace, 1939).

150. Burger, Annual Judicial Conference, Second Judicial Circuit, Buck Hill Falls, Pa. (May 10, 1980) (unpublished manuscript on file with the author).

151. Memorandum to Conference, October 28, 1961, Black Papers, Box 60, LC.

152. Included in the number of opinion pages are those for signed majority, concurring, dissenting, and per curiam opinions. For the 1960, 1965, 1970, 1975, and 1979 terms, see House Committee on Appropriations, *Departments . . . : Hearings before a Subcommittee,* 97th Cong., 2d sess., pt. 4, at 380 (Washington, D.C.: GPO, 1982). Figures for the 1938 term and tabulations for the average length of opinions are the author's.

SIX

The Court and American Life

1. Newton Minow Oral History Interview, at 27–28, UK. See also Conference Lists, Hugo Black Papers, Box 310, LC.

2. Tom Clark Oral History Interview, at 10, UK. *Brown v. Board of Education,* 344 U.S. 1 (1952) (per curiam decision on postponement of oral arguments).

3. Letter to Charles Warren, July 19, 1923, Charles Warren Papers, Box 2, LC.

4. Story related in a letter from Herbert Wechsler to Frankfurter, July 22, 1946, Felix Frankfurter Papers, Box 172, HLS.

5. Letter to Harlan, September 2, 1958, Felix Frankfurter Papers, Box 169, HLS.

6. See letter from Stone to Frankfurter, March 17, 1943, Harlan F. Stone Papers, Box 13, LC; Earl Warren Papers, Box 125, LC; and *Supreme Court Journal* for June 21, 1969.

7. W. O. Douglas, *The Court Years* 40 (New York: Random House, 1980).

8. "Frankfurter Dissent Provokes Warren to Rebuttal on Bench," *New York Times*

Al, col. 4 (March 21, 1961). For another such story, see W. J. Brennan, Jr., "Chief Justice Warren," 88 *Harvard Law Review* 1, 2 (1974).

9. W. Brennan, Jr., Remarks at Student Legal Forum, Charlottesville, Virginia, at 1 (February 17, 1959), SC.
10. Letter from Frankfurter to Reed, February 10, 1936, Felix Frankfurter Papers, Box 170, HLS.
11. Memorandum to Members of the Court, May 7, 1954, Tom C. Clark Papers, UT; Earl Warren Papers, Box 574, LC.
12. See Memorandum to the Chief Justice from the Press Office, September 1, 1948, Stanley Reed Papers, Box 174, UK; and John M. Harlan Papers, Box 498, MLPU.
13. See Letter to the Chief Justice and "Background Paper for the Chief Justice," September 22, 1969, Harlan Papers, Box 606, MLPU.
14. Note, October 12, 1970, William J. Brennan Papers, Box 487, LC.
15. W. E. Burger, foreword to M. Cannon and D. M. O'Brien, eds., *Views from the Bench: The Judiciary and Constitutional Politics* (Chatham, N.J.: Chatham House, 1985).
16. Quoted in Mitchell Tropin, "What, Exactly, Is the Court Saying?" *Barrister Magazine* 14, 68 (Spring 1984).
17. Quoted ibid., 16.
18. Quoted ibid., 68–69.
19. Quoted ibid., 67.
20. Letter to Reed about *Cox v. New Hampshire*, March 28, 1941, Reed Papers, Box 171, UK.
21. E. Warren, *The Memoirs of Earl Warren* 285 (New York: Doubleday, 1977). See also Gordon Davidson Interview, UK; and Reed Papers, Boxes 41, 43, 50, and 331, UK.
22. J. Goodale, *National Law Journal* 15 (October 15, 1979).
23. See, D. M. O'Brien, *The Public's Right to Know: The Supreme Court and the First Amendment* 134–35 (New York: Praeger, 1981).
24. Transcript of Oral Argument, Reed Papers, Box 43, UK.
25. Memo summarizing conversation with the chief justice by John Fassett for Justice Reed, Reed Papers, Box 331, UK. See also Harold Burton Papers, Box 263, LC; and Clark Papers, UT.
26. Reed Papers, Box 331, UK.
27. Law Clerks' Recommendations for Segregation Decree, Clark Papers, UT; Warren Papers, Box 574, LC.
28. Reed's notes of Conference discussion, Reed Papers, Box 43, UK. Burton's "Diaries," Box 3, LC; Felix Frankfurter Papers, HLS; and Warren Papers, Boxes 571 and 574, LC.
29. Memorandum to the Brethren, January 15, 1954, Burton Papers, Box 263, LC (quoting *Virginia v. West Virginia*, 200 U.S. 1 (1911).
30. *Griffin v. Prince Edward County School Board*, 377 U.S. 218, 219, 234 (1964).
31. Memorandum, School Openings and Desegregation, Lee White Papers, Box 5, JPL.
32. Ruby Martin Oral History Interview, at 12, JPL.
33. V. Navasky, *Kennedy Justice* 97–98 (New York: Atheneum, 1971). For a good survey of the activities and accomplishments of the Eisenhower administration in the area of civil rights, see Memorandum to the Attorney General, January 18, 1961, William Rogers Papers, Box 47; and Dwight David Eisenhower (DDE) Diaries, Box 33, EPL.
34. Memorandum on Civil Rights Legislation, White House Central Files—Execu-

tive Legislative Series, Hu, Box 65, JPL. See also Stephen Pollack Interview III, at 19; and White House Central Files—Confidential Files (WHCF-CF), Boxes 102 and 127, JPL.

35. See, generally, Lee White Papers, Box 2; and WHCF-CF, Box 102, JPL.
36. *Alexander v. Holmes County Board of Education,* 396 U.S. 1218, 1220 (1969).
37. *Alexander v. Holmes County Board of Education,* 396 U.S. 19 (1969) (per curiam). The Court had previously held, in *Green v. School Board New Kent County,* 391 U.S. 430 (1968), that "freedom of choice" in achieving school desegregation was ineffective.
38. All quotations are from justices' memos; Harlan Papers, Boxes 487, 565 and 606, MLPU; and Brennan Papers, Box 218, LC.
39. Based on figures in Appendix to Memorandum for the President, Ford Papers, WHCF—Special Files, Box 4, FPL. (The report considered districts with an "appreciable percentage" of minority students to have at least 5 percent minority students and segregated districts to have more than 50 percent nonminority students.)
40. Handwritten note of President Eisenhower, Papers as President—Administrative Series, Box 23, EPL.
41. Pollack Interview III, at 19, JPL.
42. R. Dahl, "Decision-Making in a Democracy: The Supreme Court as a National Policy-Maker," 6 *Journal of Public Law* 279, 293 (1957).
43. Ibid. and Richard Funston, "The Supreme Court and Critical Elections," 69 *American Political Science Review* 795 (1975).
44. F. P. Dunne, "On the Supreme Court's Decisions," in *Mr. Dooley in Peace and in War* (1898).
45. Letter, October 15, 1937, Stone Papers, Box 13, LC.
46. Letter, April 24, 1961, Felix Frankfurter Papers, Box 171, HLS. Memo to Conference, March 2, 1962, Clark Papers, UT. For another example of Frankfurter's appeal to the forces of public opinion, see his memorandum on *Reid v. Covert,* June 5, 1957, Warren Papers, Box 434, LC.
47. See "Institutions: Confidence Even in Difficult Times," *Public Opinion* 33 (1981); Hearst Report, *The American Public, the Media and the Judicial System* (New York: Hearst Corporation, 1983); W. Murphy, J. Tanenhaus, and D. Kastner, *Public Evaluations of Constitutional Courts: Alternative Explanations* (Beverly Hills, Calif.: Sage, 1973); and W. Murphy and J. Tananhaus, "Public Opinion and the United States Supreme Court," 2 *Law and Society Review* 357 (1968).
48. Memorandum to the President from Jim Cannon (June 1, 1976), and Memorandum from HEW Secretary David Mathews (March 29, 1974), Ford Papers, WHCF—Special Files, Box 4, FPL. See also Edmund Schmults Papers, Box 9, FPL.
49. "Text of 96 Congressmen's Declaration on Integration," *New York Times* 19 (March 12, 1956). (Five congressmen later joined the manifesto.)
50. *Cong. Record,* 97th Cong., 2d sess., S5428 (May 18, 1982) and H2852 (May 25, 1982) (daily ed.).
51. Notes and Correspondence, *Miranda* File, Warren Papers, Box 617, LC; and Abe Fortas Papers, YA. For studies of compliance with *Miranda,* see N. Milner, *The Supreme Court and Local Law Enforcement: The Impact of Miranda* (Beverly Hills, Calif.: Sage, 1971); and S. Wasby, *Small Town Police and the Supreme Court: Hearing the Word* (Lexington, Mass.: Lexington Books, 1976).
52. *Williams v. United States,* 401 U.S. 675, 677 (1971). See also *Gregg v. Georgia,* 428 U.S. 153, 180 (1976) and *Woodson v. North Carolina,* 428 U.S. 280, 299 (1976).

53. Frankfurter and Byrnes, both appointed by Roosevelt, had maintained a close relationship through the years; in 1953–1954, the latter, as governor, had made well know to Frankfurter his views that the Court would exceed its constitutional power in striking down segregation. See letters and memos, Warren Papers, Boxes 574 and 353, LC; discussion of *Cooper v. Aaron* in Chapter 5; J. Byrnes, "The Supreme Court Must Be Curbed," *U.S. News & World Report* 50 (May 18, 1956); and A. Bickel, "Frankfurter's Former Clerk Disputes Byrnes's Statement," *U.S. News & World Report* 132 (June 15, 1956) (a copy of Bickel's original and more extensive rebuttal of Byrnes's article may be found in Warren Papers, Box 353, LC).

54. See L. Powell, Jr., "Are the Federal Courts Becoming Bureaucracies?" 68 *American Bar Association Journal* 1370 (1982).

55. Memorandum on the Segregation Decree, Warren Papers, Box 574. LC.

56. J. Peltason, *Fifty-eight Lonely Men: Southern Federal Judges and School Desegregation* 9–10 (New York: Harcourt, Brace and World, 1961).

57. Transcript of Proceedings, *United States v. Reserve Mining Co.*, United States District Court, District of Minnesota, Fifth Division, No. 5-72, Civil 19, November 14, 1975, at 21–22. I am grateful to Mr. O. E. Brevin, the court reporter, for making a copy of the transcript available.

58. *Reserve Mining Co. v. Lord*, 529 F.2d 191, 185–86 (8th Cir. 1976).

59. J. W. Howard, *Courts of Appeals in the Federal Judicial System* (Princeton: Princeton University Press, 1981).

60. *Report of the Committee on Federal-State Relationships As Affected by Judicial Decisions*, reprinted in *Cong. Record*, 73d Cong., 2d sess., Appendix, A7784, A7787 (daily ed., August 25, 1958).

61. Letter, Decemeber 28, 1967, Harlan Papers, Box 301, MLPU.

62. Letter, January 29, 1968, Harlan Papers, Box 301, MLPU.

63. Letter to Clark, January 25, 1962, Clark Papers, UT.

64. See *Florida v. Meyers*, 104 S.Ct. 1852, 1854 (1984) (Stevens, J., dis. op.).

65. Nicholas Katzenbach Oral History Interview, at 41, JPL.

66. Letter, October 8, 1956, quoted by D. Fuerth, "Lyndon B. Johnson and Civil Rights" (Ph.D. diss., University of Texas, 1974); and Letter, April 2, 1957, Senate Papers, Box 289, JPL.

67. Quoted by J. Schmidhauser and L. Berg, *The Supreme Court and Congress: Conflict and Interaction, 1945–1968* 10 (New York: Free Press, 1972).

68. In *Lauf v. E. G. Shinner*, 303 U.S. 323 (1938), the Court upheld the Norris-LaGuardia Act's removal of the power of lower federal courts to issue injunctions in labor disputes.

69. *United States v. Klein*, 80 U.S. 128 (1872).

70. See *Cong. Record*, 94th Cong., 2d sess., S4128 (daily ed., April 5, 1979) and S4138 (daily ed., April 9, 1979).

71. C. H. Pritchett, *Congress versus the Supreme Court, 1957–1960*, 122–23 (Minneapolis: University of Minnesota Press, 1961).

72. B. Henschen, "Statutory Interpretations of the Supreme Court: Congressional Response," 11 *American Politics Quarterly* 441 (1983).

73. See J. Califano, *Governing America* 53–73 (New York: Simon & Schuster, 1981). The Court upheld the Hyde Amendment in *Harris v. McRae*, 448 U.S. 297 (1980).

74. Ibid., 217.

75. Dahl, supra note 42.

76. See J. Casper, "The Supreme Court and National Policy-Making," 70 *American Political Science Review* 60 (1976).

77. Herbert Brownell Oral History Interview, at 33, EPL.
78. Letter to Edgar Eisenhower, November 8, 1954, DDE Diaries, Box 8, EPL.
79. Letter to Swede Hazlett, July 22, 1957, DDE Diaries Box 25, EPL.
80. Quoted in R. Evans, Jr., and R. Novak, *Nixon in the White House* 156 (New York: Random House, 1971).
81. *American Federation of Labor v. American Sash & Door Company,* 335 U.S. 538, 555–56 (1946).
82. See N. Glazer, "Toward an Imperial Judiciary," 40 *The Public Interest* 104 (1975); D. Horowitz, *The Courts and Social Policy* (Washington, D.C.: Brookings Institution, 1977); and R. Berger, *Government by the Judiciary* (Cambridge: Harvard University Press, 1977). But see D. M. O'Brien, "The 'Imperial Judiciary': Of Paper Tigers and Socio-Legal Indicators," 2 *Journal of Law & Politics* 1 (1985).

Glossary

Advisory opinion   An opinion or interpretation of law that does not have binding effect. The Court does not give advisory opinions, for example, on hypothetical disputes; it decides only actual cases or controversies.

Affirm   In an appellate court, to reach a decision that agrees with the result reached in a case by the lower court.

Amicus curiae   A friend of the court, a person not a party to litigation, who volunteers or is invited by the court to give his views on a case.

Appeal   To take a case to a higher court for review. Generally, a party losing in a trial court may appeal once to an appellate court as a matter of right. If the party loses in the appellate court, appeal to a higher court is within the discretion of the higher court. Most appeals to the Supreme Court are within its discretion to deny or grant a hearing.

Appellant   The party that appeals a lower-court decision to a higher court.

Appellee   One who has an interest in upholding the decision of a lower court and is compelled to respond when the case is appealed to a higher court by the appellant.

Brief   A document prepared by counsel to serve as the basis for an argument in court, setting out the facts and legal arguments in support of his or her case.

Case   A general term for an action, cause, suit, or controversy, at law or equity; a question contested before a court.

Case law The law as defined by previously decided cases, distinct from statutes and other sources of law.

Certification, writ of A method of taking a case from appellate court to the Supreme Court in which the lower court asks that some question or interpretation of law be certified, clarified, and made more certain.

Certiorari, writ of A writ issued from the Supreme Court, at its discretion and at the request of a petitioner, to order a lower court to send the record of a case to the Court for its review.

Civil Law The body of law dealing with the private rights of individuals, as distinguished from criminal law.

Class action A lawsuit brought by one person or group on behalf of all persons similarly situated.

Common law The collection of principles and rules, particularly from unwritten English law, that derive their authority from long-standing usage and custom or from courts recognizing and enforcing those customs.

Concurring opinion An opinion by a justice that agrees with the result reached by the Court in a case but disagrees with the Court's rationale for its decision.

Controversies *See* Justiciable controversy.

Criminal law The body of law that deals with the enforcement of laws and the punishment of persons who, by breaking laws, commit crimes against the state.

Declaratory Judgment A court pronouncement declaring a legal right or interpretation but not ordering a special action.

De facto In fact, in reality.

Defendant In a civil action, the party denying or defending itself against charges brought by a plaintiff. In a criminal action, the person indicted for the commission of a offense.

De jure As a result of law, as a result of official action.

Dicta *See* Obiter dictum.

Discretionary jurisdiction Jurisdiction that a court may accept or reject in particular cases. The Supreme Court has discretionary jurisdiction in over 90 percent of the cases that come to it.

Dismissal An order disposing of a case without a hearing or trial.

Dissenting opinion An opinion by a justice that disagrees with the result reached by the Court in a case.

Docket All cases filed in a court.

Due process Fair and regular procedure. The Fifth and Fourteenth amendments guarantee persons that they will not be deprived of life, liberty, or property by the government until fair and usual procedures have been followed.

Error, writ of A writ issued from an appeals court to a lower court requiring that it send the record of a case so that it may review it for error.

Ex parte From, or on, only one side. Application to a court for some ruling or action on behalf of only one party.

Habeas corpus Literally, "you have the body"; a writ issued to inquire whether a person is lawfully imprisoned or detained. The writ demands that the persons holding the prisoner justify his detention or release him.

In forma pauperis In the manner of a pauper, without liability for the costs of filing cases before a court.

Injunction A court order prohibiting a person from performing a particular act.

Judgment The official decision of a court.

Judicial review The power to review and strike down any legislation or other government action that is inconsistent with federal or state constitutions. The Supreme Court reviews government action only under the Constitution of the United States.

Jurisdiction The power of a court to hear a case or controversy, which exists when the proper parties are present and when the point to be decided is among the issues authorized to be handled by a particular court.

Justiciable controversy A controversy in which a claim of right is asserted against another who has an interest in contesting it. Courts will consider only justiciable controversies, as distinguished from hypothetical disputes.

Majority opinion An opinion in a case that is subscribed to by a majority of the justices who participated in the decision.

Mandamus, writ of "We command"; an order issued from a superior court directing a lower court or other government authority to perform a particular act.

Mandatory jurisdiction Jurisdiction that a court must accept. The Supreme Court must decide cases coming under its appellate jurisdiction, though it may avoid giving them plenary consideration.

Moot   Unsettled, undecided. A moot question is also one that is no longer material, or that has already been resolved, and has become hypothetical.

Motion   A written or oral application to a court or judge to obtain a rule or order.

Obiter dictum   A statement by a judge or justices expressing an opinion and included with, but not essential to, an opinion resolving a case before the court. Dicta are not necessarily binding in later cases.

Opinion for the court   The opinion announcing the decision of a court.

Original jurisdiction   The jurisdiction of a court of first instance, or trial court. The Supreme Court has original jurisdiction under Article III of the Constitution.

Per curiam   "By the court"; an unsigned opinion of the court.

Petitioner   One who files a petition with a court seeking action or relief, including the plaintiff or appellant. When a writ of certiorari is granted by the Supreme Court, the party seeking review is called the petitioner, and the party responding is called the respondent.

Plenary consideration   Full consideration. When the Supreme Court grants a case review, it may give it full consideration, permitting the parties to submit briefs on the merits of the case and to present oral arguments, before the Court reaches its decision.

Plurality opinion   An opinion announcing the decision of the Court, but which has the support of less than a majority of the Court.

Political question   Questions that courts refuse to decide because they are deemed to be essentially political in nature, or because their determination would involve an intrusion on the powers of the executive or legislature.

Remand   To send back. After a decision in a case, the case is often sent back by a higher court to the court from which it came for further action in light of its decision.

Respondent   The party that is compelled to answer the claims or questions posed in a court by a petitioner.

Reverse   In an appellate court, to reach a decision that disagrees with the result reached in a case by a lower court.

Ripeness   When a case is ready for adjudication and decision; the issues presented must not be hypothetical, and the parties must have exhausted other avenues of appeal.

Seriatim   Separately, individually, one by one. The Court's practice was once to have each justice give his opinion on a case separately.

Standing Having the appropriate characteristics to bring or participate in a case; in particular, having a personal interest and stake in the outcome.

Stare Decisis "Let the decision stand." The principle of adherence to settled cases, the doctrine that principles of law established in earlier cases should be accepted as authoritative in similar subsequent cases.

Statute A written law enacted by a legislature.

Subpoena An order to present oneself before a grand jury, court, or legislative hearing.

Subpoena duces tecum An order to produce specified documents or papers.

Summary decision A decision in a case that does not give it full consideration; when the Court decides a case without having the parties submit briefs on the merits of the case or present oral arguments before the Court.

Tort An injury or wrong to the person or property of another.

Vacate To make void, annul, or rescind the decision of a lower court.

Writ An order commanding someone to perform or not perform acts specified in the order.

Selected Further Readings

Abraham, Henry. *Freedom and the Court: Civil Rights and Liberties in the United States*. 4th ed. New York: Oxford University Press, 1982.
———. *The Judicial Process*. 5th ed. New York: Oxford University Press, 1986.
———. *Justices and Presidents*. 2d ed. New York: Oxford University Press, 1985.
Berger, Raoul. *Government by Judiciary: The Transformation of the Fourteenth Amendment*. Cambridge: Harvard University Press, 1977.
Bickel, Alexander. *The Least Dangerous Branch: The Supreme Court at the Bar of Politics*. New York: Bobbs-Merrill, 1963.
———. *The Supreme Court and the Idea of Progress*. New Haven: Yale University Press, 1978.
———, and Benno Schmidt. *The Judiciary and Responsible Government, 1910–21*. New York: Macmillan, 1984.
Black, Charles. *Structure and Relationship in Constitutional Law*. Baton Rouge: Louisiana University Press, 1969.
Black, Hugo. *A Constitutional Faith*. New York: Knopf, 1969.
Blaustein, Albert, and Roy Mersky. *The First One Hundred Justices*. Hamden, Conn.: Archon Books, 1978.
Cannon, Mark, and David O'Brien, eds. *Views from the Bench: The Judiciary and Constitutional Politics*. Chatham, N.J.: Chatham House, 1985.
Cardozo, Benjamin. *The Nature of the Judicial Process*. New Haven: Yale University Press, 1921.

Carson, Hampton. *The History of the Supreme Court of the United States.* Philadelphia: P. W. Ziegler, 1902.

Choper, Jesse. *Judicial Review and the National Political Process.* Chicago: University of Chicago Press, 1980.

Cortner, Richard. *The Supreme Court and the Second Bill of Rights: The Fourteenth Amendment and the Nationalization of Civil Liberties.* Madison: University of Wisconsin Press, 1981.

Corwin, Edward. *The President: Office and Powers, 1787–1984.* 5th ed. New York: New York University Press, 1984.

———. *The Doctrine of Judicial Review.* Princeton: Princeton University Press, 1914.

Crosskey, William. *Politics and the Constitution in the History of the United States.* Chicago: University of Chicago Press, 1953.

Ely, John Hart. *Democracy and Distrust: A Theory of Judicial Review.* Cambridge: Harvard University Press, 1980.

Fairman, Charles. *Reconstruction and Reunion, 1864–1888.* New York: Macmillan, 1975.

Fish, Peter. *The Office of Chief Justice.* Charlottesville: University of Virginia Press, 1984.

———. *The Politics of Federal Judicial Administration.* Princeton: Princeton University Press, 1973.

Fisher, Louis. *Constitutional Conflicts between Congress and the President.* Princeton: Princeton University Press, 1985.

Frank, John. *Marble Palace: The Supreme Court in American Life.* New York: Knopf, 1958.

Frankfurter, Felix. *Extrajudicial Essays on the Court and Constitution.* Edited by P. Kurland. Cambridge: Harvard University Press, 1970.

———, and James Landis. *The Business of the Supreme Court.* New York: Macmillan, 1927.

Friedman, Leon, and Fred Israel, eds. *The Justices of the United States Supreme Court, 1789–1978: Their Lives and Major Opinions.* 5 vols. New York: Chelsea House, 1980.

Goebel, Julius. *Antecedents and Beginnings to 1801.* New York: Macmillan, 1971.

Haskins, George, and Herbert Johnson. *Foundations of Power: John Marshall, 1801–1815.* New York: Macmillan, 1981.

Hughes, Charles Evans. *The Supreme Court of the United States.* New York: Columbia University Press, 1928.

Jackson, Robert. *The Struggle for Judicial Supremacy.* New York: Knopf, 1941.

Johnson, Charles, and Bradley Canon. *Judicial Policies: Implementation and Impact.* Washington, D.C.: Congressional Quarterly, 1984.

Lewis, Anthony. *Gideon's Trumpet*. New York: Random House, 1964.

Kurland, Philip. *Politics, the Constitution, and the Warren Court*. Chicago: University of Chicago Press, 1973.

Mason, Alpheus. *The Supreme Court from Taft to Burger*. 3d ed. Baton Rouge: Louisiana State University Press, 1979.

———. *The Supreme Court: Palladium of Freedom*. Ann Arbor: University of Michigan Press, 1962.

Miller, Arthur S. *The Supreme Court and American Capitalism*. New York: Free Press, 1968.

Miller, Charles. *The Supreme Court and the Uses of History*. Cambridge: Harvard University Press, 1969.

Murphy, Bruce. *The Brandeis/Frankfurter Connection: The Secret Political Activities of Two Supreme Court Justices*. New York: Oxford University Press, 1982.

Murphy, Walter. *Elements of Judicial Strategy*. Chicago: University of Chicago Press, 1964.

———. *The Study of Public Law*. New York: Random House, 1971.

———, and C. Herman Pritchett, eds. *Courts, Judges, and Politics*. 4th ed. New York: Random House, 1986.

Pritchett, C. Herman. *The Roosevelt Court*. New York: Macmillan, 1947.

———. *Civil Liberties and the Vinson Court*. Chicago: University of Chicago Press, 1954.

———. *Constitutional Law of the Federal System*. Englewood Cliffs, N.J.: Prentice-Hall, 1984.

———. *Constitutional Civil Liberties*. Englewood Cliffs, N.J.: Prentice-Hall, 1984.

Rosen, Paul. *The Supreme Court and Social Science*. Urbana: University of Illinois Press, 1972.

Rossiter, Clinton, with Richard Longaker. *The Supreme Court and the Commander in Chief*. Ithaca: Cornell University Press, 1976.

Rostow, Eugene. *The Sovereign Prerogative: The Supreme Court and the Quest for Law*. New Haven: Yale University Press, 1962.

Schmidhauser, John. *Judges and Justices*. Boston: Little, Brown, 1979.

Schubert, Glendon. *The Judicial Mind*. Evanston: Northwestern University Press, 1965.

———, ed. *Judicial Behavior: A Reader in Theory and Research*. Chicago: Rand McNally, 1964.

———. *The Constitutional Polity*. Boston: Boston University Press, 1970.

Schwartz, Bernard. *Super Chief: Earl Warren and His Supreme Court—A Judicial Biography*. New York: New York University Press, 1983.

Shapiro, Martin. *Law and Politics in the Supreme Court*. New York: Free Press, 1964.

Sheldon, Charles. *The Judicial Process: Models and Approaches.* New York:
    Dodd, Mead, 1974.
Stern, Robert, and Eugene Gressman. *Supreme Court Practice.* 5th ed.
    Washington, D.C.: Bureau of National Affairs, 1978.
Supreme Court Historical Society, *Yearbook.* Washington, D.C.: SCHS,
    1976–.
Swisher, Carl B. *The Taney Court, 1836–64.* New York: Macmillan, 1974.
Tribe, Laurence. *God Save This Honorable Court.* New York: Random
    House, 1985.
Warren, Charles. *The Supreme Court in United States History.* 3 vols. Bos-
    ton: Little, Brown, 1922.
Westin, Alan, ed. *An Autobiography of the Supreme Court.* New York:
    Macmillan, 1963.

Index